excellent HTML

excellent HTML with an introduction to Java applets

Timothy T. Gottleber

North Lake College
Irving, Texas

Irwin McGraw-Hill

Boston Burr Ridge, IL Dubuque, IA Madison, WI New York San Francisco St. Louis
Bangkok Bogatá Caracas Lisbon London Madrid
Mexico City Milan New Delhi Seoul Singapore Sydney Taipei Toronto

Irwin/McGraw-Hill

A Division of The McGraw-Hill Companies

Excellent HTML with an Introduction to Java Applets

This book is printed on acid-free paper.

2 3 4 5 6 7 8 9 0 Q P D Q P D 3 2 1 0 9 8

ISBN 0-07-024772-2

VP/Editorial director: Mike Junior
Sponsoring editor: Rhonda Sands
Developmental editor: Kyle Thomes
Editorial assistant: Stephen Fahringer
Project manager: Natalie Durbin
Production supervisor: Pam Augspurger
Designer: Lorna Lo
Cover designer: Amanda Kavanagh
Compositor: Shepherd, Inc.
Typeface: Bembo
Printer: Quebecor Printing Dubuque, Inc.

Library of Congress Cataloging-in-Publication Data

Gottleber, Timothy T.
Excellent HTML with an introduction to Java applets / Timothy T. Gottleber.
p. cm.
Includes index.
ISBN 0-07-024772-2
1. HTML (Document markup language) 2. Java (Computer program language) I. Title.
QA76.76.H94G68 1998
005.72—dc21 98-12610
CIP

http://www.mhhe.com

table of contents

This book is dedicated to the engineers who built the Net, the Web weavers who fill it with information, and all who use it. Enjoy.

preface

To the Student

This book was written for you, the student. You want to learn how to build and maintain Web pages. You have the tool to help you do that in your hands. The author of this text is also the teacher of a class in HTML and Java applets. The students of that class provided information that will make this text useful for other students. The many technical books and reference manuals available are useful once you know what you are doing, but they are not textbooks. None were designed to be an aid in learning how to build Web pages as this book is. You are holding in your hands the results of many discussions with students as to what they wanted in a text.

There are two ways to approach learning how to code HTML. The first way is to just jump in and see what you can hack. HTML isn't that complex, and it isn't that difficult to create some simple pages with it. However, you can avoid developing some bad habits, and you can learn some great techniques by following a second, more structured approach to learning HTML. In this second approach, as presented in this text, you first learn how to use simple tags, then move on to the more complex ones. You see what you can do with just a handful of these selected, simple tags before you start using the really "slick" ones like frames or tables.

You will begin building Web pages in Chapter 2. The pages will become more and more complex as you work through the text. If you have a special need, feel free to look ahead, but remember that the exercises at the end of each chapter are designed to give you a chance to apply the new tags you learned in that chapter and refresh your memory about the tags you have already learned.

Welcome to the wonderful world of HTML! It is an exciting place that is changing even as you read this. Not long before this book went to press, the 4.0 standard was released, with further changes. Although the 4.0 standard is addressed only in the appendix of this book, everything you learn here will work for many generations of HTML. Release 4.0 is truly backward compatible. In addition, supplementary information will be found at the Web site for this book dealing with the new standard and hot new topics in HTML like DHTML (Dynamic HTML).

A principle that will be emphasized over and over throughout this text is that your job is to provide new and exciting *content* to the community we call the World Wide Web. Concentrate on the content, and let the browsers that load your pages worry about the formatting. Now go play on the Web, and if you want to see what the author's students are doing, come visit **phred.dcccd.edu** and take a look at the student pages hosted there. They are doing some wonderful things.

To the Instructor

Teaching HTML is challenging and exciting, but it can also be frustrating with only reference books and technical manuals to use as texts. This book was written because none of the other books available were designed to be used in the classroom.

Students of HTML come to class with a wide range of computer expertise, representing everything from the absolute novice to the professional programmer. This text assumes a basic level of computer literacy, but even students who are new to computing can succeed with it, albeit by putting in some serious work. An overview of the history and origins of HTML is followed by instruction in the design and development of clean, easy-to-maintain Web pages, using applets to provide some truly impressive features to the pages. Some simple tags are explained first. As the students become comfortable with the format and syntax of HTML, they are introduced to the more sophisticated tags.

You don't have to teach all of these chapters in their exact order, as most of them can stand alone. However, each chapter ends with material that gives the students grounding for the next chapter and refreshes concepts from the previous chapters. So the order of the chapters is not arbitrary.

As each new tag is introduced, there are both examples of the HTML code and screen captures showing what the code generates. This allows the students to play with HTML and compare their results to those shown in the text. Exercises at the end of each chapter allow the student to create pages using the tags they have learned. The process builds from chapter to chapter. In the author's experience, this is the best way to teach HTML. Give the students a tag, tell them how it works, and then let them use it. That way they can have actual, hands-on experience with the tags, and they seem to learn more quickly.

A wealth of ancillary tools come with this text:

- A Web site contains the applets and most of the HTML examples from the book as well as instructor notes, suggestions, and a sample syllabus. The Web site will also address the new 4.0 standard and concepts like dynamic HTML (DHTML). Go to **www.mhhe.com/cit/net/gottleber.**
- A CD is included with the book, containing the following:
  - All the applets used in the book, with a simple HTML page to drive each.

- CuteFTP, a handy file transfer protocol tool to move data across the Web.
- HomeSite, a powerful HTML editor.
- ColdFusion, a Web site development tool.
- HotDog, another HTML editor. (Some examples in the text use HotDog.)
- Most of the HTML examples from the text.
- MapEdit, a wonderful tool for producing image maps easily and quickly.
- PaintShop Pro to create art for the pages.
- WinZip, a useful tool for compressing HTML and images before shipping them across the Web.

The applets and the HTML examples each have an index page in the respective subdirectory on the CD. You or your students can access any of the applets by pointing your browser at **D:\applets\applets.html,** assuming that D is your CD-ROM drive. The applets index will give you a choice of each of the applets, but you must be running a platform that supports Java, such as UNIX, Linux, Windows95, Windows NT, or the Macintosh operating system.

Likewise, you can access the HTML examples by pointing your browser at **D:\htmlexamples\html.htm.** The HTML index gives access to the different chapter indices, each of which provides the HTML for the figures in that chapter. In some cases there is more than one example of the same HTML, or some HTML examples that are very similar, which are included for completeness and to keep in step with the text. You can run the HTML code from any browser that supports the HTML 3.2 standard; you need not have a Java-compatible platform to use the HTML examples that don't contain applets.

The CD contains a complete version of HotDog 2.5, the HTML editor highlighted in the book. A trial version of HotDog 4.5 is also included. The remaining software on the CD is made up of trial versions of the products. They are full-feature software, but they expire after 30 days. For that reason you may wish to wait until a couple of weeks into the semester before having your students install them. Students should not use the features of the page-development tools until the final project. Up to that point, they should use HotDog only as an ASCII editor. This way they learn how the actual HTML goes together, as well as the syntax and the order of the various tags. If they begin by using all the features of an HTML development tool, they become dependent upon those features and then encounter difficulty if they need to modify their code on the server.

For example, creating the correct path to an image can be tricky. If the students have to hand-build the path, they learn how HTML renders the address. If all they have to do is click on the target icon and then browse for the correct filename, they won't necessarily learn how to create the correct path. There are other editing tools available for download from the Web. Explore. You might find others that you really like. The most important thing about this or any text is that it should free you to focus on your teaching. Enjoy it, enjoy your students, and have fun!

Acknowledgments

Creating a book is a time-consuming process. First and foremost I want to thank my wife, Patti and son, Richard, for the time they sacrificed to allow me time to write, and for the support they provided throughout the whole process. Thanks, you two, I owe you!

Next, I wish to thank my students. They suffered through this process, too, working the exercises, listening to the lectures, and commenting on the content.

I also want to thank Dr. David England and Dr. Angie Runnels for allowing me to pursue this project.

The folks at McGraw-Hill were wonderful: Rhonda, Kyle, Natalie, and Steve were always there, encouraging and supporting. This book would not have been possible without their continued support. A special thanks to Maggie, way up North; she wrestled my words around until they made sense.

Sincere thanks go out to the following reviewers for their valuable input: Stephanie Low Chenault, College of Charleston; H. E. Dunsmore, Purdue University; Tim Eichers, Northern Virginia Community College; David Eppright, University of West Florida; Linda Hemenway, Santa Rosa Junior College; William Hix, Motlow State Community College-Tennessee; Barbara Hotta, University of Hawaii Leeward Community College; Oliver Lawrence, College of Du Page; C. E. Tapie Rohm, Jr., California State University-San Bernardino; John Smiley, Pennsylvania State University.

Finally, a word of thanks to Patty Larkin, Melissa Etheridge, Buddy Mondlock, Richard Wagner, Edvard Grieg, LVB, and Johann S. Bach for the music that kept me sane.

CHAPTER **one**

AN HTML OVERVIEW

The first part of this book focuses on **HyperText Markup Language** (**HTML**). This is the tool used to build Web pages. After studying HTML, you will be able to build, change, and maintain your own pages on the World Wide Web. As in almost any aspect of the world of computing, HTML authors use some special vocabulary. If you find a word that you don't understand, please check in the glossary at the end of this book. Knowing the meaning of the special terms used with HTML is very important. Often, half the battle in learning a new skill is learning the vocabulary of that skill.

What HTML Isn't

Before we look at what HTML is, it is important to make sure you understand what HTML *isn't*. First, HTML *isn't* hard to learn or use! Just like anything new, it looks a little strange when you first see it, but in a short time you can be reading and writing HTML like a pro. Second, HTML *isn't* a true programming language. In other words, it is not a language used to write Web programs. We will get into programming when we explore Java. HTML also *isn't* a page description language, or a **WYSIWYG** (**What You See Is What You Get**) word processor or desktop publishing tool. HTML is used to define the **content** of a document (what it says), but not the layout (how it looks). You can determine what the document says, but not precisely how it looks when displayed.

The terms *document* and *page* are often used interchangeably when talking about the World Wide Web. They don't mean exactly the same thing. HTML is used to create electronic documents that can be read on many different systems using software called a **browser**. The browser translates the HTML codes into a presentation on the screen. The **page** is what you see when the document is displayed on the screen. Technically, the **document** is the actual HTML you write, and the page is how it looks when viewed. Most Net cruisers don't make that distinction, so you may see the terms used interchangeably.

One fundamental fact of HTML is that while the author controls the *content,* the browser controls the *layout* of a document (with one exception that we will look at later). You can spend lots of time hand-editing (inserting extra spaces, tabs, blank lines, and such) to make your page look great, but most browsers will remove all those spaces, and all your careful work will be lost. The HTML term for extra spaces, tabs, and carriage returns is **white space**. HTML browsers usually compress all the white space into a single space.

What's in a Name

Now that we know what it is not, let's look at what HTML is. We will start with the name. The **H** stands for "hyper." A **hyper document** is one that contains links to other "things" or places either within or outside the document. A **link** is the general term for a specially marked place on the screen that will cause something to happen when you activate it. Clicking (with a mouse button) on a link can open another HTML document, move you to another place in the current document, display a picture, play a sound, or run a video clip.

As you move from hyper document to hyper document, the browser builds a chain of the pages you have visited so that you can easily go back and revisit one. Since the browser builds a chain, each page you have visited could be called a link in that chain. As an **HTML author**, or **Web weaver**, you will code links from your documents to other documents, both on your computer and across the world. For example, if this were a hyper document, and if the author had built in a link that defined the word **link,** that word would appear in a different font and/or underlined, and/or in a different color. If you moved your mouse pointer to that spot on the page and clicked the mouse button, that link would open a small page that defined the word *link* for you.

Here is an example: Suppose you go to the University of Virginia's Electronic Text Center, where many books are online. At that site you see the screen presented in Figure 1.1.

- Canfield, Dorothy : Ivanhoe and the German Measles [Illust.] (30 KB)
- Carleton, S.: The Tall Man (40 KB)
- Carleton, S.: The Lame Priest (40 KB)
- Carleton, S.: The Whale (30 KB)
- Carr, Mildred : Letter from Mildred Carr in Liberia to James Miner [Illust.] (6 KB)
- Carroll, Charles: Concerning Cheapness (20 KB)
- Carroll, Lewis: Alice in Wonderland (165 KB) TOC
- Carroll, Lewis: Through the Looking-Glass and What Alice Found There (195 KB) TOC
- Carroll, Lewis: The Hunting of the Snark: an Agony in Eight Fits [Illust.] (45 KB)
- Cary, Elisabeth Luther: Recent Writings By American Indians [Illust.] (20 KB)

Figure 1.1 Part of a page from the University of Virginia's online library.

You want to read *Alice in Wonderland,* so you move your mouse pointer to that title (the seventh entry on the screen) and press the left mouse button. The next thing that appears on your screen is the first page of the electronic text, as shown in Figure 1.2.

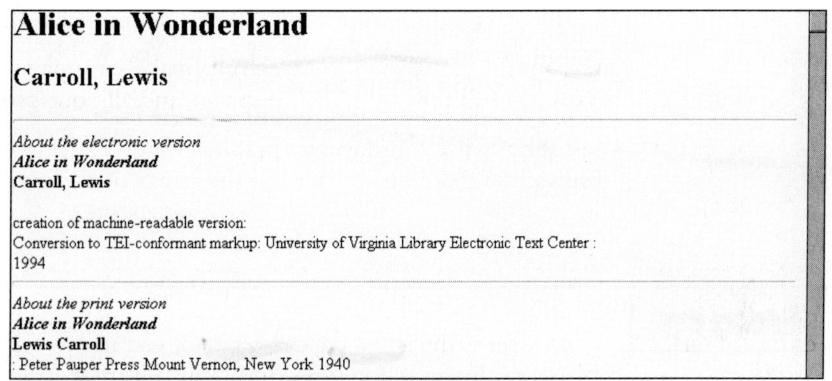

Alice in Wonderland

Carroll, Lewis

About the electronic version
Alice in Wonderland
Carroll, Lewis

creation of machine-readable version:
Conversion to TEI-conformant markup: University of Virginia Library Electronic Text Center :
1994

About the print version
Alice in Wonderland
Lewis Carroll
: Peter Pauper Press Mount Vernon, New York 1940

Figure 1.2 The first page of *Alice in Wonderland,* the electronic text version.

The title on the previous page was a *link* to the actual document.

Hyper documents are often considered more useful than standard text documents because the user can explore relationships among the ideas, or get definitions, by clicking on the links the author provides. Some people predict that in the future you will be reading "books" like this one over the World Wide Web rather than on paper.

Let's continue with the meaning of the letters in HTML. The **T** stands for "text." HTML is a type of **Standard Generalized Markup Language (SGML)**. It is **portable,** meaning it allows all sorts of computers, all across the world, to view documents created in any SGML. Another way to say this is that HTML allows portability across platforms. The term **platform** describes a particular type of computer, running a particular version of a specific operating system, browser, and so on. For example, an IBM PC running Windows 95 and Netscape Communicator is one type of platform. A Macintosh running the System 7 operating system and Netscape 3.1 is a different type of platform. Adding pictures, sounds, or video to a document can make it more interesting, but not all the browsers can support those features.

The **ML** in HTML stands for "markup language." This term comes from the publishing industry. Another example of a markup language is proofreaders' marks. Editors use symbols like ¶, the paragraph mark, to indicate a change in the way the text appears on the page. In HTML we use the <P> symbol to indicate the start of a new paragraph. We can use HTML to change the general way the text is laid out, but we are always at the mercy of the browser used to view our HTML document for the exact format. Some browsers recognize only a subset of the HTML codes and ignore the others. There is little consistency among the various browsers. For example, some browsers will display headings like this:

This is a heading

Others will display the same heading like this:

This is a heading

Any one browser will, however, be consistent within itself in the way it displays text marked up in a particular way.

One central concept of HTML development is that *you are responsible for the content, but the browser handles the layout*. You will have limited control of the format. So you should focus on the content, the information you are making available, and leave the formatting to the browser. As you develop your pages, test them with your favorite graphical browser. But also test them with a text browser so that you can address the needs of both types of users.

Browsers

A browser is the software, or program, you use to cruise the World Wide Web. Netscape, Internet Explorer, and Lynx are three examples of browser programs. Browsers can be either text-based, like Lynx, or graphical, like Netscape and Internet Explorer. The browser program translates the HTML language and builds, or renders, the image on the screen for you. Graphical browsers like Netscape and the Internet Explorer can display pictures, play sounds, and show animations. They are **multimedia** presentation tools. Figure 1.3 shows the Dallas County Community College District Web page as seen with Netscape. It took 16 seconds to appear on the computer used by the author of this book.

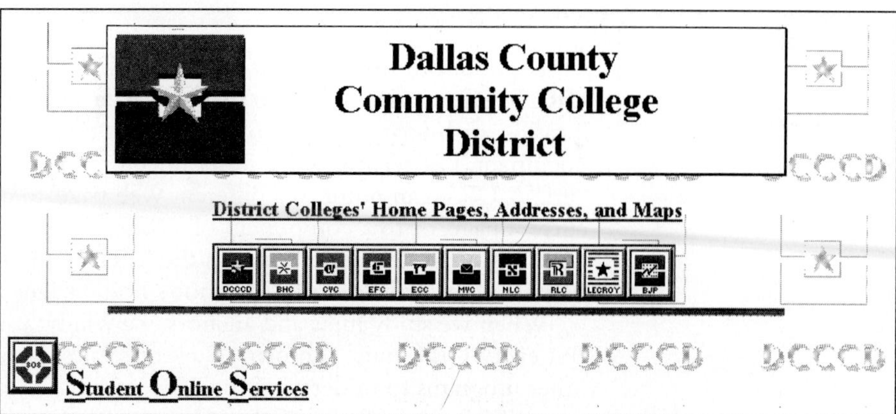

Figure 1.3 The DCCCD home page viewed with a graphical browser.

Text-based browsers like Lynx display only the text of the document and cannot show the pictures, play the sounds, or show the videos. Figure 1.4 shows the Dallas County Community College District Web page as it looks when displayed with the Lynx browser. It took less than a second to appear on the computer used by the author of this book. Why did it take so much less time with the Lynx browser than with Netscape? Because none of the graphics files were transferred.

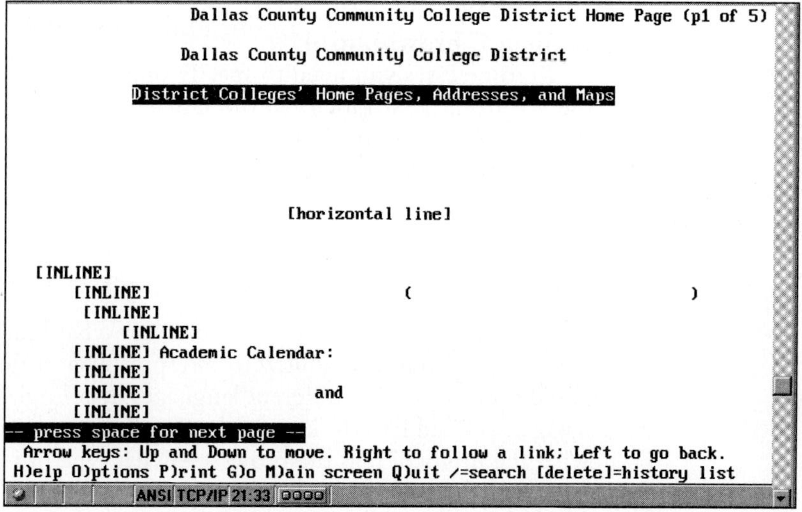

Figure 1.4 The DCCCD home page viewed with text-based browser.

Some people have access only to a text browser or have computers that can support only a text browser. Many World Wide Web experts often use a text browser or turn off the automatic downloading of images because text is transferred across the Internet much faster than pictures. Cruising with Lynx is a whole lot faster than with a graphical browser.

What Is a URL?

Throughout our discussion of the World Wide Web, we will be using the term **URL**. URL stands for **Uniform Resource Locator**. Simply, it describes the location, or Internet address, of the specific resource we want to use for our document. The term URL is pronounced as three letters, "You are ell" not "erl." A URL can point to a different Web page, to another location in the current page, or to a component of a page, like an image. For example, **http://home.netscape.com/** is the URL of the Netscape home page, and **http://www.yahoo.com/** is Yahoo's home page.

When we study links and anchors, we will be using different kinds of URLs. But every URL must conform to a set of rules. These rules allow browsers and other programs to understand the URL and use it to reliably move the data across the Internet from one location or page to another. When you create your Web page, it will have a URL that is unique to that page. That unique URL, or address, will allow anyone on the World Wide Web to find your page and view the information you place there.

The general form of a full URL is

protocol://domain name/path/filename

For example, the page from the Electronic Text Library at the University of Virginia that lets you browse for authors with a last name that starts with C is

http://etext.lib.virginia.edu/modeng/modengC.browse.html

In this example, the protocol is **http:**, the domain name is **etext.lib.virginia.edu**, and the path and filename is **/modeng/modengC.browse.html.**

In some cases you need to specify only part of a URL. For example, to go to the Electronic Text Library at the University of Virginia, you would need to specify only the protocol and the domain name, **http://etext.lib.virgina.edu/.** Let's look at each of the three parts of the URL and see what they mean.

Protocol

The **protocol** of a URL tells the browser what kind of resource it is accessing. The browser must know how to interpret what it finds. It is as if your browser could translate several different languages into English. Before it could translate a page, it would have to know what language it was translating from. That is what the protocol tells the browser—what type of resource it will be using. There are seven common protocols, shown in Table 1.1.

Domain

The **domain name** is the second part of the URL. It specifies the physical location of the file or information resource. A **domain** is the computer that runs the server software to handle the protocol specified in the first part of the URL. The domain portion of the URL starts immediately after the colon or the two slashes ("//") that end the protocol. The domain portion ends with a single slash. You can specify the domain either by its IP address or by using a domain name that stands for the site's IP address.

Protocol	Example	Description
file:	**file:///C|foobar.htm**	A file you want the browser to read. Usually the file is local or is on the same computer as the document that points to it. Notice it has three slashes, not two, and the drive letter "C" is followed by a vertical bar, not a colon.
ftp:	**ftp://ftp.fancyfoo.stuff/foobar.txt**	A resource you want to bring back to the current computer. Usually this is used if you want your users to be able to download or copy a file to their computers.
gopher:	**gopher://deep.gopher.hole/**	This URL transfers control to a gopher site and opens that gopher space, or gopher hole.
http:	**http://unreal.place.com/**	You will most often see links that point to other Web pages. The link is specified as a **HyperText Transfer Protocol** (**http**) link so the browser knows it is looking for another Web page.
mailto:	**mailto:someone@somewhere.net**	This URL will start a mail program *if the browser supports mailto URLs.* This is often used to request feedback about a Web page. Notice that there are no slashes.
news:	**news:alt.some.cool.newsgroup** **news:C6491Rt@netplace.net**	*If the browser supports Usenet news URLs,* the first example will open the news reader and begin reading that newsgroup. The second example will just open the article specified from the newsgroup. Each article is given a specific number to identify it. Notice that there are no slashes.
telnet:	**telnet://user:password@server:port** **telnet://server:port**	The first example will login remotely at the computer specified, using the username and password supplied. *This is very dangerous, because your username and password are visible in the HTML code.* In the second example, the browser should prompt for a username and password before making the connection. It is a safer alternative. Always remember to tell your users what username and password to use if you don't supply one.

Table 1.1 Types of protocols.

IP stands for **Internet Protocol**. IP addresses are four sets of one, two, or three digits separated by periods. They define the Internet address of the particular machine pointed to by the URL. An example of an IP address is 198.95.251.5. It identifies a specific computer somewhere on the World Wide Web. If you choose to use a domain name, a special program called a **DNS**, or

Domain Name Server, will try to translate the domain name into an IP address. If it cannot translate the domain name, you will see the annoying "DNS unable to translate domain name" message.

Since most people find numbers harder to remember than names, it is easier to tell someone to download software from **home.netscape.com** than 198.95.251.53, the IP address. Domain names can be very long. They usually end in a two- or three-character extension. Some of the common extensions are

Extension	Meaning
.edu	an educational site, usually a college or university
.com	a commercial site or business
.gov	government sites like the White House or Senate
.org	nonprofit organizations
.net	usually an **ISP** (**Internet Service Provider**)

Some of the extensions also indicate the country of the domain. For example, a domain name that ends in **.au** indicates an Australian site, and one that ends in **.fr** indicates a location in France.

If you want to look at the main page for a domain, you can usually specify just the protocol and domain without a path or filename. For example, if you want to see Netscape's home page, you can type the following into the target for your browser: **http://home.netscape.com/**. If you want to look at Yahoo's home page, use **http://www.yahoo.com/**.

Path and Filename

Let's use the following example: **http://etext.lib.virgina.edu/modeng/modengC.browse.html**. The last part of this URL is the path and file we are interested in. If the resource you are connecting to is a file, then the URL will end in a filename. In our example, the HTML document is called **modengC.browse.html**. It is located in a directory or subdirectory called **modeng**.

URLs are the heart of navigation across the World Wide Web, and we will use them throughout our exploration of HTML.

HTML Terminology

Like any other specialized skill, using HTML requires that you learn some specific terms. Some of the terms are logical, and some are, well, a little odd. If you're going to read books about HTML, talk with people about HTML, or cruise the Net to find out more about HTML, you will need to learn a handful of specialized terms.

Tags

One of the first terms you will run across is **tag**. Tags are HTML codes that are enclosed in angle brackets (< and>). These tags are used to format the text. For example, the <BR> tag adds a line break into the text. You will learn more about specific HTML tags in the chapters that follow.

Tags come in two general types: empty tags and containers. The tag <BR> is an example of an **empty tag**. It does not hold or surround anything, so it is called empty. **Containers** start with a beginning tag, contain some text that is modified by the container, and end with an ending, or closing, tag. The closing tag looks like the beginning tag except that it has a slash preceding its name. Following is an example of a container that causes the text within it to appear in italics. <I> is the beginning tag, and </I> is the closing tag.

```
<I> This text is in italics </I>
```

This would produce the following when viewed by most browsers:

This text is in italics

Attributes

Empty or beginning container tags can contain other HTML elements called **attributes**, which are special codes that modify the tags. For example, the empty tag <HR> causes a horizontal line, or rule, to appear on the page. You can specify the length of the line, its size (how thick it is), and whether it starts on the right margin, is centered, or starts on the left margin. To specify these different values, you include attributes within the tag itself. For example, if you want to place a horizontal rule across your document that is as wide as the page and one pixel thick, you would put the following tag in your document:

```
<HR SIZE=1>
```

Notice that the attribute, SIZE, is enclosed within the angle braces and thus is inside the beginning tag.

Most of the tags you use will have attributes that modify the way they work. Sometimes there are several possible attributes, and the tag can be complex. For example, the beginning tag of the <BODY> container has nine different attributes. Occasionally a particular attribute is used by only one browser. Other browsers will usually ignore attributes they don't support.

Containers

The other type of tag, a container, has both a beginning tag and an ending tag. Between the beginning and ending tags is information that is controlled by the container. A very useful container is the bolding container. It looks like this in HTML:

```
<B>This text is bold</B>
```

This would produce the following when viewed by most browsers:

This text is bold

The bolding tag simply makes the text it holds, or contains, appear in a bold font. If a bold font is not available, the browser may make the text appear in reverse video or underlined. Remember, the actual presentation of the text is up to the browser. Notice that the bolding container starts with a tag that looks like an empty tag, <B>, and ends with a slightly different tag. The ending tag has the right, or forward, slash before the tag character (</B>). Ending tags have no attributes. It is very important to place the ending tag correctly. In this case, if we left off the ending tag, the browser would bold the rest of the text it encountered.

Good HTML authors always close any container that should be closed for their particular version of HTML. Some containers are migrating to the status of empty tags, in which case the closing tag is almost always skipped. This is an example of the constantly changing face of HTML. New tags are added, older tags are deprecated, and the way the tags are used also evolves. The elements of a list are a good example of evolving tag use. The <LI> element is really a container, but the newer versions of most browsers can infer the closing tag, so it is universally omitted now.

Another useful container is the paragraph container (<P>). The paragraph container has one attribute, **ALIGN**, which allows you to have your paragraph aligned to the left, center, or right. The browser will usually choose to align the text on the left margin. In other words, left alignment is usually the default value. A **default value** is the value a program will choose if the user does not specify one.

The align attribute is part of the opening, or beginning, tag. Let's look at an example of this container so that you can see how tags and attributes look in actual HTML code. Don't worry if some of the codes you see appear a little odd to you—you are just beginning your exploration of HTML, and as in learning any new language, it will take a little time to figure it out.

If we put the code in Figure 1.5 into an HTML document, it would look like Figure 1.6 in Netscape:

```
<P ALIGN=RIGHT>
Right is Right
</P>
<P ALIGN=CENTER>
Center is Middle
</P>
<P ALIGN=LEFT>
Left is Left
</P>
<P>
Left is also the Default
</P>
```

Figure 1.5 Sample HTML code showing attributes and containers.

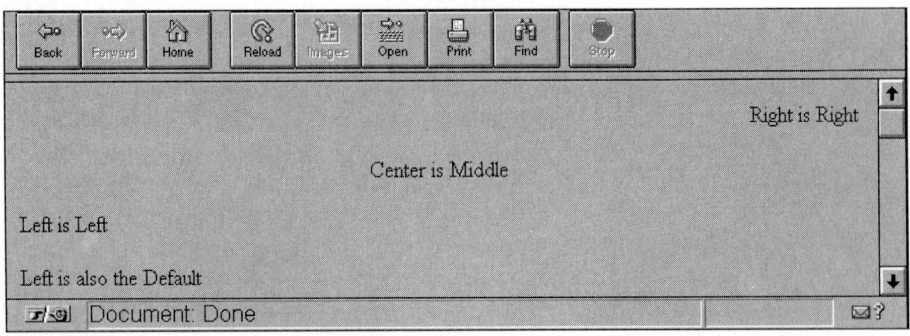

Figure 1.6 Sample Netscape screen showing how alignment affects paragraph placement.

One of the more interesting and yet sometimes confusing features of most HTML browsers is their ability to infer, or guess, when you want to close a container. For example, the code in Figure 1.7 will produce exactly the same result (shown in Figure 1.6) as the code in Figure 1.5. Compare the two codes and find the differences.

```
<P ALIGN=RIGHT>
Right is Right
<P ALIGN=CENTER>
Center is Middle
<P ALIGN=LEFT>
Left is Left
<P>
Left is also the Default
```

Figure 1.7 Sample HTML code with another view of containers.

That's right, there are no closing paragraph tags in Figure 1.7. The browsers guess, or infer, that when you start a new paragraph, you want to close the previous one. Some books you read will say that the ending paragraph tag is not necessary and will advise you to ignore it. They will point out that you can usually let the browser infer when to close containers. But this can lead to very strange-looking pages, because sometimes the browser won't guess correctly and will close a container too early or too late. Other times, the browser will not guess at all. For example, with the heading containers, the browser will happily include the rest of your page in a heading if you fail to close the container. Wise Web weavers have learned that in most cases it is best to close their containers. It takes only a few keystrokes to do so, and it can save you from some very strange-looking results.

HTML Command Format

The <BODY> container provides a good example of the general format of an HTML command. It is used to contain the main portion of an HTML document. We will explore exactly how to use this container when you build your first Web page. For now we will use it to examine the format of an HTML command.

```
<BODY bgcolor=yellow text=blue > ...The body of the page...</BODY>
    | ---- attributes ------|
|-----beginning tag -----------||---contents of container---||-ending tag-|
```

You can see from the preceding example that there are three parts to an HTML container. The beginning tag, which may have attributes, is the first part. The text held by the container is the second part. The ending tag is the third part. If you choose not to use an attribute, the browser reading the document will choose a value, the default, for you. The general format of an empty tag is just like the beginning of the container. We will explore both types of tags in more detail in the next chapter.

Browsers and HTML

Several browsers are available for reading HTML documents. They are loosely grouped into graphical and text-based styles. It is important to you as a Web weaver to understand a little of how the browsers will work with the documents you create. Accordingly, we discuss some of the more popular browsers in this section. However, because of the ever changing nature of the Web, tomorrow there may be a new browser available, or one of the ones discussed here may no longer exist. As a user, you can simply pick the browser you like best, but as a Web weaver, you need to try your pages with at least two different browsers to see how they work.

Netscape

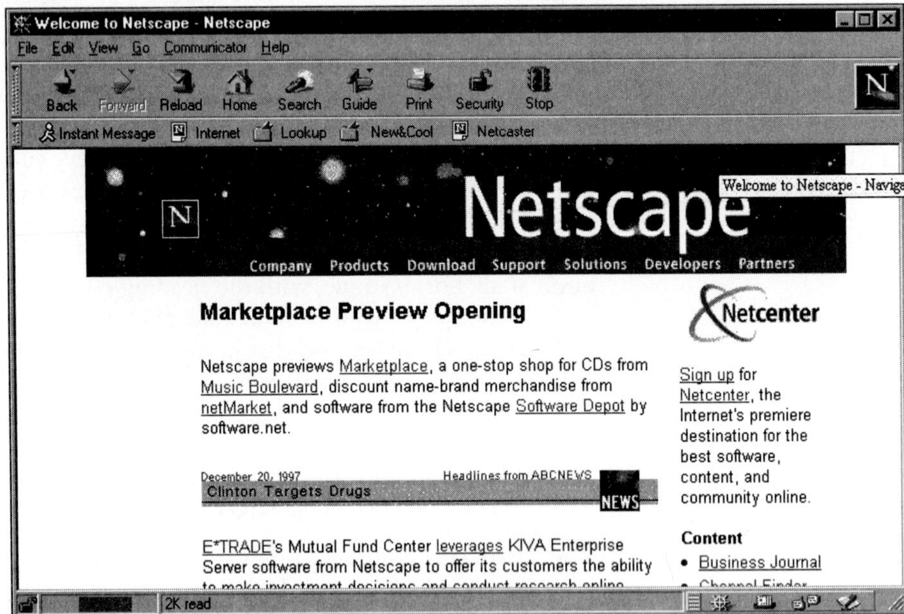

Figure 1.8 Netscape Communications Corporation's home page.

Currently Netscape (Figure 1.8) is the most popular browser on the World Wide Web. It is available from Netscape Communications Corporation and is free to students and faculty. Netscape is always being upgraded to perform more tasks and to run more quickly. In addition to the current release of Netscape, there is a beta release as well. The term **beta** means a new, experimental version of a software package. Users who are experienced with a software program often select a beta version to try new features before they become part of the current release. You can download Netscape from Netscape's home page at **http://home.netscape.com**. The term **downloading** means copying a computer-readable file from another computer to your computer.

Internet Explorer

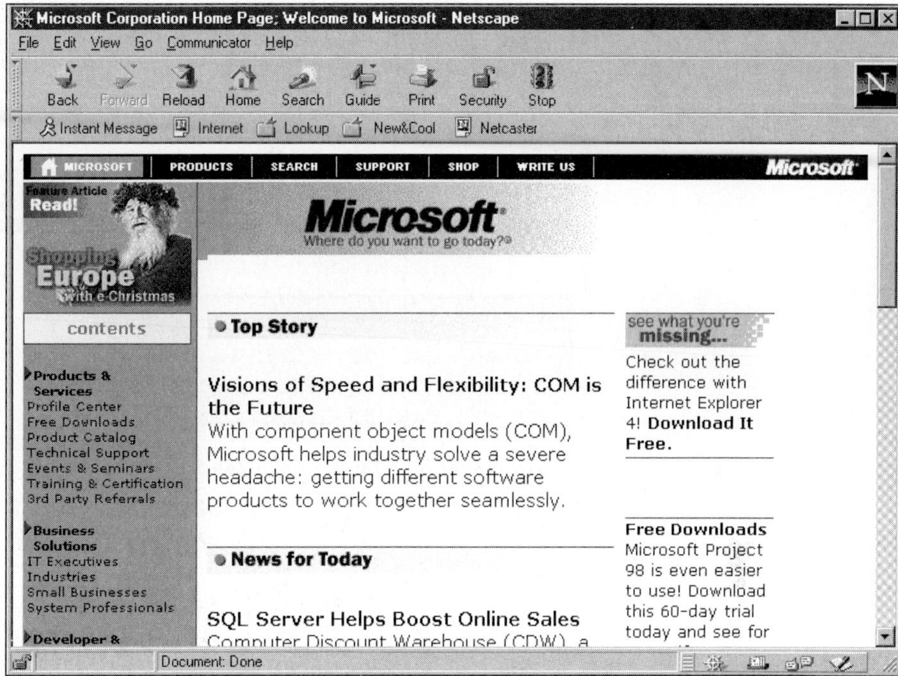

Figure 1.9 Microsoft's home page.
Microsoft® is a trademark of the Microsoft Corporation.

Microsoft's Internet Explorer (Figure 1.9) is another graphical browser, like Netscape. These two browsers are the two players in the current "browser war" that is being fought on the Net. Both Netscape and Microsoft are attempting to have the number one browser, and so both are enhancing their products to make them more attractive to the user community. This means that you need to keep informed of the new features available with each release of either of these packages.

NCSA Mosaic

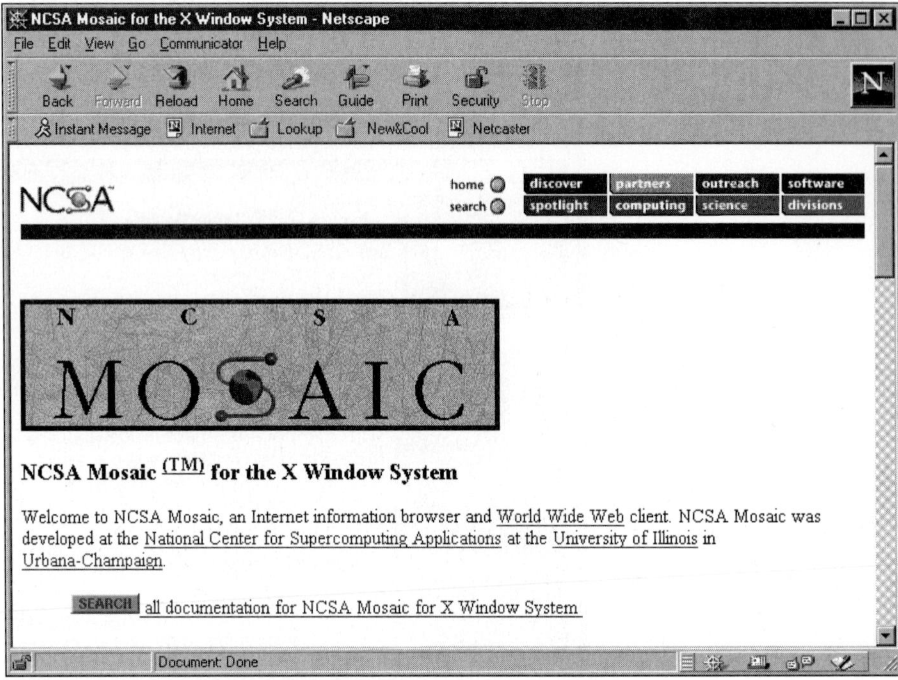

Figure 1.10 NCSA Mosaic's home page.

The NCSA Mosaic (Figure 1.10) used to be the premier browser for the World Wide Web. It has been replaced by Netscape because Netscape has more features and more quickly adapts to requests from the user community. Mosaic was the first full-color browser and, as such, is given credit for making the Web as popular as it is today.

Lynx

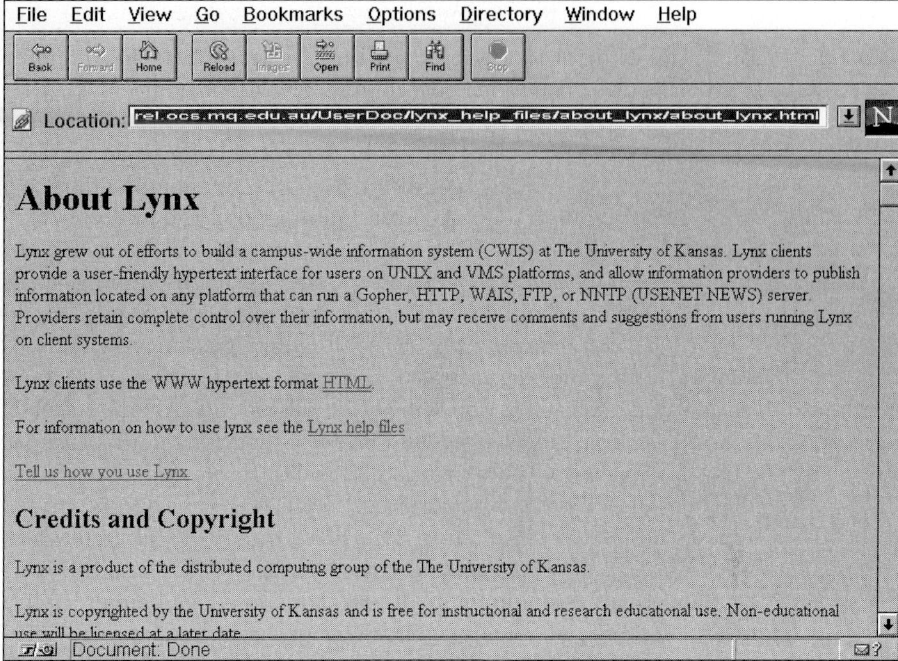

Figure 1.11 A Lynx source page, no graphics!

Lynx "links :-)" is a text-only browser. There is strong support for this browser in a community of dedicated Lynx users. They rightly maintain that the Web exists to share information, and that information can be more quickly shared if we don't have to wait for large graphic files to cross the Web. Many sophisticated Web cruisers use Lynx or another text browser when they want to access lots of information quickly. They use graphical browsers only for recreation on the Web or when they have to obtain an image. Considerate Web weavers will always have a copy of Lynx or another text-based browser available to check out their pages in text-only mode.

Netscape for Macintosh

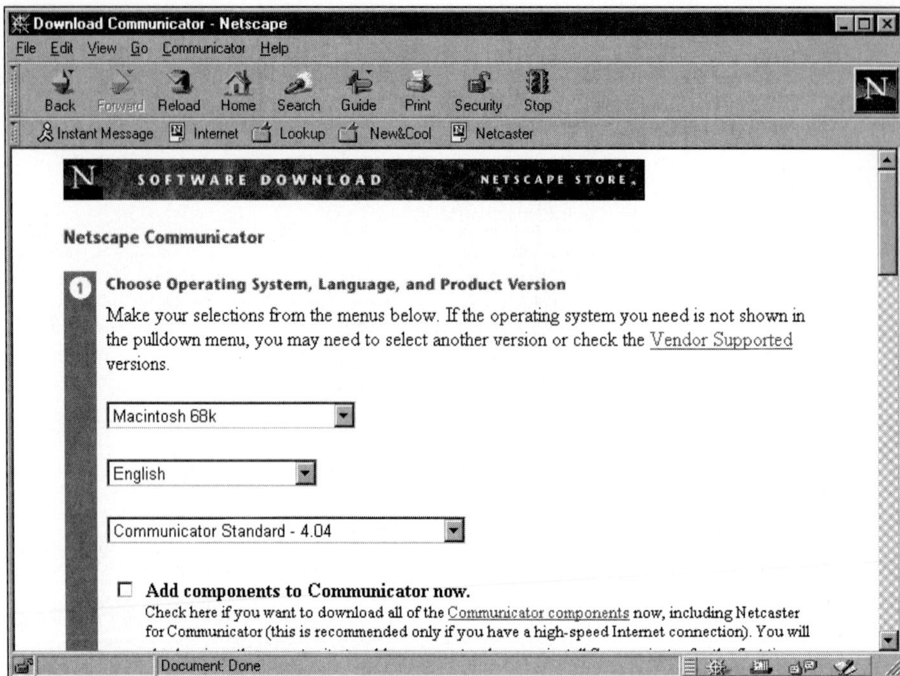

Figure 1.12 Downloading Netscape for Macintosh.

Netscape, as we have seen earlier in this chapter, is currently the most popular browser for Intel or PC platforms. They also have a version of their browser that is designed for the Macintosh platform. Figure 1.12 shows the download screen for the Macintosh browser. Unless you want to use a browser that is only available for the Macintosh platform, Netscape is an ideal choice as it is so widely used.

Cyberdog

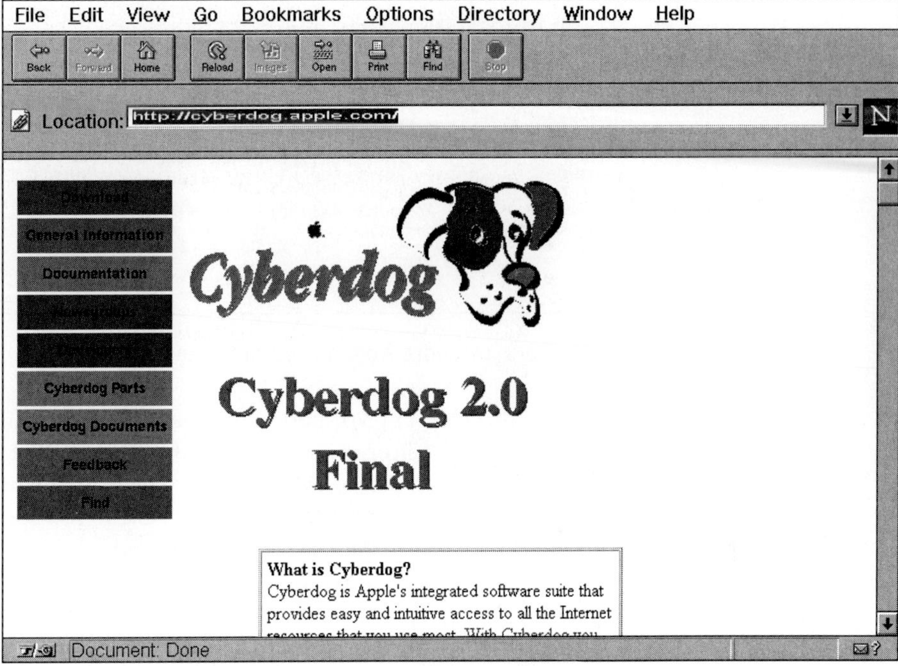

Figure 1.13 Cyberdog's home page, another Mac browser.

Cyberdog (Figure 1.13) is another browser available for the Macintosh platform. It is optimized to take advantage of the special abilities offered on the Macintosh. Currently you can download it for free.

Necessary Tools

To become a Web weaver, you need only three tools. A simple ASCII editor, an HTML viewer (software that lets you see what your document will look like to a browser), and an ISP (Internet Service Provider) to "host" your page. An ISP will put your document in a directory that is on a site with a recognized domain so other people can browse your page from across the Internet. Making your page available on a known domain is called **hosting** your page. Let's look at these three tools.

ASCII Editor

The first requirement for building Web pages is an editor that produces plain ASCII files as output. **ASCII** stands for **American Standard Code for Information Interchange**. An **ASCII editor** produces a standard ASCII file, or a file with just the text but with no embedded word-processing codes. Most word-processing software will add formatting, font, and other types of codes to the document. Browsers don't know what to do with those extra characters. Figure 1.14 shows some of the codes that appear in a word-processed file. As you can see, they make little sense!

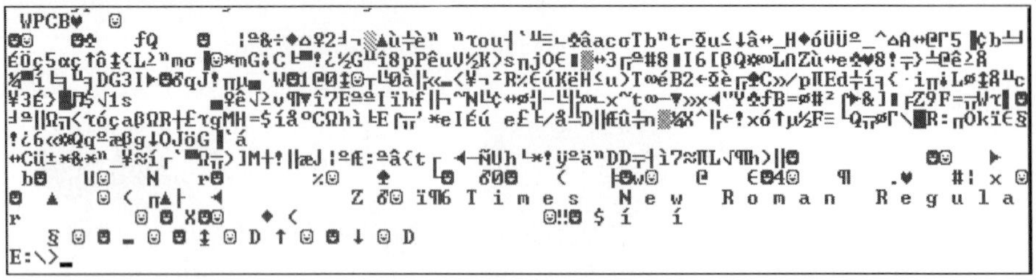

Figure 1.14 Codes from a word-processed file.

To produce HTML code, you need a simple editor. If you are using a Unix system, the vi editor is an excellent choice. The Notepad editor in Windows will also work. Most of the word processors, like Microsoft Word or WordPerfect, can save a file as plain ASCII if you specifically ask them to. You will need to select the "save as" option and ask for DOS text. Almost any word-processing or editing package can be used, but it is sometimes easier to produce HTML code with a simple editor. There are add-ons for some of the more popular word processors that enable them to act as HTML editors. Later in this chapter we will discuss specialized HTML editors.

HTML Viewer

There are three different ways you can view your document to see how it will appear on the World Wide Web. One of the easier ways to preview your documents is to use the browser you normally use to cruise the Web. Most browsers will allow you to specify the source of the HTML documents you are browsing. For example, in Netscape you can simply click on the **File** tool and then click on **Open** and type in the name of the file you just created. Or you can use the Browse feature to find your new document (touching the Control key and the O key at the same time will also invoke this option). Remember to save your document with an extension of **.htm** in DOS or **.html** in Unix so that viewer software will recognize it as an HTML document. For example, an HTML document called **compare.htm** on a DOS computer would be called **compare.html** on a Unix system.

Another way to view your software is to download a viewer option for your word processor. Several free packages add this feature to word processors like Microsoft Word version 6.0. Using this type of viewer you can see what your new document may look like on the page. You can check your choice of colors, fonts, and local images. But because these viewers are not connected to the Internet, they will not be able to link to other sites across the World Wide Web.

In addition to browsers and word-processor add-ons, several stand-alone HTML viewers are available for downloading from the Net. HTML Viewer is a package for Macintosh computers that allows the user to view HTML documents without having an online connection. I-View is a similar product for IBM and IBM-compatible PCs.

You should also have one of the text-only viewers so that you can see what your page will look like to users with text-only browsers like Lynx. Responsible Web weavers always produce pages that are accessible and usable with either graphical or nongraphical browsers.

ISP (Internet Service Provider)

Most people don't maintain a full-time, high-speed connection to the Internet, so they need an organization with that type of connection to make their Web pages accessible to users all across the Internet. Companies that specialize in providing World Wide Web access are called Internet Service Providers, or ISPs. Your college may provide you with Web space and in so doing will host your page on the World Wide Web. However, there is an expense associated with building, hosting, and maintaining a Web site, so many colleges don't allow their students to have college-supported Web pages. Check with the data-processing services department of your college.

Internet service providers can be expensive or relatively inexpensive. The cost usually depends on the services they provide. Inexpensive ISPs will normally host your page and provide you access to the Net but will usually require you to download and install the client software you want to use. **Client software** is a program like Netscape that is resident on your computer but interacts with other programs or data across the Net. Some of the common client packages are **ftp** (**File Transfer Protocol**), which allows you to move files across the Internet; **telnet**, which allows you to work remotely on computers across the Net as if you were at that computer's location; and browsers like Netscape or Internet Explorer.

Some ISPs charge you monthly for your Web space. Others include a fixed amount of space in their pricing but charge for any additional space. For example, one ISP charges students $49.95 per year for Internet access. The students must download all the client software they need. The ISP will host their Web pages of up to 2 megabytes in size as part of the yearly fee. If a student needs more space for a Web page, the cost is $1.95 per megabyte per month. There is no additional charge for connect time, e-mail messages sent and received, or any other services. However, technical support is available only during office hours, Monday through Friday.

Another ISP charges $19.95 a month. For this charge the subscriber gets several disks of software and detailed instructions on how to install it. This ISP will help the subscriber install a Web page and will be very active in supporting it for an additional charge of $2.50 per megabyte per month. Technical support is available 24 hours a day, seven days a week. There is a small fee for each e-mail message sent or received. Several other services, like a stock market data service, are provided for a fee.

These two different ISPs illustrate some of the significant differences in service and price that are available. If you are able to download and install software on your computer, and if you don't need much technical support, one of the budget-priced ISPs will probably meet your needs. On the other hand, if you want more support, and if you would like to have software sent to you rather than having to download it, you may wish to subscribe to one of the larger, more expensive ISPs.

Nice-to-Have Tools

You can get by with the tools mentioned in the previous section, but there are three other HTML tools that will make the job of building and maintaining Web pages much easier. First, although you can build Web pages with a simple ASCII editor, it is much easier and faster to use a special **HTML editor** to write your document. Second, you can take an existing file built with a word processor and run it though an **HTML text-file converter** to create an HTML document from the plain text. (Some HTML editors can also do this job.) Finally, to ensure that your Web page works correctly, you can use one of the **HTML verifiers** to make sure your links are valid and your HTML syntax and grammar are correct. Let's look at these different tools individually.

HTML Editor

Many HTML editors are available on the Internet. Some are free, some are shareware, and others are commercial products. Three of the most popular HTML editors are Soft Quad's HoTMetaL Pro, Sausage Inc.'s HotDog, and the HTML editor that is built into Netscape Gold 3.0. Figures 1.15–1.17 show how the same, short HTML file looks in each of these editors. Figure 1.18 shows how it appears in the Netscape browser.

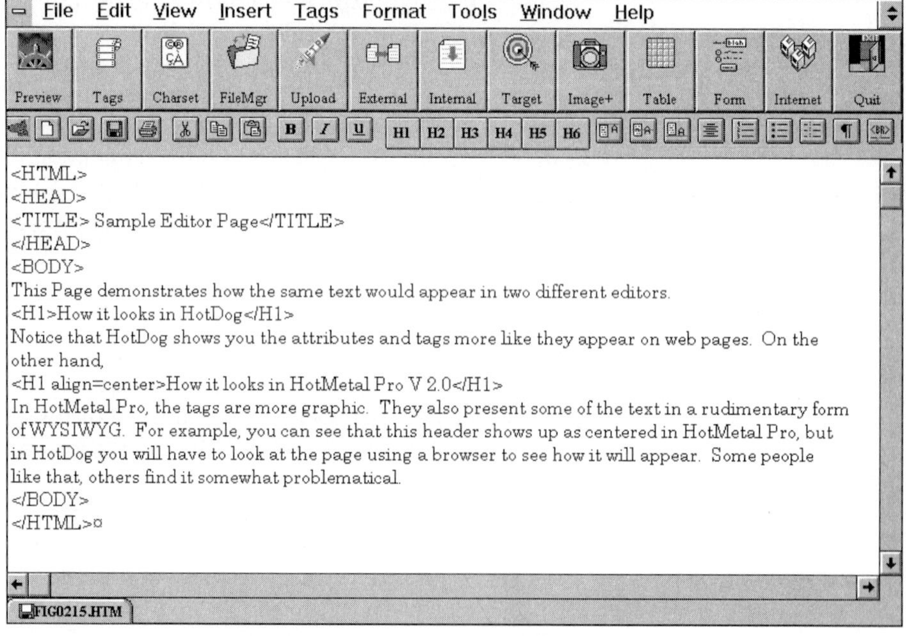

Figure 1.15 A sample document shown in the HotDog HTML editor.

As you can see in Figure 1.15, the HotDog editor shows you all the HTML tags in the document. The advantage of this style of editor is that since you actually see the codes, and not simply the result, it is somewhat simpler to edit, or modify, the document. A disadvantage is that you need to use another tool to see how the document will look. HotDog has a preview package, but you still need a browser to see in detail how the page will look.

The HoTMetaL Pro editor has a different approach. Figure 1.16 shows the same file as it looks in HoTMetaL Pro, which uses a more graphical representation than HotDog for some of the tags but does not show most of the attributes. HoTMetal does, however, show you how the document may look when viewed by a browser. Yet, HoTMetaL doesn't represent all of the browsers, so the document may appear very differently on some browsers. For example, the first heading, "How it looks in HotDog," looks as if it is centered in HoTMetaL. It isn't really coded that way, but that is how HoTMetaL chooses to represent that heading level.

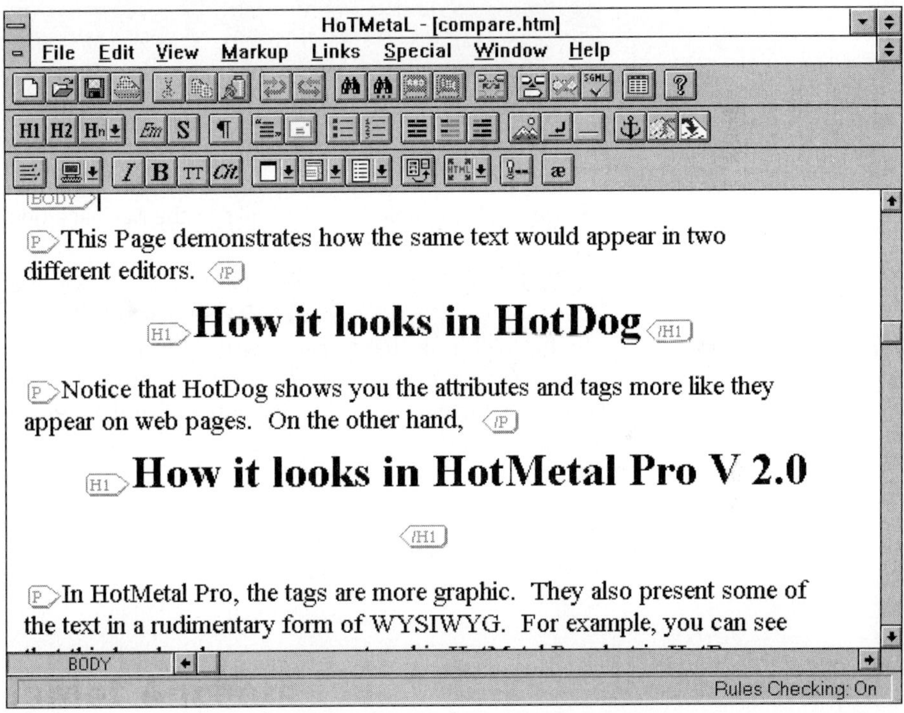

Figure 1.16 A document as it appears in the HoTMetaL editor.

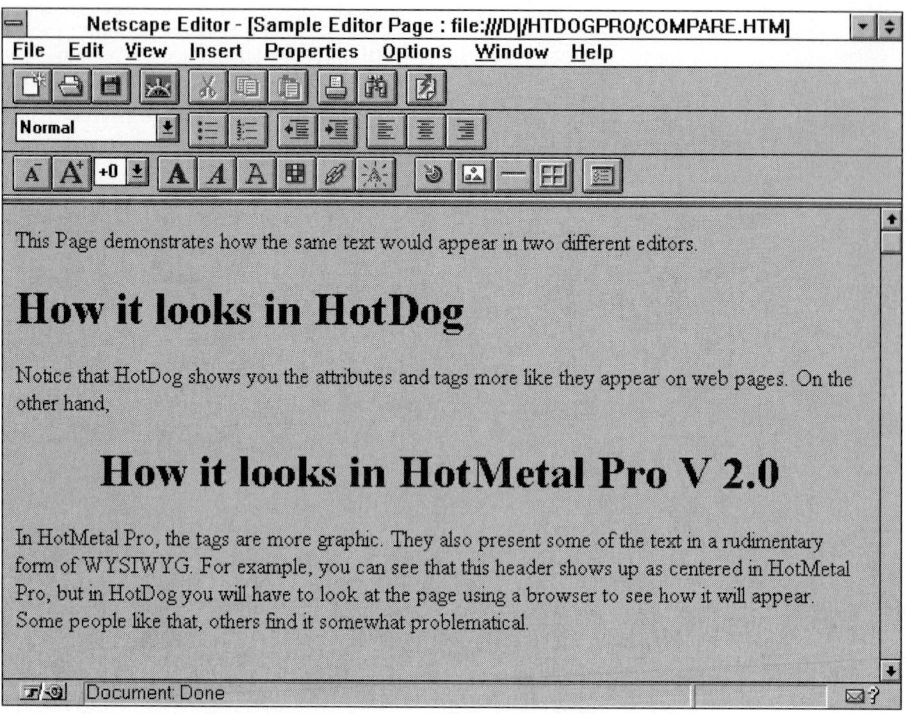

Figure 1.17 A sample file as it looks in the Netscape Gold 3.0 editor.

Figure 1.17 shows this file as it looks with the HTML editor that is part of Netscape Gold 3.0. This HTML editor is the most graphical. It shows you what the file will look like in the Netscape browser. This type of editor produces a page that may be more difficult to edit, simply because you can't see any of the codes. Obviously, if you are extremely familiar with HTML, you can infer the coding from the WYSIWYG screen of the Netscape Gold 3.0 editor, but editing with this device may be more difficult for new HTML designers.

Now look at Figure 1.18 to see how the page would appear when viewed with the Netscape browser.

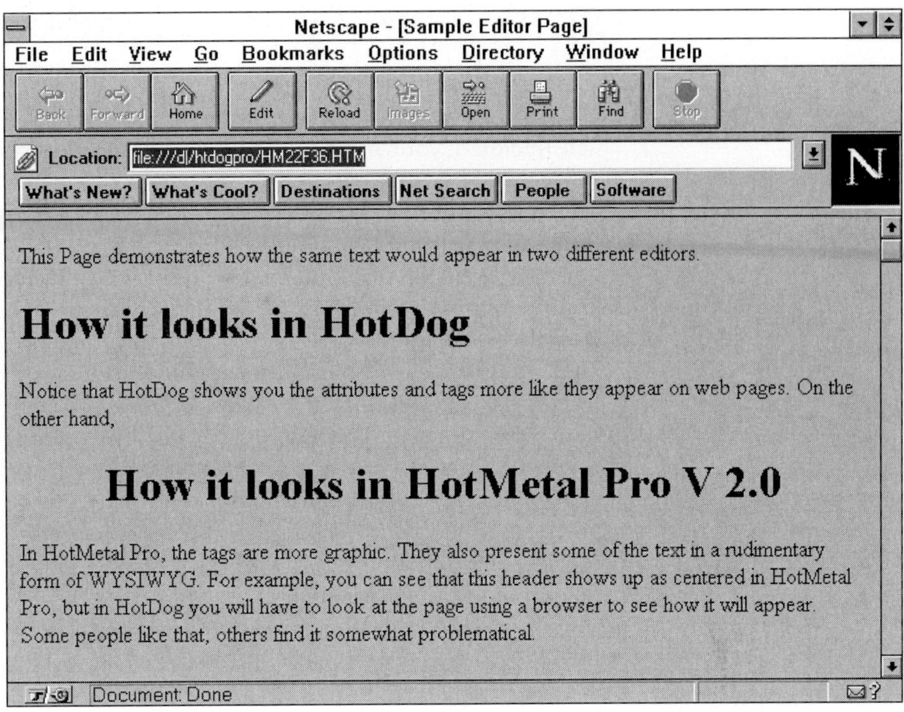

Figure 1.18 The sample HTML document as it appears in the Netscape browser.

To summarize, editors like HoTMetaL Pro give you some idea of the format of the page as you build it. On the other hand, editors like HotDog let you see more of the file while you are editing it, and the resultant file looks more like the source code you see when you view the source of Web pages across the Net. The Netscape editor is the most WYSIWYG of the three types described here. With the Netscape editor, the file you are working on looks very much like it will when viewed with the browser.

Which style you choose is a personal decision. Any of the products are excellent tools. However, tools that let you see as much of the code as possible, like HotDog, enable you to better understand the relationship between the HTML code and what ends up on the browser's screen. WYSIWYG editors are fun, but they are hard to use to solve a problem.

HTML Text-File Converters

Several tools can be used to embed HTML codes within an existing text file and make it an HTML document. Some of these tools are designed for the Microsoft word processor, MS Word, either version 2.0 or version 6.0. The ANT HTML converter and the GT_HTML converter are both available for downloading from the Internet. Quarter Deck Corporation produces the commercial converter, Web Author. In addition to these specialized conversion tools, most of the major HTML authoring packages can also take a text file as input and imbed HTML codes within it to make it an HTML document.

HTML Verifiers

Before publishing your page on the World Wide Web, you must make sure that it works. If you have some links that don't connect, or some containers that are left unclosed, your users may end up with results you didn't intend. To solve these problems, you can personally test each link and exercise each part of your page to ensure that it performs as expected. However, if you have a large set of pages with hundreds of links, it would take a lot of time to do the testing. Some tools are available on the World Wide Web that will check your pages for errors, testing each link and making sure the syntax is correct. One of the better HTML verifiers, or verification programs, is called Weblint ("It will pick the fuzz off your Web pages"). You can also visit Doctor HTML or WebTech to have your pages evaluated. If you are building a large Web site or for some other reason cannot take the time to evaluate all your links and syntax, you might want to use one of these verification services.

Places to Get Neat Stuff on the Net

An astounding number of Web sites provide software that works with HTML. What follows is only a partial listing of the available software. As you know, URLs change from day to day, so if one of these sites is no longer available, you can conduct a search and find other sites that are more current. This list is a place to start, not an exhaustive one.

Browsers

Netscape (http://home.netscape.com) This is one of the favorite browsers for the Web. You can download the most recent version of this browser, and if you are associated with a school, you can register your copy for free. From this site you can download the Netscape browser for several platforms including both Macintosh and PC platforms.

Internet Explorer (http://www.microsoft.com) This is the other "big" browser in the browser wars. You can download the most recent version of this browser free from Microsoft.

Lynx (http://www.ukans.edu/about_lynx/about_lynx.htm and **ftp://ftp2.cc.ukans.edu/pub/DosLynx/readme.htm)** This is one of the most often used nongraphical or text only browsers. You should test your page with a nongraphical browser so you can address the needs of those users who don't believe that a picture is worth a thousand words. The first URL given here tells you about Lynx, and you can download it from the second URL.

WebExplorer (http://www.raleigh.ibm.com) This is IBM's entry into the browser wars. It is far less popular than the big two, Netscape and Internet Explorer, but some folks really seem to like this browser.

Cyberdog (http://cyberdog.apple.com) This is one of the more popular Macintosh browsers available for downloading.

HTML Editors

A wide selection of HTML editors exists. Many are shareware or freeware, and some are commercial packages. Several are tools that add features to word processors like Microsoft Word. The following list is just a small sample of the available products.

HotDog (**http://www.sausage.com**) This one of the better HTML editors if you want to see HTML presented as the language rather than as the outcome. If you purchase the professional version, it includes a page viewer, so you don't need a browser. However, the page viewer is limited in the attributes it accepts. Therefore, it is best to have a browser available to view the page.

HoTMetaL (**http://www.sq.com**) This editor is preferred by nearly half the HTML community because it has very strong validation, or verification, routines. It tries to be somewhat WYSIWYG, which distracts some Web weavers. You will need a browser to view your page.

PageSpinner (**http://www.algonet.se**) This is one of the more common Macintosh editors.

Arachnid (**http://www.uiowa.edu**) This is a very popular Macintosh HTML editor. There are fewer Macintosh editors than those built for the Intel chip (IBM PCs), but Macintosh users are very loyal to their particular favorite.

Conversion Programs

If you need to convert an existing electronic file into an HTML document, you can use an HTML editor or one of the following conversion tools.

ANT HTML (**http://www.mcia.com/ant/antdesc.htm**) This tool works with both Word for Windows and Word for Macintosh.

WP2X (**http://www.milkway.com/People/Michael.Richardson/wp2x.html**) This tool is designed to work with WordPerfect documents.

GT_HTML (**http://www.hatech.edu/work_html**) Like ANT HTML, the GT_HTML works with both the Windows and Macintosh versions of Microsoft Word.

Cyberleaf (**http://www.ileaf.com/ip.html**) This tool works with Microsoft Word, WordPerfect, or Framemaker files.

HTML Verifiers

It is important to ensure that your Web page contains valid links and correct syntax. You can use MOMspider, Doctor HTML, and/or Weblint at the URLs listed.

MOMspider (**http://www.ics.uci.edu/pub/websoft/MOMspider**)

Doctor HTML (**http://www.sai.msu.su/admin**) You need to be patient if you use Doctor HTML. It may take a little while for the analysis of your site to be sent back to you.

Additional Search Sites

Many new and better HTML tools will become available as more and more people begin to use the Web to transfer information. Following are some of the more popular search tools for exploring the Web to find additional resources.

Yahoo (**http://www.yahoo.com**)

Metacrawler (**http://metacrawler.cs.washington.edu:8080**)

Altavista (**http://altavista.digital.com**)

Metasearch (**http://www.highway61.com**)

CHAPTER **two**

YOUR FIRST WEB PAGE

Now that you know some of the terminology used in HTML, it's time to build a simple page. The purpose of the World Wide Web is to share information. It's purpose is not to show off artistic skills, nor is it to duplicate existing information. Your page should provide unique information to the users in a way that is easy to understand and pleasant to view. Remember that not all the users will have graphical browsers, so build a page in a way that is usable in both graphic and text-only modes. Let's look at some of the tags you can use to build a page.

Types of Markup Tags Used in HTML

In HTML there are two major types of markup tags: empty tags and containers. **Empty tags** are used for page formatting. **Container tags** are used to manipulate or control the contents placed within them.

An empty tag has no closing tag and so does not enclose any text. It starts with a left angle bracket (<) followed immediately by the tag identifier, or name. Next come any attributes—special words that modify the way the tag works—separated by spaces. The tag ends with a right angle bracket (>). For example, **<HR WIDTH="50%">** is an empty tag that puts a line across the screen. The attribute, WIDTH="50%", determines how long the line is, in this case 50 percent of the screen width.

Containers start with a beginning tag, which is formatted like an empty tag. They also have an ending tag that marks the end of the text they contain, or surround. The ending tag starts with a left angle bracket, has a slash (/) preceding the tag identifier, and ends with a right angle bracket (**</HTML>** is an example of an ending tag). There are no attributes on an ending tag, and the tag identifier or name must be preceded by a slash (/).

The beginning container tag that surrounds the whole Web page is **<HTML>**. It is closed by the </HTML> tag. All the contents of a Web page or document must be enclosed by the <HTML> *contents of page* </HTML> container.

Empty Tags

Empty tags do not have a corresponding ending tag. Three examples of empty tags follow.

The line break tag, **
,** causes the browser to stop the current line and move the cursor to the left margin. It functions like a carriage return on a keyboard. It is often used for formatting text or inserting blank lines. For example, a poem would be encoded as shown in Figure 2.1. Figure 2.2 shows how it would look on a browser.

```
Robert Frost wrote: <BR>
"Two roads diverged in a yellow wood, <BR>
And sorry I could not travel both <BR>
And be one traveler, long I stood <BR>
And looked down one as far as I could <BR>
To where it bent in the undergrowth;"
```

Figure 2.1 HTML code for line breaks.

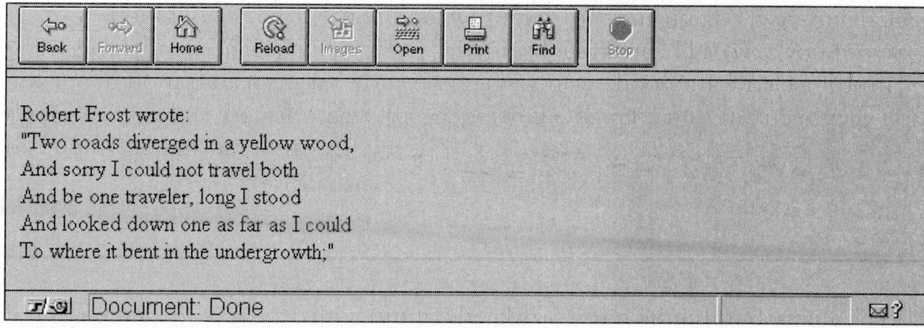

Figure 2.2 Netscape's presentation of line breaks.

<HR>

The horizontal rule tag, **<HR>**, puts a horizontal line, or rule, across the screen. This is an empty tag. It has four attributes you can use to modify the way the line appears on the screen. Even though the tag contains attributes, it is called an empty tab because it has no closing or ending tag. Figure 2.3 shows how three of the attributes are used. Figure 2.4 shows how it looks using Netscape.

```
<HTML>
<HEAD>
<TITLE>Poem with horizontal lines </TITLE>
</HEAD>
<BODY>
Robert Frost wrote
<HR SIZE=2 ALIGN=LEFT WIDTH="50%">
"Two roads diverged in a yellow wood, <BR>
And sorry I could not travel both <BR>
And be one traveler, long I stood <BR>
And looked down one as far as I could <BR>
To where it bent in the undergrowth;"
<HR SIZE=2 ALIGN=LEFT WIDTH="50%">
</BODY>
</HTML>
```

Figure 2.3 HTML code for horizontal rules.

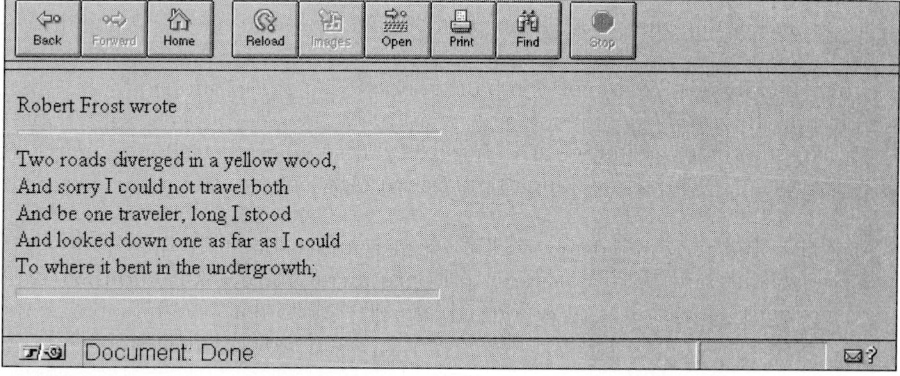

Figure 2.4 Netscape's presentation of horizontal rules, showing the different widths of rules in a document.

The **WIDTH** attribute sets the length of the line. In this example, both lines are one half, 50 percent, of the screen width. The **ALIGN** attribute defines the horizontal placement of the line on the page. The **SIZE** attribute determines how thick the line is. The default line is the width of the screen, side to side, 3 pixels thick. The term **pixel** stands for picture element. It is one of the many tiny dots that make up the display on your computer screen. Usually one pixel is about the size of one point of type on a standard 75 dot-per-inch display. Typical typefaces are about 12 points, or 12 pixels tall. The pixel is the smallest addressable unit of space on a screen.

In Figure 2.4, the first line is only 2 pixels thick. The second line is 6 pixels thick, twice the normal thickness of a line. In both cases the length of the line (WIDTH attribute) is half the screen wide, or 50 percent of the screen width. WIDTH can be expressed in either the number of pixels or as a percentage of the actual screen size. It is usually better to use the percentage measure because it will look the same regardless of the screen size. If you use an absolute width, setting WIDTH to a fixed number of pixels, the browser will use that length regardless of screen size. That may change the appearance of your screen on different computers or with different browsers.

We start both lines at the left margin, as specified by our ALIGN attribute (ALIGN=LEFT). The default for alignment is *centered,* so we need to specify *left* alignment to bring the lines to the left margin.

<P>

You may see examples of HTML code that appear to have other empty tags. One of the more common is the paragraph tag, **<P>**. In version 2 of HTML, the paragraph tag was an empty tag and allowed only an alignment attribute. In version 3 of HTML, the paragraph tag was changed to a container. In most cases, you should code both the beginning and ending tags on all containers. Because HTML tries to be as friendly as possible, it will close any unclosed tag if it can infer, or guess, a closing location. That can cause very unpredictable output if you modify a page that uses unclosed containers. So be careful to always close your containers. Some syntax-checking programs will catch open containers for you. An editor like HotDog will display both the opening and closing tags on containers to make your job a little easier.

Figure 2.5 presents an example of the way an open paragraph container can cause formatting problems. Notice that there is no closing paragraph tag, </P>. Figure 2.6 shows how that page would look using the Netscape browser.

```
<HTML>
<HEAD>
<TITLE> Container demo </TITLE>
</HEAD>
<BODY>
<H1>Sample paragraph</H1>
<P>Here is the first paragraph of my document.  I intend to
have this paragraph continue for at least three more lines.
I am using this paragraph to demonstrate how the insertion of
other information within an open container can change the way
the text looks.  Notice that this paragraph has no closing
container.  This should be the last line of the paragraph.
</BODY>
</HTML>
```

Figure 2.5 HTML code with an open paragraph container.

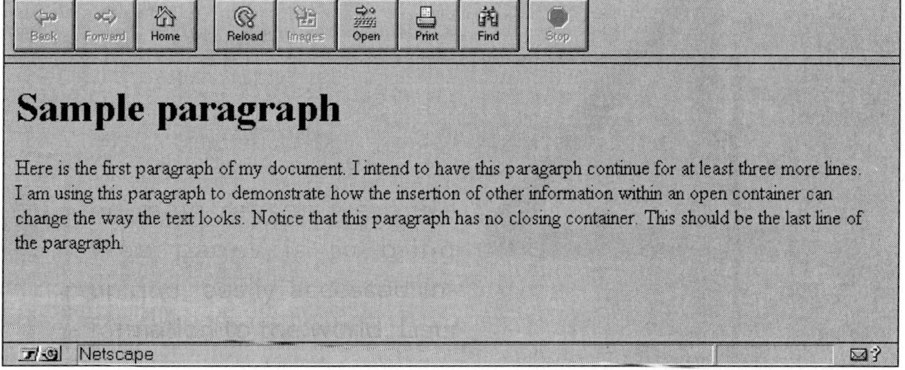

Figure 2.6 Netscape's presentation of the open paragraph.

So far the page looks fine. However, if we try to add a second paragraph by simply manipulating the text the way we would in a paper, as shown in Figure 2.7, we don't get the results we expect. Figure 2.8 shows how the file looks in Netscape.

```
<HTML>
<HEAD>
<TITLE> Container demo </TITLE>
</HEAD>
<BODY>
<H1>Sample paragraph</H1>
<P>Here is the first paragraph of my document.  I intend to
have this paragraph continue for at least three more lines.
I am using this paragraph to demonstrate how the insertion of
other information within an open container can change the way
the text looks.  Notice that this paragraph has no closing
container.  This should be the last line of the paragraph.

Now I am going to add an additional paragraph.  See, it
starts on a new line with a blank line between.
</BODY>
</HTML>
```

Figure 2.7 HTML code in which text is added to an open container.

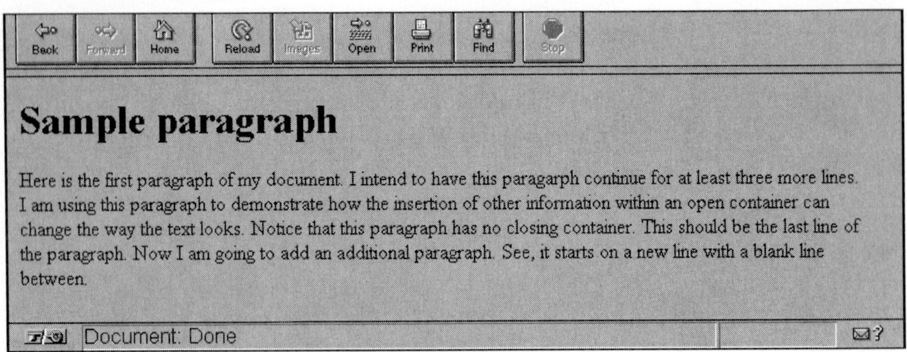

Figure 2.8 Netscape's presentation of the new paragraph after an open container, showing unexpected formatting.

Because we failed to close the first paragraph, the additional text we inserted was added to that first paragraph. Browsers will remove any white space (extra blanks, tabs, line feeds, and so on) in order to present the text as concisely as possible. We can easily fix the problem by just adding a closing tag to the end of our first paragraph, as shown in Figure 2.9.

```
<HTML>
<HEAD>
<TITLE> Container demo </TITLE>
</HEAD>
<BODY>
<H1>Sample paragraph</H1>
<P>Here is the first paragraph of my document.  I intend to
have this paragraph continue for at least three more lines.
I am using this paragraph to demonstrate how the insertion of
other information within an open container can change the way
the text looks.  Notice that this paragraph has no closing
container.  This should be the last line of the paragraph.
</P>
Now I am going to add an additional paragraph.  See, it
starts on a new line with a blank line between.
</BODY>
</HTML>
```

Figure 2.9 HTML code for adding a closing tag to the first paragraph.

Notice in Figure 2.9 that the first paragraph is now closed by the paragraph ending tag, </P>, and we removed the line that separated the two paragraphs in our HTML source. The browser puts the extra line in, as you can see in Figure 2.10. Simply adding an ending tag solved our problem.

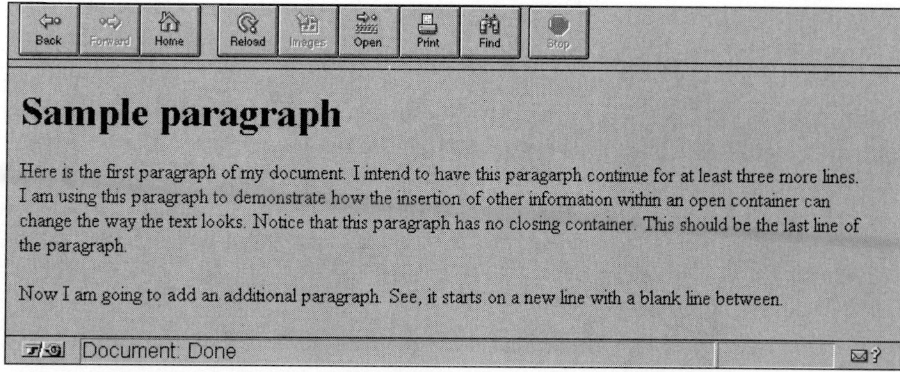

Figure 2.10 Netscape's presentation of how a paragraph break appears after the closing tag is added.

Adding a closing tag solved our problem, but there are other ways we could have achieved the same result. As we discussed, a browser will try to guess where closing tags belong, so if we were to write the HTML code as shown in Figure 2.11, the result would look the same. The browser has to guess where we want the first paragraph to end because there is no closing tag. It guesses, or infers, that we want to close the first paragraph before we open the new one. Although it guesses correctly this time, it might not another time. Therefore, one of the rules of good Web weaving is to close your containers so that the browser doesn't have to guess.

```
<HTML>
<HEAD>
<TITLE> Container demo </TITLE>
</HEAD>
<BODY>
<H1>Sample paragraph</H1>
<P>Here is the first paragraph of my document.  I intend to
have this paragraph continue for at least three more lines.
I am using this paragraph to demonstrate how the insertion of
other information within an open container can change the way
the text looks.  Notice that this paragraph has no closing
container.  This should be the last line of the paragraph.
<P>Now I am going to add an additional paragraph.  See, it
starts on a new line with a blank line between.
</BODY>
</HTML>
```

Figure 2.11 HTML code with a second opening tag but no closing tag.

Containers

Most of the markup tags in HyperText Markup Language are called containers. These tags have an opening tag and a closing tag with text or graphics between. The text or graphics between the two tags is controlled, or modified, by the container. Any attributes a container uses, like the WIDTH="50%" on the <HR> container in the previous example, are always included in the beginning tag. Ending tags do not have attributes.

First Containers

The following are some of the first containers we use to create a Web page. They are common to almost every page found on the Web.

<HTML>

The first container we will use is the **<HTML>** tag. This identifies the type of document we are creating, as well as marking the beginning and ending of our Web page. The <HTML> tag can have one attribute, called VERSION, but it can cause problems with some browsers, so most experts advise against its use.

If you look at Figure 2.5 and then Figure 2.6, you can see the use of the <HTML> tag. Browsers may recognize HTML tags in either uppercase or lowercase; however, the standard describes them as uppercase only, so you should code them in uppercase. In this text, we will show the HTML tags in uppercase to follow the standard, and to help distinguish them from the actual text. Many experienced Web weavers code their HTML like this because it makes it much easier to read and maintain. Nevertheless, as you explore the Web, you will run across pages where all or most of the tags are lowercase. This is just an author preference; the browsers don't care.

<HEAD>

The **<HEAD>** container tag has no attributes and serves only to contain the other tags that make up the header. The whole <HEAD> container is always placed between the <HTML> tag and the <BODY> tag. Because it is always located in this area of the document, the <HEAD> and </HEAD> tags can be inferred by some browsers. Therefore, you may find Web pages without a <HEAD> container. Generally, you should not depend on the browser to infer the location of a tag, because it may not guess the way you want it to. The <HEAD> container may contain any of the following tags that define and manage the content of the document:

TAG	FUNCTION
<BASE>	Sets the base URL for the document; used if the URL of the document is not the base for the other URL references.
<BASEFONT>	Sets the size of the font for the document. The default is 3.
<ISINDEX>	Indicates that the page can be searched.
<LINK>	Defines the relationship between the current document and another document on the Web.
<META>	An additional tag that can specify additional Web server name/value pairs. It is seldom used.
<NEXTID>	An historical entry in the HTML standard—don't use it.
<TITLE>	The only tag that is *required* in the <HEAD> of the document. Very imporant because it should accurately describe your page.

Some of these tags will be of value later to tie several pages together. For now, let's just look at the <TITLE> container.

<TITLE>

The **<TITLE>** container has no attributes. It is used to identify the title of the document you are building and must be put inside the <HEAD> container. Figure 2.12 shows a sample <TITLE> in the HTML code. Figure 2.13 shows how it looks when presented by the Netscape browser.

```
<HTML>
<HEAD>
<TITLE> This is the Title</TITLE>
</HEAD>
<BODY>

</BODY>
</HTML>
```

Figure 2.12 HTML code for a title.

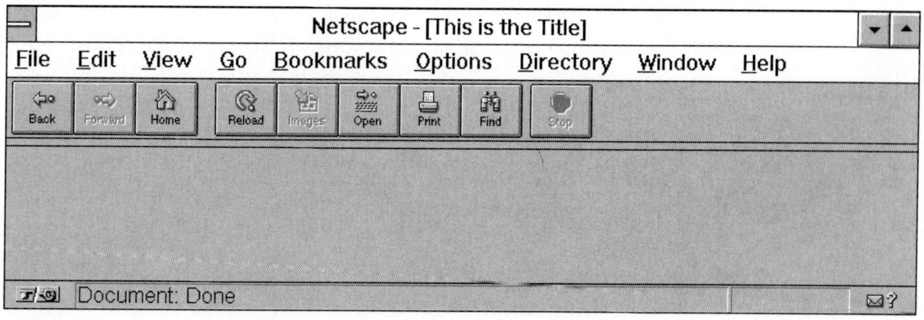

Figure 2.13 Netscape's presentation of a title.

Notice that Netscape displays the title along the top identifier bar. Many people confuse headings with the title and thus look for the title to be displayed in the body of the page. Most browsers, if they display the title at all, display it outside the actual text area of the page. The title is a required part of a Web page, and it is also very important for three reasons:

1. The title may be used in the Bookmarks file or a Hot Links file of the people who visit your page. It should help them define the contents of the page so they can return when needed.
2. An Internet search engine or cataloging program may return only the title as a description of your page. People may make the decision whether to visit your page or not based on this information.
3. People who are surfing the Net and come upon your page should have some idea of the contents when they arrive.

For all these reasons, it is important to have a good, accurate title. However, your title should also be brief, as many browsers, like Netscape, place the title in the bar across the top of the screen. Long titles may be cut off and hence look strange. Examples of some good titles, which explain the page, follow:

```
<TITLE> Basic HTML commands </TITLE>
<TITLE> Radical Rhonda's Super Home Page </TITLE>
<TITLE> Pictures of Green Sea Turtles </TITLE>
```

The following titles are not good because either they do not describe the page enough for Web cruisers or they are so long that they will be cut off by the browser:

```
<TITLE> Stuff </TITLE>
<TITLE> My Home Page </TITLE>
<TITLE> Really Cool Pictures of Turtles I Have Taken While On Vacation
</TITLE>
```

The title must be plain text. Do not use any text modifiers like bolding or underlining; they will be ignored. Choose a title that will draw interest to your page and accurately reflect the contents.

<BODY>

Before version 3 of HTML was released, the **<BODY>** tag had no attributes. Anything within the <BODY> . . . </BODY> container was called the "body content." This container holds the majority of your page. HTML version 3.0 introduced a series of attributes to give the author greater control over the appearance of the document. Some of these attributes are currently available in only one specific browser. Be very careful if you select one of those attributes, as other browsers may ignore the attribute, and your page may not appear as you intended.

Other attributes will change the way specific elements of your page, like the link colors, are displayed. If you change things the user is used to, you may reduce the usefulness of your page. Generally it is best to allow the browser to default, or choose for itself, these values. For example, most graphical browsers show unfollowed links in bright blue and links the user has followed in a darker, purple-blue color. If you were to reverse these colors on your page, you could really confuse the user. The attributes of the <BODY> tag are described next.

BGCOLOR

The **BGCOLOR** attribute controls the background color of the page. It is expressed as a mixture of red, green, and blue (RGB). Each of these colors has an intensity range of 0–255, with zero representing none of that color and 255 representing the most intense value for that color. There is a little twist with HTML, though—these color numbers must be expressed as hexadecimal (base 16) numbers. (The digits are 0123456789ABCDEF.)

Two easy ways of converting the decimal RGB number to a hexadecimal are (1) using a calculator that supports hexadecimals and (2) using a table. Some of the numbers are simple: 255 decimal = FF in hex, and zero decimal = 00 in hex.

Some of the colors available are

White	FFFFFF
Bright red	FF0000
Bright green	00FF00
Bright blue	0000FF
Yellow	FFFF00
Magenta	FF00FF
Cyan	00FFFF
Black	000000

To make life a little easier, two of the browsers support color names rather than just the hexadecimal numbers. A list of some of those names is included in Appendix A of this text. Currently only Netscape, version 2.0 and above, and the Internet Explorer use the color names, and the use of color names is not consistent from version to version of the browsers. The Internet Explorer uses a small subset of the names. The following code shows how the background color is coded:

```
<BODY BGCOLOR="yellow">
     or
<BODY BGCOLOR="#FFFF00>"
```

FFFF00 is the code for yellow.

When you decide to add colors to your page, you can spend a significant amount of time trying to get them just the way you want them—and you can create some absolutely horrible combinations. For example, bright red letters on a bright blue background are very distracting. A background color that does not contrast well with your text color can make your page very hard to read. You also need to remember that the readers of your page can configure their browsers to automatically set different colors and override all your hard work.

BACKGROUND

The **BACKGROUND** attribute allows you to place a picture or image in the background of your page. The Netscape and Internet Explorer browsers will display the image you select and will **tile**, or repeat, the image both vertically and horizontally to fill the whole background. The effect is similar to the wallpaper in Windows. You should select a dim, subtle image for your background. If the background is too intense or too bright, it will distract from or interfere with the text and other images you have on your page.

If you choose a background image, your choice of background color (BGCOLOR) will be hidden unless your background image has transparent areas. (We will discuss transparent images when we look at using images as indicators for links.) The value specified in the background attribute is the path, or URL, for the background image you have selected. It should be a small image because it will need to be moved across the Internet to your viewer's location. Figures 2.14 through 2.16 show a sample background, the code to invoke it, and the way the page looks with that background in place. (Note that the black line around the image in Figure 2.14 is not part of the actual GIF. It is there only to outline the small image on the page.)

Figure 2.14 A background image. It is a light image.

```
<HTML>
<HEAD>
<TITLE> Container demo </TITLE>
</HEAD>
<BODY BACKGROUND="rock.gif" >
<H1>A page with a sample background</H1>
<P>This background image is repeated, or tiled, to fill the
page.   Use a background that is not going to interfere too
badly.
</BODY>
</HTML>
```

Figure 2.15 HTML code for a background.

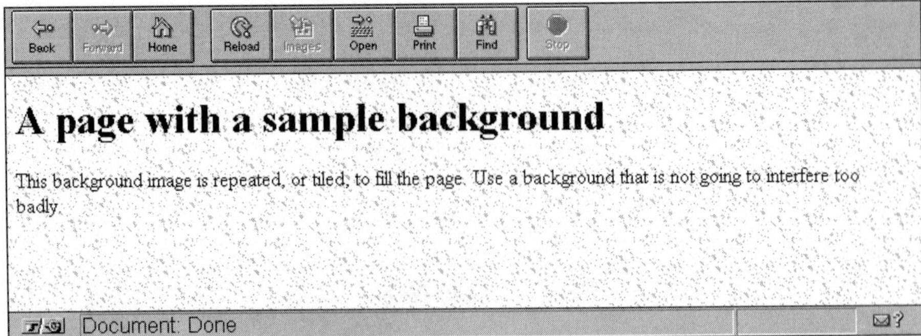

Figure 2.16 Netscape's presentation of a background, showing how the image is tiled, or duplicated.

Avoid building large, full-screen, images, because they will be slow to load and will increase the congestion on the Internet. Your URL for an image should point to the machine that hosts the page. Don't have your URL point to a file across the Net, because that can greatly increase the time it takes to load your page. For example, in the HTML code in Figure 2.15, the image from **rock.gif**, a file that resides on the author's computer, is used. When the browser starts to build the page, it need look only to this file to create the background. However, if this file were located on another machine, somewhere across the Net, the URL would look like this: **file://an.othersystem.net/pub/bground/rock.gif.** In this case, the browser would have to establish communication with the **an.othersystem.net** machine, look in the **/pub/bground directory**, and copy the image in the file **rock.gif** back to the current computer before it could build the background for the page. This really increases the traffic on the Internet and will slow the browser down as it builds the page.

One of the best ways to get nice backgrounds is to find them on the Net. Many sites offer public-domain background files (usually in **GIF**, **Graphic Interchange Format**, or **JPEG**, **Joint Photographic Experts Group** format.) You can use your browser to collect the background and save it on your own machine. Then you can use that background in your own page. If you choose to use another Web weaver's work, ask permission. Usually the page will contain a way to e-mail the person who built the page. Ask the owner of the work if you can use the background on your page. Most of the time the authors are pleased that you want to use their work.

There is a cardinal rule to remember about background images: Any background image will interfere to some extent with reading the text on the page. Make sure your background image is worth even a slight degradation of the readability of your page.

BGPROPERTIES

The **BGPROPERTIES** attribute is currently recognized only by Internet Explorer. BGPROPERTIES works in conjunction with the BACKGROUND attribute. The value is always "fixed," meaning it causes the background to freeze in the browser image so it will not scroll with the rest of the window contents. If you wish to use it, you would code it like this:

```
<BODY BGPROPERTIES=fixed>
```

TEXT

The **TEXT** attribute sets the color for all the text on the page except the text enclosed in an anchor, <A>, container. We will explore anchors in the next chapter. You need to ensure that your text color works with your selected background color or background image. To help the readability of your page, it should contrast nicely and not clash. For example, the following color selections would create a page that is difficult to read:

```
<BODY BGCOLOR="#AAAAAA" TEXT="#777777">
```

Figure 2.17 shows what this code would produce in Netscape. As you can see, a poor choice of BGCOLOR and TEXT can make a page almost impossible to read.

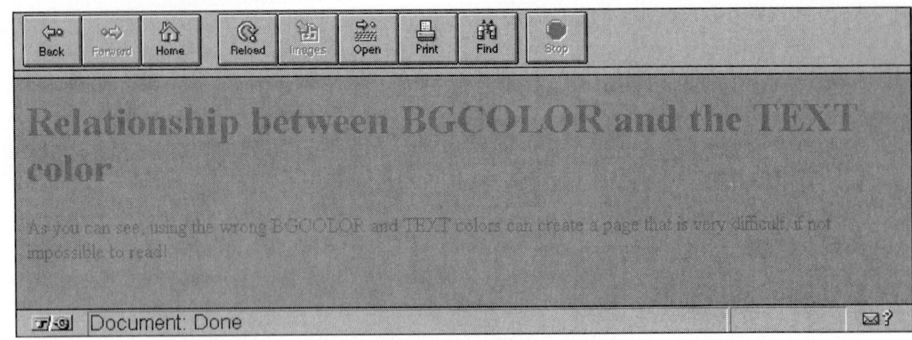

Figure 2.17 Netscape's presentation of BGCOLOR and TEXT choices that cause readability problems.

As you cruise the Net, you will come across some pages that are very difficult to read because the author of the page made a poor text-color selection. Text color is selected just like background color, using a hexadecimal value like "#FFFF00", or a color name like "yellow" if you are targeting the Netscape or Internet Explorer browsers.

ALINK, LINK, VLINK

These three attributes are used in the following way:

ALINK—controls the color of the active link, or the link that is being targeted by the mouse. This attribute is currently used only by Netscape; the others ignore it.

LINK—controls the color of all the hyperlinks the user has not yet followed.

VLINK—controls the color of all the links the user has already followed at one time or another.

It can be very confusing and frustrating for your users if you change these colors. Most browsers keep the link colors constant, and users come to depend on those colors. For example, as mentioned earlier, on most browsers, the links not yet chosen are blue and the links that have been visited are dark purple. Using the attributes LINK and VLINK, you could reverse those values, making the followed links blue and those not yet visited dark purple. That could be very confusing for your users.

If you have a special need to change these colors, remember to make them different from the text color, and different among themselves. You can specify the colors just as you did with the text and background colors, using either a hexadecimal value or a color name. The following example sets the color of the unused links as red, and those that have been visited to bright green.

```
<BODY LINK="FF0000" VLINK="00FF00">
```

But, remember, you should change the default colors only if you have a compelling reason to do so.

LEFTMARGIN, TOPMARGIN

The **LEFTMARGIN** and **TOPMARGIN** attributes are currently supported only by the Internet Explorer. LEFTMARGIN sets the starting place for the rest of the page, setting a margin in pixels. TOPMARGIN, also measured in pixels, sets the space at the top of the screen, below which the text will begin.

A Few Considerations

Using lots of colors and fancy images, you can produce a Web page that is a work of art. However, there are some things that can go wrong with that approach:

1. You will usually increase the time it takes to load your page. This can frustrate your users and may also increase congestion on the Internet. If you use a large image as the background, that will add substantial time to the load time. And, remember, not all your users are tied directly to the Internet. Some depend on 9600 baud modem lines and pay for each minute of connect time. They may not appreciate a beautiful background image that takes 30 minutes to download.
2. Your page may look wonderful on a computer with a high-resolution screen and 256 available colors. But if your user has a machine with fewer available colors, or a monochrome monitor, your pretty screen may become unusable. If you use colors in your page that the local machine does not have available, the local browser may be forced to "dither" the image. **Dithering** is the process of replacing one uniform color with repeating patterns of other colors that approximate the initial color. This can make your text very difficult or impossible to read, or just plain ugly.
3. Even though you are using a wonderful image as your background, you might want to reconsider using an image at all. Putting text on top of an image makes the text harder to read.
4. If you use a background image, the browser must fill in that image as the user scrolls through the page. This process by the browser can lead to slower scrolling.
5. The colors you choose, while beautiful on your computer, may not be available on a 16-color VGA Windows machine. In replacing your pretty colors with those available for that machine, the browser may set the background color and the text color to the same value. The result will be impossible to read!

A careful selection of colors and images can create a wonderful Web page. As you cruise the Net, you will find many examples of beautifully crafted pages. The careful use of colors and images allows you to express yourself artistically and enables you to create unique HTML documents. Playing with color and form is great fun. However, as you play, keep in mind that the real purpose for most Web pages is to transmit information. If colors and images get in the way of the transferal of information, then perhaps you need to rethink your layout.

At this point it is important to address the idea of Web page design. Usually the minds that are capable of excellent coding and HTML development aren't the same kinds of minds that are capable of excellent layout and page design. It is tempting to use all the "bells and whistles" possible when developing a page, often to the detriment of the actual content. If you are developing a professional

Web page, it is almost a necessity to consult with a graphics designer. The designer can tell you which colors go together well, how much "white space" you should have on your page, where to place images for greatest effect, and so on. Your users will appreciate the result.

Comments

Before we go on with building our first page, it is time to discuss one important tool. As you write your Web page, it is very important to include small, informative **comments** that explain why you have done what you have done. These comments will not show up when your page is browsed, but they will appear when the source is viewed. Many authors make the mistake of putting in comments that tell what they did but not why:

```
<BODY LINK="FF00FF" VLINK="00FF00"
<!-- Make the Link colors FF00FF and the vlink 00FF00 -->
```

That comment, (enclosed in the <!-- --> container), tells me what has been done, but the same information can be read from the HTML. A much better set of comments would be

```
<BODY LINK="FF00FF" VLINK="00FF00"
<!-- Set LINK to Magenta and VLINK to Green -->
<!-- Use these colors to match the Schools color choices -->
```

Now we know what colors were chosen and why they were chosen instead of the default colors.

Your comments should not be designed for other readers as much as to document your choices for yourself. It is very frustrating to come back to modify your page at some later date and have no earthly idea why you have built some particular construct the way you did. Well-written comments can guide you back through your logic and remind you of why you did what you did.

It is also handy to place comments that show where you found the images and backgrounds you used. That way, should you lose them from your local disk, they can easily be retrieved again. It is also a nice way to give credit to those other Web authors who have allowed you to use their artwork.

Comments should be only one line long and should not contain any other HTML tags. A comment container starts with <!-- and ends with a -->. Note that this ending tag is different from any we have seen so far. The following is an example of a comment that might follow a header:

```
<!--  The color "#FF0077" is a nice dusky rose -->
```

This comment will be seen only if the user elects to view the source code of the page. Careful, consistent use of comments will help you as you maintain your page. Comments will also help users who want to understand how you achieved your results.

Headings

A document that contains page after page of unbroken text can be very difficult for a user to read. Web pages should be broken up with appropriate headings to divide the text flow into manageable pieces. HTML allows six different levels of headings (**<H1> </H1> . . . <H6> </H6>**). The way the headings are displayed depends on the browser used to read the document. Some browsers will display the headings in different sizes of fonts. Others may indicate a header by bolding it, underlining it, moving it about the page, or changing its color. In addition, users can sometimes set how a browser will display headings.

The code in Figure 2.18 specifies six different headings, which are shown in Figure 2.19 the way Netscape would display them.

```
<H1> This is the first heading </H1>
This text follows the first heading.
<H2> This is the second heading </H2>
This is the text that follows the second heading.
<H3> This is heading level 3 </H3>
Text that follows heading level 3.
<H4> This heading is level 4 </H4>
This is the text under that heading.
<H5> This is heading level 5 </H5>
Text following the fifth heading level.
<H6> This is the lowest level heading, level 6 </H6>
Here is text beneath the lowest heading.
```

Figure 2.18 HTML code for six different heading levels.

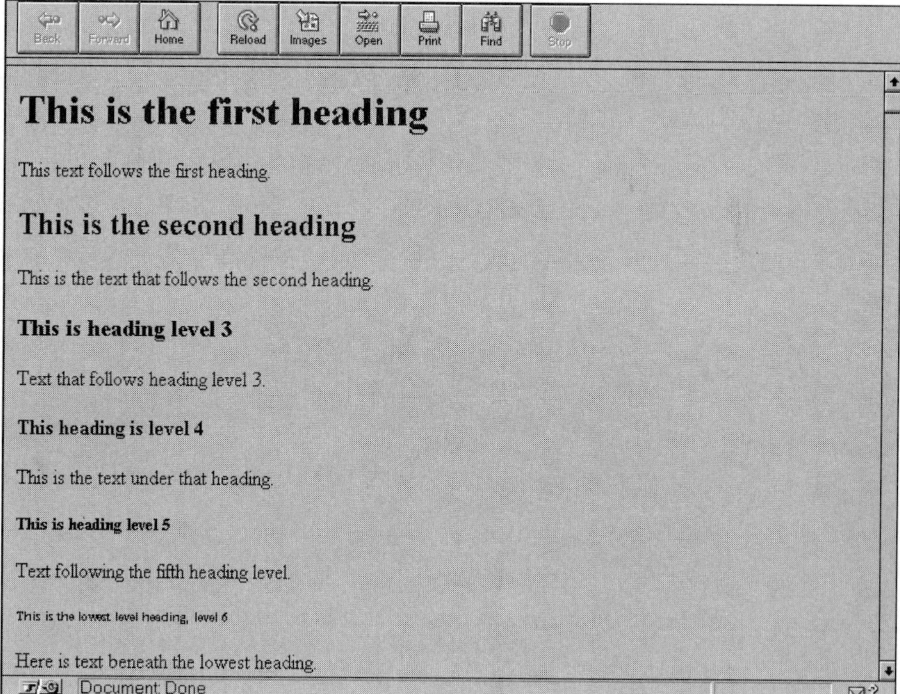

Figure 2.19 Netscape's presentation of some different heading levels.

The headings each start a new paragraph and provide some formatting. But you can't rely on this feature. If the browser used to view your page shows the different headers only by color, then your formatting will be lost. Do not attempt to use headings to control how the text looks on the page. Remember, the browser is in charge of the look—you should worry only about the content.

A level 1 (<H1>) heading is often used at the start of the body of the page or document. It should restate the title. Other headings are used to divide the text into manageable sections and to help users high-scan through the page to find the information they are seeking.

Remember that you must always use the closing heading tag to end your heading. The browser cannot guess where you want your heading to end, so it cannot supply the ending tag for you. If you forget to close a header, you might be unpleasantly surprised with the result. Look what happens in Figure 2.20 when a header is added without the ending tag. Without the tag that would have closed the first heading after Robert Frost's name, Netscape views the rest of the document as part of the heading. You will run across this problem from time to time as you cruise the Net.

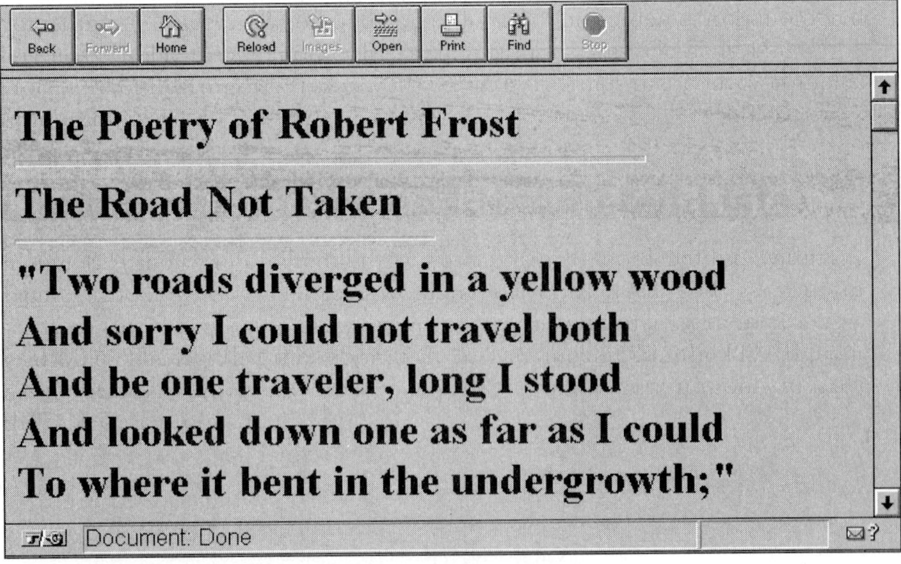

Figure 2.20 Netscape's presentation of an unclosed heading.

Headings can be aligned, just like horizontal rules (<HR>). Alignment is the only attribute for this container. However, headings can contain a wide variety of other HTML elements. For example, a heading may contain link anchors <A>, images <IMG>, line breaks <BR>, horizontal rules <HR>, style changes (<CITE>, <CODE>, <EM>, <KBD>, <SAMP>, <STRONG>, <VAR>), and font modifiers (<B>, <I>, <U>, <STRIKE>, <TT>, <FONT>). In practice, font or style changes, while allowed, are usually overridden by the browser because the font and style of the heading text is already prescribed by the browser.

It is sometimes interesting to add small images to headings. Some of the more effective ones are logos, bullets, or small icons. Figure 2.21 presents the code for a small page that has blinking buttons as part of a header. Figure 2.22 shows how this looks in Netscape.

```
<HTML>
<HEAD>
<TITLE> Fancy Headings demo </TITLE>
</HEAD>
<BODY>
<H1>Demo of some fancy Headings...</H1>
<H2><IMG SRC="file:///d|/html/images/grblnk.gif">   Images
are nice</H2>
We can always use pictures to spice up our pages.  However,
we must be aware of the price we pay to use them.  Images are
slower to download, and can cause overhead when used.
<H2><IMG SRC="file:///d|/html/images/grblnk.gif">  Buttons
are fun</H2>
It seems that nearly everybody likes buttons.  As you cruise
the web you will find many examples of fancy buttons.  These
happen to blink!
</BODY>
</HTML>
```

Figure 2.21 HTML code for images as part of a header.

Figure 2.22 Netscape's presentation of images incorporated into headings.

Helping your user navigate through the page is important. Remember that the main reason to put a page on the Web is to provide information as quickly and efficiently as possible. Making navigation less complex, and thus helping users find what they want, is very important.

Paragraphs

When you write a regular-text document, like a term paper, you divide the text into sections called **paragraphs**. To do that, you end the line and perhaps insert a blank line on your page like this:

The space you see above this line is called white space. In computer jargon, **white space** is defined as one or more spaces or tabs. Web browsers treat all white space the same. Therefore, if you had an HTML document with a partial line of text, three blank lines, and another partial line of text, a browser would close up the lines and make them flow into each other. For example, the text in Figure 2.23 would produce the result shown in Figure 2.24.

```
<HTML>
<HEAD>
<TITLE>Whitespace Demo </TITLE>
</HEAD>
<BODY>
This is a
line of


text

with
lots                of          white

space
</BODY>
</HTML>
```

Figure 2.23 HTML code with a lot of white space, both tabs and new lines.

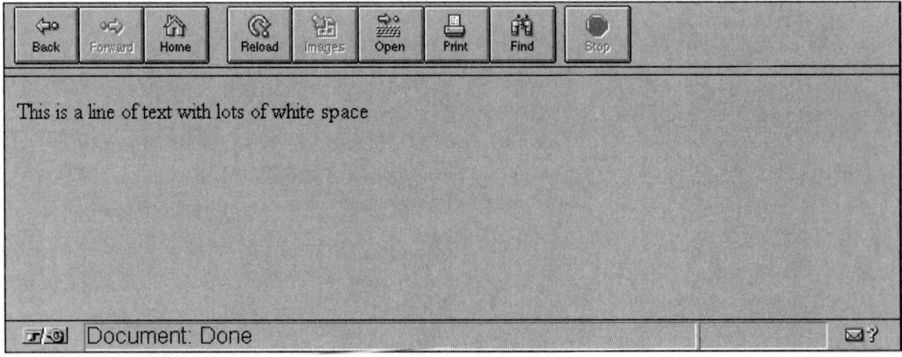

Figure 2.24 Netscape's presentation of a lot of coded white space compressed into one blank per instance of white space.

Since you can't insert blank lines to break up paragraphs, you need some other tool to divide the text into logical sections. We have seen that headings can divide the text, but headings are intended to break the page into large units. It is possible with some browsers to use multiple line breaks,
s, to insert several blank lines, but it is considered very poor form to insert more than two
s in one place. Always remember that you are concerned with the content, and the browser handles how the text is placed on the page.

One way to divide text into logical blocks is to place the text blocks into paragraph containers, <P> . . . </P>.

As we saw at the beginning of the chapter, in the earlier versions of HTML, the paragraph was an empty tag like <HR> and <BR>. It was used to mark the beginning of a paragraph, and there was no closing tag. You will find some older documents on the Web that are marked in this manner. It is good practice to close all your paragraph containers, even though the closing tag can be guessed, or inferred, in some cases. If you are putting blocks of text between headings, the closing heading tag will start a new paragraph. With some browsers it may not matter if you put the <P> tags at the beginning and ending of the paragraph after the heading tags, but with others the tags may generate extra white space. Consequently, this practice is usually discouraged.

When the <P> tag was changed from an empty tag to a container, it also gained the ALIGN attribute. Like horizontal rules and headings, a paragraph can be aligned left, center, or right. Left alignment is the default; it is what the browser uses if you don't specify which type of alignment you want.

A paragraph container can contain some other tags. For example, it may contain links (<A>), images (<IMG>), font changes (<B>, <FONT>, <I>, <STRIKE>, <TT>), line breaks (<BR>), and style changes (<CITE>, <CODE>, <EM>, <KBD>, <SAMP>, <STRONG>, <VAR>). However, if the browser encounters any other tag in a paragraph, like a heading tag, it assumes that the closing paragraph tag is missing and ends the paragraph for you—whether you wanted the paragraph closed there or not.

We will explore several other text-formatting tags in later chapters, but it is time for you to begin building a Web page.

Exercises

2.1. Type in the following small HTML file. If you are using an HTML editor like HotDog, some of the tags will be inserted for you by the editor. If you are using another editor, remember to save your text as plain ASCII. (Enter the text just like it is shown; you will modify it in a moment.)

```
<HTML>
<HEAD>
<TITLE> My first Web Page! </TITLE>
</HEAD>
<BODY>
This is my first web page!
My name is &;your name here&gt;
And I think this is really neat!
</BODY>
</HTML>
```

Now load your browser, and call up this HTML script. It should look something like the following:

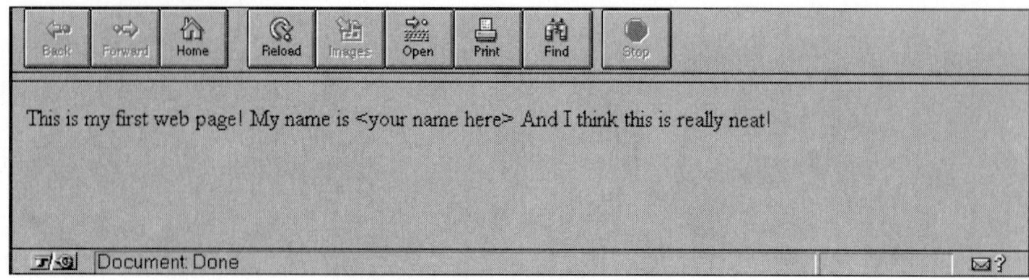

Now, looking at your screen, check the following:

a. Is your title (up there on the Netscape line) correct?
b. Do you have only one line of text on the page?
c. Is the word "And" capitalized?

(We capitalized the word "And" so you could see how the browser took care of the format.)

If you answered no to any of these questions, go back and fix your HTML document. Remember that you should have closing tags for all containers. Now make the document appear in the browser in three lines.

2.2. Build an HTML document that produces the following Web page:

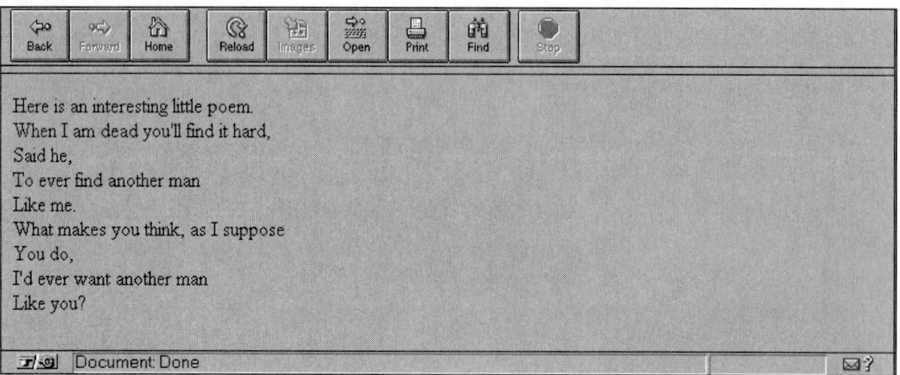

Notice the line breaks. After you build the HTML document and verify that it looks like this, be sure to save it. We are going to add to it. Remember, your location will be different.

2.3. Starting with the document we built in Exercise 2, change your code to produce the following page. You will need to use headings and paragraphs. Because your browser may not display headings just like the sample shown here, please check your results with your instructor or fellow class members.

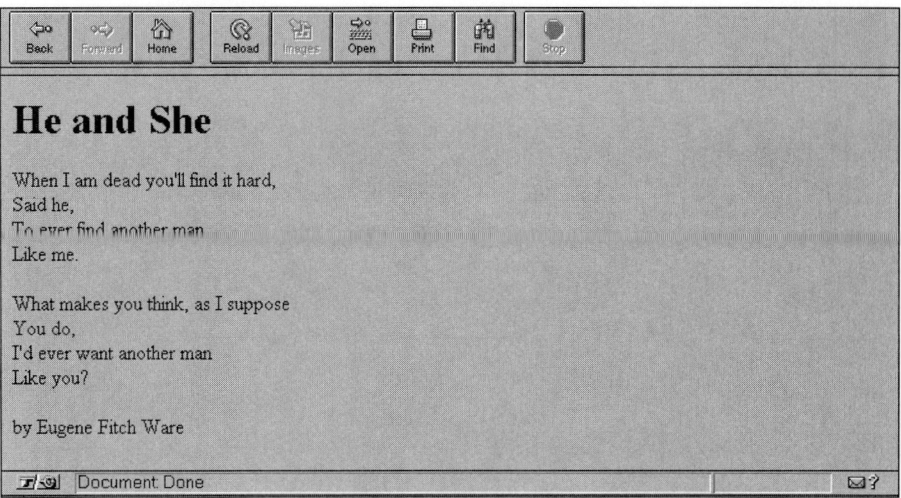

2.4. Produce the following document. Change the data in the page to your own information.

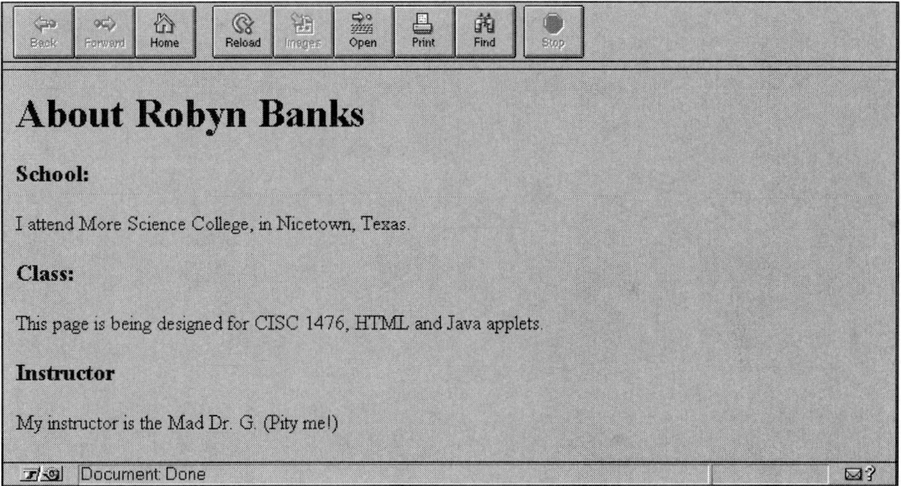

All of this information should fit on one page. (Hint:You may need to adjust the heading levels you use to make it fit.)

2.5. Experiment with the way the browser eliminates white space.You may wish to build the HTML document in Figure 2.23 to use as a test document. Prove to your satisfaction that you can insert blank lines with the <P> tag. Experiment with multiple blank lines. If possible, use at least two different browsers in your research. If you have several browsers available, put a paragraph break after a heading to see if it generates extra white space.

CHAPTER three

LET'S BE A LITTLE MORE CREATIVE

In the last chapter we built a simple, static Web page. A **static Web page** contains no links within the document or to other documents, no graphics, and no way for users to interact with the page. Now it is time to allow the users some control over where they go on the page rather than simply scrolling up and down. We also need to allow the users to move from page to page of the document. To do this, we need to incorporate links into the file. Linking is an important step in Web page development because it adds the *hyper* to the term *hypertext*.

Why Is Hypertext Hyper?

A **hypertext document** contains elements called **links** that allow users to click their mouse button on a particular part of the screen and perform some action. The actions can include (1) moving to another part of the document; (2) opening and displaying an image, text, or sound file; and (3) opening a document from somewhere else in the world across the Internet. In this chapter we will deal with simple links to places within our current document as well as to other documents in our current directory. We will examine linking across the Internet in a later chapter.

Documents having dynamic links to other documents or to places within the same document date back to the 1980s. The Apple Macintosh supported HyperCard, which was a powerful hyper language allowing the user to create **buttons** within a document that would, when clicked, load an image, play a sound, or open and display another text file. The documents were called **stacks**, and each page or screen was a **card** in that stack. Different cards could be linked together. The language used to create the buttons was a true programming language, and rather sophisticated to write.

HTML is an instance, or subset, of IBM's Standard Generalized Markup Language (SGML). It enables you to build documents that allow the dynamic linking of several pages. If you use an HTML editor like HotDog, most of the actual HTML coding is taken care of for you. In any case, links (Figure 3.1) will enable your user to pick up definitions, play sounds, view pictures and video, or move about through a collection of documents with a simple click of a mouse button. Now let's look at how we create links.

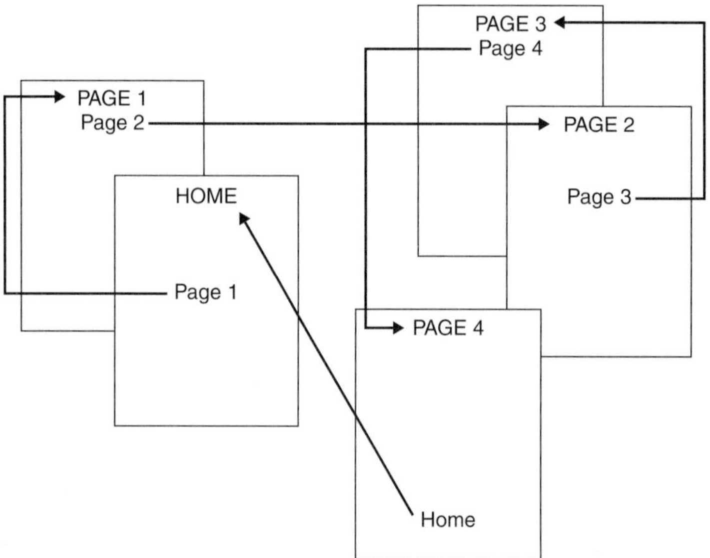

Figure 3.1 Example of how several documents or pages may be linked together.

The Anchor Tag, <A> . . . </A>

The anchor tag, **<A>**, is a container that serves as the basis for all the links we are going to create in this section. It has several attributes. We will explore two of them here. Later, when we address links across the Internet, we will address some of the other attributes.

There are several ways to refer to the relationship between the document housing the link and the document pointed to by the link. In some texts you will find the terms *head* for the place where the link starts and *tail* for the place the link points to. In others you may find the terms *start* and *destination* for these two locations. These terms may be confusing, so in this book we will use the **source** to indicate the origin of a link and **target** to indicate the end of the link. Thus our links start at the source and end at the target.

Format of an Anchor

We will use anchor containers two ways in this chapter. First we will use them as a way to place a tag, or name, indicating a target within our document. Then we will use an anchor container to allow our user to transfer to a particular document or a place within the current document by clicking on the text within the anchor.

It is important to remember that the anchor can be used within another container. In other words, we could put an anchor within a heading container if we wanted the header to be the target of a link. It is bad HTML style, though, to put a heading container within an anchor. Proper style would be as follows:

```
<H2 align="right" > <A NAME="PP" > Phred's Page </A> </H2>
```

Here the anchor is contained within the heading, and "Phred's Page" will appear the way the browser presents a level 2 heading. If users select a link to PP, they be will transfered to this heading. On the other hand,

```
<A NAME="PP" > <H2 ALIGN="RIGHT" > Phred's Page </H2> </A>
```

is an example of bad style because the anchor contains another container, in this case a level 2 heading. Some browsers will try to close the anchor container before opening the heading container. That action could cause unpredictable results. Let's look at some examples to see how the anchor should be used.

Target Anchors

If we want to allow the user to jump from point to point within the same document, or to jump to a specific point in another document, we must have a tool to label the **target anchor** for the link. The <A> anchor with the NAME attribute provides a tag that will serve as a target. The code is presented in Figure 3.2.

```
<HTML>
<HEAD>
<TITLE>Intra-page Links </TITLE>
</HEAD>
<BODY>
<H1>Poetry Selections </H1>
This page contains some of the poetry written by some of my favorite
poets.
Please take a minute to sample their work.  Most of these poets write in
one
of the recognized rhyming styles.
<P>
This is a list of the poets shown on this page: </P>
<H3>Robert Frost</H3>
<H3>Unknown</H3>
<H3>Edward Arlington Robinson</H3>
<H3>Margaret E. Bruner</H3>
<HR align="center" width="75%" size=6>
All of these poets can be found in "Poems That Live Forever" published
by Doubleday.
<H2 align="center"><A NAME="RF">Robert Frost</A></H2>Target anchor
<H3>The Road Not Taken</H3>
   <!--Text of poem omitted for clarity of example -->
H2 align="center"> <A NAME="UNK">Unknown</A> </H2>Target anchor
<H3>Growing Smiles</H3>
   <!--Text of poem omitted for clarity of example -->
<HR align="center" width="50%" size=6>
<H2 align="center"><A NAME="EA">Edward A. Robinson</A></H2>Target anchor
<H3>Richard Cory</H3>
   <!--Text of poem omitted for clarity of example -->
<HR align="center" width="50%" size=6>
<H2 align="center"><A NAME="MB"> Margaret E. Bruner</A></H2>Target anchor
<H3>Epitaph for a Cat</H3>
   <!--Text of poem omitted for clarity of example -->
</BODY>
</HTML>
```

Figure 3.2 HTML code for target anchors.

Notice in Figure 3.2 that the bold parts of the code are the target anchors. It will be possible to create a link to any of these four anchors. In the next section we will build the links to these targets.

When creating a target anchor, you may imbed it within another container, as shown Figure 3.2. The anchors are within the level 2 headings. The NAME attribute is used to identify a section or fragment of the page. In this example we have the RF section, the UNK section, the EA section, and the MB section. Notice that the NAME attribute is short in our example. RF is the name for the target fragment by Robert Frost. The text that is contained within the anchor container will show on the screen in a format governed by any other containers that enclose it. In our example, each author's name is formatted as a level 2 heading, so the target displayed by the anchor,

```
<H2 ALIGN="LEFT"><A NAME="RF" > Robert Frost </A> </H2>
```

would appear as follows when viewed by Netscape:

Robert Frost

When users click on a link that points to this anchor, they will be transfered to this heading in the document.

If you want to have working links that appear as you design them, you must maintain the integrity of your containers. In the preceding example, it would be easy to make the mistake of closing the heading before closing the anchor, like this:

```
<H2 ALIGN="CENTER"> <A NAME="Neat"> A Neat Thing </H2> </A>
```

Notice that the heading container is closed before the anchor container. Some browsers could get confused and miss the closing anchor tag, thus keeping the anchor open. Other browsers will detect this crossed container as an error and not set up the anchor at all. In either case, the results will not be what you expect. Close your containers in the order you build them, with inner containers closed before outer containers.

Intrapage Source Anchors

The other form of anchor we will discuss in this chapter are source anchors. There are really three types of links: intrapage links, intrasystem links, and intersystem links. In this chapter we will discuss the first two. The **intrapage link** is a link within a single document or page. This is the element of HTML that gives it the ability to actually transfer control to some other part of the current document. Any source anchor contains the special attribute, **HREF**, discussed next.

HREF

Figure 3.3 shows an excerpt from a Web page that contains some source links. As you can see, this use of the anchor container has the attribute HREF, which stands for **H**ypertext **REF**erence. The HREF attribute identifies the pointer, or pathway, to the target of the link. The target of a link is a Uniform Resource Locator (URL). In this case the URL is local to, or within, the document we have created. The URL allows the user to jump to a selected poet with the click of a mouse button. The form of the local URL is the name of the anchor, exactly as it appears in the NAME= attribute, preceded by the octothorp, or number symbol (#).

```
<BODY>
<H1>Poetry Selections </H1>
This page contains some of the poetry written by some of my
favorite poets.
Please take a minute to sample their work.  Most of these
poets write in one of the recognized rhyming styles.
<P>
This is a list of the poets shown on this page: </P>
<H3><A HREF="#RF">Robert Frost</A></H3>
<H3><A HREF="#UNK">Unknown</A></H3>
<H3><A HREF="#EA">Edward Arlington Robinson</A></H3>
<H3><A HREF="#MB">Margaret E. Bruner</A></H3>
```

Figure 3.3 HTML code for HREF attributes for intrapage links.

Many computer systems are case-sensitive, so you should be careful to have the URL exactly match the target. A case-sensitive system recognizes the difference between uppercase and lowercase letters. For example, the target "RF" and the target "Rf" are different on a system that recognizes the case of the letters. On a case-insensitive system, like DOS, both targets are considered the same. If you used a target of "Rf" in your NAME= attribute, you should also have an HREF= of "Rf".

Always enclose the URL in quotation marks. There are some special cases when that is unnecessary, but most of the time the quotation marks are required, and it is a good habit to develop.

The text between the end of the opening tag and the beginning of the ending tag is the text the user will see that indicates a link exists. Always use the closing </A> anchor tag, as it cannot be inferred by the browser.

As you remember from the last chapter, the link text will be a different color and may be specified by the LINK attribute of the <BODY> container. In Netscape, it will also be underlined. Figure 3.4 shows how this part of the page will look in the browser.

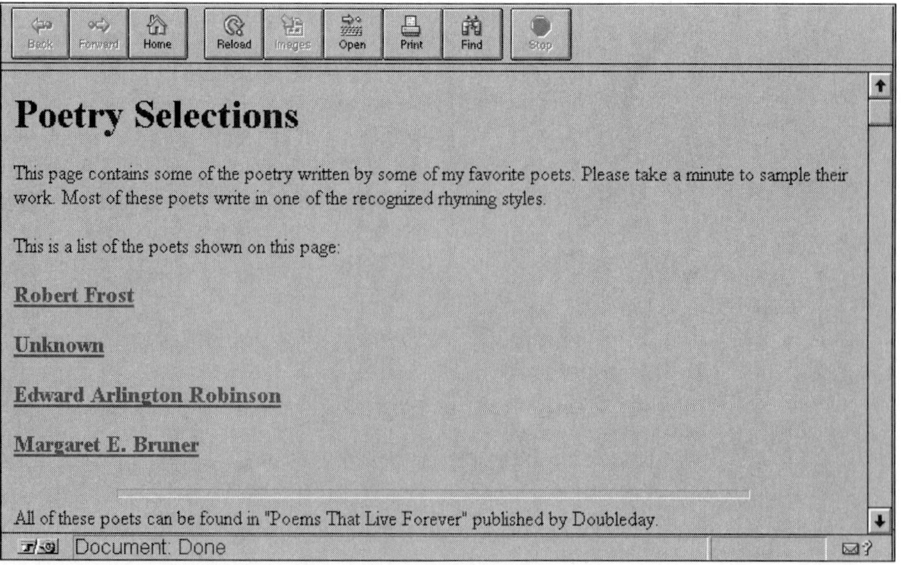

Figure 3.4 Netscape's presentation of source anchors.

Notice that the text we have chosen for our hyperlink is also enclosed in a heading. This makes the link easy to see and gives a nicely formatted list of links. The fact that the link text is a different color and is underlined tells the user that it is a link. Also, when the user moves the cursor over the link, it becomes a pointing finger rather than the normal arrowhead. This change in the pointer is another indication that the text under it is a link.

This type of intrapage link is common when you are presenting a large volume of related information—for example, a large document where the table of contents contains the intrapage links. These links will allow users to select the sections they wish to view, click on them, and immediately see their selections without having to page down through the document. If you are building a menu for your page, you can also use this technique. Remember that the user can always scroll through the whole document using the scroll bar on the right side of the page. What you are doing with this type of internal link is providing an easy way for the user to navigate around the page.

Intrasystem Source Anchors

If you choose to write a long hypertext document, you may be causing unnecessary problems for the user. First, a long document is slower to download than a short one. Second, a set of short documents may be easier for users to navigate among because they can easily return to the master, or central, document from any of the other documents. Finally, one of the rules of programming and structure says you should have each thing you create do *one* thing well. A large hypertext document providing information on 14 different topics is not doing *one* thing well. A much more structured format for the information would be 14 smaller hypertext documents, each presenting one of the facets of the information in a well-organized fashion, and one document serving as a menu for the others. And in addition to being easier for the user, smaller documents will be easier for you to maintain.

Figure 3.5 presents the pertinent section of the page we used before, modified to reflect this preferred style of development. Each HREF now points to a separate file that was created by cutting apart the previous large document. You will notice that the URL no longer starts with an octothorp, or number

```
<H1>Poetry Selections </H1>
This page contains some of the poetry written by some of my
favorite poets.
Please take a minute to sample their work.  Most of these
poets write in one of the recognized rhyming styles.
<P>
This is a list of the poets whose work is available for your
pleasure:
</P>
<H3><A HREF="RFpoem.htm">Robert Frost</A></H3>
<H3><A HREF="UNKpoem.htm">Unknown</A></H3>
<H3><A HREF="EApoem.htm">Edward Arlington Robinson</A></H3>
<H3><A HREF="MBpoem.htm">Margaret E. Bruner</A></H3>
```

Figure 3.5 HTML code for HREF attributes for intrasystem links.

sign. That tells the browser that the reference is now to another file rather than a target within the current document. The only differences in coding an intrasystem URL rather than an intrapage URL are (1) the absence of the octothorp and (2) the fact that the URL is now a path to a file rather than simply a target within the document.

Figure 3.6 shows how the code in Figure 3.5 would look in a browser. Notice that the links are still underlined. You cannot tell just by looking at the link whether it points within the document, across documents on the same system, or across the Internet. From the browser's point of view, a link is a link.

When you specify the path that the browser should take to find a document, you can use either an absolute or relative path name. Both have a purpose and use, so let's discuss each of them.

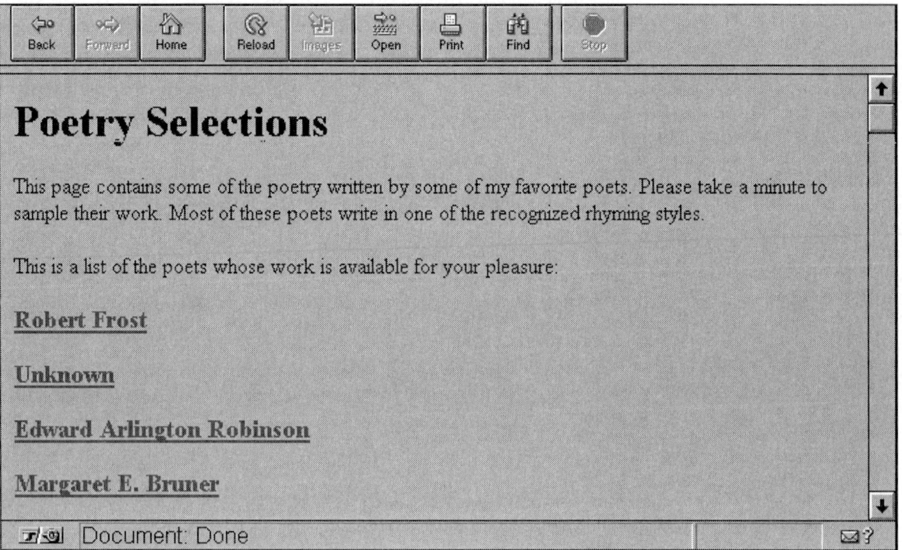

Figure 3.6 Netscape's presentation of intrasystem links.

Absolute Path Names

Absolute path names always start with a slash (/) and contain the full path to the document you are referencing. The browser knows that you are using an absolute path when the path name starts with the slash. There are a couple of important points about absolute path names. First, the majority of the servers on the Internet are running the UNIX operating system. Therefore, the way we specify paths is more UNIX-like than DOS-like. In UNIX the right, or forward, slash (/) is used to divide the parts of a path name. You will need to use this convention when coding absolute path names. In addition, when you specify a drive letter, you should follow it with the vertical bar (|) rather than the colon as you are used to in DOS. Table 3.1 provides some absolute path names from three different operating systems, showing how they would be coded.

Absolute Path Name	What It Tells the Browser
`HREF="/home/users/html/RFpoem.html"`	The file is on a UNIX system, in the directory **/home/users/html**. The filename is **RFpoem.html** (UNIX allows longer filenames.)
`HREF="/D|/html/poems/RFpoem.htm"`	This is a DOS example. Here the file is on the D: drive, in the directory **/html/poems**. Note that the absolute path starts with a slash, as is required. DOS limits file extensions to three characters, so our **.html** file is saved as **.htm.**
`HREF="/Hard Disk 2/HTML Poems/RFpoem.html"`	This time the file is on a Macintosh system. It is on the second hard drive, in the directory **HTML Poems**.

Table 3.1 Samples of absolute path names.

As you can see in the table, the path name looks a little different on different operating systems. However, an absolute path must always tell the browser exactly where to find the file because it specifies the full and complete path name.

While it may seem a good idea to always specify a full path name, let's look at another way to tell the browser how to find the files it needs, using relative path names.

Relative Path Names

A relative path starts from the directory in which the browser is currently working, the directory that contains the current document. Relative path names must not start with a right, or forward, slash, because the right slash is the first character of absolute path names. When specifying a relative path, you again tell the browser exactly where to look to find the file it needs. The difference between an absolute and a relative path is that the relative path starts from the current position in the file structure. The simplest relative path names point to target files contained in the same directory as the source document, and this is the ideal. You can see examples of that type of relative link in Figure 3.5. In that example we direct the browser to look in the same directory where it found the current page to find **RFpoem.htm**. Table 3.2 provides some sample relative path names.

As you can see in comparing Table 3.1 with Table 3.2, in most cases the relative path is a shorter target than the absolute path. Relative path names are usually faster for the browser to use as well.

Relative versus Absolute Path Names

At first glance, it would seem much better to always use absolute path names rather than relative path names for linked material. Yet, most experts agree that just the opposite is true. To explain why, we need to first point out that whenever possible you should have all the files you are referencing in the same

Relative Path Name	What It Tells the Browser
`HREF="RFpoem.htm"`	This file is in the current directory. This is the simplest relative path-naming scheme.
`HREF="poems/ABpoem.html"`	In this case the target is in the directory or folder called **poems,** which is a subdirectory of the current directory.
`HREF="lit/poetry/BCpoem.html"`	Here the target is in the subdirectory or folder called **poetry,** which is in the subdirectory or folder called **lit,** which is in the current subdirectory or folder.
`HREF="../CDpoem.html"`	This is the way we direct the browser to move back or up one directory or folder. Here we are saying that the file we want is in the parent directory for the current directory. The .. notation says to move up or back one level.
`HREF="../../poems/DEpoem.htm"`	Here the target is located up two levels and is in the subdirectory or folder called **poems** at that level.
`HREF="../D|/English/poems/EFpoem.htm"`	Here the source document was in the directory **C:/html,** and the target is on another drive on the system. In this case the absolute path would be shorter.

Table 3.2 Samples of relative path names.

directory. That way the browser doesn't have far to look to find the files. Also, you can easily move the files as a group if you are changing from one server to another. Now, all the files are in one directory, then short, relative path names like those shown in Figure 3.5 are most efficient. Furthermore, if you use relative path names, it is easier to maintain your Web page because you won't need to keep changing your path names when you move your files from directory to directory.

One-Way Streets

One of the common problems you will discover as you cruise the Web is the lack of good backward pointers linking multiple pages back to a main page. When testing a set of pages, many Web weavers start at their first page and then use the "Back" button in their browser to move from a subpage back to the main page. This works just fine if all the users will start at the first page of the series. However, this model has a flaw if any users find one of the target pages and place the URL of that target page in their Bookmarks file. When those users come back to that page in a different browsing session, they will be unable to return to the main page. Why? Because their browser no longer holds the "Back" pages in memory, or **cache**. It is very frustrating to be on a subpage of the page you want, with no way to return to the main page except to either search for it again or, if you remember the URL, enter it again.

You should never create such one-way traps for your users. Always include a "back to the main page" link in each of your documents. That way you provide linkage in both directions for your users. They may choose the "Back" feature of their browser, but they also have the opportunity to return to the main page through a designated button.

The "Click Here" Faux Pas

Many new Web weavers fall victim to the classic error of button design called the "click here" faux pas. You will encounter it most often on newly created Web pages. As you peruse the page, you will find sentences that say things like, "**Click here** to go to the next page," or, "**Click here** to see pictures of my dog," and so on. Obviously, the author wants the user to realize that there are links available on the current page. However, because the author doesn't really understand how the browser displays links, he or she feels compelled to explicitly tell the user that there are links available. It looks far more professional to say, "You can go to the **next page**," or "See pictures of **my dog**", or even, "Take a peek at my new **computer**." Be subtle with your links. The users understand how their browsers display links—give them some credit. Oh, and if you want to see some exercises, **click here**.

Exercises

3.1. Retrieve the page you created in Exercise 2.4. Insert at least three anchor targets within the document. Then create links to each of the targets. Make sure all of them work. Remember that each of the targets should be on a different set of text within the document, separated by enough text to force the browser to jump from one anchor to the next. You won't be able to demonstrate that your links work if you have only one page of text, because the browser will not be forced to change pages.

3.2. Modify the page you created in Exercise 3.1 by removing three of the sections and placing them into separate files. An easy way to do that, if you are using an HTML editor like HotDog, is to cut the text out of the first document, open a new page, and paste the text you cut out into the new document. Create a set of links to the new pages. Make sure all the links work.

3.3. Move one of the pages you created in Exercise 3.2 to a directory or folder at least two levels away from the source document. Modify the link to that page to reflect the new path. Make sure that the link is an absolute path reference, not a relative one. Also make sure the link works.

3.4. Ensure that each of the pages you have created in your little web has a link that points back to the main page. Ensure that each of those links works. Now add a link to each of those pages that points to at least one other page in your set. Test each of those links.

3.5. Examine your pages, and also the pages of two classmates, to ensure that none of you have fallen into the "click here" trap. Add a "click here" button so you can see how it looks—and remember to avoid it.

3.6. If you have a connection to the Web, cruise the Net and find at least one example of a page that violates one of the guidelines we discussed. Notice how hard it is to use that page. Save the URL and share it with your classmates.

CHAPTER **four**

Bringing Order to the Chaos

The main reason we build Web pages is to bring unique, easily accessed information to the world. Lists are one way to organize information for easy access. People use lists to organize information in their day-to-day lives, and we can supply that form of organizational tool to them in our Web pages.

Plain-Text Lists

We can build what appear to be lists of information by using the <BR> command to force a line break after each item in the list. To use this "brute force" method to create a list of three items, we could use the code in Figure 4.1.

```
<HTML>
<HEAD>
<TITLE>List 1 </TITLE>
</HEAD>
<BODY>
The following shows a brute force way to build a Christmas
list:<BR>
1.  Partridge in pear tree<BR>
2.  French Hens<BR>
3.  Calling Birds<BR>
</BODY>
</HTML>
```

Figure 4.1 HTML code showing the "brute force" method of building a list.

As you can see, the Web weaver must put in the numbers and do the layout to make the list look like a list. Figure 4.2 shows how that code looks in a browser.

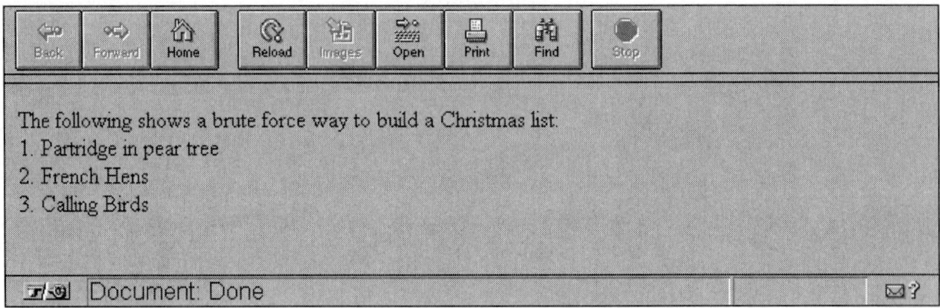

Figure 4.2 Netscape's presentation of the "brute force" list.

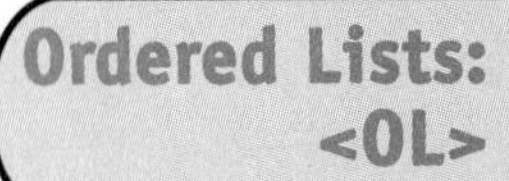

Ordered Lists: <OL>

Since lists are an easy tool for most people to use, HTML has special list-making tags. There are five different kinds of lists, but only three of them are commonly used. The first type of list is the simple **ordered list** (**<OL>**). This is a rather sophisticated tag, and it has some interesting attributes.

The easiest way to code the ordered list is to simply enter the <OL> container tag and then enter the individual list items, each preceded by the <**LI**> (list item) container. (Note: Although the list item, <LI>, is actually a container, for all practical purposes we will treat it as an empty tag because closing it doesn't have any advantages. All the current browsers automatically close a <LI> tag when they find another <LI> or the end of the list.) This is one of the examples of a container that seems to be migrating into an empty tag. Figure 4.3 shows how our sample list would be coded using the <OL> container.

```
<HTML>
<HEAD>
<TITLE>List 2 </TITLE>
</HEAD>
<BODY>
The following shows a more efficient way to build a Christmas
list:
<OL>
<LI> Partridge in pear tree
<LI>French Hens
<LI> Calling Birds
</OL>
</BODY>
</HTML>
```

Figure 4.3 HTML code for a simple ordered list.

Two new HTML tags are involved with the ordered list: the ordered-list container, <OL> . . . </OL>, which encloses the list, and the list-item container, <LI>, used to start each new list element. The simple form of the ordered list causes most browsers to put a number at the beginning of each list item. The default is the Arabic numerals, and the default starting number is 1. Figure 4.4 shows how this list would look using the Netscape browser.

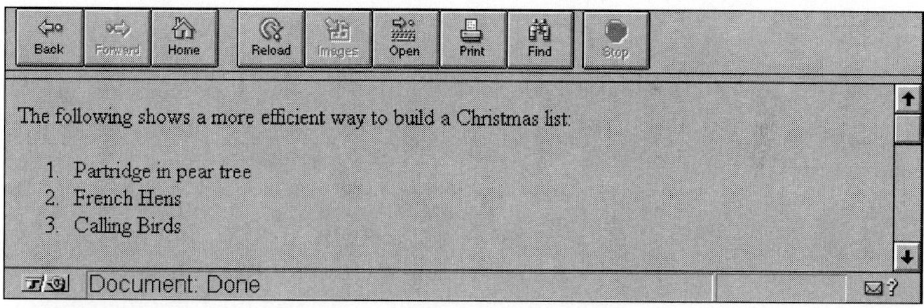

Figure 4.4 Netscape's presentation of a simple ordered list.

One advantage of using the list container over coding a list using line breaks (<BR>) becomes obvious when you try to insert an element into the middle of the list. For example, in our Christmas list example, we are missing the turtledoves! There need to be two turtledoves before the three French hens. Using the "brute force" method, we would have to perform the following steps to modify the list:

1. Type in the new line between lines 1 and 2.
2. Renumber the line numbered 2 as 3.
3. Renumber the line numbered 3 as 4.

That would result in the HTML code shown in Figure 4.5. Figure 4.6 shows what this code would produce in Netscape.

```
<HTML>
<HEAD>
<TITLE>List 1 </TITLE>
</HEAD>
<BODY>
The following shows a brute force way to build a Christmas
list:<BR>
1.  Partridge in pear tree<BR>
2.  Turtledoves
3.  French Hens<BR>
4.  Calling Birds<BR>
</BODY>
</HTML>
```

Figure 4.5 HTML code for a modified "brute force" list.

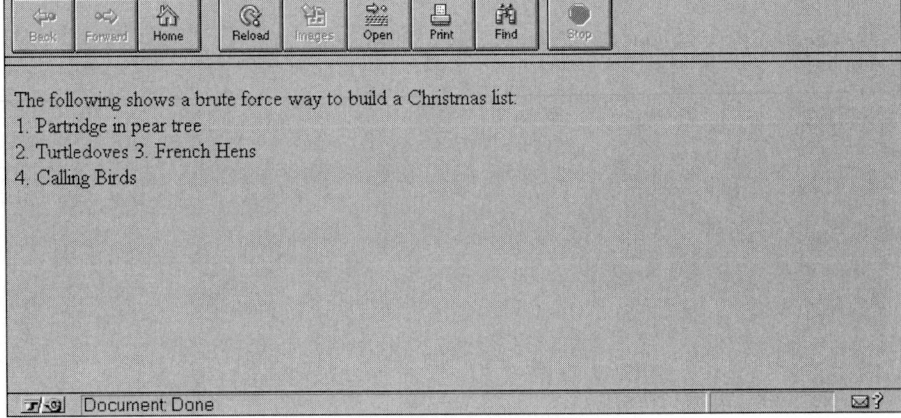

Figure 4.6 Netscape's presentation of the modified "brute force" list.

Bah-Humbug! We forgot to put the <BR> after the new entry. Now we have to edit it again. If we had used an ordered-list container, all we would have had to do was insert a new <LI> tag and the new entry. The browser would have updated the numbers for us, and we would not have needed to remember the <BR> either. Figure 4.7 shows how this would look in code form. Figure 4.8 shows how the code would look in the browser.

```
<HTML>
<HEAD>
<TITLE>List 2 </TITLE>
</HEAD>
<BODY>
The following shows a more efficient way to build a Christmas
list:
<OL>
<LI> Partridge in pear tree
<LI>Turtledoves
<LI>French Hens
<LI> Calling Birds
</OL>
</BODY>
</HTML>
```

Figure 4.7 HTML code for an ordered list.

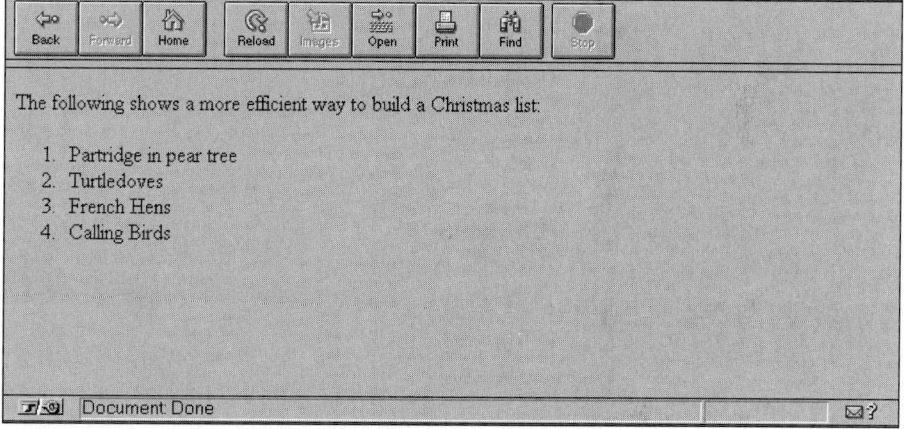

Figure 4.8 The updated ordered list as seen in Netscape.

Since it is so much easier to use the ordered list container and because people order their worlds in lists, most Web weavers find this one of the more common containers they have on their pages. The ordered list has several attributes that make it even more useful for specific tasks.

START

It is sometimes handy to have a list start at some number other than one. For example, you may wish to list the steps in a task, with some discussion interspersed among the steps. You could code the first list container that describes the first 3 steps, type your discussion, and then start a second list that begins with the number four. Here is an example of some HTML code that illustrates this. Notice how the START attribute is used in the second and third lists.

```
<HTML>
<HEAD>
<TITLE> List 3 </TITLE>
</HEAD>
<BODY>
There are 8 steps to change the oil in your Saturn:
<OL>
<LI>Find a comfy place to park the car, in the shade in
summer, in the sun in winter.
<LI>Get the waste oil pan, filter wrench, and 14mm box end
wrench ready.
<LI>Find 4 quarts of 5W-30 oil and a Saturn oil filter.
</OL>
It is really important, or so the folks at Saturn tell me, to
use 5W-30 oil and genuine Saturn oil filters.
<OL START=4>
<LI>Remove the oil drain plug, and drain the old oil into the
waste oil pan.
<LI>Remove the old filter...then clean up the mess you made.
<LI>Replace the oil drain plug after the oil stops dripping.
<LI>Put the new oil filter on, 1/4 turn past finger tight.
</OL>
Always remember to put just a bit of  oil on the rubber
gasket before you put the oil filter back on.  This will make
a better seal, and help you get the filter tightened
correctly.
<OL Start=8>
<LI>Put 4 quarts of 5W-30 oil into the engine.
</OL>
</BODY>
</HTML>
```

Figure 4.9 HTML code for the START attribute.

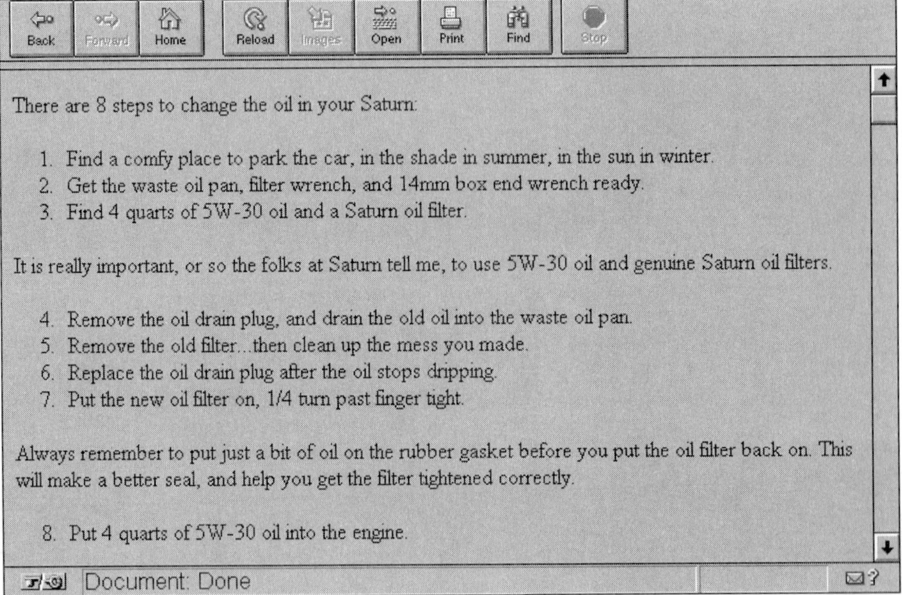

Figure 4.10 Netscape's presentation of lists that use the START attribute.

As you can see, using the START attribute allows the browser to build the lists, but the author can still control the ordering of the numbers. This is a very handy tool.

TYPE Attribute

Besides letting you decide what number your list is to start with, HTML also provides a way for you to change the style of the numbers or letters of the list elements. Table 4.1 shows the different number and letter styles provided by the **TYPE** attribute. Figures 4.11 through 4.14 show four versions of the same table, showing four of the five different TYPE styles. These four examples show how the different TYPEs change the style of the "numbering." This attribute will be handy for making outlines, as we will see later in the chapter, when we put lists inside lists.

TYPE	GENERATED STYLE	EXAMPLES
A	Uppercase letters	A. B. C. D.
a	Lowercase letters	a. b. c. d.
I	Uppercase Roman numerals	I. II. III. IV.
i	Lowercase Roman numerals	i. ii. iii. iv.
1	Arabic numerals (default)	1. 2. 3. 4.

Table 4.1 Number and letter styles of the TYPE attribute.

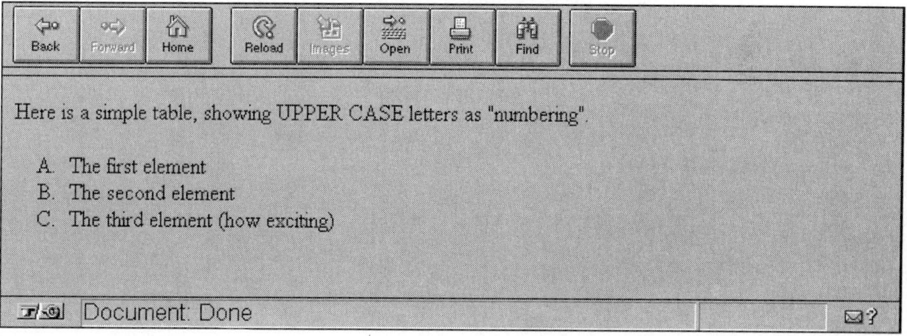

Figure 4.11 TYPE=A for list.

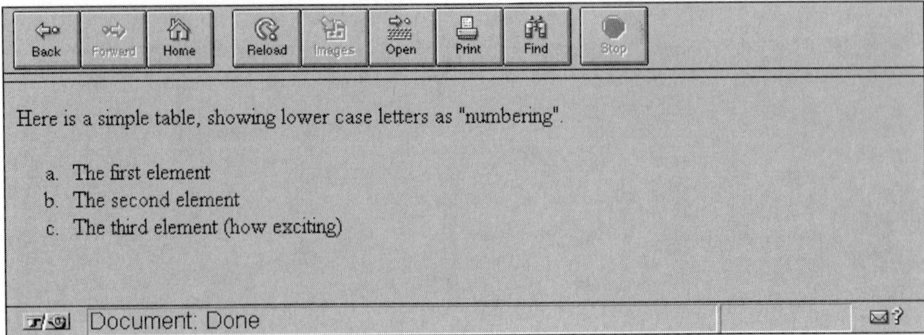

Figure 4.12 TYPE=a for list.

Figure 4.13 TYPE=I for list.

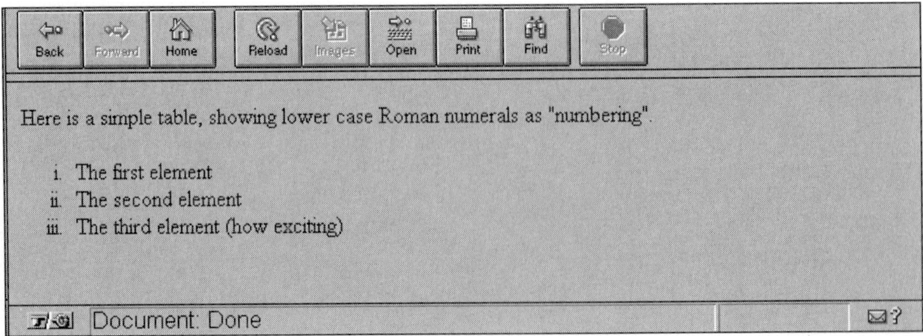

Figure 4.14 TYPE=i for list.

<LI>

You have already seen the way the **<LI>** container is used to indicate elements of a list. While the <LI> tag is really a container, browsers can always infer the end of this container by what follows, so it is unnecessary to code the </LI> closing tag. Not coding the closing tags also makes it easier to modify the list, so wise Web weavers will omit the closing tag for this particular container. The <LI> container is an example of a tag that is migrating to the status of an empty tag.

The <LI> container can contain almost anything if it defines an element of an ordered or unordered list. It can contain paragraphs of text, image, and even other lists. If the list item is within a directory or menu list, that directory or menu list cannot contain other lists or blocked elements like paragraphs or forms.

The <LI> container is a universal container. It is used with all of the different types of lists except definition lists, discussed at the end of this chapter. What the <LI> tag generates differs depending on the type of list for which it defines an element. For example, in an ordered list, the <LI> tag specifies a list element that is preceded by a number or letter. In an unordered list, it specifies a list element preceded by one of the different types of bullet.

TYPE

The **TYPE** attribute of the <LI> container is very much like the TYPE attribute of the <OL> container. However, whereas the list TYPE specified the style of the numbers for the whole list, the TYPE attribute on a single list item changes the style of the numbering for only that item. The list in Figure 4.15 shows the different values for the TYPE attribute, with each list item having its own TYPE. Figure 4.16 shows how the code looks when rendered by Netscape.

```
<HTML>
<HEAD>
<TITLE> List5-all </TITLE>
</HEAD>
<BODY>
The following list shows each type of list item, and
describes what it is.
<OL>
<LI TYPE=A>This element is of type A
<LI TYPE=a> This element is of type a
<LI TYPE=I> This element is of type I
<LI TYPE=i> And this element has a type i
</OL>
</BODY>
</HTML>
```

Figure 4.15 HTML code for a list showing four of the various <LI> TYPE attributes.

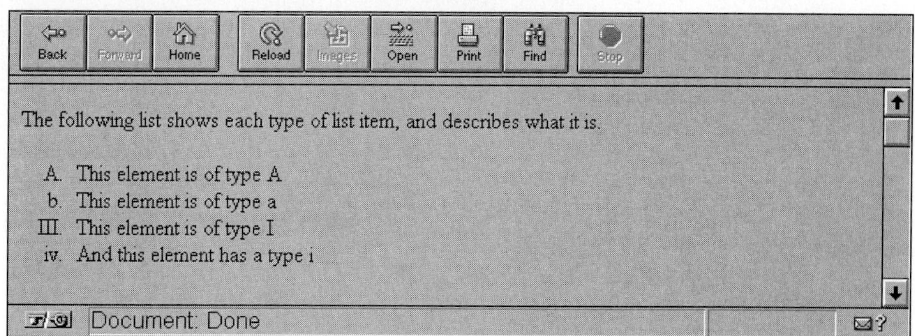

Figure 4.16 Netscape's presentation of a list showing four of the various <LI> TYPE attributes.

VALUE Attribute

Like the START attribute of the <OL> tag, the VALUE attribute of the <LI> tag can specify a particular starting value that will serve as the new base number for the rest of the items in the list—unless a subsequent item specifies another value. It is important to remember that at the start of a list you should use the START attribute, but within the list you should use the VALUE attribute. Misusing the VALUE attribute can cause confusing results. Figure 4.17 shows an example of the misuse of the VALUE attribute. Figure 4.18 shows its very confusing result.

```
<HTML>
<HEAD>
<TITLE> List6-all </TITLE>
</HEAD>
<BODY>
The following list shows each type of list item, and
describes what it is.
<OL>
<LI VALUE=5>This is the first element of the list.
<LI VALUE=1> The second element
<LI VALUE=11> The third element
<LI TYPE=i> The fourth element changes number type, but not
VALUE
<LI VALUE=1> and the last element has VALUE 1 too, notice
that the type continued!
</OL>
</BODY>
</HTML>
```

Figure 4.17 HTML code showing misuse of various <LI>VALUE and TYPE attributes.

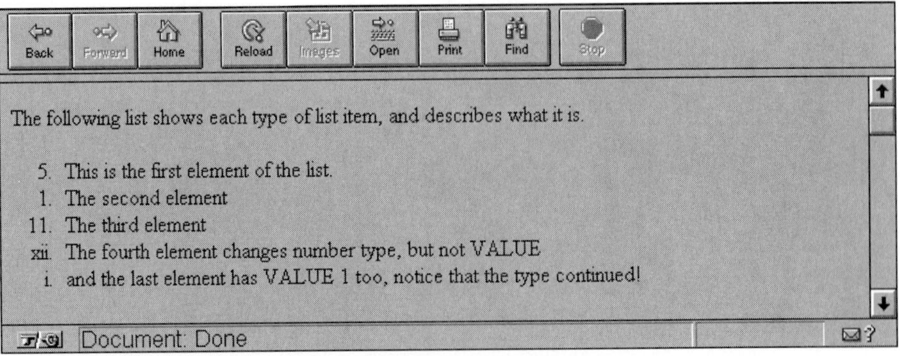

Figure 4.18 Netscape's presentation of a list resulting from misuse of various <LI> VALUE and TYPE attributes.

As you can see from this example, each time either the VALUE or the TYPE of the elements was changed, that change was propagated from that point down the list until there was another change. You need to be very careful when changing the TYPE or VALUE for list elements. It is rare that you will need that flexibility.

If you are trying to build clean, fully HTML-compliant code, you should never include any text or other items within a list that are not part of the actual list. For example, in Figure 4.8 we could have tried to include the descriptive paragraphs within the list yet keep them outside the actual list elements. That way we would not have had to restart the numbering on successive lists. However, most browsers would have had a problem with that, and it could have resulted in a very difficult read. Figure 4.19 shows how we could code the oil-change example without changing lists. *This is* <u>not</u> *HTML-compliant* code. It is shown to illustrate a *bad* example! In other words, don't try this at home.

```
<HTML>
<HEAD>
<TITLE> List 3 </TITLE>
</HEAD>
<BODY>
There are 8 steps to change the oil in your Saturn:
<OL>
<LI>Find a comfy place to park the car, in the shade in
summer, in the sun in winter.
<LI>Get the waste oil pan, filter wrench, and 14mm box end
wrench ready.
<LI>Find 4 quarts of 5W-30 oil and a Saturn oil filter.

<P>It is really important, or so the folks at Saturn tell me,
to use 5W-30 oil and genuine Saturn oil filters.</P>

<LI>Remove the oil drain plug, and drain the old oil into the
waste oil pan.
<LI>Remove the old filter...then clean up the mess you made.
<LI>Replace the oil drain plug after the oil stops dripping.
<LI>Put the new oil filter on, 1/4 turn past finger tight.

<P>Always remember to put just a bit of  oil on the rubber
gasket before you put the oil filter back on.  This will make
a better seal, and help you get the filter tightened
correctly.</P>

<LI>Put 4 quarts of 5W-30 oil into the engine.
</OL>
</BODY>
</HTML>
```

Figure 4.19 HTML code showing the INCORRECT way to put text blocks within a list.

Notice in Figure 4.19 that we needed to enclose the comment paragraphs in the paragraph container. In the current version of the Netscape browser, this code would generate the same screen as did the code in Figure 4.8. However, this is not good HTML practice!

Unordered, or Bulleted, Lists: <UL>

Sometimes you will want to make a list of items that have no necessary order. In cases like this, you can have the browser build an **unordered list**, also called a **bulleted list**. For example, we may want to create a list like the one shown in Figure 4.20.

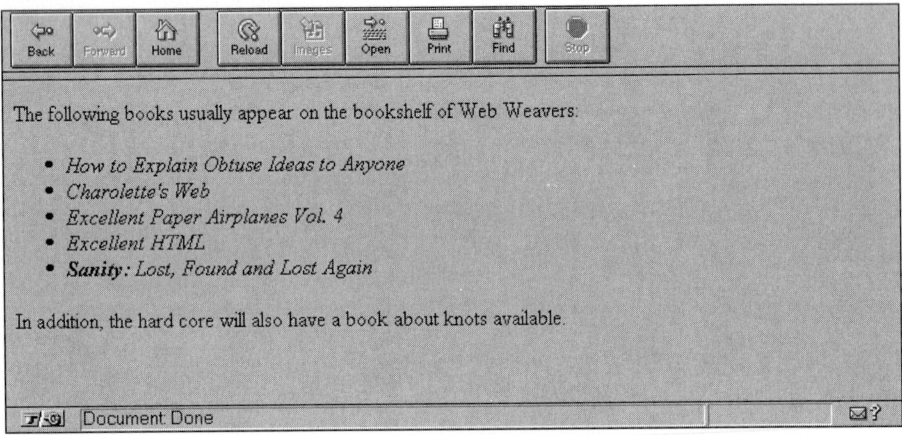

Figure 4.20 Netscape's presentation of an unordered list.

Notice that the list elements are preceded by bullets rather than numbers or letters, but otherwise the format of this list is very similar to that of the ordered list. Figure 4.21 presents the code used to produce this list.

```
<HTML>
<HEAD>
<TITLE> Unordered List </TITLE>
</HEAD>
<BODY>
The following books usually appear on the bookshelf of Web
Weavers:
<UL>
<LI><EM>How to Explain Obtuse Ideas to Anyone</EM>
<LI><EM>Charlotte's Web</EM>
<LI><EM>Excellent Paper Airplanes Vol. 4</EM>
<LI><EM>Excellent HTML</EM>
<LI><EM><STRONG>Sanity</STRONG>: Lost, Found and Lost
Again</EM>
</UL>
In addition, the hard core will also have a book about knots
available.
</BODY>
</HTML>
```

Figure 4.21 HTML code for an unordered list.

It is possible to change the shape of the bullets in an unordered list by using the TYPE option, but only Netscape currently supports this feature.

Another option for both the ordered and unordered lists is the **COMPACT** attribute. It is supposed to make the list smaller by compressing line spacing between the list items. However, most browsers ignore this attribute, so it is of little value to code it.

<LI> in Unordered Lists

As we have seen, the <LI> tag is used to identify list items in an unordered list just as it is used in an ordered list. There are, however, some small differences in the way the <LI> attributes are evaluated. The code in Figure 4.22 shows the same list items used in Figure 4.17 that demonstrated the misuses of the TYPE and VALUE attributes Here they are shown as they would appear in an unordered rather than an ordered list. Figure 4.23 shows their result.

```
<HTML>
<HEAD>
<TITLE> Unordered List with typed items </TITLE>
</HEAD>
<BODY>
This is an unordered list, but each list element has either a
type or value attribute:
<UL>
<LI VALUE=5>This is the first element of the list.
<LI VALUE=1> The second element
<LI VALUE=11> The third element
<LI TYPE=i> The fourth element changes number type, but not
VALUE
<LI VALUE=1> and the last element has VALUE 1, too; notice
that the type continued!
</UL>
As this example shows, unordered list elements don't
recognize values or types that indicate either letters or
numbers.
</BODY>
</HTML>
```

Figure 4.22 HTML code showing misuses of VALUE and TYPE attributes in an unordered list.

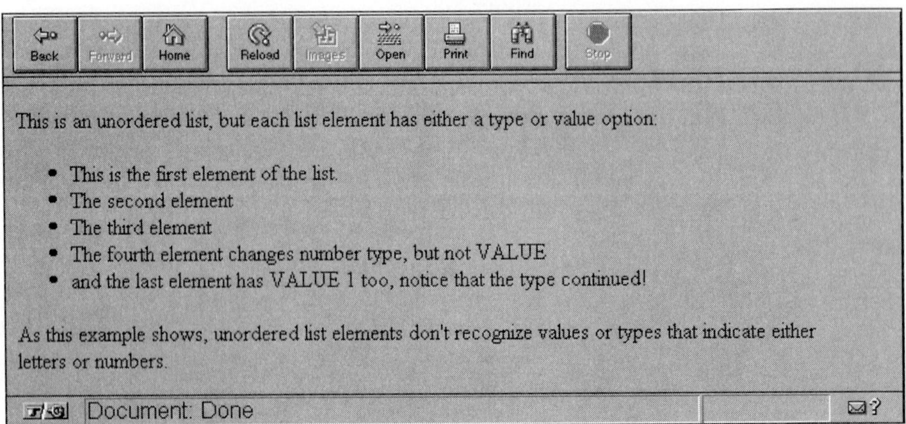

Figure 4.23 Netscape's presentation of an unordered list, showing misuse of the VALUE and TYPE attributes.

Lists of Lists (Nesting)

Sometimes it is necessary to build lists of lists. In both ordered and unordered lists, it is possible to put another list (a sublist) inside a list element. This procedure of **nesting** lists allows you to build structures that convey complex relationships.

Combining Ordered and Unordered Lists

Figure 4.24 shows an ordered list that has two small unordered lists within it. Figure 4.25 shows how Netscape would render this HTML code. As you can see from this example, the browser indents the list within a list to increase readability. The fact that the subordinate lists are indented in the HTML code has no bearing on how the browser displays it. This indention is only to make the code easier to read.

```
<HTML>
<HEAD>
<TITLE> Lists within Lists! </TITLE>
</HEAD>
<BODY>
When packing a briefcase to go to school, be sure to:
<OL>
<LI> Pack Yoda, the lap top.
    <UL>
    <LI> Get the power cord and transformer
    <LI> Find the box of disks
    <LI> Check on the PCMCIA cards
    </UL>
<LI> Check that the Day-Timer is there
    <UL>
    <LI> Check that it is the right month
    <LI> Check that it is the right year
    </UL>
<LI> Take correct text books
<LI> Make sure LUNCH is packed!
</OL>
</BODY>
</HTML>
```

Figure 4.24 HTML code for unordered lists contained within ordered lists.

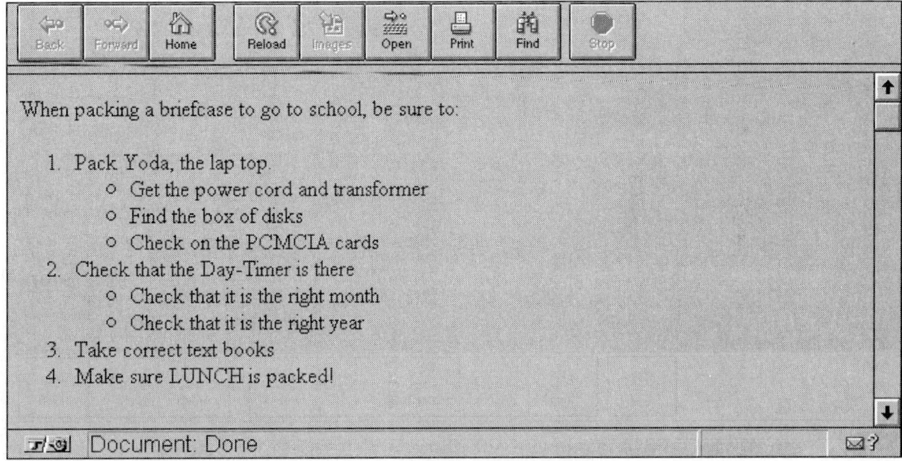

Figure 4.25 Netscape's presentation of a list within a list.

Nesting Unordered Lists

In nested unordered lists, most browsers use different bullet types to show that some elements are subordinate to others. The code in Figure 4.26 has three levels of nested unordered lists.

```
<HTML>
<HEAD>
<TITLE> Lists within Lists! </TITLE>
</HEAD>
<BODY>
When packing a briefcase to go to school, be sure to:
<UL>
<LI> Pack Yoda, the lap top.
       <UL>
       <LI> Get the power cord and transformer
       <LI> Find the box of disks
                <UL>
                <LI>  Get this semester's homework disk
                <LI>  Get the grading software disk
                <LI>  Make sure the games disk is packed!
                </UL>
       <LI> Check on the PCMCIA cards
       </UL>
<LI> Check that the Day-Timer is there
       <UL>
       <LI> Check that it is the right month
       <LI> Check that it is the right year
       </UL>
<LI> Take correct text books
<LI> Make sure LUNCH is packed!
</UL>
</BODY>
</HTML>
```

Figure 4.26 HTML code for nested unordered lists.

In Netscape this code would generate the page shown in Figure 4.27. Notice that the browser uses different bullets on each of the different levels generated.

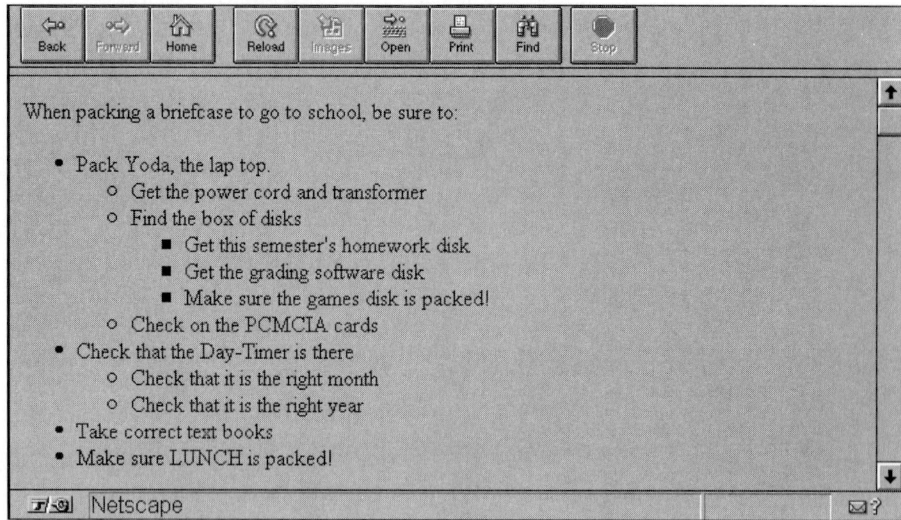

Figure 4.27 Netscape's presentation of nested unordered lists.

Nesting Ordered Lists

Nesting ordered lists allows the creation of outlines. For example, if we change the HTML code in Figure 4.26 to use ordered lists, the result would be as shown in Figure 4.28.

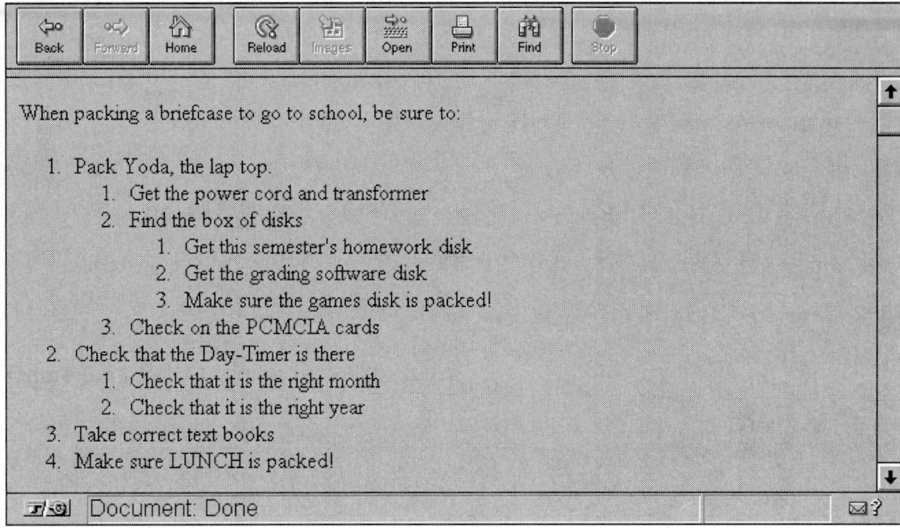

Figure 4.28 Netscape's presentation of nested ordered lists.

Hmmmm. Figure 4.28 is not quite what we had in mind. Although it does indeed show a nested list of ordered lists, it isn't all that readable. What we need to do is change the <TYPE> attribute of the various lists to show subordination. It is best to use the standard outline order (I. , A. , 1. , a.). Figure 4.29 presents the HTML code that will make the list more understandable. Notice that we need to specify the TYPE attributes only for the opening of each list, not for each element. Figure 4.30 shows how the code looks in Netscape.

```
<HTML>
<HEAD>
<TITLE> Ordered lists within lists! </TITLE>
</HEAD>
<BODY>
When packing a briefcase to go to school, be sure to:
<OL TYPE="I">
<LI> Pack Yoda, the lap top.
    <OL TYPE="A">
    <LI> Get the power cord and transformer
    <LI> Find the box of disks
          <OL TYPE="1">
          <LI>  Get this semester's homework disk
          <LI>  Get the grading software disk
          <LI>  Make sure the games disk is packed!
          </OL>
    <LI> Check on the PCMCIA cards
    </OL>
<LI> Check that the Day-Timer is there
    <OL TYPE="A">
    <LI> Check that it is the right month
    <LI> Check that it is the right year
    </OL>
<LI> Take correct text books
<LI> Make sure LUNCH is packed!
</OL>
</BODY>
</HTML>
```

Figure 4.29 HTML code for nested ordered lists using attributes.

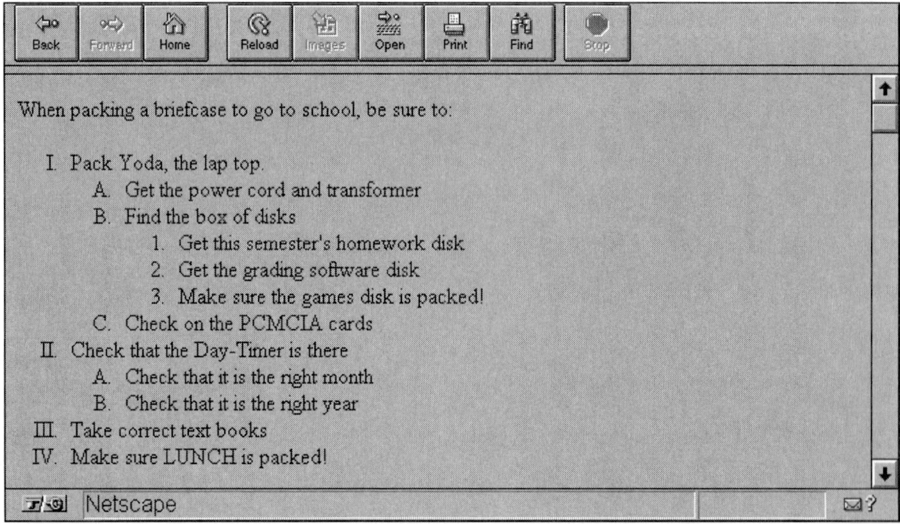

Figure 4.30 Netscape's presentation of nested ordered lists using TYPE attributes.

Using ordered or unordered lists can make your page more understandable to your users. In later examples you will see why lists are becoming a standard feature of many of the pages on the Web. As you cruise the Net, look for examples of lists, both good and bad.

Readability

This is a good time to bring up readability. As your HTML code gets longer and more complex, you will find that it saves you both time and effort if you take readability into account as you build the page.

Inserting a couple of blank lines around a particular structure, like a list, makes it just a little easier to find and yet requires little time and effort. Likewise, it is simple to insert a tab or two in front of subordinate items to show their relative relationship. Also, putting each logical part of the HTML code on a separate line makes the code easier to read and understand. The code in Figure 4.31 violates all of these readability rules. Although it is very short, you can see how much more difficult it is to read than the previous examples of HTML code.

```
<HTML><HEAD><TITLE> Ordered lists within lists!
</TITLE></HEAD><BODY>When packing a briefcase to go to
school, be sure to:<OL TYPE="I"><LI> Pack Yoda, the lap
top.<OL TYPE="A"><LI> Get the power cord and transformer<LI>
Find the box of disks<OL TYPE="1"><LI>  Get this semester's
homework disk <LI>  Get the grading software disk<LI>  Make
sure the games disk is packed!</OL><LI> Check on the PCMCIA
cards</OL><LI> Check that the Day-Timer is there<OL
TYPE="A"><LI> Check that it is the right month <LI> Check
that it is the right year</OL><LI> Take correct text
books<LI> Make sure LUNCH is packed!</OL></BODY> </HTML>
```

Figure 4.31 HTML code written with minimal readability.

If you look closely, you will find that this is the same HTML code that generated the ordered lists within lists of Figure 4.30. All the blank lines, tabs, and extra carriage returns have been removed. This code will generate the same nested lists as the code in Figure 4.29, but it is harder to read and understand and would be much more difficult to maintain.

Simple formatting techniques like these will make it much easier for you to find your way around in your HTML code. Good formatting will also make it easier for other people to see what you have done. As your pages get longer and more complex, making them readable will become ever more important. You can puzzle out the code shown in Figure 4.31, but if you were faced with 20 pages of code all jammed together like that, it could be a daunting task. Some Web weavers build whole sites of pages like this, and they are for all intents and purposes unreadable. This example also brings home the point that while the Web weaver controls the content, the browser controls the format, because the jammed together HTML code will generate exactly the same page in Netscape as the more readable code will.

Definition Lists

Most browsers also support another form of list, called a **definition list,** which presents data formatted like a glossary or a dictionary. It is the ideal format to present lists of words or concepts and their meanings. Figure 4.32 presents the code for a definition list describing the various types of lists. As you can see in figure 4.33, the browser does some nice formatting of the text.

```
<HTML>
<HEAD>
<TITLE> A definition list </TITLE>
</HEAD>
<BODY>
<H2>The Three Common types of HTML lists:</H2>
<DL>
<DT> Ordered Lists
     <DD>An ordered list contains several elements, each of
     them preceded by a number, letter, or Roman numeral.
     The TYPE attribute describes the character used to
     precede the list element, and the VALUE attribute can
     start or change the numbering sequence.
     </DD>
 <DT>Unordered Lists
     <DD> Unordered lists show a series of elements, preceded
     by some form of bullet character.  Most browsers show
     subordinate lists indented and preceded by a different
     bullet element.
     </DD>
 <DT>Definition Lists
     <DD>  A definition list is used to display a word or
     phrase, followed by the definition or explanation of
     that word or phrase.  They are commonly used in
     dictionary or glossary lists.
     </DD>
</DL>
</BODY>
</HTML>
```

Figure 4.32 HTML code for a definition list.

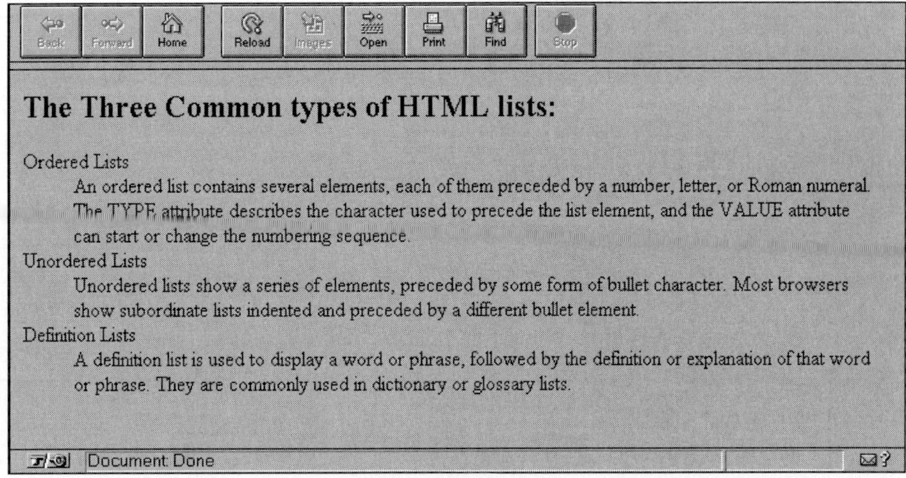

Figure 4.33 Netscape's presentation of a definition list.

Looking at the code, you can see that the definition list uses different tags than the other two types of lists we have studied. The formatting, again, is just to improve readability and has no bearing on the way the browser presents the lists.

<DL>

Definition lists are enclosed within the **<DL>** (definition list) container. The </DL> ending tag is *never* omitted. Each element of a definition list is composed of two different parts, the word or phrase to be defined followed by the definition. Each of the parts of an element has a particular HTML tag to define it. A definition list does not use the <LI> (list element) tag unless the definition itself contains an ordered or unordered list. If you consult a manual, you will find that the <DL> container supports the COMPACT attribute. Few if any browsers still recognize this attribute, so it has little or no value.

<DT>

The **<DT>** (define term) tag indicates the term that is to be defined. It is valid only within a <DL> container. Although the <DT> tag is formally considered a container, it is almost always used as an empty tag, like <LI>. The <DD> tag that immediately follows the end of the <DT> tag serves to alert the browser to close the <DT> container. While it is technically possible to follow the <DT> tag with a long expression, the traditional use is to use a single word or short phrase. There are no attributes on the <DT> tag.

<DD>

The **<DD>** (define definition) tag is coded immediately following the word or phrase associated with the <DT> tag. It marks the beginning of the definition segment of the <DL> list entry.You can code any HTML construct within the definition portion of the list. However, since your users generally expect this type of format to be used for definitions and the like, you should restrict your content to the succinct definition or explanation of the word or phrase shown by the <DT> tag.There are no attributes associated with this tag.

Obsolete List Forms

As you cruise the Web, and look at code, you will see a couple of other types of lists.These lists were used with older versions of HTML and are generally not handled differently or uniquely by the browsers, so are considered obsolete.

Menu Lists

The **<MENU>** container was used to represent items in a pull-down menu format rather than in an unordered list. Sometimes the browser eliminated the leading bullet or presented the information in multiple columns. Each element was indicated by the <LI> tag, as in both ordered and unordered lists. Most browsers present this list just like an unordered list.

Directory Lists

The **<DIR>** tag was originally designed to display lists of file names, like the DOS dir command. Most browsers now treat it as an unordered list, but if they don't, the browser expects very short (20 characters or less) entries for each <LI> in the list.As with other lists that use the <LI> element, the TYPE attribute, if recognized, specifies the type of bullet for a <DIR> list. In some of the older versions of the browsers, elements in a <DIR> list could be displayed in multiple columns.As you can see, Netscape doesn't handle these lists any differently than an unordered list.

Figure 4.34 presents the HTML code for <MENU> and <DIR> lists.The Netscape screen in Figure 4.35 shows both types of lists. Notice that they look like simple unordered lists.

```
<HTML>
<HEAD>
<TITLE> Obsolete Lists </TITLE>
</HEAD>
<BODY>
<H3>A MENU type list</H3>
<MENU>
    <LI> First menu element
    <LI> Second menu element
    <LI> Third menu element
</MENU>
<H3>A DIRECTORY type list</H3>
<DIR>
    <LI> READ.ME
    <LI> README.TO
    <LI> README.3
```

Figure 4.34 HTML code to create <MENU> and <DIR> lists.

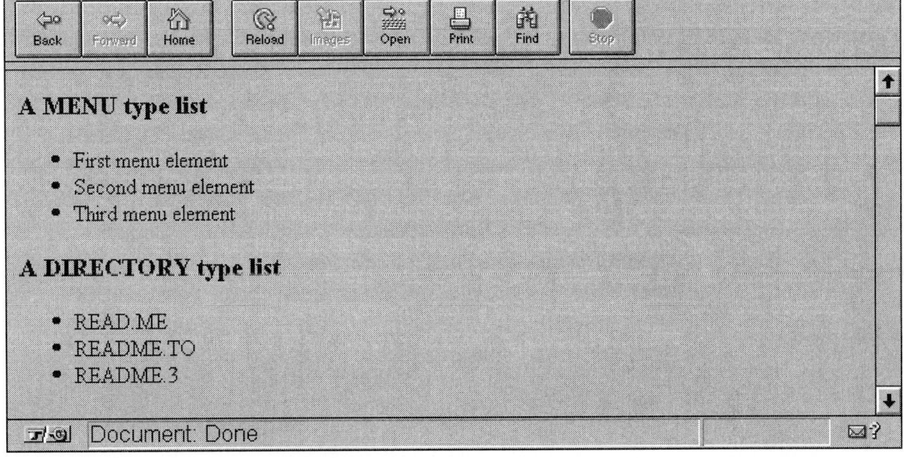

Figure 4.35 Netscape's presentation of <MENU> and <DIR> lists.

Exercises

Perform each step *in order.* Neither skip nor combine steps!

4.1. Create the following list:

a. List six of your favorite music CDs. Use only the <BR> tag, and number the items from 1 to 6.

b. Add an entry between items 4 and 5, then renumber the list.

c. Change the list from Arabic numbers to lowercase letters (a–g).

4.2. Duplicate the three steps from Exercise 4.1, but this time use the ordered list <OL> container. Perform all three steps in the same order.

4.3. Using multiple list containers, create the following outline:

I. Lists
  A. Ordered
    1. Type
      a. Alpha
        i. Uppercase
        ii. Lowercase
      b. Arabic numbers
      c. Roman numerals
        i. Uppercase
        ii. Lowercase
    2. Start
  B. Unordered
    1. Type

Note: The unordered list uses type to change the type of bullet. It only works in Netscape right now.

      a. Square
      b. Disk
      c. Circle
II. Examples

Remember that nothing but <LI> items should occur within the <OL> and <UL> containers!

4.4. Create a set of nested, unordered lists at least four levels deep, and observe how the browser changes the bullets for different levels. For example:

o Outermost level
  - Second level
    ★ Third level
      + Fourth Level 1
      + Fourth Level 2
    ★ Third level
  - Second level
o Outermost level

YMMV★ on the different bullets selected. That is what you are discovering!

4.5. Cruise the Net and find and capture at least two examples of excellent uses for lists. Document where you captured them, and create a separate page for those two lists. They should WOW your classmates and your instructor! Be sure to leave a note telling the Web Weaver of those sites that you are borrowing their lists.

★ Your Mileage May Vary.

CHAPTER five

MAKING THINGS A LITTLE DIFFERENT

5

Although the cardinal rule of HTML is that the author controls the content and the browser controls the format, there are some things you can do to try to control how your text appears on the screen. Actually, there are a few things you can do that will make your text look *very* different. In this chapter you will learn how to ask the browser to make your text look different and how to format the text in special ways.

Styles

The term **style** describes a way to set off a group of characters from the surrounding text block. There are two general forms of style: logical style and physical style. For the purposes of this book, we will define those two different types of style this way: **Logical styles** describe the way the text within the container is used. **Physical styles** describe the way the text is to look in a browser. Since the browser is in control of the way the text actually appears, the HTML code can only attempt to provide formatting direction. All we can say with any degree of certainty is that any particular style will be rendered the same way each time by any particular browser. For example, one browser may render all level 1 headings, <H1>, as bold and in large font. Another browser may render all such headings as centered and underlined but in the same size font as the rest of the document.

Physical Styles

The physical styles discussed here are intended to change the actual format of the text as it is displayed by the browser. While our general rule is that we control the content and the browser controls the format, the following tags are designed to actually give us some control of the format where possible. Some browsers will recognize these tags, and some will ignore them. Minimal use of physical tags helps ensure a better, more consistent page.

Boldface: <B>

The boldface **<B> . . . </B>** physical-style container causes any text enclosed to be displayed as **bold**. It is like the bold attribute found in most word processors. The example following this section will illustrate each of these physical styles. The logical style of **<STRONG> . . . </STRONG>** is one that most often creates a bold font. It will be discussed under "Logical Styles."

Italics: <I>

One way to cause text to appear in *italics* is to use the **<I> . . . </I>** container. This is like the italics option found in most word processors. The logical style of **<EM> . . . </EM>** (discussed later) is most often used to produce this result.

Monospaced Text: <TT>, <CODE>, <KBD>

When showing how code looks, or when showing HTML tags, some authors use **<TT> . . . </TT>** for a typewriter or Teletype font to produce a monospaced font like Courier. In a **monospaced font,** each character takes up the same amount of space. The opposite is a **proportionally spaced font**, like the one this book is printed in, where, for example, a *w* takes up more space than an *l*. This gives `the text a different appearance` that can be quite striking.

Several other styles also produce a monospaced font. For example, **<CODE> . . . </CODE>** and **<KBD> . . . </KBD>** were designed for special applications where you want to represent, respectively, computer code or keyboard input. They are falling from favor and should not be used anymore.

Underlining: <U>

Another physical tag is the underline tag, **<U> . . . </U>,** which underlines the text enclosed within the container. There is no specific logical-style tag that produces underline. Depending on the browser, several of the logical tags may produce underlined text.

Figure 5.1 shows the code for the four physical tags discussed thus far. Figure 5.2 shows how the Netscape browser displays these physical-style containers. As you can see, it is possible to combine physical styles so that you can underline, bold, and italicize the same text. However, notice the words "your text." They are bold, italicized, underlined, and in a monospace font. That combination doesn't really look monospaced. Apparently, the browser did not have a bold, italicized, underlined, monospaced font available, so it did the best it could. Even with physical styles, the actual formatting of the text is under the control of the browser, and there is no browser standard to require support for combined styles. Therefore, a considerate Web weaver will use the logical-style alternative whenever possible.

```
<HTML>
<HEAD>
<TITLE> Physical style examples </TITLE>
</HEAD>
<BODY>
The following paragraphs are each enclosed in a different
physical tag.  This is designed to show how the various tags
look when viewed by the Netscape browser.
<P><B>This paragraph is enclosed in the bold container.  It
is a paragraph of bold text. </B>
</P>
<P><I>This paragraph is enclosed in the italics container.
You can see how italics look using this tag.
</I>
</P>
<P><TT>This is the typewriter or monospaced font.  Usually a
font like courier is used for this.</TT>
</P>
<P><U>This paragraph is all underlined.  It is contained
within an underline container.</U>
</P>
<P>And of course, <B>you can <I> combine styles <U> as well
to really emphasize <TT> your text </TT></U></I></B>
Remember, it is usually better form to use the logical tags
rather than the physical tags.
</BODY>
</HTML>
```

Figure 5.1 HTML code for the first four physical-style containers.

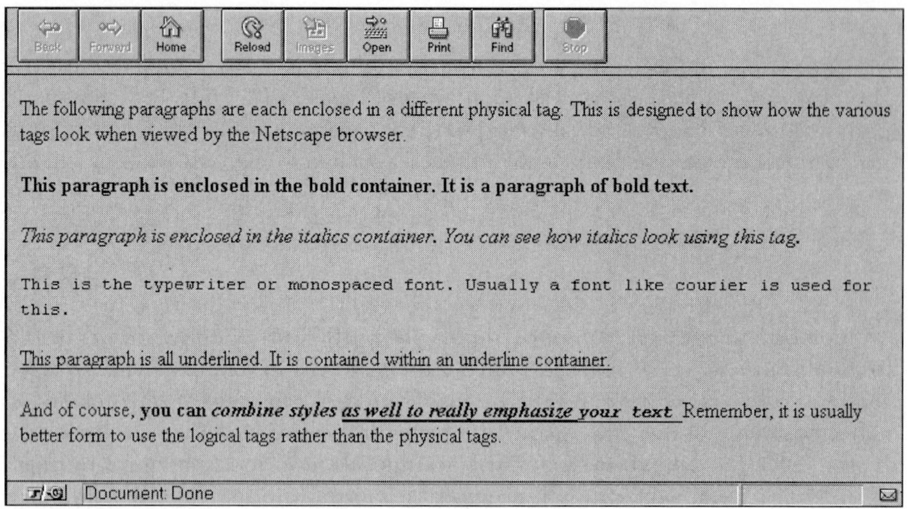

Figure 5.2 Netscape's presentation of the first four physical styles.

Big Text: <BIG>

Some of the physical-style tags are browser-specific. For example, **<BIG> . . . </BIG>** (big text) is currently only a Netscape extension. You can nest several <BIG> containers to increase the size of the text up to the browser's maximum size. The code in Figure 5.3 produces a line of text in which the words get bigger and bigger because of the <BIG> containers nested within each other. As we close each of the <BIG> containers, the text decreases in size again. There is a maximum "bigness"—currently a size 7. Normal text is size 3.

```
<HTML>
<HEAD>
<TITLE> An example of <BIG></TITLE>
</HEAD>
<BODY>
This <BIG> text <BIG> gets <BIG> bigger <BIG> and <BIG>
bigger </BIG> but </BIG> there </BIG> is </BIG> a maximum
</BIG> size.
</BODY>
</HTML>
```

Figure 5.3 HTML code for the Netscape extension <BIG>.

Figure 5.4 shows how Netscape renders the HTML code. The text gets bigger, in steps of 1, from size 3 to size 7. Notice that the <BIG> tags coded after the browser reaches size 7, at the word "and," are ignored.

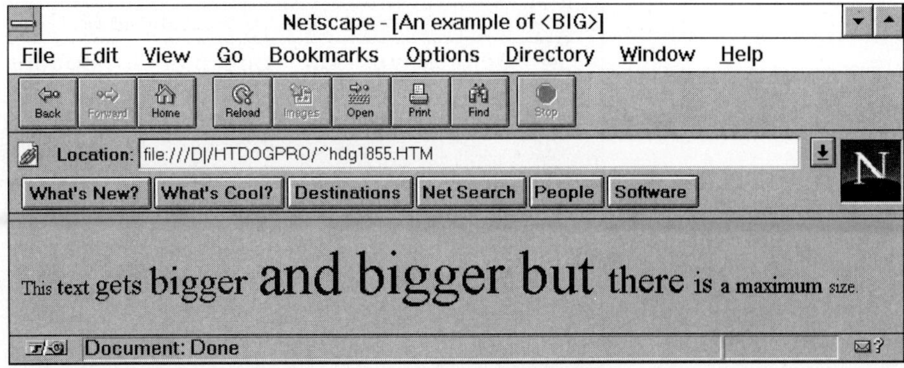

Figure 5.4 Netscape's presentation of text enclosed in <BIG> containers.

Small Text: <SMALL>

Just as Netscape allows you to make text bigger, you can make text smaller as well. Making text larger can increase readability. Making text smaller is usually used only for special applications. Like <BIG>, the **<SMALL> . . . </SMALL>** container can be nested to make the text smaller and smaller. Figure 5.5 gives an example of code for small text. Notice how the readability is affected. Figure 5.6 shows how Netscape renders the HTML code. Remember, normal-size text is considered size 3. Size 1 is the smallest text size. Therefore, we would expect only two reductions in text size, not three. And as we can see from Figure 5.6, our predictions are correct. There are only three text sizes shown on the screen. Readability can suffer when text gets smaller, so be careful in using this container.

```
<HTML>
<HEAD>
<TITLE> An example of <SMALL></TITLE>
</HEAD>
<BODY>
This <SMALL> text <SMALL> gets <SMALL> smaller </SMALL> but
</SMALL> there's </SMALL> a minimum </SMALL> size.
</BODY>
</HTML>
```

Figure 5.5 HTML code for the <SMALL> container.

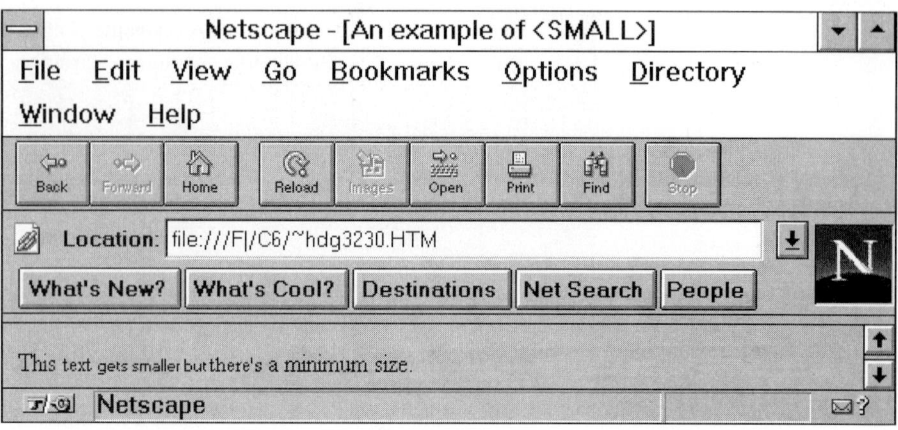

Figure 5.6 Netscape's presentation of text enclosed in <SMALL> containers.

Subscripts and Superscripts: <SUB>, <SUP>

Subscript and superscript tags, **<SUB>** and **<SUP>,** are most often used in scientific and mathematical notations. Subscripts don't always appear in the same size and font as the text line. They are set one-half line below the normal text flow. Superscripts are sometimes the same size and font as the current text line but other times are rendered in a smaller font. They are set one-half line above the normal text flow. Figure 5.7 shows examples of both. Notice the excessive use in the second paragraph. This is an obvious example of abuse of the tags. Figure 5.8 shows how the code is rendered by Netscape. Notice that Netscape shows both subscripts and superscripts in a smaller font than the normal text.

```
<HTML>
<HEAD>
<TITLE> An example of Sub and Super Scripts</TITLE>
</HEAD>
<BODY>
In this line, the word <SUB>subscript</SUB> is below the
line, and <SUP>superscript</SUP> is above. <P>You
<SUB>can</SUB><SUP>make</SUP><SUB> your</SUB> <SUP>text</SUP>
<SUB>look</SUB> <SUP>silly,</SUP> too!</P>
</BODY>
</HTML>
```

Figure 5.7 HTML code for subscripting and superscripting.

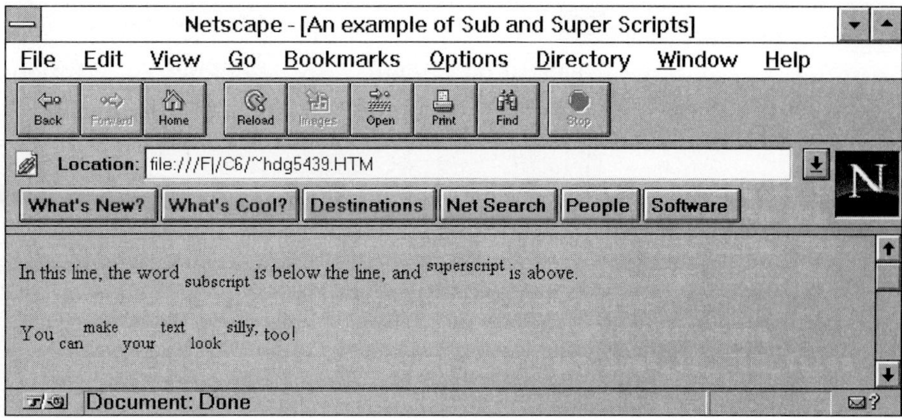

Figure 5.8 Netscape's presentation of subscripts and superscripts.

Strike-Through Text: <STRIKE>

Most of the browsers will display text with a line through it, called "strike-through text" or "strike-out text." This is most often used to show text that has been removed from or replaced in a document. Legal documents use this feature, and it is sometimes handy in other documents to show what has been removed or replaced. Internet Explorer supports **<S> . . . </S>,** an abbreviated form of the **<STRIKE> . . . </STRIKE>** container. HTML 3.2 replaces the <STRIKE> . . . </STRIKE> container with the <S> . . . </S> container.

Figure 5.9 shows the code for strike-through (or "out") text, and Figure 5.10 shows how Netscape presents this code. Look closely at Figure 5.10. Notice how the horizontal line goes beyond the words, also marking through the spaces on either side of the word. This is a messy look. It happened because the author was not careful in constructing the code. In Figure 5.9, notice that there are spaces on either side of the word within the <STRIKE> container. Now see the difference in the HTML snippet shown in Figure 5.11.

```
<HTML>
<HEAD>
<TITLE> <STRIKE> sample</TITLE>
</HEAD>
<BODY>
In this line, the words<STRIKE> strike out </STRIKE> have a
line through them.
That is called strike out.
</BODY>
</HTML>
```

Figure 5.9 HTML code for the <STRIKE> container.

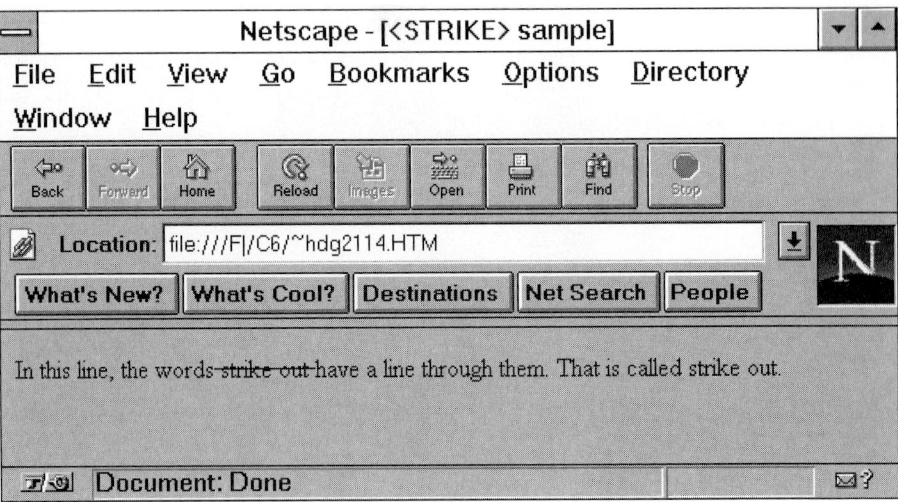

Figure 5.10 Netscape's presentation of the <STRIKE> container.

```
<BODY>
In this line, the words <STRIKE>strike out</STRIKE> have a
line through them. That is called strike out.
</BODY>
```

Figure 5.11 Better HTML coding of the <STRIKE> container.

Only the words "strike out" are enclosed by the container. Observe the difference in the result in Figure 5.12. This is our first example of need for careful placement of container tags.

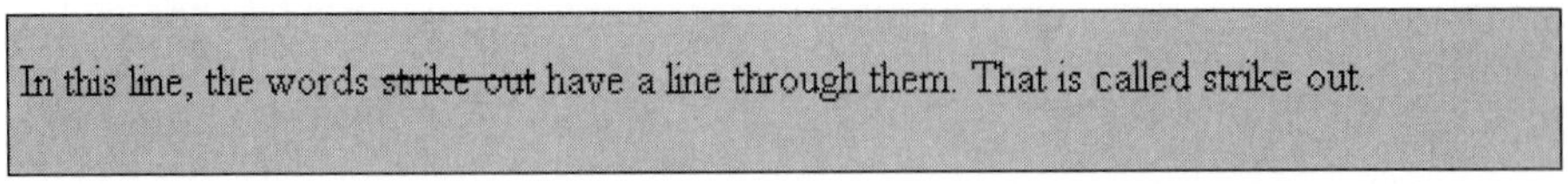

In this line, the words ~~strike out~~ have a line through them. That is called strike out.

Figure 5.12 Netscape's presentation of the more carefully crafted <STRIKE> container.

Blinking Text: <BLINK>

Blinking text is the last of the physical tags we will discuss. It is last for a very good reason: you should use this tag only when circumstances *force* you to use it. The **<BLINK> . . . </BLINK>** container causes the text within it to blink on and off. This effectively calls attention to the text that is blinking, but it very quickly begins to annoy the user. Many Web weavers feel this tag should not be used at all because it is so aggravating. It is impossible to portray the vexation this tag produces in a simple, static screen, but if you look at the code in Figure 5.13, you can imagine the awful screen that all this blinking text would produce.

```
<HTML>
<HEAD>
<TITLE> <BLINK> (shudder) example</TITLE>
</HEAD>
<BODY >
<BLINK>
On this screen, every line blinks.  They all blink at the
same rate, so it seems <BR> that the whole screen is flashing
on and off.  If I were to use ugly colors <BR> as well, I
could construct a totally awful page.<BR>
Don't use blink unless you absolutely must!
</BLINK>
</BODY>
</HTML>
```

Figure 5.13 HTML code for the (ugh) <BLINK> container.

Logical Styles

Logical styles, also called **content-based styles,** require the Web weaver to consider not what the page should look like, but rather how the particular text sequence is supposed to be used. This marks a change in thinking, away from the simple word-processing mentality and toward a more consistent and user-centered way of presenting information. The following logical styles can convey more information than the physical tags in the previous section because they not only change the appearance of the text, but also explain why the text was set off from the body of the page. Use logical styles whenever you can, marking text according to how it is to be used rather than how you expect it to look. This principle will probably become more important as future versions of the browsers become more complex and intelligent and have more expressive formatting capabilities.

The fact that a particular group of characters is enclosed within a specific logical container is what is important, not how the browser chooses to display those contents. For example, a scholar may search through many Web pages, pulling out the examples of character strings that are enclosed within <CITE> containers. That the Web weaver chose to enclose the text within that particular tag conveys the information that the text in the container is a citation. That information is more important than how the text appears on the page. With this idea of conveying information in mind, you need to choose your logical styles carefully and consistently.

Strongly Emphasized Text: <STRONG>

The **<STRONG> . . . </STRONG>** container is used to bring strong emphasis to the enclosed text. Many browsers will bold the contents, but that is not the required change. This is the most emphatic tag. It usually stands out more than the <EM> tag, discussed next.

Emphasized Text: <EM>

Text enclosed in the **<EM> . . . </EM>** container is supposed to be emphasized, but this tag indicates a milder form of emphasis than the <STRONG> tag indicates. Currently most browsers will render this text in italics. Figure 5.14 presents code for both the <STRONG> and the <EM> containers.

```
<HTML>
<HEAD>
<TITLE>Logical containers</TITLE>
</HEAD>
<BODY >
When you use the EM tag, <EM>the text is usually put in
italics </EM> <BR> and when you use the STRONG tag,
<STRONG>the text is normally bold</STRONG>. <BR>  It is
possible to <EM>code the STRONG container within the EM
container to produce <STRONG>bold italics.</STRONG></EM>
</BODY>
</HTML>
```

Figure 5.14 HTML code for <EM> and <STRONG> containers.

Notice in Figure 5.14 that you can enclose one logical container inside another to achieve combined effects. Remember that all combinations are not necessarily supported, and, just as with the physical-style combinations, you may not see exactly what you expect. Figure 5.15 shows how this code is represented by Netscape.

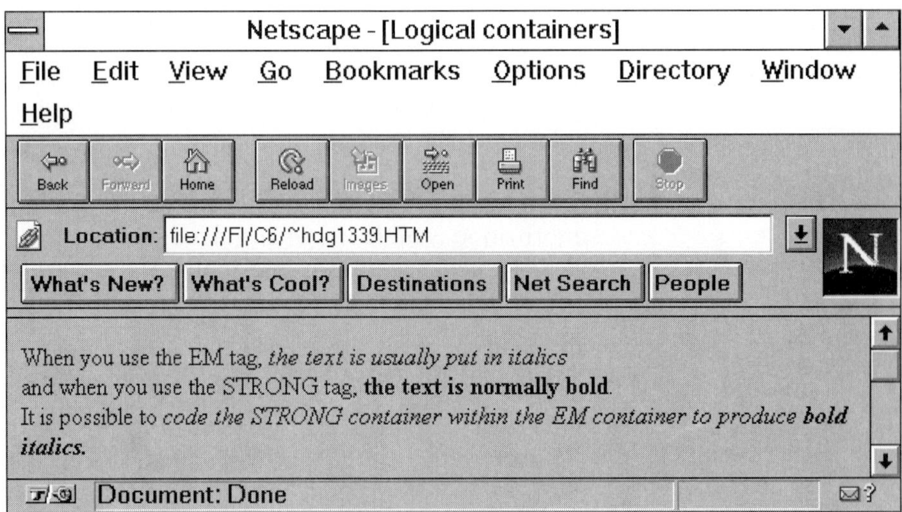

Figure 5.15 Netscape's presentation of <STRONG> and <EM> containers.

Computer Code: <CODE>

The **<CODE> . . . </CODE>** container was at one time widely used to present actual computer code on the page. This tag is falling out of favor with many Web weavers, so you might consider using the <TT> (typewriter or Teletype) container instead. The <TT> container was discussed earlier under "Monospaced Text." As HTML continues to evolve, new tags appear and other tags are dropped. The <CODE>, <KBD>, and <SAMP> tags are all being dropped. The browsers will continue to support them for some time, but Web weavers who are on top of the game usually avoid them. An exception might be if you want to use the <CODE> container to show some C code or Java code. Normally, this type of thing is shown in a monospaced font. Figure 5.16 shows how <CODE> might be used to present the first C program most people learn. Figure 5.17 shows the result in Netscape.

```
<HTML>
<HEAD>
<TITLE> <CODE> example </TITLE>
</HEAD>
<BODY>
The first program most people write in <STRONG>C</STRONG>
class is<BR>
<CODE>
#include &LT stdio.h &GT<BR>
int main(void)<BR>
{<BR>
printf("Hello World \n");<BR>
return 0;<BR>
}<BR>
</CODE>
</BODY>
</HTML>
```

Figure 5.16 HTML code for the <CODE> tag.

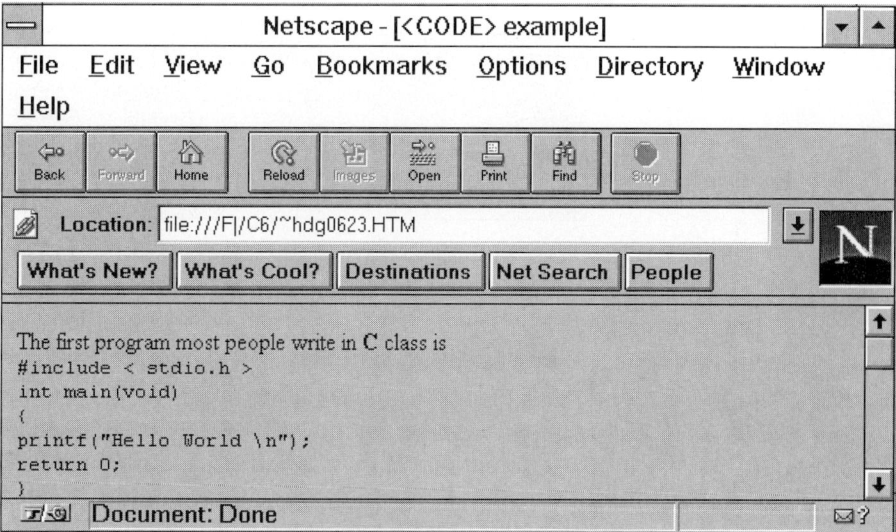

Figure 5.17 Netscape's presentation of the <CODE> tag.

Citations: <CITE>

When you put a bibliographical citation in your document, you can enclose it in the **<CITE> . . . </CITE>** container. This will help your user find the actual documents you make reference to. Figure 5.18 presents the code for a citation. Figure 5.19 shows how the citation looks in the Netscape browser. As you can see, citation tags usually produce italics. But the importance of the citation is that it points the sophisticated user to your references, not that it changes the text to italics.

```
<HTML>
<HEAD>
<TITLE> <CITE> example </TITLE>
</HEAD>
<BODY>
One of the better reference books for HTML is <CITE>HTML The
Definitive Guide </CITE>  written by Musciano and Kennedy,
and published by O'Reilly & Associates, Inc.
</BODY>
</HTML>
```

Figure 5.18 HTML code for the <CITE> tag.

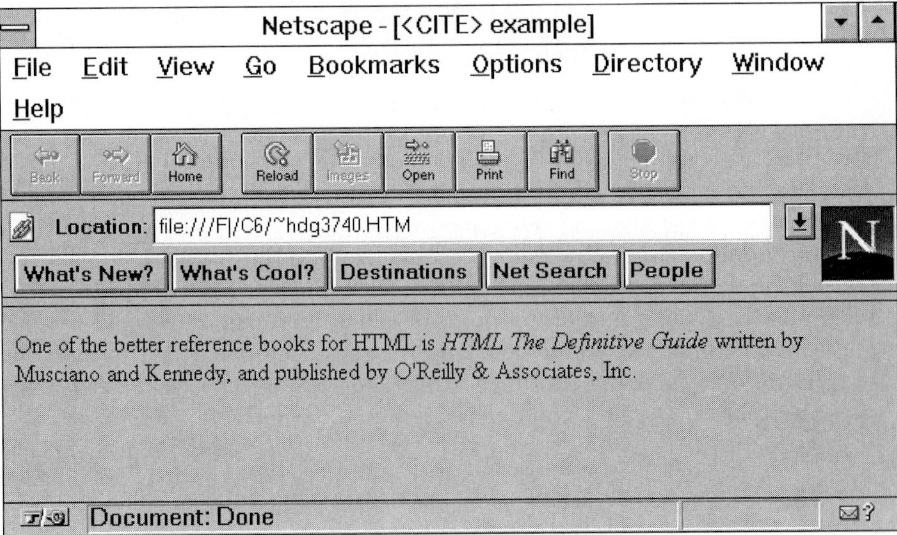

Figure 5.19 Netscape's presentation of the <CITE> tag.

Definitions: <DFN>

The **<DFN> . . . </DFN>** container is currently supported only by Internet Explorer, but the conscientious Web weaver will use it anyway, because it sets apart a definition, whether or not it will be rendered in a particular font. In Internet Explorer the text in the <DFN> container is italicized, but in

Netscape it appears in standard font because Netscape doesn't recognize the container. Figure 5.20 shows some HTML code using <DFN>. Figure 5.21 shows the result in Netscape, and Figure 5.22 shows the result in Internet Explorer.

```
<HTML>
<HEAD>
<TITLE> An example of the <DFN> tag </TITLE>
</HEAD>
<BODY>
The definition of a term, <DFN> defined as the explanation of
the meaning of the term, </DFN> can be illustrated in
Internet Explorer, but not in Netscape.
</BODY>
</HTML>
```

Figure 5.20 HTML code for <DFN> tag.

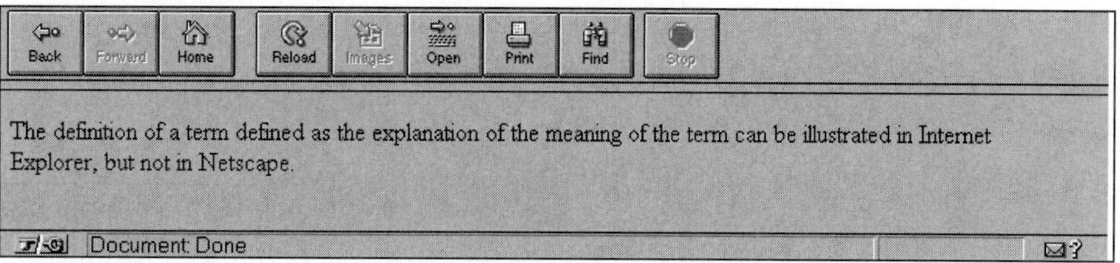

Figure 5.21 The <DFN> tag does not produce a difference in Netscape.

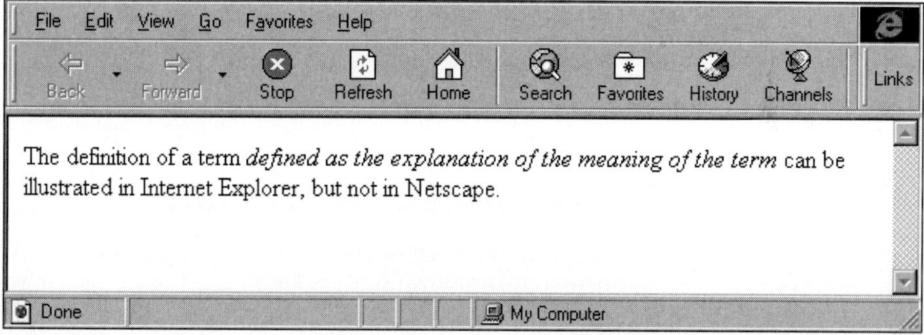

Figure 5.22 The <DFN> tag appears in italics when displayed by Internet Explorer.

Variable Values: <VAR>

The **<VAR> . . . </VAR>** container is most frequently used with a tag like <PRE> to show something that the user is supposed to input. Like the outdated <CODE> tag, this one is usually used when showing computer input or a computer program. Figure 5.23 presents the code for the <VAR> container. Figure 5.24 shows how Netscape renders it.

```
<HTML>
<HEAD>
<TITLE> Variables </TITLE>
</HEAD>
<BODY>
The VAR tag  is used to show input from the user, that will
change.  For example:  On the input line, put your
<VAR>Name</VAR> and your <VAR>E-mail address</VAR> so we can
contact you.
</BODY>
</HTML>
```

Figure 5.23 HTML code for the <VAR> tag.

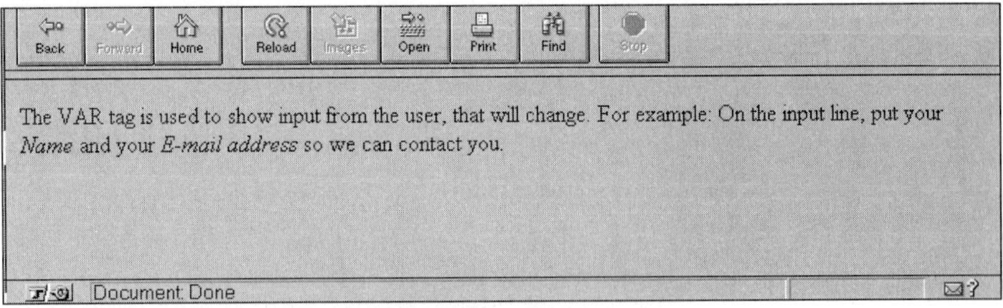

Figure 5.24 Netscape's presentation of the <VAR> tag.

Block Quotes: <BLOCKQUOTE>

In a formal paper or article, a long quotation is set off in a separate paragraph that is indented on both sides. Sometimes it also appears in a different font from the rest of the text. You can create the same effect with some of the browsers using the <BLOCKQUOTE> . . . </BLOCKQUOTE> container. Although the exact rendering will vary among the different browsers, the <BLOCKQUOTE> container will usually indicate that the text contained within it is a quotation. Figure 5.25 presents the code for a block quote Figure 5.26 shows how Netscape will render this coding.

```
<HTML>
<HEAD>
<TITLE> Block quotes </TITLE>
</HEAD>
<BODY>
A famous person once said, when talking of life:
<BLOCKQUOTE>There were many paths that led up into those
mountains, and many passes over them. But most of the paths
were cheats and deceptions and led nowhere or to bad ends;
and most of the passes were infested by evil things and
dreadful dangers.
</BLOCKQUOTE>
<CITE>p. 64 <U>The Hobbit</U> by J.R.R. Tolkien</CITE><BR>
While this is not exactly what most of us face on a day to
day basis, it can be considered possible that J.R.R. Tolkien
was speaking of the modern world when he penned those lines.
</BODY>
</HTML>
```

Figure 5.25 HTML code for block quotes to highlight long quotations.

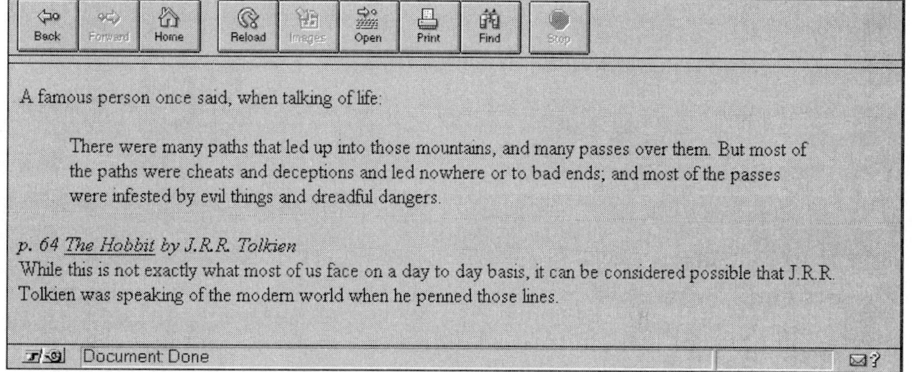

Figure 5.26 Netscape's presentation of a <BLOCKQUOTE> tag.

Notice that the paragraph is indeed indented on both margins. Netscape does not change the font of the text, but it does add space both above and below the quoted paragraph. This browser also correctly formats the text and does not add quotation marks.

Addresses: <ADDRESS>

Any Web document you create should have your address, or at least the address of a responsible party located somewhere on the page. Usually this address is located at or near the bottom of the page, at one of the margins. It should contain the name and an e-mail address of the Web weaver and, in the case of a commercial site, the name, address, and e-mail address (if possible) of the owner or responsible party representing the business. In other cases you may wish to use the **<ADDRESS> . . . </ADDRESS>** container to put your own name and address into a page so people can use both **snail mail** (regular postal service) and e-mail to contact you.

Figure 5.27 presents the code for the <ADDRESS> container. We have a new type of link here, the MAILTO. Don't worry about it right now. We will examine this link when we look at linking across the Net. It is included here for completeness. Look at the way Netscape renders this code in Figure 5.28.

```
<HTML>
<HEAD>
<TITLE> Addressing </TITLE>
</HEAD>
<BODY>
If you have comments or questions, please contact<BR>
<ADDRESS><A HREF="MAILTO:ttg@phred.dcccd.edu">
Your Humble Author <BR></A>
North Lake College<BR>
5001 MacArthur Blvd.<BR>
Irving, TX  75038-3899</ADDRESS>
</BODY>
</HTML>
```

Figure 5.27 HTML code for an <ADDRESS> container. Notice the
s used for lineup.

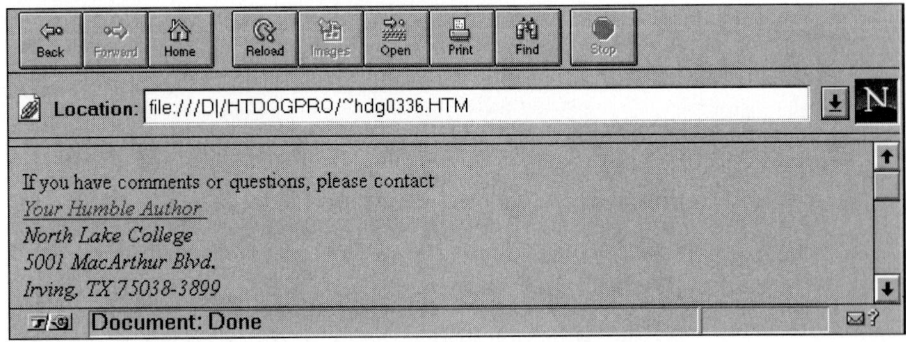

Figure 5.28 Netscape's presentation of an <ADDRESS> container.

Special Font Handling

In addition to the styles described in the previous section, the new HTML standard allows the Web weaver to actually control the font in all or part of a document. The "big two" browsers, Netscape and Internet Explorer, seem to be leading the charge into new and better features. For example, both support a set of font sizes that start at size 1 and run all the way through size 7. Font size 3 is the standard, beginning size. As you saw with the <BIG> and <SMALL> tags, you can both increase and decrease the size of the font displayed. According to the documentation, the relationship between the different virtual font sizes is about 20 percent for each change. For example, font size 4 is supposed to be 20 percent larger than font size 3 (the standard size), and font size 1 is supposed to be 40 percent smaller than font size 3. We will see that this does not necessarily hold true for all browsers. Again, the browser controls the format.

In the discussion of the <BASEFONT> tag that follows, you will see how these different sizes relate to one another. Internet Explorer also allows the Web weaver to change the actual font used. However, that option is dangerous unless the Web weaver knows that the font specified is available on all the machines accessing the page. The only time you can be sure that a specific font is available on all machines is when the page is being designed for use on an **intranet** within a company, where all of the machines are set up the same way.

Changing the Document's Font: <BASEFONT>

The **<BASEFONT>** tag changes the size of the font in a page. It is usually used as an empty tag, although it is really a container. When a browser encounters the </BASEFONT> tag, it resets the font size to the default 3 rather than simply terminating the current <BASEFONT> value.

This tag has only one attribute, SIZE, and it is a required attribute. The size can be set to any integer value between 1 and 7. Figure 5.29 shows how the size of the basefont can be coded to change the way the text looks (very similar to the way <BIG> and <SMALL> are used).

```
<HTML>
<HEAD>
<TITLE> A demonstration of <BASEFONT> </TITLE>
</HEAD>
<BODY>
This line is shown in the normal font<BR>
<BASEFONT SIZE=1>  And this line in a tiny font (SIZE=1).<BR>
<BASEFONT SIZE=2>Now the font should be 20% larger (SIZE=2)<BR>
<BASEFONT SIZE=3>Back to the normal size 3<BR>
<BASEFONT SIZE=4>Now start to grow (SIZE=4)<BR>
<BASEFONT SIZE=5>Up 20% to SIZE=5<BR>
<BASEFONT SIZE=6>Size is up to 6<BR>
<BASEFONT SIZE=7>SIZE=7 The biggest basefont size<BR>
</BODY>
</HTML>
```

Figure 5.29 HTML code for <BASEFONT> used to increase the size of the text.

Figure 5.30 shows how the Netscape browser displays text with a changing <BASEFONT>. If it seems to you that the change from SIZE=4 to SIZE=5 in Figure 5.30 is really about a 20 percent step whereas the change from SIZE=6 to SIZE=7 is greater than 20 percent you are absolutely correct. Even though the documentation claims that each size increase is only 20 percent, the browser actually controls how the text appears, and it does not always follow the 20-percent rule.

Now notice in Figures 5.31 and 5.32 how the size of the font drops back to 3 when the </BASEFONT> tag is reached. We would expect that closing the container would change the basefont back to the previous size, in this case 5. However, as Figure 5.32 shows us, when the browser encounters the closing </BASEFONT> tag, the size of the text changes back to the default, size 3.

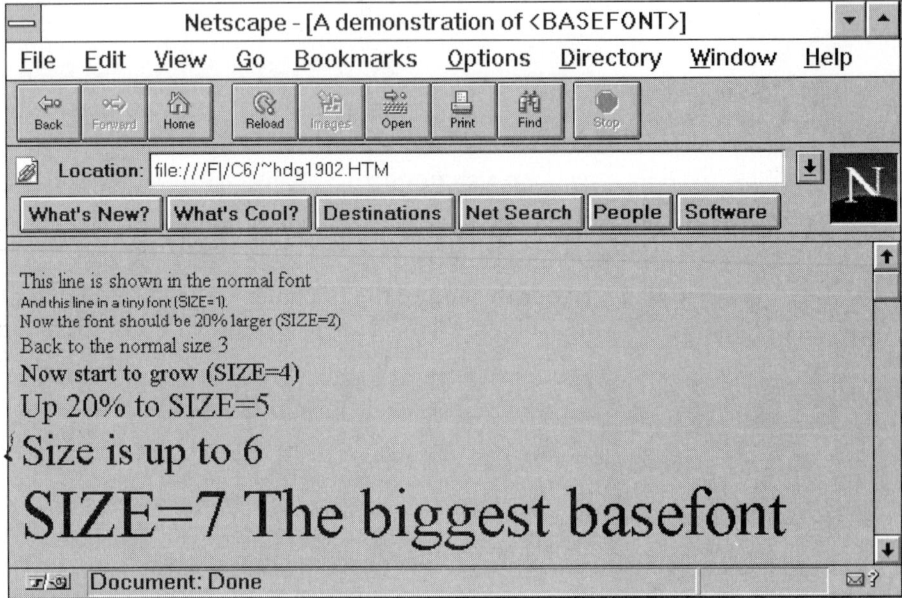

Figure 5.30 Netscape's presentation of <BASEFONT>, showing how the size of the text changes with different basefonts.

```
<HTML>
<HEAD>
<TITLE> A demonstration of <BASEFONT> </TITLE>
</HEAD>
<BODY>
This line is shown in the normal font<BR>
<BASEFONT SIZE=5> Change the basefont size to 5 <BR>
<BASEFONT SIZE=7> Up to size 7, now we add the close tag
</BASEFONT>
and the text drops back to 3, not 5 as we expect.
</BODY>
</HTML>
```

Figure 5.31 HTML code for changing the basefont, then closing the container.

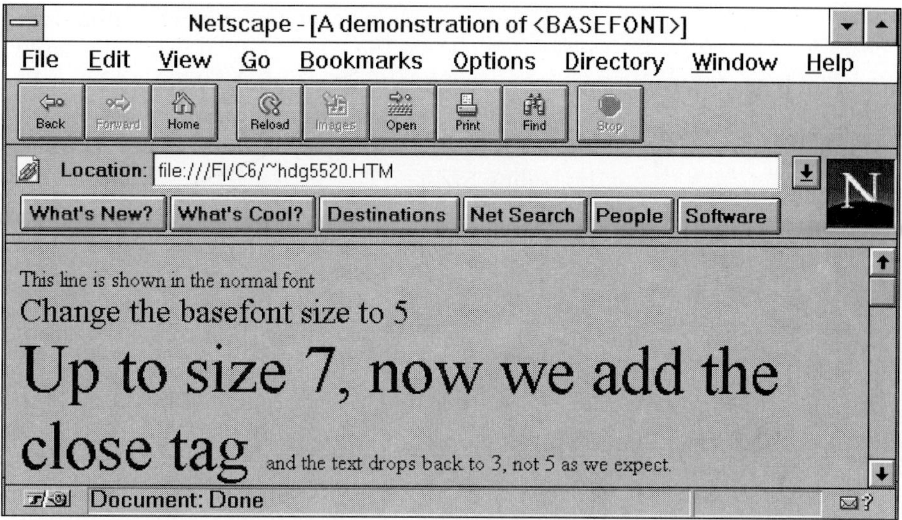

Figure 5.32 Netscape's presentation of </BASEFONT> showing how the font size drops back to size 3 after the closing tag.

The <BASEFONT> tag applies to all the text that follows it until the browser encounters another <BASEFONT> tag, a closing </BASEFONT> tag, or the end of the document. The SIZE option of the <BASEFONT> tag also allows relative rather than absolute size specification. For example, you can code a SIZE of +1 rather than calculating the absolute value. Figures 5.33 and 5.34 show a series of single-step size increases from the default to the maximum, and then back down to the minimum.

```
<HTML>
<HEAD>
<TITLE> <BASEFONT> with increments</TITLE>
</HEAD>
<BODY>
This line is shown in the normal font<BR>
<BASEFONT SIZE=+1> Change the basefont size to 4 <BR>
<BASEFONT SIZE=+1> Up a size <BR>
<BASEFONT SIZE=+1> Up a size <BR>
<BASEFONT SIZE=+1> Up a size to the maximum<BR>
<BASEFONT SIZE=-1> Down a size <BR>
<BASEFONT SIZE=-1> Down a size <BR>
<BASEFONT SIZE=-1> Down a size <BR>
<BASEFONT SIZE=-1> Down a size <BR>
<BASEFONT SIZE=-1> Down a size <BR>
<BASEFONT SIZE=-1> Down a size now at the minimum 1<BR>
</BODY>
</HTML>
```

Figure 5.33 HTML code for changing the basefont size by increments rather than absolute value.

As you can see from Figure 5.34, changing the base font up and down with relative values has the same result as using absolute values. What is important to notice is that the effect is cumulative, or additive. Each time you +1 or -1, the font changes from the *preceding value*. You can, of course, make relative steps larger than 1. For example, you could increase the size of the text from 3 to 5 by coding SIZE=+2.

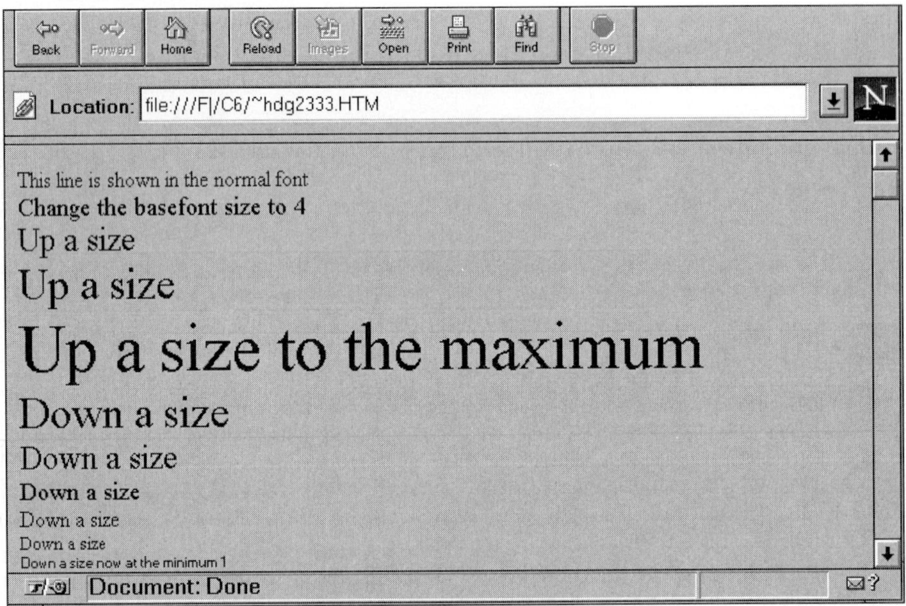

Figure 5.34 Netscape's presentation of <BASEFONT>, showing a change in size by increments rather than absolute values.

Normally a Web weaver will place the <BASEFONT> tag in the head of the document, but it can be placed anywhere in the document, and it can be used several times.

Changing the Font for a Block of Text: <FONT>

The <BASEFONT> tag is useful for changing the size of the font for the whole page, or at least a substantial portion of it. But what should you do when you want to change the size—or the color or typeface—of the font for a small part of the page, perhaps even just a character or two? In these cases, the **<FONT> . . . </FONT>** container is used. Because this is a container, you should always code the closing container tag, </FONT>. There are two common attributes for this tag: COLOR and SIZE.

COLOR

The color of the text enclosed in the container is set by the **COLOR** attribute, just as you learned to set text color in the <BODY> tag. You can use a six-digit hexadecimal number, with each successive pair of numbers representing the red, green, and blue (RGB) components of the desired color. Or you can use the "standard" color words shown in Appendix A. The hexadecimal values are recommended because your results will generally be more consistent with them.

SIZE

The <FONT> container allows you to change the size of the contained text. You can code this **SIZE** attribute just as you coded the SIZE attribute for the <BASEFONT> tag. There is one critical difference, however, if you use relative size values. As you saw, in the <BASEFONT> tag, the relative size values are incremental. *In the <FONT> container, each relative calculation is based on the default, or the value set by the preceding <BASEFONT> tag.* That means that the same set of relative size increases coded for <BASEFONT> will keep the text in <FONT> at size 4 (3 + 1) for each line.

Figure 5.35 shows code that tries to increase the font size four times, intending to move it from size 3 to size 7. The code then tries to decrease the font size six times, from size 7 to size 1. Figure 5.36 shows what Netscape does with this code. As you can see, the size increases from the base size of 3, but each incremental value adds to the *base font* size. This is a very significant difference between the way the <BASEFONT> and the <FONT> tags use relative size values. Because of the possible confusion generated, wise Web weavers specify the <FONT> SIZE value as an absolute number rather than a relative one.

```
<HTML>
<HEAD>
<TITLE> <FONT> with size increments</TITLE>
</HEAD>
<BODY>
This line is shown in the normal font<BR>
<FONT SIZE=+1> Change the FONT size to 4 <BR>
<FONT SIZE=+1> Up a size <BR>
<FONT SIZE=+1> Up a size <BR>
<FONT SIZE=+1> Up a size to the maximum<BR>
<FONT SIZE=-1> Down a size <BR>
<FONT SIZE=-1> Down a size <BR>
<FONT SIZE=-1> Down a size <BR>
<FONT SIZE=-1> Down a size <BR>
<FONT SIZE=-1> Down a size <BR>
<FONT SIZE=-1> Down a size now at the minimum 1<BR>
</BODY>
</HTML>
```

Figure 5.35 HTML code changing the <FONT> size by increments rather than absolute value.

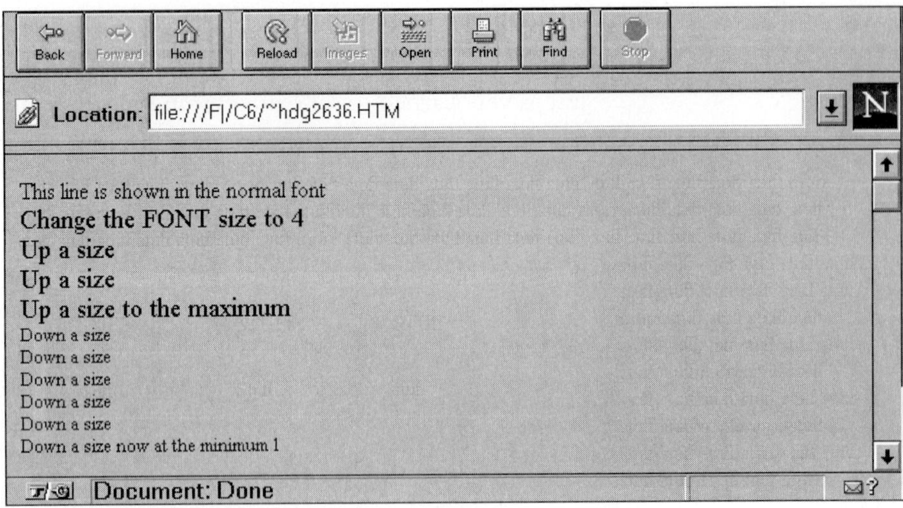

Figure 5.36 Netscape's presentation showing that the <FONT> tag does not perform additive relative size increases.

FACE Attribute

Both Netscape and Internet Explorer allow the rash Web weaver to attempt to alter the actual typeface of the text, within some defined parameters. The **FACE** attribute of the <FONT> tag allows for the specification of a series of different typefaces for the text contained within the container. Usually the Web weaver will specify a series of different typefaces, hoping that the target machine contains one of them. If none of the specified typefaces are available on the target machine, the browser will use the default typeface. One very dangerous situation arises when the target machine has a typeface name that matches the name in your HTML code but that renders an unreadable page. For example, if the Wingdings font had been renamed Desdemona, and the page contained the code `<FONT FACE="Desdemona, Braggadocio">`, the resulting page would appear as if it were written in a secret code (see Figure 5.37). While this might be handy for leaving secret messages, it would fail the test of providing easily accessed information. Figure 5.38 shows how this code would look in Netscape.

```
<HTML>
<HEAD>
<TITLE>  Playing with FACE </TITLE>
</HEAD>
<BODY>
This line is shown in the normal font<BR>
<FONT FACE="Wingdings, Desdemona">
It is critical that you use fonts that your user will have.
This is a big question!
</FONT>
Now that you know that critical bit, have a good day! :)
</BODY>
</HTML>
```

Figure 5.37 HTML code changing the typeface of the text so that it looks like a "secret message."

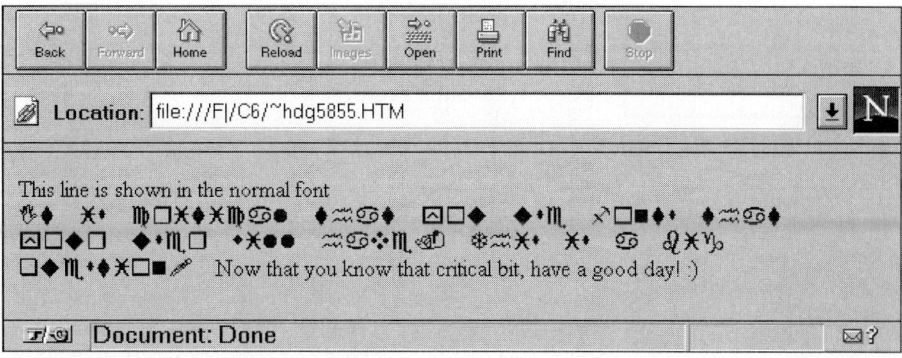

Figure 5.38 Netscape's presentation of the FACE code, looking like a "secret message."

This last example seems to bring us over the edge into the realm of typesetting rather than Web weaving. There may be an exceptional condition that demands that you change the typeface, but this particular feature should be used only in the extreme case. Figure 5.39 shows an example of the FACE code taken to an extreme. Figure 5.40 shows how it looks in Netscape. (Note: This example is not necessarily good practice for Web weavers, but it does create some visual interest). Use the FACE attribute very sparingly, if at all.

```
<HTML>
<HEAD>
<TITLE>  A bad example </TITLE>
</HEAD>
<BODY>
<FONT SIZE=6 Color="#DD00CC" FACE="Braggadocio">
W</FONT>elcome to my page!
</BODY>
</HTML>
```

Figure 5.39 HTML code for an extreme example of the use of the FACE attribute.

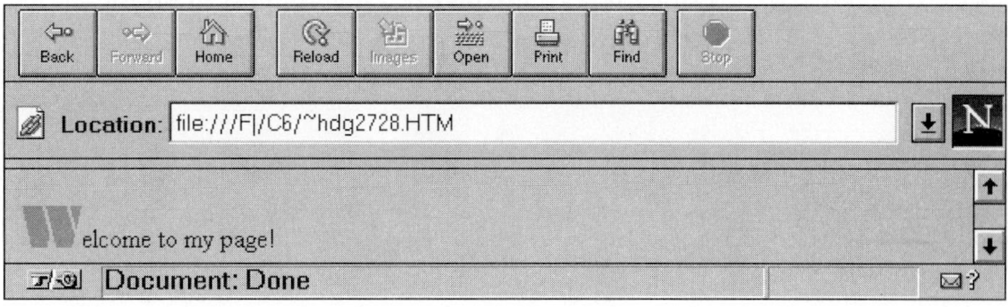

Figure 5.40 Netscape's presentation of an extreme example of the FACE attribute.

Turning Off Formatting

Sometimes it is necessary to prevent the browser from altering the way a portion of the screen looks.

<PRE>

The **<PRE> . . .</PRE>** container is designed to present a block of text without enforcing additional formatting by the browser. In a <PRE> container, supernumerary (extra) blanks are not removed. This container has one optional attribute, **WIDTH,** which determines how many characters fit on a single line. This is a request to the browser, not an absolute demand. Lines that are longer than the width of the browser pane will extend outside the browser pane, requiring the user to scroll right in order to read all of the text. The **browser pane** is that part of the screen that is normally visible to the user without scrolling to the right. The common browsers will support lines longer than their normal pane if they are required to by the HTML code. Usually it is a bad idea to force text beyond the browser pane, because it may be overlooked by the user. Also, it places an additional burden on users because they have to scroll to access all the information you are providing.

You should not use tags that cause a paragraph break within the <PRE> container because it may cause inconsistent behavior across browsers. Some browsers may interpret these tags as simple line breaks, whereas others may infer a </PRE> tag before the break and end the container. Style tags are allowed within a <PRE> block, so if the text within the block contains characters like the ampersand (&) or the greater than (>) and lesser than (<) signs, you will need to use the special symbols for them to avoid having the browser simply ignore them.

Usually a <PRE> block is used to protect and illustrate tabs or other formatting for computer programs and the like. Don't use the <PRE> container simply to avoid having the browser format your text.

Figure 5.41 presents the code for a <PRE> block. This set of instructions was coded using the default tab stops set by the HotDog HTML editor. Figure 5.42 shows what the browser does with this code. Notice how the browser used a much larger tab value than did the HTML editor. If you are going to use the <PRE> container, it is a good idea to use spaces rather than tabs to perform your alignment.

```
<HTML>
<HEAD>
<TITLE> <PRE> example </TITLE>
</HEAD>
<BODY>
The following is part of a simple awk script.  It is
important to use correct indention to show which parts are
subordinate.<BR>
<PRE>
BEGIN {
       count=0
       printf("User ID     Login Shell      User Name\n\n")
      }
{
       printf("%s\t\t%s\t\t%s\n",$2,$7,$1)
}
</PRE>
</BODY>
</HTML>
```

Figure 5.41 HTML code for the <PRE> tag.

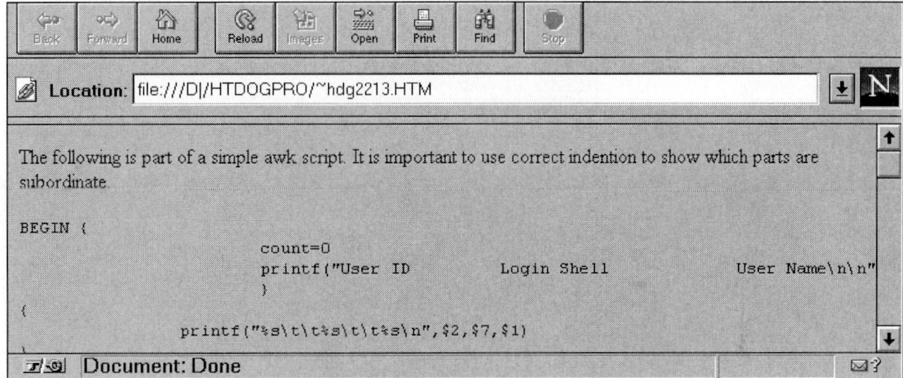

Figure 5.42 Netscape's presentation of the <PRE> tag.

Figure 5.43 presents the same code but with spaces rather than tab characters. Notice how, in Figure 5.44, the browser still expands the spaces more than we intended. This again brings home the idea that the browser is the final authority when it comes to layout.

```
<HTML>
<HEAD>
<TITLE> <PRE> example </TITLE>
</HEAD>
<BODY>
The following is part of a simple awk script.  It is
important to use correct indention to show which lines are
subordinate.<BR>
<PRE>
BEGIN {
   count=0
   printf("User ID        Login Shell        User Name\n\n")
   }
{
   printf("%s\t\t%s\t\t%s\n",$2,$7,$1)
}
</PRE>
</BODY>
</HTML>
```

Figure 5.43 HTML code for the <PRE> tag with spaces used rather than tabs.

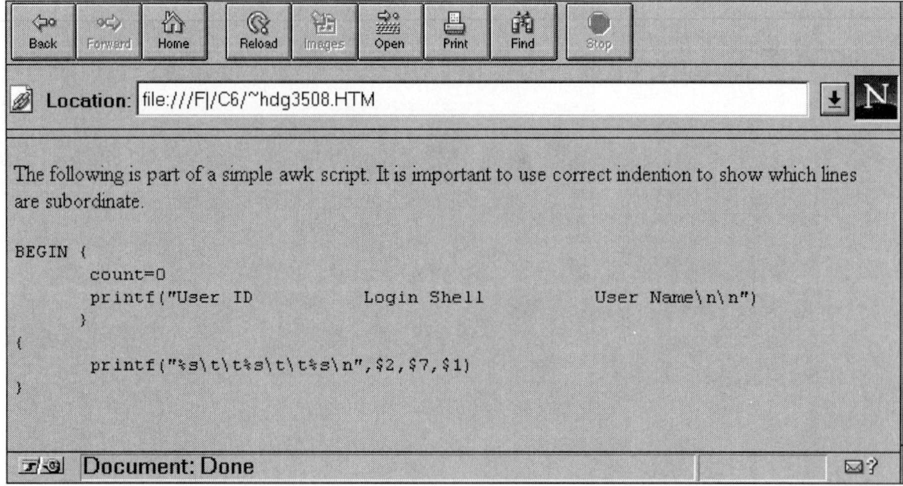

Figure 5.44 Netscape's presentation of the <PRE> tag with spaces used in the code.

As you can see in Figure 5.44, the browser still added more spaces, than we desired, but with a little creative playing you can make at least one browser line up the text the way you want it to. Notice that in the HTML code, the words "count" and "printf" start under the "I" of BEGIN, yet they are aligned under the open French brace ({) when the browser displays them.

When you start to work on exact alignments, you can spend a lot of time trying to get things "exactly right," just as you can waste huge amounts of time trying to get "just the right color" for your text or background. Generally, you should spend your time and energy on the content, not the format of the pages. Gee, where have you heard that before?

Deprecated Tags: <LISTING>, <XMP>

Two additional tags (containers) that are similar to the <PRE> container are the <LISTING> and <XMP> containers. They were popular in Netscape 2.0 but have fallen out of favor and may not be supported beyond Netscape 3. The differences are subtle. The **<LISTING>** tag is like the <PRE> tag, with a WIDTH=132 attribute. The **<XMP>** (for eXaMPle) tag is also like <PRE>, with a WIDTH=80 attribute. The only real difference between these two tags and <PRE> is that they don't support all the formatting options of <PRE>, so you don't need to use special characters like (<, >, and &) to include the <, >, and & characters. Because these two tags are most likely going to disappear, the wise Web weaver won't use them.

Stopping the Tagging: <PLAINTEXT>

If you get tired of having to use tag after tag, you can turn off the recognition of all the rest of the tags on your page by entering the <PLAINTEXT> tag. This is an empty tag. There can be no closing tag because no tags are recognized after this one.

<PLAINTEXT> is most often used to allow existing ASCII documents to be displayed by a browser without worrying about markup tags that might be included in the text. The first versions of the browsers had some problems with ASCII text, and this was a valuable tag at one time. Most of the time it is no longer necessary today. Figure 5.45 presents the code for the <PLAINTEXT> tag. Figure 5.46 shows its effect in Netscape. Notice that there is no closing tag on the <PLAINTEXT> container, because *all* tags that follow it are ignored. The <PLAINTEXT> tag is not a common one, but it can be useful to create pages that show the actual structure of HTML. Use is very sparingly.

```
<HTML>
<HEAD>
<TITLE> Plaintext example </TITLE>
</HEAD>
<BODY>
On this page, I will code some regular tags, <BR>
Then will code the plaintext tag, and repeat the tags coded <BR>
before it.
<H3>Here is a level 3 heading</H3>
<PLAINTEXT>
On this page, I will code some regular tags, <BR>
Then will code the plaintext tag, and repeat the tags coded
<BR> before it.
<H3>Here is a level 3 heading</H3>
</BODY>
</HTML>
```

Figure 5.45 HTML code for the <PLAINTEXT> tag, for illustration only.

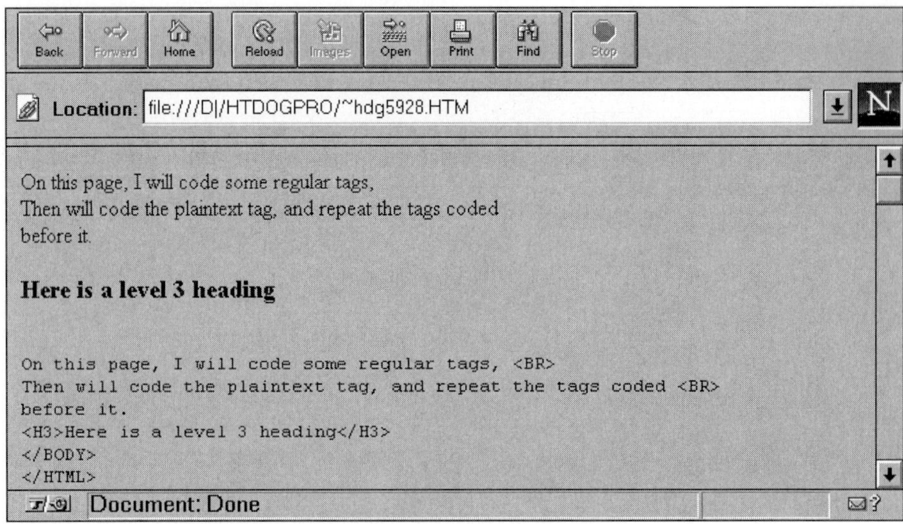

Figure 5.46 Netscape's presentation of how the <PLAINTEXT> tag stops the processing of all other tags.

Lines on the Page: <HR>

Using horizontal lines, or rules, to separate the various sections of your pages produces a nice visual effect and is a functional tool as well. The tag used to draw horizontal rules across your screen is **<HR>**. This tag causes a line break and then resets paragraph alignment to the default, the left. Most browsers will insert the line immediately below the current line. Following that line, the text will continue.

The code in Figure 5.47 places a simple horizontal rule across the page. This little chunk of code demonstrates placing the default line between two lines of text. The default line is 3 pixels thick and looks three-dimensional. It stretches from one side of the screen to the other and looks as if it were chiseled into the screen. Figure 5.48 shows how the default line looks in Netscape.

```
<HTML>
<HEAD>
<TITLE> Rules, Rules, Rules</TITLE>
</HEAD>
<BODY>
This page illustrates a simple horizontal rule.  There is a
rule below this line
<HR>
And the rule should be above this line.
</BODY>
</HTML>
```

Figure 5.47 HTML code for a simple horizontal rule.

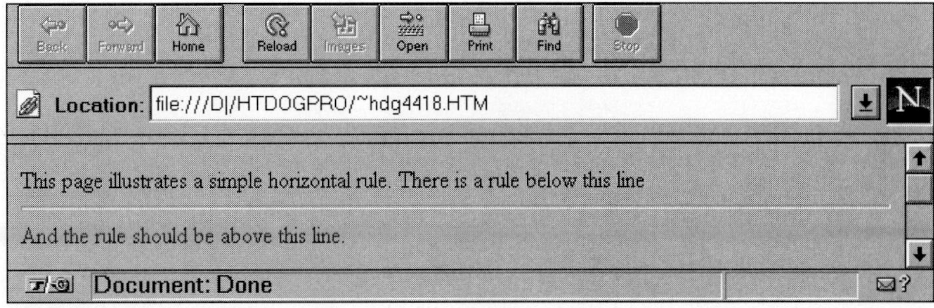

Figure 5.48 Netscape's presentation of a simple, default horizontal line.

Although the simple horizontal rule is a good visual break all by itself, there are several attributes that can add interest and impact to it, making the <HR> tag even more valuable.

SIZE

The **SIZE** attribute of a horizontal rule is really the thickness of the line in pixels. You can specify any thickness from 1 to very large numbers, but usually a divider that is thicker than 50 or 60 pixels is more distracting than valuable. Figure 5.49 presents the code for four horizontal rules of different sizes. As you can see in Figure 5.50, the 1-pixel line doesn't look three-dimensional in Netscape, but it does provide a nice visual break. The 50-pixel line is rather too big and distracting.

```
<HTML>
<HEAD>
<TITLE> Rules and more Rules</TITLE>
</HEAD>
<BODY>
There are 4 horizontal rules below<BR>
This one is size 1
<HR SIZE=1>
This one is size 3
<HR SIZE=3>
This one is size 20
<HR SIZE=20>
This one, size 50
<HR SIZE=50>
</BODY>
</HTML>
```

Figure 5.49 HTML code for four horizontal rules.

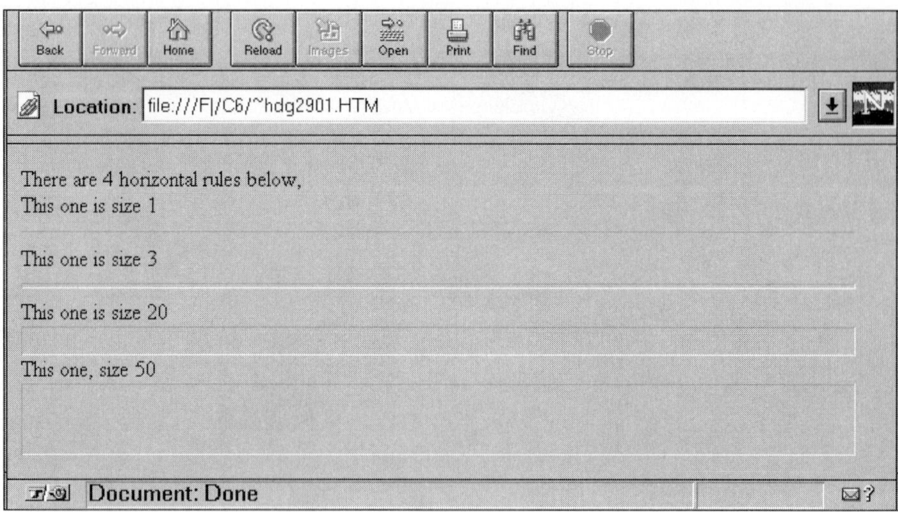

Figure 5.50 Netscape's presentation of different sized horizontal rules.

WIDTH

The **WIDTH** attribute of a horizontal rule describes how far across the screen it extends. There are two ways to code **WIDTH**: in pixels, called **absolute width,** or as a percentage of the total screen width, called **relative width**. Figure 5.51 presents the code for some rules of varying widths. Figure 5.52 shows how these rules look in Netscape. When you use a percentage value, always enclose the value in quotation marks. If a browser interprets the percent sign as a special character, it may cause an error in your page, and you may also lose some of the content from your page.

```
<HTML>
<HEAD>
<TITLE> Rules III </TITLE>
</HEAD>
<BODY>
The following rule is 100 pixels wide.
<HR WIDTH=100>
The rule below is 250 pixels wide.
<HR WIDTH=250>
The rule below is 20% of the screen width.
<HR WIDTH="20%">
Finally, this rule is 45% of the screen width.
<HR WIDTH="45%">
</BODY>
</HTML>
```

Figure 5.51 HTML code for rules of different widths, both absolute and relative.

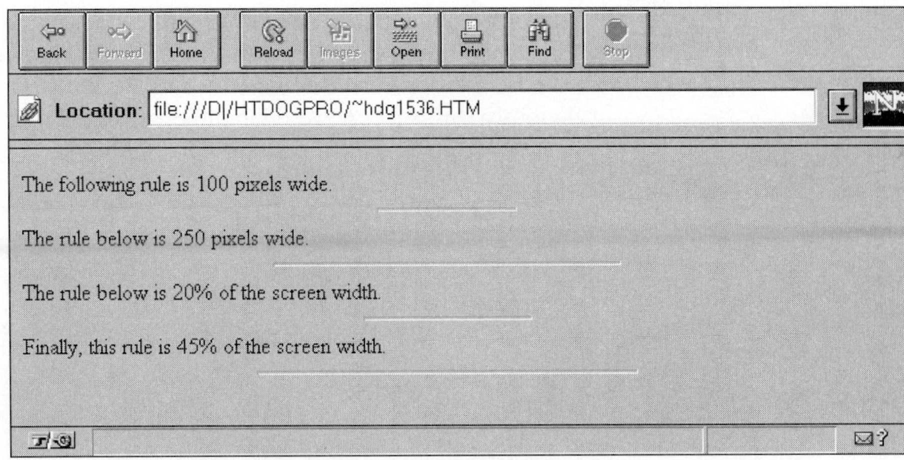

Figure 5.52 Netscape's presentation of rules of different widths.

Most professional Web weavers recommend using percentage values for almost all width attributes in the <HR> tag. If you code an absolute number of pixels, the browser will display that number. If the user has a low-resolution screen, the line may be longer than you intend. For example, on a monitor with a display 1280 pixels wide by 1060 pixels tall, a 100-pixel line would only be 7.8 percent of the screen. However, on a monitor with a display 800 pixels wide by 600 pixels tall, the same absolute line length would be 12.5 percent of the screen. On the other hand, with relative addressing, 10 percent of the screen will always be 10 percent of the screen, regardless of resolution.

The majority of the browsers will center any rule that is less than the full width of the window. If you want to change the alignment, you can specify three different values of the ALIGN attribute, discussed next.

ALIGN

The three **ALIGN** attribute values are *right, left,* and the default, *center.* By combining headings with differently aligned rules, you can create some interesting effects. For example, the code in Figure 5.53 creates interest easily. Figure 5.54 shows how it looks in Netscape.

```
<HTML>
<HEAD>
<TITLE> Aligned Rules </TITLE>
</HEAD>
<BODY>
<H3 ALIGN=RIGHT >Check These Offers</H3>
<HR WIDTH="24%" ALIGN=RIGHT>
<H3 ALIGN=CENTER>These are special</H3>
<HR WIDTH="22%">
<H3 >More Specials</H3>
<HR ALIGN=LEFT WIDTH="18%">
</BODY>
</HTML>
```

Figure 5.53 Examples of the three alignments.

The ALIGN attribute was not used in the second example because the default for the alignment is *center.* By the same token, alignment was not coded in the last header, because *left* is the default, and that is what was needed. Obviously, this is a contrived example; however, some very powerful Web pages use right-aligned rules to draw the user's eye.

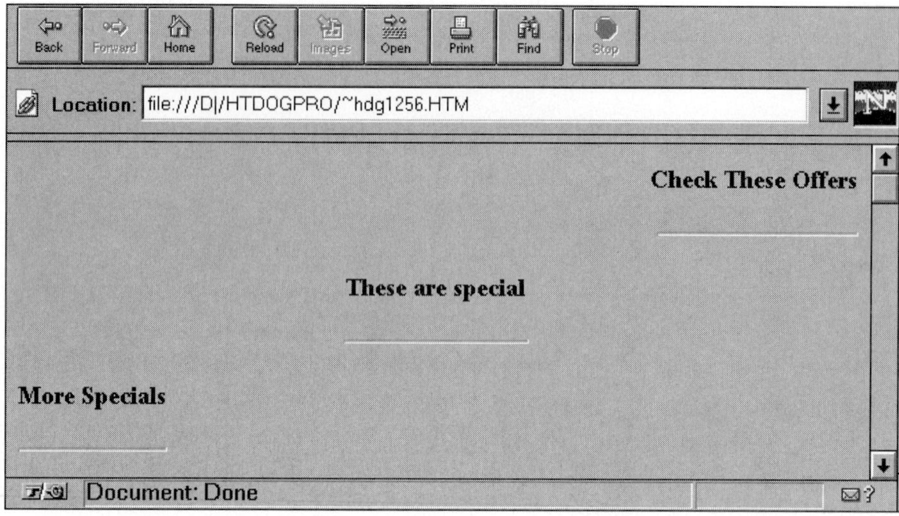

Figure 5.54 Netscape's presentation of the different alignments.

One way to provide a consistent appearance for your pages is to use a standard header and footer on each page. If you set these off with a horizontal rule, it will help your page appear neat and orderly.

NOSHADE

There may be times when you don't want the rule to have a three-dimensional, chiseled look in Netscape or Internet Explorer, but would rather have it appear as a two-dimensional line, like it would be shown on the other graphical browsers. To accomplish this, simply add the **NOSHADE** attribute to the <HR> tag. The code in Figure 5.55 creates two rules that are identical with the exception of having NOSHADE coded on the second. Figure 5.56 shows how they look in Netscape. As you can see, the normal horizontal rule looks like a three-dimensional image, and the one with the NOSHADE attribute looks like a popsicle stick. The NOSHADE attribute is very striking when used sparingly.

```
<HTML>
<HEAD>
<TITLE> Rules with NOSHADE</TITLE>
</HEAD>
<BODY>
<H3 >The following rule is a normal, 3D rule:</H3>
<HR WIDTH="50%" SIZE=12>
<H3 >The following rule has the NOSHADE option set</H3>
<HR WIDTH="50%" SIZE=12  NOSHADE>
</BODY>
</HTML>
```

Figure 5.55 Coding the NOSHADE option on the <HR>.

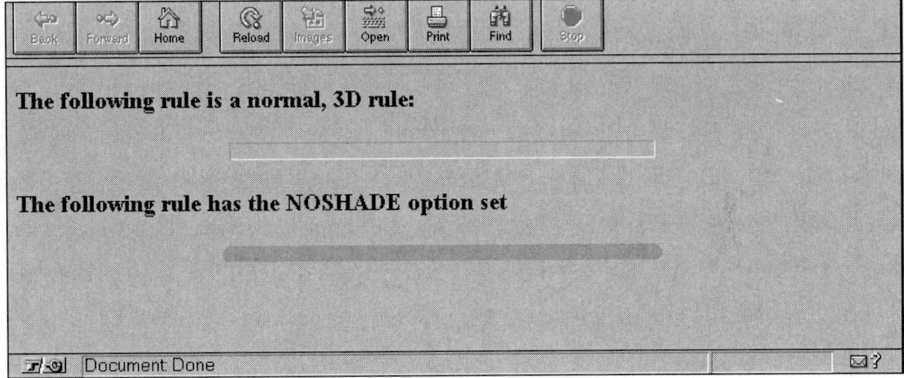

Figure 5.56 Netscape's presentation of the NOSHADE attribute.

Special Characters

One drawback with powerful browsing agents like Netscape and Internet Explorer is that they will try to interpret every recognizable character sequence as if it were a set of tags. For example, were we to convert this document into HTML and try to show it on a browser, a line that said:

"The format of a standard tag is <tag> with the < starting the tag and the > closing it."

wouldn't look like that when displayed, because the browser would try to resolve the <s and the >s. Being unable to do so, it would ignore them. Let's see how that would actually look. Figure 5.57 shows the HTML code for the previous several lines of text. All that is changed in the code is the addition of two line breaks to set the quoted statement off from the rest of the text. Figure 5.58 shows what Netscape makes of this code.

```
<HTML>
<HEAD>
<TITLE> Special Characters I </TITLE>
</HEAD>
<BODY>
For example were I to convert this document into HTML, and
try to show it on a browser, a line that said:<BR>
"The format of a standard tag is <tag>  with the < starting
the tag and the > closing it."<BR>
wouldn't look like that when displayed because the browser
would try to resolve the <s and the >s.  Being unable to do
so, it would ignore them.  Let's see how that would actually
look.
</BODY>
</HTML>
```

Figure 5.57 HTML code using special characters.

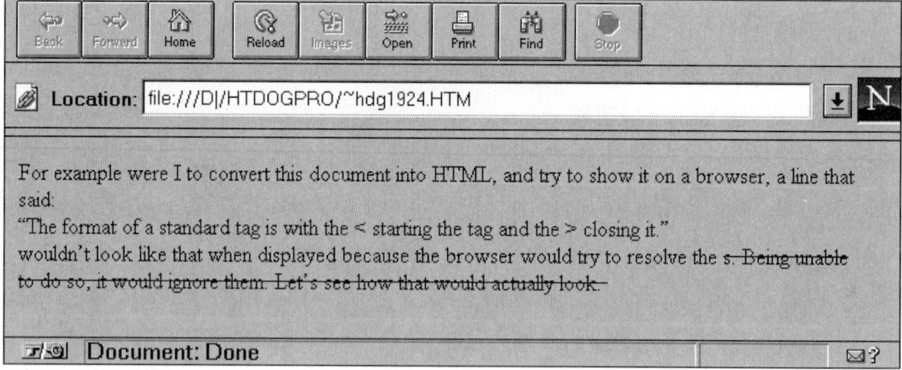

Figure 5.58 Netscape's presentation of special characters.

This is even more interesting than we might have expected. Not surprisingly, "<tag>" is not shown because the browser can't figure it out and so ignores it. But the string "<s and the >" has been interpreted as an <s> (strike-through) tag, with some unknown attributes, so the rest of the text is shown in strike-through font. Obviously, we shouldn't use spurious special characters.

There are times when special characters are needed. We might want to illustrate how to code something in HTML, or we might want to use other special characters like © (copyright), ™ (Trade Mark), ® (Registered Trade Mark), & (ampersand), or even Ð (the Icelandic eth). The designers of HTML anticipated this need and created a whole set of symbols ranging from currency symbols like ¥ (the yen) to simple typographical symbols like . . . (the ellipsis). Most of the common symbols can be coded two ways—either as a named entity or as that character's numeric position in the Latin-1 standard character set. The **Latin-1 character set,** designed by the International Standards Organization (ISO), is a list of common letters, numbers, symbols, and punctuation marks used in Western languages. Each symbol has a numeric value, and some also have names. (The common ASCII character set is a subset of Latin-1.) For example, the ampersand (&) has a numeric value of 38 and the standard name of &.

When you code any symbol, you start with an ampersand and end with a semicolon. After the ampersand, you put the standard name or an octothorp (#) followed by the numeric value. That sounds confusing, but it is simple when you look at some examples. Figure 5.59 shows how the first two sentences of the paragraph before this one would look in HTML.

```
<HTML>
<HEAD>
<TITLE>Special Characters II </TITLE>
</HEAD>
<BODY>
There are times when special characters are needed. We might
want to be able to illustrate how to code something in HTML,
or we might want to use other special characters like &copy;
(copyright), &#153;  (Trade Mark), &reg;  (Registered Trade
Mark), &#38; (ampersand), or even &ETH; (the Icelandic eth).
The designers of HTML anticipated this need and created a
whole set of symbols ranging from currency symbols like &yen;
(the yen) to simple typographical symbols like &#133; (the
ellipsis).
</BODY>
</HTML>
```

Figure 5.59 HTML code for special characters.

About half the special characters are coded using their standard names, and about half are coded using their numeric values. Notice that in each case the special-character coding starts with an ampersand and ends with a semicolon. Figure 5.60 shows how the Netscape browser displays this code. Notice that except for the line length, sentences in Figure 5.60 look just like the ones in this text. Some of these codes will work in some browsers but not others. Even with this kind of coding, presentation is dependent on the browser—and in some cases, such as with alternate typefaces, the presentation is dependent on the constraints of the hardware the browser is running on.

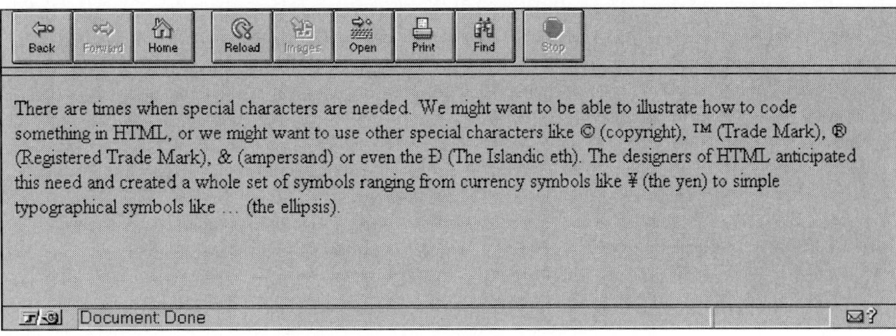

Figure 5.60 Netscape's presentation of some special characters.

Line Breaks

Back in Chapter 2 you learned how to insert new line characters into your document with the <BR> tag. Now we need to explore that tag in a little more detail. In addition, there is a tag that prevents the browser from breaking the line and another tag that allows a line break at specific places if the text has extended past the margin of the browser pane.

Normally you will use the <BR> tag simply to insert a line break into your page. We saw examples of this usage in Chapter 2 when we wrote some lines of poetry. However, when we combine images with our text, we can also use line breaks to cause the text to flow alongside the image. We will discuss images in depth in Chapter 7. For now, though, we will focus on the use of <BR> tags to manipulate the text around images, as shown in Figures 5.61 and 5.62.

```
<HTML>
<HEAD>
<TITLE> Line Breaks </TITLE>
</HEAD>
<BODY>
This line should come before the image, and ends with a line
break <BR>
<IMG SRC="alice.jpg" WIDTH=150 HEIGHT=150 ALIGN=left>  This
text should appear next to the image and should scroll
alongside that image.  By the way, the little cutie on the
left is Alice Blue Brown, a miniature horse that lives with
your humble author. <BR CLEAR=LEFT>
Sweet Alice Blue Brown<BR>
Notice that the line above looks like a caption.
</BODY>
</HTML>
```

Figure 5.61 HTML code for several different <BR> tags.

In Figure 5.61 the first <BR> causes the kind of line break we saw in Chapter 3. The second <BR> uses a CLEAR=LEFT option to cause the browser to force a line break and then resume printing when the left margin is clear. This causes the text "Sweet Alice Blue Brown" to appear on the left margin, right under the picture (see Figure 5.62). In this way it looks like the caption to the photograph. The final <BR> starts a new line with the "Notice" sentence.

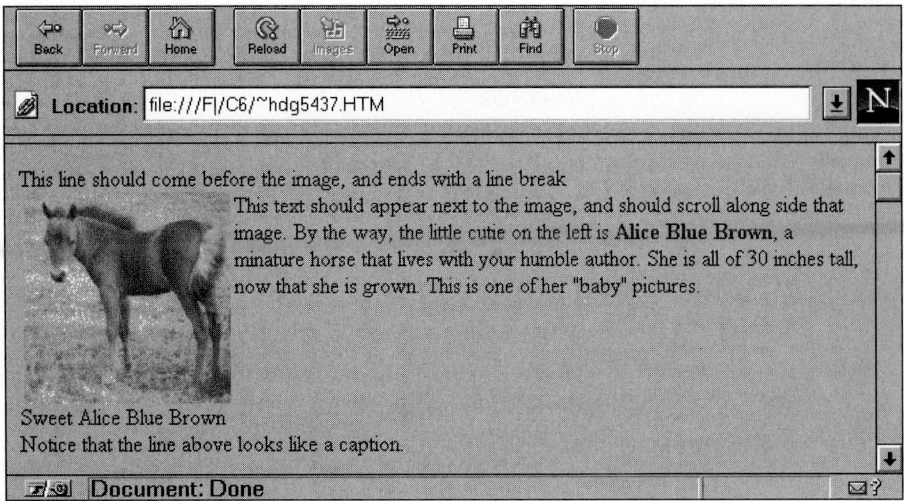

Figure 5.62 Netscape's presentation of several different <BR> tags.

While it is relatively easy to line up an image on the left margin, it is more difficult on the right, simply because you don't know how wide the browser's window will be and therefore don't know when the <BR> is correctly placed.

If you want to be sure to clear out all the previous alignments, you can issue a <BR CLEAR=ALL> to reset the breaks to the default. This CLEAR=ALL option is handy to prevent subsequent paragraphs from running up against an image and confusing the reader.

<NOBR>

Sometimes it is necessary to display a long line—for example, a line the user should input into the computer. Figure 5.63 presents the code for instructions on inputting a long line of computer code (to use the Find command in UNIX). Don't worry about understanding how Find in UNIX works; just look at the code in Figure 5.63 and the generated display in Figure 5.64. Notice that the display could be confusing for a new user to understand because of the formatting of the lines. Is she supposed to type the first line, then touch the return key and type the second line? Or should she type this as one long line? Actually, this example is particularly confusing in that the user could type the first part of the line, then touch the return key, and the command would work but not in the right way. To keep the meaning clear, this line of text must remain as a single line, regardless of the width of the browser window.

```
<HTML>
<HEAD>
<TITLE>Non-breaking lines </TITLE>
</HEAD>
<BODY>
In some cases, especially when you need to present a long
line for the user to duplicate, it can be confusing if the
line is broken.  The user may not know whether to use the
multi-line format, or enter it as just one long line.  For
example, if this were a UNIX tutorial, the user might be
instructed  to type the following line:<BR>
<TT>prompt% find /home/machine/user_list/mydir -name
"sample_program*.html" -print &gt; /tmp/list_of_HTML_files
</TT>
</BODY>
</HTML>
```

Figure 5.63 HTML code for a long line of computer code.

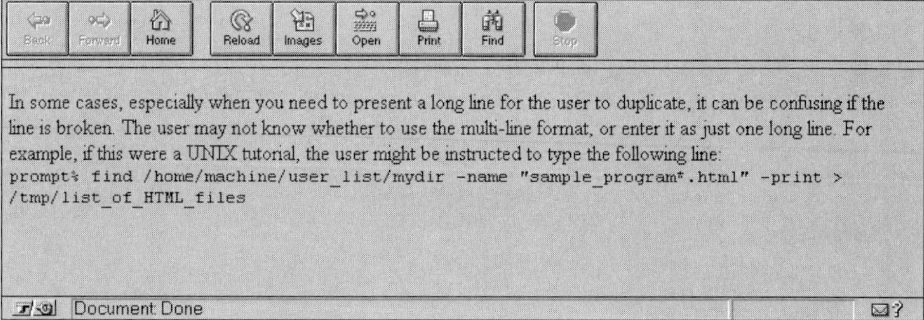

Figure 5.64 Netscape's presentation of a long line with a browser-induced line break.

To create a single, unbroken line, you can code the **<NOBR> . . . </NOBR>** container. Text within the container will not be wrapped at the right edge of the browser window but instead will continue off the right side of the screen, requiring the user to scroll to the right to finish the line. This is most often used to display (1) a line of computer code, (2) a computer input prompt and the associated command as it ought be typed, or (3) some line of text that would be confusing if it were broken over a line boundary.

Although it is difficult to explain this on paper, look at the code in Figure 5.65 and then at the rendering in Netscape in Figures 5.66 and 5.67. The only difference between the code in Figure 5.65 and the code in the previous example in Figure 5.63 is the inclusion of the <NOBR> container around the line of UNIX code and the removal of the <BR> that preceded the <NOBR>. Yet look at the difference these changes make in Figures 5.66 and 5.67.

```
<HTML>
<HEAD>
<TITLE>Non-breaking lines II</TITLE>
</HEAD>
<BODY>
In some cases, especially when you need to present a long
line for the user to duplicate, it can be confusing if the
line is broken. The user may not know whether to use the
multi-line format, or enter it as just one long line. For
example, if this were a UNIX tutorial, the user might be
instructed to type the following line:<NOBR>
<TT>prompt% find /home/machine/user_list/mydir -name
"sample_program*.html" -print &gt; /tmp/list_of_HTML_files
</TT></NOBR>
</BODY>
</HTML>
```

Figure 5.65 HTML code for the <NOBR> tag.

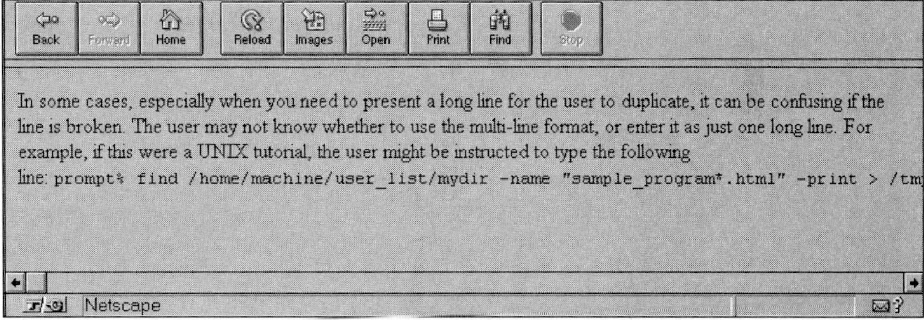

Figure 5.66 Netscape's presentation of the left side of the long line.

If you compare the screen capture in Figure 5.66 with previous examples, you will see that a scroll bar and arrows have been added to the bottom of the display. The scroll bar and arrows are Netscape's way of telling you that the screen information extends to the right, beyond the browser pane. (Figure 5.67 shows the rest of the line.) The <NOBR> also causes a <BR> before the line if it is longer than the browser window. It is a very intelligent little tag.

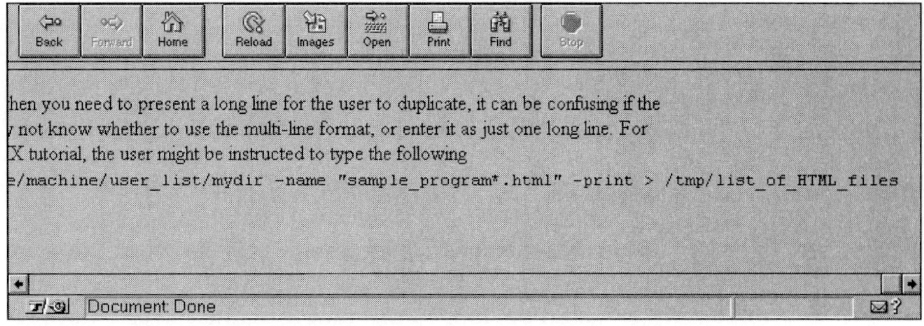

Figure 5.67 Netscape's presentation after the user has scrolled to the right to pick up the rest of the line.

In this example, the user needn't wonder how to code the line. However, he must use the scroll bar or scroll arrows to see the right side of the line. If he doesn't notice the scroll bar, he might miss the right end of the line. That is the trade-off you need to make: reducing confusion but pushing data beyond the right margin of the browser window.

To make matters more complex, you can code a <BR> inside a <NOBR> container, and most browsers will honor it. If you need to code breaks into your <NOBR> container, consider the <WBR> tag, discussed next.

<WBR>

The **<WBR>** tag is probably the most sophisticated style element we have encountered so far. This tag allows you to insert a conditional break in lines contained within a <NOBR> container. The <WBR> tag will cause a break (carriage return/line feed) in a line contained within a <NOBR> container if the line has extended beyond the right margin of the browser window. You won't use this tag every day, but you will need it when you want your text to be an unbroken line as much as possible, yet without requiring your user to camp out on the right scroll key. Figure 5.68 presents the code for using the <WBR> tag.

```
<HTML>
<HEAD>
<TITLE>Word breaks</TITLE>
</HEAD>
<BODY>
<NOBR>
This text is contained in a non-breaking line, just to show
how the &lt;WBR&gt; <WBR> works with different <WBR>widths of
browser windows.  There have been <WBR> three  word breaks so
far.  Notice that they don't force a break, they simply allow
it. <NOBR>
</BODY>
</HTML>
```

Figure 5.68 HTML code for the <WBR> tag.

There are three <WBR> tags in Figure 5.68. They will force a word break if the text extends beyond the right margin of the browser window. Figure 5.69 shows how Netscape renders this code in a wide window. The first word break is skipped because the line is not long enough to extend to the right margin. The second break, after the word "different," is used, because otherwise the text would have scrolled off the right margin. The third break, after the word "been," is used, because otherwise this text likewise would have scrolled off the right margin. Even though this last break makes the document look odd, the browser follows the rule of breaking before extending the line beyond the right margin.

See Figure 5.70 for better placement of the word breaks. The same code was used, but the browser window was narrowed. The word break after "different" could be skipped this time, because the break after the word "been" allowed the line to stop before the right margin. Obviously, the text looks better this way.

You won't use the <WBR> tag often, but it is a handy one to know about.

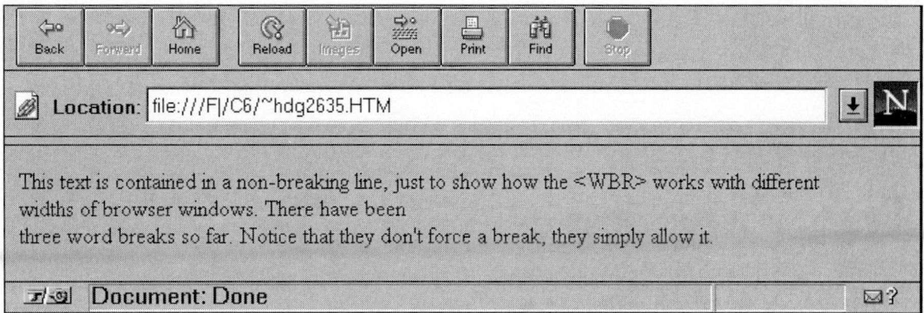

Figure 5.69 Netscape's presentation of a nonbreaking container with <WBR>s coded, in a wide browser window.

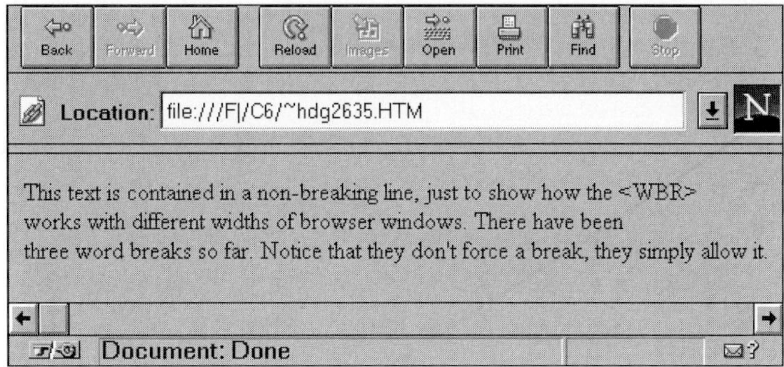

Figure 5.70 A non-breaking container with <WBR>s coded, in a narrow browser window.

Exercises

5.1. Create a page that demonstrates the ten physical-style tags. (Yes, you can use the <BLINK> tag—just this once!)

5.2. Create a separate page that demonstrates and explains the seven logical-style tags.

5.3. Add to or build a page that demonstrates the different uses for the <BASEFONT> and the <FONT> tags, showing both absolute and relative sizing as well as the proper use of color.

5.4. Build a short list, eight to ten items long, set off above and below from the surrounding text by a nice pair of centered horizontal rules. The list should show different special characters and how they are coded.

5.5. Add a section to the list in Exercise 5.4 that demonstrates the <BR>, <NOBR>, and <WBR> containers.

5.6. Experiment with the use of the <PRE> container. Within that container, explain how and why it could be used.

CHAPTER six

TABLES AND TABLE ISSUES

The table is one of the most concise, direct, and efficient tools for presenting certain types of data. Numeric data, data that show a relationship, any data that are usually displayed in a spreadsheet—all are excellent candidates for an HTML table. In addition, tables are a great way to present related data like pictures with their descriptions. The table feature became standard in release 3 of HTML, and was one of the first features extended into HTML 2 because of its utility.

We saw in Chapter 4 how lists could help our user collect information efficiently. Now let's look at the way tables can also help us in our task of presenting information in the most efficient manner possible. Before tables were built into HTML, the only reasonable ways to create tabular data were to use a <PRE> container or to capture the data in an image. The <PRE> tag could not provide the power or the flexibility gained with the table tags.

What's in a Table

Tables are composed of *rows* running across the screen, and *columns* that run up and down:

```
  C
R O W
  L
  U
  M
  N
```

The intersection of a row and a column is called a **cell**. Most browsers consider each cell a unique entity, and they arrange the data to fit within the space allowed by that cell. Some special formatting provisions and extensions exist that we will discuss later in this chapter, but for the most part, you can think of each cell as a unique, albeit small, page unto itself. Every table must have at least one row and at least one cell. Everything in a table is contained within a cell except the caption.

Tables are referred to by row first and by column second. A "2 by 3 (or 2×3) table" has two rows and three columns. As you begin to code tables, you will see why this convention is followed. You must first declare a row and then declare the elements of each column in that row. Each cell in a table has a row and column address, with the row address coming before the column address.

Nearly anything you can put into an HTML document can be put into the cell of a table, including other tables. You can put in images, rules, headings, lists, and even forms. In addition, you can use a type of table to build columnar pages. With all this power available, it may seem that tables have no missing features; however, there are some things tables don't quite do yet (at least as far as HTML 3.2 is concerned).

1. Not all the browsers will flow data around a table the way they will an image, although Netscape and Internet Explorer will. This is a small problem, but it can cause some formatting inconveniences with some browsers. Tables usually use the formatting of the text flow in which they are placed, so you can justify the data in each cell right, left, or, if the table is contained within a <CENTER> container, center.
2. You can align the data in any individual cell, but you can't align across cells. That means you can't line up the decimal points in a column of numbers, even if they have the same number of digits. But, again, as the Web weaver, you should be more concerned with content than format. Let the browser handle the formatting. You are providing information, and pretty is not as important as accurate.

3. The border and rule lines, if you choose to use them, are all the same size in a table. Some of the more progressive browsers, like Netscape and Internet Explorer, allow you to alter the thickness of the border and ruler lines, but all of them are set to the same size (width).

4. No running headers and footers can be used in tables. Since a page can be infinitely long, this is not a problem unless you are printing the page. Then running headers would be nice—but, again, this is a minor nuisance.

Table-Building Tags

The whole world of tables contains only five, relatively sophisticated tags:

1. **<TABLE> . . . </TABLE>** encloses the table.
2. **<TH> . . . </TH>** defines the table headers.
3. **<TR> . . . </TR>** defines the table rows.
4. **<TD> . . . </TD>** surrounds the actual table data.
5. **<CAPTION> . . . </CAPTION>** allows you to place a caption either above or below the table.

Figure 6.1 presents the code for a simple table so that you can see how all the parts fit together. We will discuss each of the table tags in detail, but it's worthwhile to look at a simple table first. As you can see, the coding for a table is just a little more complicated than anything we have considered so far. It is a *very* good idea to draw your table on paper before you start coding it so that you know how many rows and columns you need and what headings you want to use. As your tables get more complex, this design step will be more and more important. Drawing the table on paper will end up saving you a great deal of time.

```
<HTML>
<HEAD>
<TITLE> Simple Sample Table </TITLE>
</HEAD>
<BODY>
The table following is just a simple 2 x 3 table.  It has
very few fancy attributes, but it does  show how the parts of
the table fit together.
<TABLE
      BORDER=5
      WIDTH="75%">
<CAPTION ALIGN=BOTTOM> A simple table example </CAPTION>
<TR>
      <TD>Row1/Column1 </TD> <TD> R1/C2 </TD> <TD> R1/C3 </TD>
</TR>
<TR>
      <TD>R2/C1</TD><TD>R2/C2 </TD><TD>R2/C3 </TD>
</TR>
</TABLE>
The table in this example has 6 cells.
</BODY>
</HTML>
```

Figure 6.1 HTML code for a simple table.

Figure 6.2 shows how the table code in Figure 6.1 appears in Netscape.

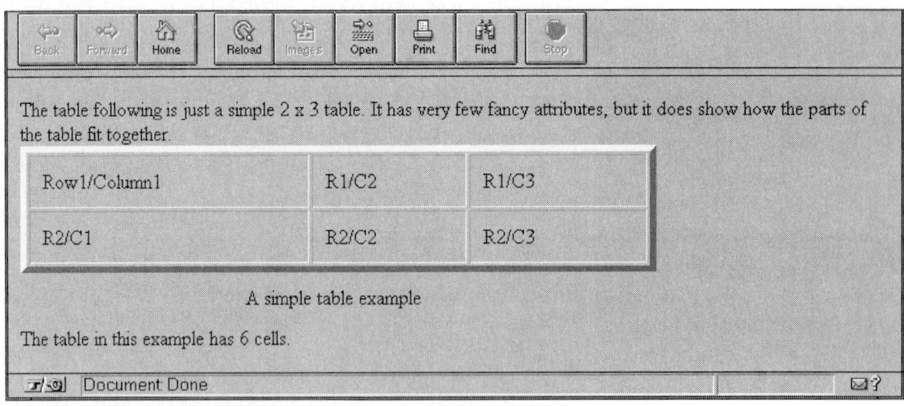

Figure 6.2 Netscape's presentation of a simple table.

The only special attribute used in this example is BORDER, which makes the outer frame around the table a little larger. The WIDTH attribute of the table is set to 75 percent of the width of the screen, and there is a caption beneath the table. Otherwise, this is a plain-vanilla table meant to give you the basic idea of how a table is built.

<TABLE>

The **<TABLE> . . . </TABLE>** container surrounds the whole table. The browser will stop the current text flow, break the line, insert the table at the beginning of a new line, then restart the text flow on another new line following the table. Normally the table picks up the alignment of the current paragraph, so most tables are aligned left. If the paragraph containing the table is centered, <P ALIGN=CENTER>, or if the <CENTER> tag precedes the table, then the table could be aligned in the center of the page.

Even though a cell in a table can contain any other HTML structure that can appear on a page (obviously tags like <HTML>, or <BODY> won't work in a table), only the <TR> and the <CAPTION> containers are allowed and recognized within the <TABLE> container. A demonstration table of "stuff" on a page of "stuff" is shown in Figure 6.3. This table has no attributes coded.

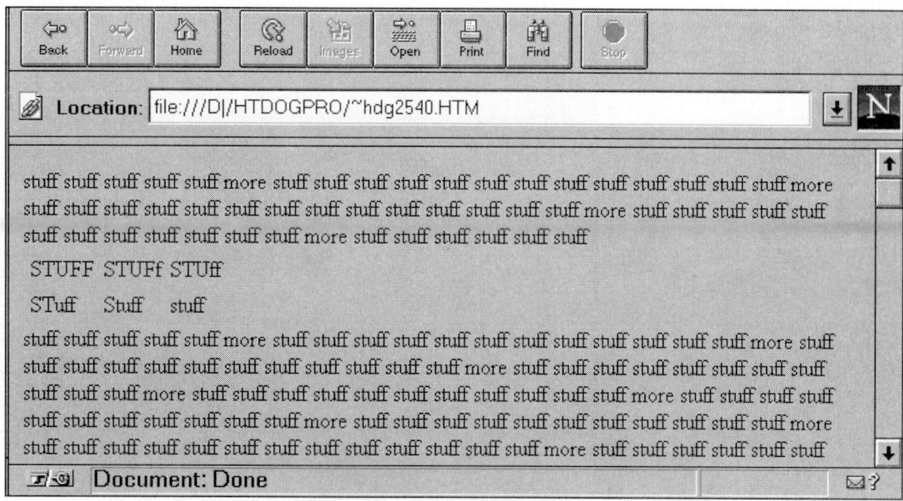

Figure 6.3 Netscape's presentation of a demonstration table with no attributes coded; it is a 2×3 table.

ALIGN

Tables are objects, like images, that are placed within the browser window. However, unlike images, tables are not part of the normal text flow. Instead, they signal a break in the flow. Normally text flows above or below a table but not next to it. You can change that with the **ALIGN** attribute, which specifies the margin to which the table is justified, with the text flowing around the table if there is room. Usually the ALIGN attribute is used with the WIDTH attribute, which we will discuss later.

Alignment of text around the table takes precedence over alignment of the paragraph that contains the table. Figures 6.4 and 6.5 show the same simple table we saw in Figure 6.3 except that it is aligned on the left and right margins, respectively. Notice how the text now flows around the table.

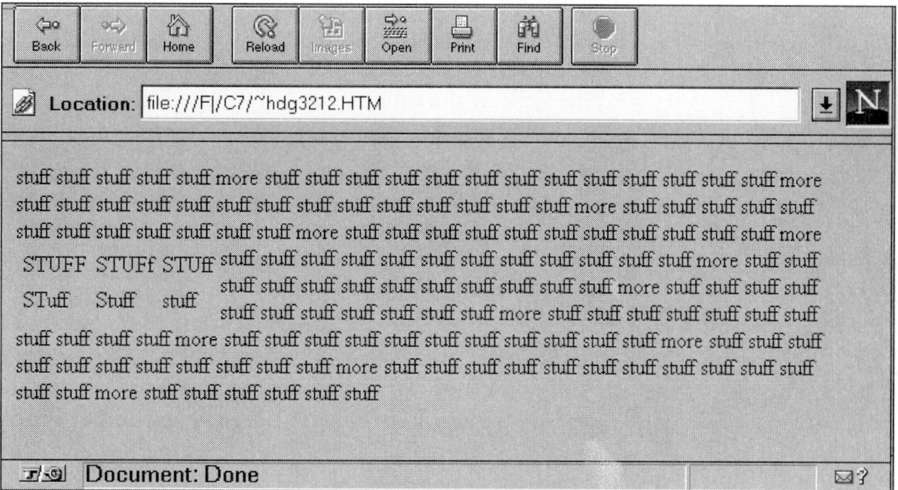

Figure 6.4 Netscape's presentation of a demonstration table with the ALIGN=LEFT attribute coded.

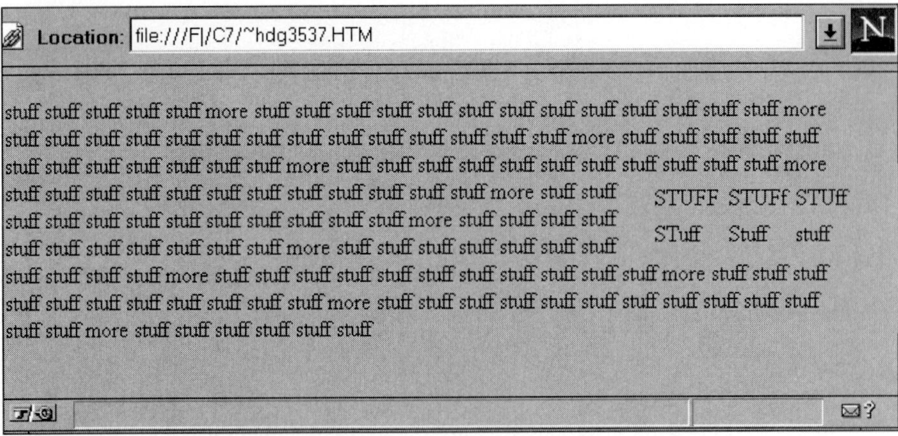

Figure 6.5 Netscape's presentation of a demonstration table with the ALIGN=RIGHT attribute coded.

BGCOLOR

It is possible, at least with Internet Explorer and Netscape, to change the color of the background for the text inside the table using the **BGCOLOR** attribute. Like other places where you can code color, you can use either the standard color names or the hexadecimal codes for the table background. As with the background color on your page, you should make sure that the background color of your table will work with the color of the font used for the text. The text should be easily readable. Internet Explorer seems to continue the background color down to serve as a background for the <CAPTION> containers as well; Netscape does not.

BORDER

The **BORDER** attribute allows you to tell the browser whether or not to put a border around the table and also between each cell. It further specifies how wide to make the border around the table. The default value for this attribute is 1, meaning there will be a 1-pixel border around the table and around each of the cells in the table. Currently there is no way to code for a border around the table but not between each cell, or vice versa. If you code a number larger than 1, the browsers will make a wider border around the table, but the division between cells will still be a 1-pixel border (unless you code a CELLSPACING attribute, discussed later). If you code a zero, there will be no border around the table but there will still be a thin border, the color of the background of the page, between the cells.

Figure 6.6 shows a simple border; all that was coded here was the BORDER attribute with no size. The border is composed of three different colors. In Netscape these colors are usually based on the background color of the document. The outside border has a three-dimensional effect, as if it were raised up from the plane of the document. If you choose the wrong background color for your page, you can lose part of the border coloring. If your background is too dark, you will lose the bottom and right sides of the border.

If your background is too light, you will usually lose the upper and left sides of the border. Figure 6.7 shows the same test table but with a BORDER=5 attribute coded.

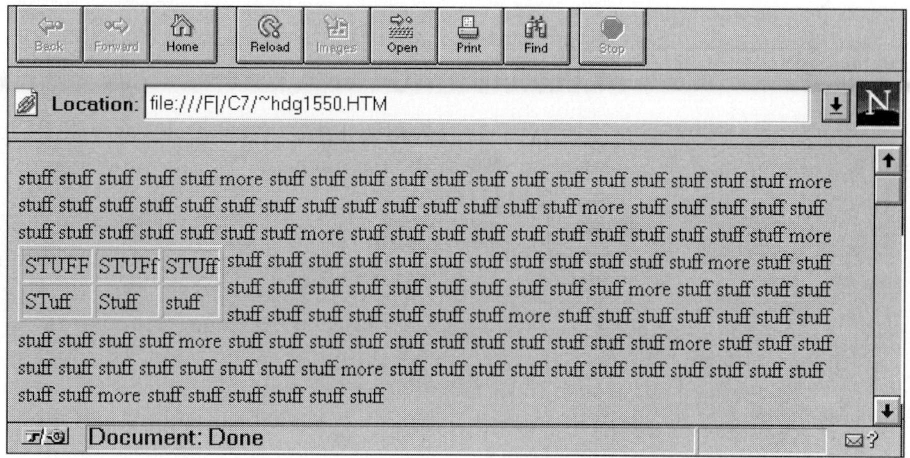

Figure 6.6 Netscape's presentation of a demonstration table with the BORDER and ALIGN=LEFT attributes coded.

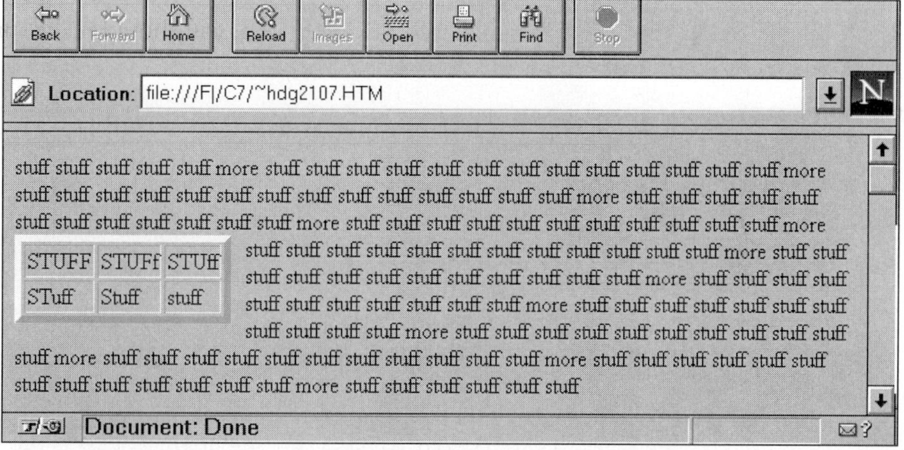

Figure 6.7 Netscape's presentation of a demonstration table with the ALIGN=LEFT and BORDER=5 attributes coded.

Internet Explorer allows you to code different colors for the three values used in the border using the **BORDERCOLOR, BORDERCOLORLIGHT,** and **BORDERCOLORDARK;** Netscape does not yet support these options.

It is important to realize that each new release of either of the two major graphical browsers, Netscape or Internet Explorer, incorporates some of the tags and attributes that had been unique to the other browser. In this way the "standard" is increased even without official sanction. For example, before release 3 of Netscape, the BGCOLOR attribute was an option only for Internet Explorer. Now it is supported by both of these browsers. Before release 3 of Internet Explorer, the CELLPADDING attribute was supported only by Netscape. Now it is supported by both browsers. In this way more and more features are available to the Web weaver as the browsers continue to evolve.

CELLPADDING

Both Netscape and Internet Explorer allow you to determine the amount of space between the data in a cell and the cell border. This value is set using the **CELLPADDING** attribute. The default padding is 1 pixel. You can set it higher to make the data appear to float in the middle of the cell, or you can set it to zero to make the cells as small as possible. On previous figures showing the demonstration table, notice how the "f" of "stuff" seems to touch the border of the cell. The space between the "f" and the border is 1 pixel, the default value for the space around the data. Let's see what happens when we add an attribute of CELLPADDING=10 to the table. In Figure 6.8, notice how the size of the table has increased. This padding of 10 pixels makes the data seem to float in the center of the cells, and it increases the space on all sides of the data.

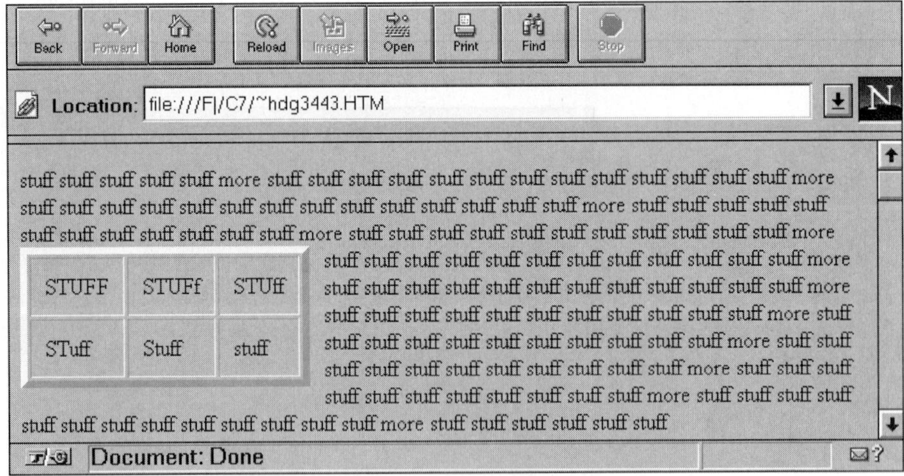

Figure 6.8 Netscape's presentation of a demonstration table with CELLPADDING=10, ALIGN=LEFT, and BORDER=5 attributes coded.

CELLSPACING

Another area you can control in tables is the distance between its cells. The **CELLSPACING** attribute allows the Web weaver to set the distance between the cells and also between the border of the table and the cell. This attribute can make each element of the table stand out. The browser handles the spacing between cells a little differently than the spacing between the border and the outside cells. Normally the browser puts 2 pixels of border between cells and along the outer edge of the table. If you code the BORDER option, the browser increases the space between the internal cells by 2 to allow for the embossed effect, while the spacing between the outer cells and the border increases by the size of the BORDER value. Setting the CELLSPACING to zero will create the narrowest possible interior cell borders. Let's look at a couple of examples of different CELLSPACING examples.

Figure 6.9 shows the result of CELLSPACING=5. Notice how the embossed lines between the cells have increased in width and definition. Now let's take away the CELLSPACING altogether by setting CELLSPACING=0. As Figure 6.10 shows, even though the CELLSPACING is set to zero, the fact that the BORDER attribute is set requires that the CELLSPACING be at least 2 pixels—one for the dark line and one for the light line to give the three-dimensional, embossed look. With the border coded, this is the smallest CELLSPACING available. This is yet another example of how the browser overrides the explicit instructions coded in the document. The browser controls the format, and the Web weaver controls the content.

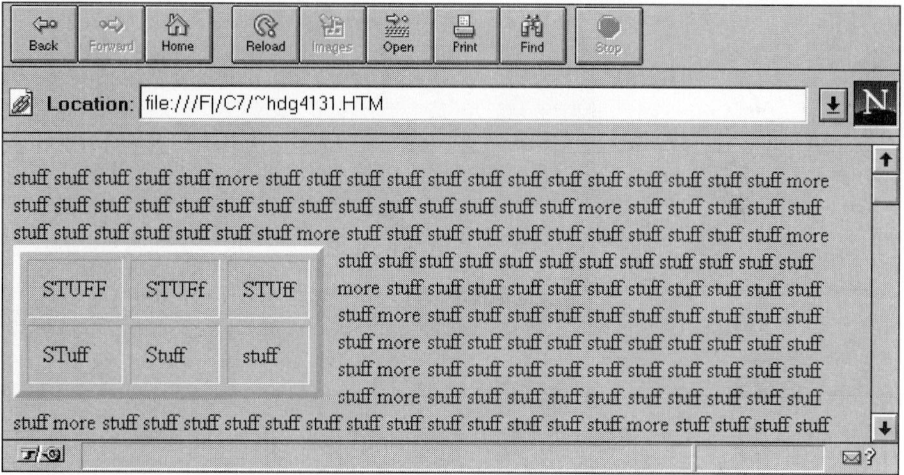

Figure 6.9 Netscape's presentation of a demonstration table with CELLSPACING=5, CELLPADDING=10, ALIGN=LEFT, and BORDER=5 attributes coded.

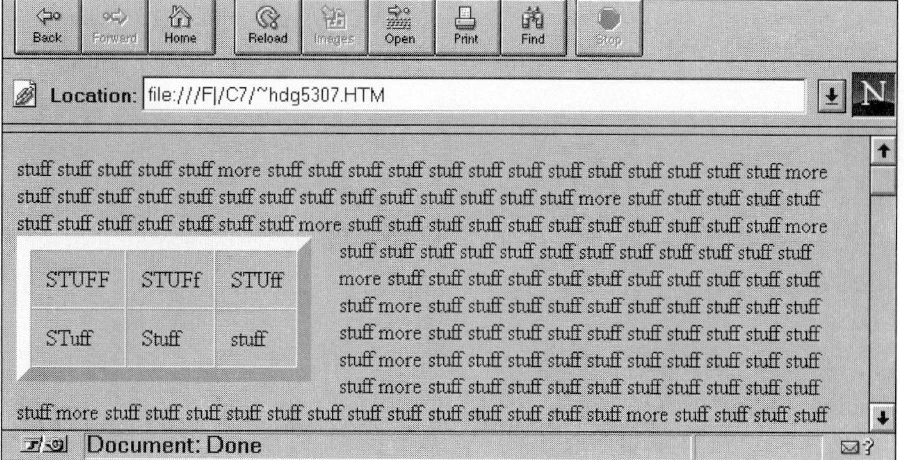

Figure 6.10 Netscape's presentation of a demonstration table with CELLSPACING=0, CELLPADDING=10, ALIGN=LEFT, and BORDER=5 attributes coded.

HSPACE

The **HSPACE** attribute (horizontal space) tells the browser how much room to leave between the table and the text or margin on either side of it. The wider the HSPACE, the more the table stands out from the margin and from the text beside it. If you have coded an ALIGN attribute in your table, the HSPACE attribute will determine how far the table is from (1) the margin and (2) the text that is wrapping around the table. *The HSPACE attribute is not recognized unless the ALIGN attribute is also coded.*

Figure 6.11 shows our demonstration table with an HSPACE=10 attribute added to the <TABLE> tag. As you can see, the text has been shifted right, away from the table, and the table itself has also moved right, away from the left margin by 10 pixels. These figures were taken from a monitor with fairly high resolution.

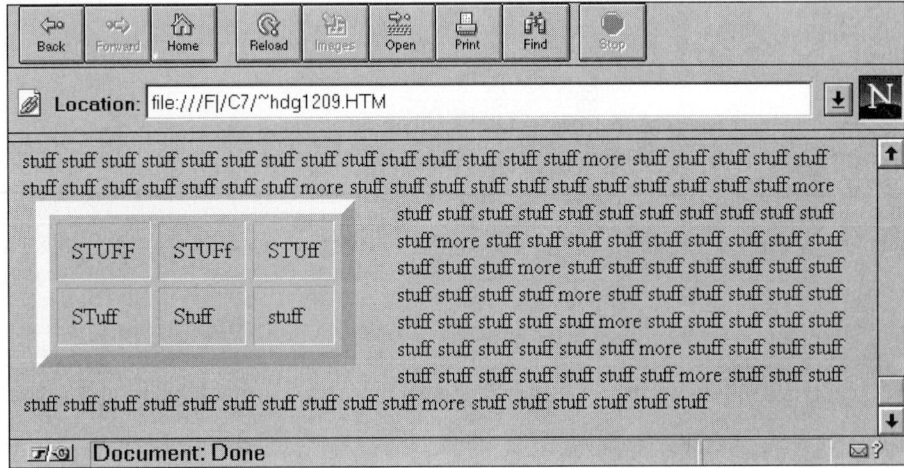

Figure 6.11 Netscape's presentation of a demonstration table with HSPACE=10, CELLSPACING=5, CELLPADDING=10, ALIGN=LEFT, and BORDER=5 attributes coded.

VSPACE

The **VSPACE** attribute (vertical space) controls how close the table lies to the top or bottom of the window and also how close the surrounding material—text or images—lies to the top and bottom of the table. Like HSPACE, VSPACE seems to have an effect only when the ALIGN attribute is invoked. Figure 6.12 shows our table with a VSPACE of 15. The table is becoming more usable now. It is easier to read because it has some space around it. The only part of the table we haven't yet controlled is the actual width of the table, discussed next.

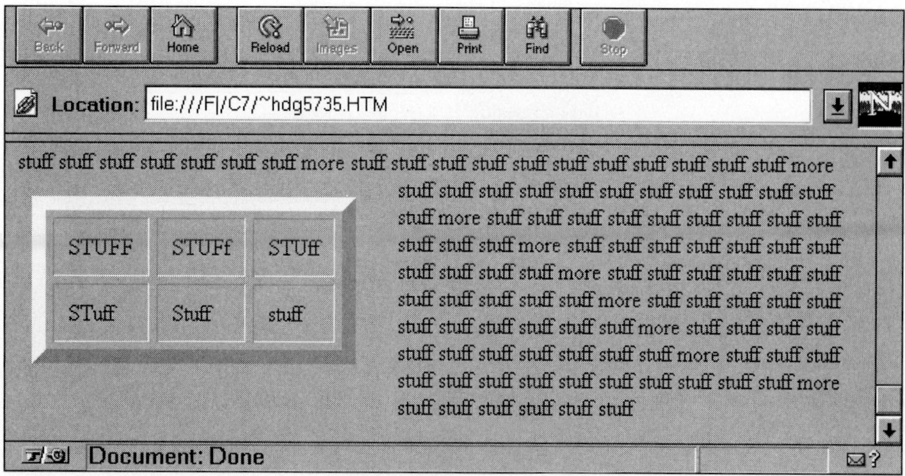

Figure 6.12 Netscape's presentation of a demonstration table with VSPACE=15, HSPACE=10, CELLSPACING=5, CELLPADDING=10, ALIGN=LEFT, and BORDER=5 attributes coded.

WIDTH

The **WIDTH** attribute controls how wide a table is—that is, how much of the horizontal browser-window real estate is covered by the table. Normally the browser will make the table wide enough to present the data you have put into the table, with a little padding. You cannot make the table smaller than the minimum necessary to present the information you have coded. You can, however, make the table wider than necessary.

As with the horizontal rule (<HR>), there are two ways to code the WIDTH attribute for a table: either as a fixed number of pixels or as a percentage of the screen width. Good practice is to always code in percentages, because different monitors have different resolutions (pixels per inch), so some pixels are bigger than others. This can lead to problems if you are expecting to put a particular amount of text next to a table and have coded in pixels. On a low-resolution screen (big pixels), there will not be as much room next to the table as on a high-resolution screen. Coding your table width as a percentage of the screen will often eliminate this problem. Figure 6.13 shows a version of our table coded so it takes up over half the screen. Using WIDTH="65%" will make the table just over half the screen wide regardless of the resolution of the monitor.

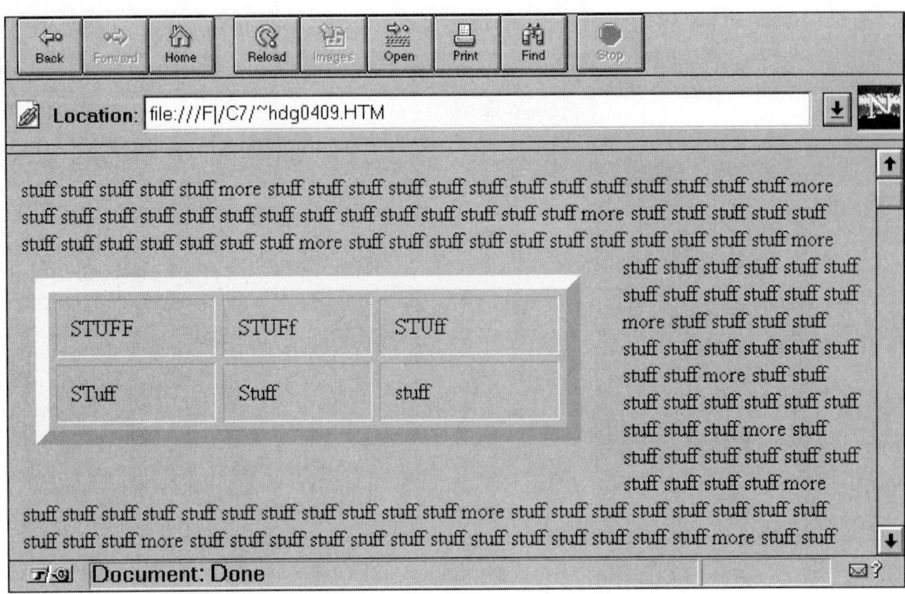

Figure 6.13 Netscape's presentation of a demonstration table with WIDTH="65%", VSPACE=15, HSPACE=10, CELLSPACING=5, CELLPADDING=10, ALIGN=LEFT, and BORDER=5 attributes coded.

The table takes up 65 percent of the width of the browser window. You cannot use the WIDTH attribute to make the table smaller than is necessary to display the data. For example, if we coded a WIDTH of "5%", the table would still be as wide as it is in Figure 6.12. The WIDTH attribute cannot be used to compress the table.

VALIGN

The VALIGN attribute is currently supported only by Internet Explorer. It allows the user to set the vertical alignment for the data in all of the cells of the table. In the other browsers this attribute must be set for each row or each cell. We will examine this attribute in detail in the next section, when we discuss the VALIGN attribute for the <TR> (table row) tag.

Table Rows: <TR>

In HTML, tables are built row-first. Each row defines and contains the cells within it that make up the columns. The **<TR> . . . </TR>** container surrounds the data tags that contain the content of a table. Some Web professionals feel you need not code the </TR> closing tag, because the browser can infer one when it reaches another <TR> or an end-of-table, </TABLE>, tag. Skipping the closing tag is not a good idea, because it may cause a compatibility problem with later versions of the browsers. Also, the lack of a closing tag makes finding the end of a particular row just a little harder.

Some of the attributes for the <TR> tag look suspiciously like attributes for the <TABLE> tag, but they have different meanings when used with the <TR> tag. As an example, let's look at the ALIGN attribute.

ALIGN

When used within the <TABLE> tag, the **ALIGN** attribute determines the justification of the table and whether text will flow next to the table. When used within the <TR> tag, ALIGN specifies the horizontal alignment of the data within the cells comprising this row. An alignment specified for a particular row affects only the cells in that row, not the cells in other rows. Thus, you can use the ALIGN attribute to set the common alignment for the row and then change the alignment of one or more particular cells on a cell-by-cell basis.

You will need to set the alignment of the data within cells only if you don't want to use the defaults. Netscape and Internet Explorer use a default *center* alignment for headers and a left alignment for data. Mosaic uses a default *left* alignment for both headers and data. So, for example, if you want all the data in a particular row centered rather than left-justified, you can code the ALIGN attribute in the <TR> tag to set center alignment for all of the cells in that row. Figure 6.14 shows a table with the three different alignments. This table is coded with WIDTH="50%" to give enough space in the cells to really see the alignment. The table also has additional spacing and a small border to set it off.

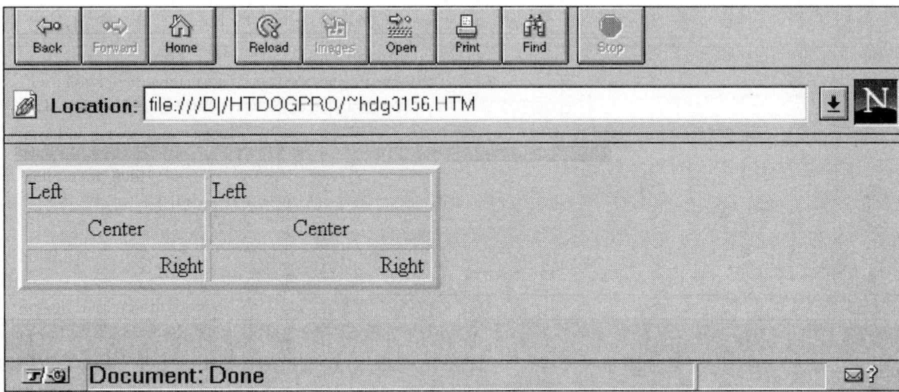

Figure 6.14 Netscape's representation of a simple table, showing row-wise alignment options.

BGCOLOR

The **BGCOLOR** attribute for the <TR> tag acts the same as the BGCOLOR attribute for the <TABLE> tag except that it applies only to the particular row in which it is coded. Using this attribute, you can change the color of each row of your table. Use this judiciously, if at all! With very little effort you can create hideously ugly tables. One acceptable use for this attribute is to set off the header row from the body of the table. Another is to divide a table horizontally by placing a colored row across it.

Figure 6.15 shows how color can be used to highlight the headings in a table. As you can see, it is possible to code a different color for each row of a table. But it is not usually a good idea to code multiple colors in a table unless those colors signify something to the user. Carefully used to actually convey information, the BGCOLOR attribute is a powerful feature.

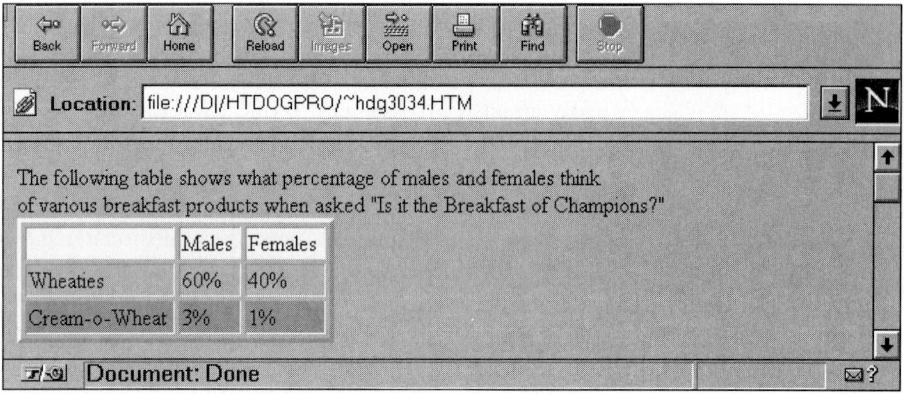

Figure 6.15 Netscape's presentation of a table showing row-wise BGCOLOR.

BORDERCOLOR

Like the attributes for tables, the attributes of BORDERCOLOR, BORDERCOLORDARK, and BORDERCOLORLIGHT in Internet Explorer allow you to specify the three colors for the borders of a row. This option should be used only as a last resort or if your client demands it, because the chances of creating a disharmonious page are great. The colors you see on your screen are not necessarily the colors your users see. Their monitors may have different color renderings because of different resolutions. The next time you are in a computer store where they have many monitors all displaying the same screen, notice the vast difference in the quality, richness, brightness, and clarity of the colors on the various monitors. You will probably see some that show bright, strong yellows, for example, where others show a much softer, paler hue.

VALIGN

The **VALIGN** attribute is an extension of the common browsers. It is not recognized by the Mosaic browser, but it is by the "big two." This attribute instructs the browser regarding the vertical placement of the data within the cells in that row. There are four different values available for this attribute. The default is *center.* Then, in addition to *top* and *bottom,* there is a *baseline* value that aligns the data with the bottom of the first row of text in any other cells.

Figure 6.16 shows a table with these different alignments. A different VALIGN value was used for *each cell* to illustrate how they all look. Remember, the default for VALIGN is centered, so you need to code it only if you want other than centered data.

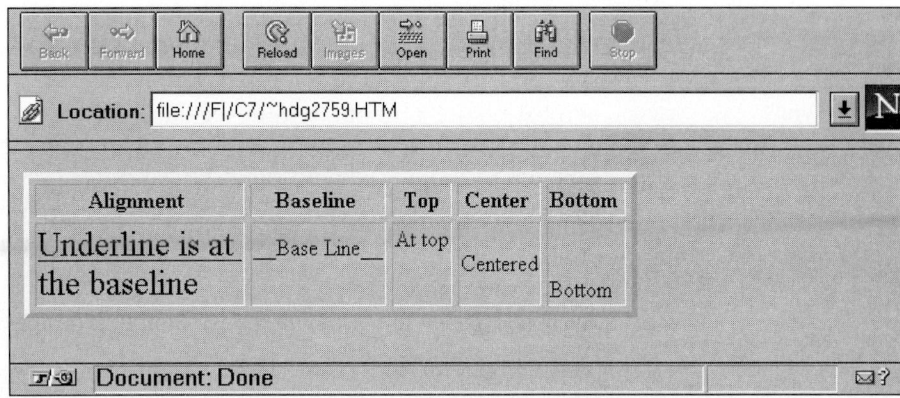

Figure 6.16 Netscape's presentation of a table showing the different VALIGN values.

Table Data and Table Headers: <TD>, <TH>

We have finally reached the containers that will hold the actual data in the table. The **<TD> . . . </TD>** and **<TH> . . . </TH>** tags surround the table data (<TD>) or table heading (<TH>) information for the table. Each instance of these containers describes one cell in the table.

The Netscape browser renders the <TH> headers in a bold font and centers them. The other browsers treat both <TD> and <TH> containers identically, so there is no advantage to using one over the other. The best guess for the future is that the <TD> containers will consistently be handled differently from the <TH> containers, so the wise Web weaver will learn to use them as they were intended to be used.

The table in Figure 6.17 has exactly the same data coded in both formats. The right cell has the data in a <TD> container, and the left cell has the data in a <TH> container. As you can see, Netscape bolds and centers information in the headers and left-justifies information that is table data. Using the correct container will help assure the compliance of your page with future releases of the browsers.

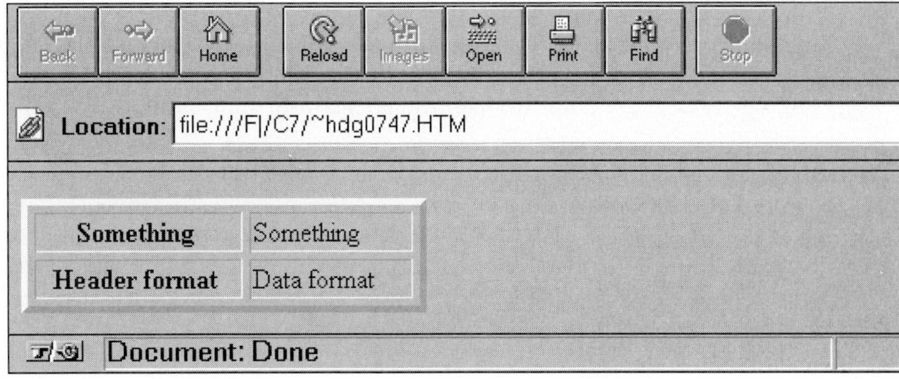

Figure 6.17 Netscape's presentation of <TH> and <TD> codes.

There is an order of precedence for the attributes of a table. Attributes coded at the cell level have precedence over those at the row level. Attributes coded at the row level have precedence over those coded at the table level. Consequently, you have quite a bit of control over the elements of a table. Some of the attributes available for the <TD> and <TH> tags are identical in name and function to those used with the <TR> tag. Others are unique to the <TD> and <TH> tags, giving you even more control over the appearance of the table. First let's look at the attributes that are common with other table tags.

ALIGN

The **ALIGN** attribute for <TD> and <TH> works exactly like the ALIGN attribute for <TR>, with the exception that the alignment is just for the cell it is coded for. The alignment of the next cell reverts to the alignment specified by the row. If that alignment is not set, it reverts to the alignment set by the table itself. Like the ALIGN attribute of the <TR> container, this ALIGN attribute can be set to one of three values: *left, right,* or *center.*

BGCOLOR

Like the BGCOLOR attribute for either the <TABLE> or <TR> tags, the **BGCOLOR** attribute for <TD> and <TH> allows you to set the background color, in this case for a particular cell. You can set the color with either a color name or a hexadecimal code. The color you code within this tag applies only to the cell described. The other cells of the row will be the color set in the <TR> tag or, if that has not been set, in the <TABLE> tag. As always, when using color you need to be very careful not to create a visual unpleasantness. The BGCOLOR attribute may be of use in creating a table with one or two cells highlighted to bring attention to their contents.

Border Colors

Like the **BORDERCOLOR, BORDERCOLORDARK,** and **BORDERCOLORLIGHT** attributes for the <TR> tag, these same attributes can be used for the <TD> and <TH> containers. Thus, you can specify these attributes for each individual cell. As we have observed before, this attribute is currently supported only by the Internet Explorer and can easily create very unattractive combinations. It may be of value if you need to highlight one cell, but in almost all cases, it is sufficient to use background colors or even text colors to gain the effects you want without using the border colors.

VALIGN

The **VALIGN** attribute is functionally identical to its namesake associated with the <TR> tag. It allows for vertical alignment of the data within a single cell of the table. It is useful for altering the way the data in one specific cell are presented. The alignment of data or headings in subsequent cells is not affected. Actually, using this attribute allowed the creation of the table in Figure 6.16.

Let's look at the code for that table, in Figure 6.18. You can see how all the elements fit together to present the data and headings. But there is an error in the table. Look closely at the code and see if you can pick it out.

```
<HTML>
<HEAD>
<TITLE> Alignment in tables </TITLE>
</HEAD>
<BODY>
<TABLE
      BORDER=4
      CELLSPACING=4
>
<TR  >
     <TH>Alignment </TH>
     <TH>Baseline </TH>
     <TH>Top</TH>
     <TH>Center </TH>
     <TH>Bottom </TH>
</TR>
<TR>
     <TD> <FONT SIZE=+2><U>Underline is at </U><BR>the
     baseline</FONT></TD>
     <TD VALIGN=BASELINE> __Base Line__</TD>
     <TD VALIGN=TOP> At top</TD>
     <TD VALIGN=CENTER> Centered</TD>
     <TD VALIGN=BOTTOM> Bottom</TD>
</TABLE>
</BODY>
</HTML>
```

Figure 6.18 HTML code for a simple table, showing the VALIGN attribute.

Right, the closing </TR> for the final row is missing. The table works just fine, but the code could cause confusion for someone. It would have been better to have closed that container.

How you lay out the actual HTML code for a table makes a big difference in how easy it is to understand—and, more importantly, how easy it is to change. In Figure 6.18 each level of table tag is indented to its own level, and the data and headings are each on a line by themselves. Figure 6.19 shows the very same code with the physical formatting removed. It will generate exactly the same table, but it is much more difficult to read, understand, and change.

```
<HTML>
<HEAD>
<TITLE> Alignment in tables </TITLE>
</HEAD>
<BODY>
<TABLE BORDER=4 CELLSPACING=4><TR  ><TH>Alignment </TH>
<TH>Baseline</TH><TH>Top</TH><TH>Center </TH><TH>Bottom </TH>
</TR><TR><TD> <FONT SIZE=+2><U>Underline is at </U><BR>
the baseline</FONT></TD><TD> VALIGN=BASELINE> __Base Line__
</TD><TD VALIGN=TOP> At top</TD><TD VALIGN=CENTER>
Centered</TD><TD VALIGN=BOTTOM> Bottom</TD></TABLE>
</BODY>
</HTML>
```

Figure 6.19 Unformatted HTML code for the VALIGN table example.

It is much easier to notice that the closing </TR> is missing in Figure 6.18 than in Figure 6.19. Formatting your code properly will make your code more readable by others and will help you debug it or make changes in it.

WIDTH

The **WIDTH** attribute is the first we will discuss that is different when applied to the <TH> and <TR> tags. As in the other uses of WIDTH, you can code it as an absolute number of pixels, which will change with the varying resolutions of the monitors, or you can code it as a percentage. But it differs from the WIDTH attribute for the <TABLE> tag in that when you code it as a percentage, that percentage is of the *width of the table,* not the width of the page.

Remember that the width you set for a particular cell, *sets the width for that column in the whole of the table.* As is true for the table's width, you cannot set a width that is less than the browser determines is the minimum necessary to display the existing contents of the cells in that column. If you happen to code more than one different width in the same column, the browser will take the largest value for the whole column. If you code a width, it is best for maintenance and readability to code it on the first occurrence of that column in the table.

Figure 6.20 shows a four-column table in which the two center columns take up 40 percent of the width of the table and the two outer columns take up 20 percent. Figure 6.21 shows the result in Netscape. This table also illustrates the difference between heading cells and data cells. The first row consists of all heading cells and the second row of data cells.

```
<HTML>
<HEAD>
<TITLE> Cell Widths </TITLE>
</HEAD>
<BODY>
<TABLE
      WIDTH="80%"
      CELLPADDING=5
      BORDER
>
      <TR>
           <TH>Col 1</TH>
           <TH WIDTH="40%">Col 2</TH>
           <TH WIDTH="40%">Col 3</TH>
           <TH>Col 4</TH>
      </TR>
      <TR>
           <TD>Col 1</TD>
           <TD>Col 2</TD>
           <TD>Col 3</TD>
           <TD>Col 4</TD>
      </TR>
</TABLE>
</BODY>
</HTML>
```

Figure 6.20 HTML code showing the WIDTH attribute for a cell.

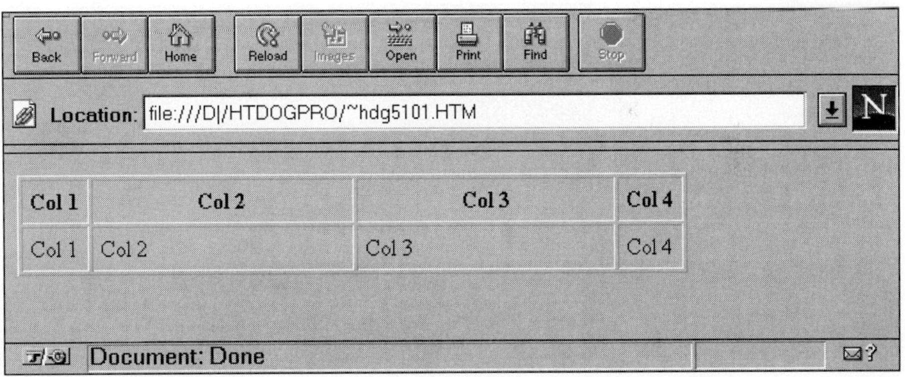

Figure 6.21 Netscape's presentation of the WIDTH attribute for a cell.

If we try to code a column with a width too small for the data or heading, the browser will ignore our request and present the data in the space necessary. This is the same way the browser works if we try to code a table width too narrow to allow the browser to present the data. In both cases the browser ignores the WIDTH attribute. Here is an example: The table coded in Figure 6.22 is smaller than the one in Figure 6.20, and the second row is coded with WIDTH="5%". That is clearly too narrow to display the data.

Figure 6.23 shows how the browser will render the code. Obviously, the width of the second column is greater than 5 percent of the width of the table.

```
<HTML>
<HEAD>
<TITLE> Cell Widths </TITLE>
</HEAD>
<BODY>
<TABLE
      CELLPADDING=5
      BORDER
      WIDTH="40%"
>
      <TR>
           <TH>Col 1</TH>
           <TH WIDTH="5%">Col 2</TH>
           <TH WIDTH=40%>Col 3</TH>
           <TH>Col 4</TH>
      </TR>
      <TR>
           <TD>Col 1</TD>
           <TD>Col 2</TD>
           <TD>Col 3</TD>
           <TD>Col 4</TD>
      </TR>
</TABLE>
</BODY>
</HTML>
```

Figure 6.22 HTML code for cell width.

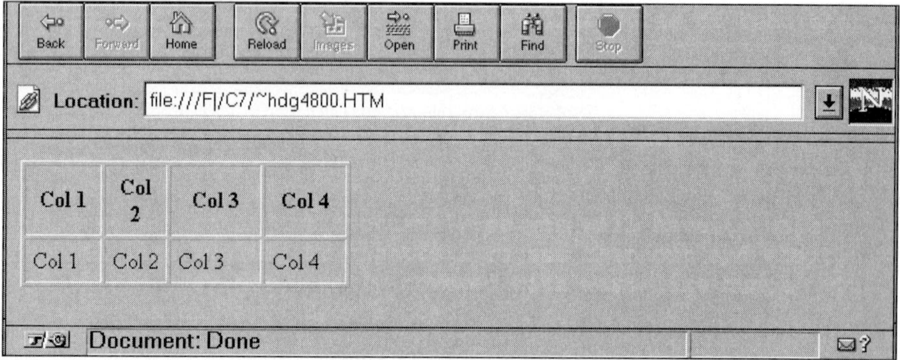

Figure 6.23 Netscape's presentation of cell width forced by the browser.

The browser has forced the width to be greater because it needed more space than "5%" to present the data. However, it did try to honor the width request by splitting the heading so the column could be as narrow as possible.

The next set of attributes are those unique to the actual data or headings in the table. These attributes control the layout of the cells and of the text within the cells.

COLSPAN

There are times, usually with headings, that some information needs to span more than one column. To arrange for that, you need to code the **COLSPAN** attribute and tell the browser how many columns you want the particular cell to span. Figure 6.24 presents a short HTML segment that creates a small table with a couple of headers that span multiple columns. Remember, either <TD> or <TH> cells can have this attribute.

```
<HTML>
<HEAD>
<TITLE> Spanning Columns  </TITLE>
</HEAD>
<BODY>
Here is a simple table illustrating how column spanning can
be used:
<TABLE
      WIDTH="45%"
      BORDER
>
      <TR BGCOLOR="#DDDDDD">
          <TH COLSPAN=2> I span 2 cols </TH>
          <TD> 1 Col </TD>
          <TH COLSPAN=3> I span 3 cols </TH>
      </TR>
      <TR BGCOLOR="CCCCCC">
          <TD>Cell 2,1</TD>
          <TD>Cell 2,2</TD>
          <TD>Cell 2,3</TD>
          <TD>Cell 2,4</TD>
      </TR>
</TABLE>
</BODY>
</HTML>
```

Figure 6.24 HTML code for the COLSPAN attribute.

The first and third cells in this table span more than one column. The first cell spans the two columns defined by the cells beneath, Cell 2,1 and Cell 2,2. The second cell in the first row spans a single column. The third heading presents us an interesting situation. It is supposed to span three columns. However, there is only one column below that cell. In this case, the browser will span across the existing column but won't add columns to make the COLSPAN work.

Figure 6.25 shows how Netscape renders this code. As you can see, the first cell that spans two columns works perfectly. This is how the code was designed to be used. In the second case, the cell that is to span three columns has only one column in the table below it. Since the browser won't generate new columns to fulfill the requirements of a COLSPAN, there is only one cell, and a small blank space, below the second COLSPAN cell.

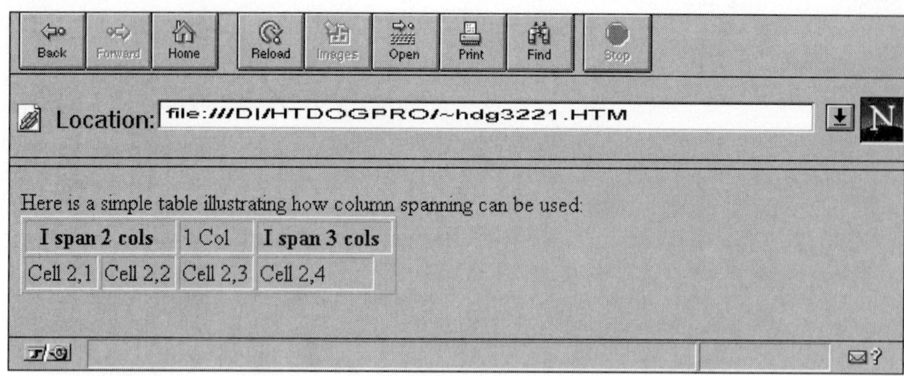

Figure 6.25 Netscape's presentation of the COLSPAN attribute.

ROWSPAN

HTML allows the creation of a cell that spans multiple rows. The **ROWSPAN** attribute creates a cell that spans two or more rows. This attribute is useful for creating headings and legends for the cells in a table. The ROWSPAN attribute is set to an integer number equal to the number of rows the cell is to span. Figure 6.26 shows a simple table with the ROWSPAN attribute set. Notice that all that has been changed is the coding for ROWSPAN in the first cell description. Other than that change, the table definition is identical to the one in Figure 6.24. However, the browser renders it significantly different, as shown in Figure 6.27.

```
<HTML>
<HEAD>
<TITLE> Spanning Rows  </TITLE>
</HEAD>
<BODY>
Here is a simple table illustrating how row spanning can be
used:
<TABLE
      WIDTH="45%"
      BORDER
>
      <TR BGCOLOR="#DDDDDD">
            <TH ROWSPAN=2> I span 2 Rows </TH>
            <TD> 1 Col </TD>
            <TH COLSPAN=3> I span 3 cols </TH>
      </TR>
      <TR BGCOLOR="CCCCCC">
            <TD>Cell 2,1</TD>
            <TD>Cell 2,2</TD>
            <TD>Cell 2,3</TD>
            <TD>Cell 2,4</TD>
      </TR>
</TABLE>
</BODY>
</HTML>
```

Figure 6.26 HTML code for the ROWSPAN attribute.

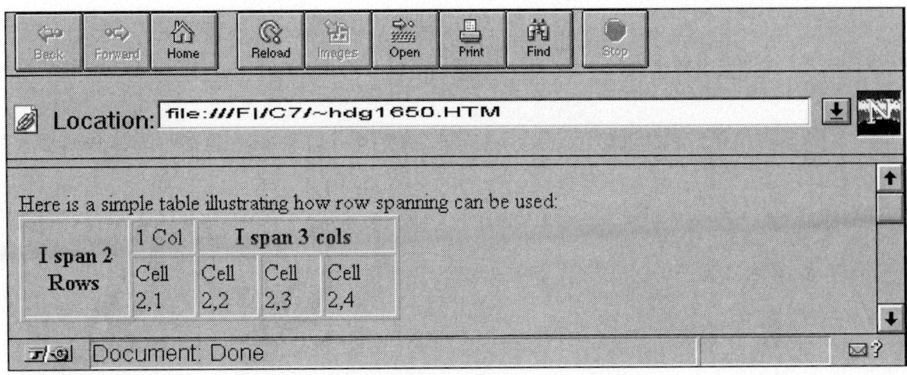

Figure 6.27 Netscape's presentation of the ROWSPAN attribute.

Because we effectively added another column when we created the cell that spanned two rows, our heading cell that spans three columns is now correctly aligned. As we saw with the COLSPAN attribute, if we code ROWSPAN greater than the number of rows remaining, the browser will not add rows to grant our request. Figure 6.28 provides an example. Here the ROWSPAN value is 3. There are only two rows in this table. Figure 6.29 shows how Netscape renders that code. It ignores the excessive ROWSPAN value. If we add another row to the table, the leftmost cell will span the new row to honor our request. With larger tables, cells that span both rows and columns can create interesting effects.

```
<HTML>
<HEAD>
<TITLE> Spanning Rows  II </TITLE>
</HEAD>
<BODY>
Here is a simple table illustrating excessive row spanning:
<TABLE
       WIDTH="45%"
       BORDER
>
       <TR BGCOLOR="#DDDDDD">
           <TH ROWSPAN=3> I span 3 Rows </TH>
           <TD> 1 Col </TD>
           <TH COLSPAN=3> I span 3 cols </TH>
       </TR>
       <TR BGCOLOR="CCCCCC">
           <TD>Cell 2,1</TD>
           <TD>Cell 2,2</TD>
           <TD>Cell 2,3</TD>
           <TD>Cell 2,4</TD>
       </TR>
</TABLE>
</BODY>
</HTML>
```

Figure 6.28 HTML code for a ROWSPAN that exceeds the number of rows.

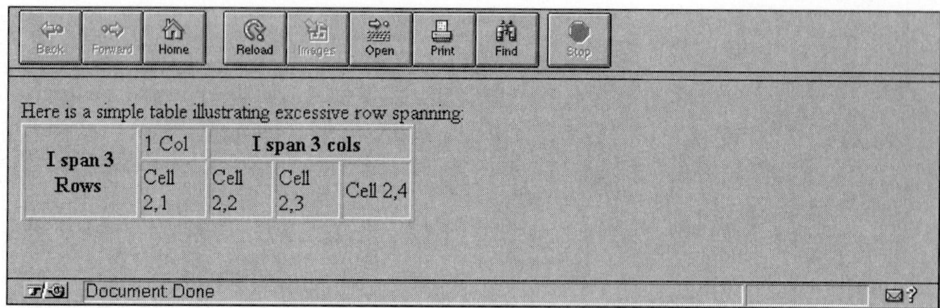

Figure 6.29 Netscape's presentation of an overly large ROWSPAN attribute.

Long Lines: <NOWRAP>

Normally the browsers will wrap the contents of a cell across multiple lines to make the data fit, visibly, in the requisite cell. However, there are times when it is necessary to prevent the browser from wrapping lines. As we saw with the <NOBR> container, there are situations in which a broken line could be confusing for the users. The container used in the table definition is **<NOWRAP>**.

The code in Figure 6.30 shows how the NOWRAP container is used. Notice that the second of the two cells in this simple table contains only three more characters than the first. Figure 6.31 shows how they look in a browser. Normally the two cells of the table would be of equal width. However, since the NOWRAP attribute was coded for the second cell, the browser is forced to make that cell large enough to display the whole line of text without wrapping it. As a result, the second cell is much larger than the first.

```
<HTML>
<HEAD>
<TITLE> Unwrapped table </TITLE>
</HEAD>
<BODY>
This table illustrates the NOWRAP attribute<BR>
<TABLE
      WIDTH="60%"
      BORDER
      CELLSPACING=5
>
      <TR>
         <TD> This code will be wrapped within the cell </TD>
         <TD NOWRAP> This code will NOT be wrapped within the
         cell </TD>
      </TR>
</TABLE>

</BODY>
</HTML>
```

Figure 6.30 HTML code for the NOWRAP attribute.

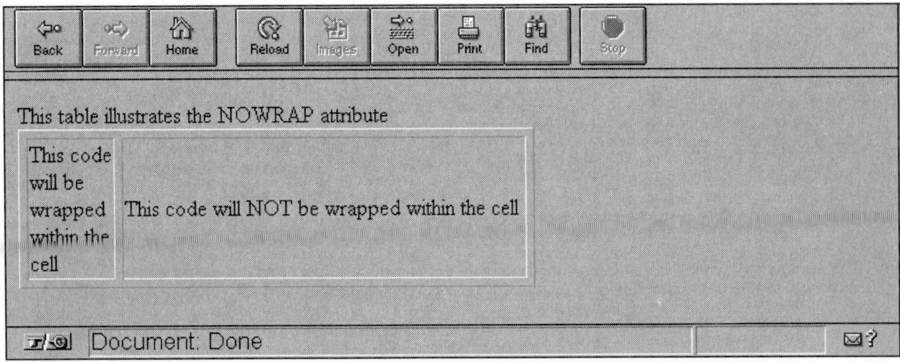
Back
Forward
Home
Reload
Images
Open
Print
Find
Stop
This table illustrates the NOWRAP attribute
This code will be wrapped within the cell
This code will NOT be wrapped within the cell
Document: Done

Figure 6.31 Netscape's presentation of the NOWRAP attribute.

<CAPTION>

Most tables need a caption to explain their contents. The extended browsers, Netscape and Internet Explorer, both recognize the <CAPTION> tag and place the contents above the table. Like any of the cells in the table, the <CAPTION> can contain anything that can be placed in the <BODY> of an HTML document, but the wise Web weaver will constrain the contents of the <CAPTION> tag to a description of the table.

Note that the </CAPTION> closing tag is *never* omitted. Also note that the <CAPTION> container can be placed anywhere in the <TABLE> container, but by convention it is usually placed at the beginning of the <TABLE> container, before the other content. The actual positioning of the caption is very browser-dependent. Netscape and Internet Explorer place the caption above the table, centered with respect to the table edges. Mosaic also places the caption above the table but centers it with respect to the edges of the browser window—a slight difference. Mosaic makes the caption bold whereas the other two major browsers don't.

ALIGN and VALIGN

All of the browsers support placement of the caption either above or below the table, but they can't agree on the details of how to accomplish this relatively simple task. All of them default to placing the caption above the table. Netscape and Mosaic use the **ALIGN** attribute, with a value of *below,* to place the caption under the table. Internet Explorer, on the other hand, uses the **VALIGN** attribute, with values of *top* and *bottom,* to put the caption above or below the table. (The other two browsers ignore the VALIGN attribute.) Internet Explorer uses the ALIGN attribute to control the horizontal positioning of the caption, aligning it *left, center,* or *right.* Consistency is so nice.

Figure 6.32 shows the code to place a caption on a simple table. Notice that the caption is not aligned, so it should appear above the table. The <CAPTION> container is coded immediately after the end of the <TABLE> tag. Figure 6.33 shows how Netscape displays the code. The caption is centered above the table. That is the default. Figure 6.34 shows how the table would look if the ALIGN=BOTTOM attribute were coded in the <CAPTION> tag.

```
<HTML>
<HEAD>
<TITLE> A table with color </TITLE>
</HEAD>
<BODY>
The following table shows what percentage of males and
females think <BR>
of various breakfast products when asked "Is it the Breakfast
of Champions?"<BR>
<TABLE
      BORDER=3
      CELLSPACING=3
>
 <CAPTION>Breakfast preferences by gender</CAPTION>
      <TR  ALIGN=CENTER>
            <TD><BR></TD>
            <TD> Males </TD>
            <TD> Females </TD>
      </TR>
      <TR >
            <TD> Wheaties </TD>
            <TD> 60% </TD>
            <TD> 40% </TD>
      </TR>
      <TR >
            <TD> Cream-o-Wheat </TD>
            <TD> 3% </TD>
            <TD> 1% </TD>
      </TR>
</TABLE>
</BODY>
</HTML>
```

Figure 6.32 HTML code for the <CAPTION> attribute.

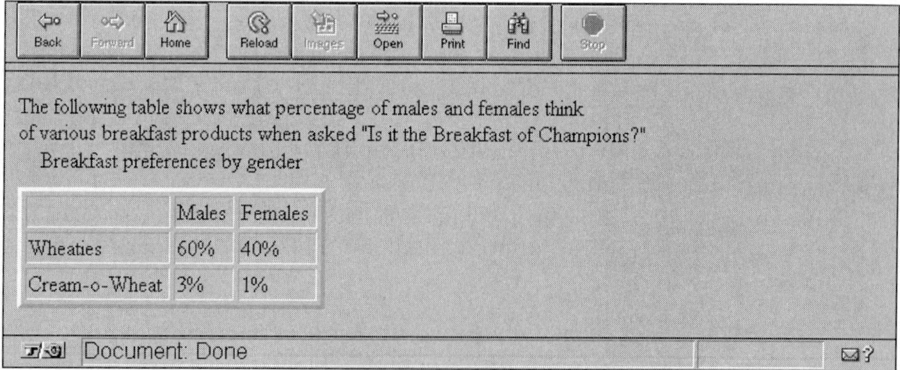

Figure 6.33 Netscape's presentation of the <CAPTION> attribute.

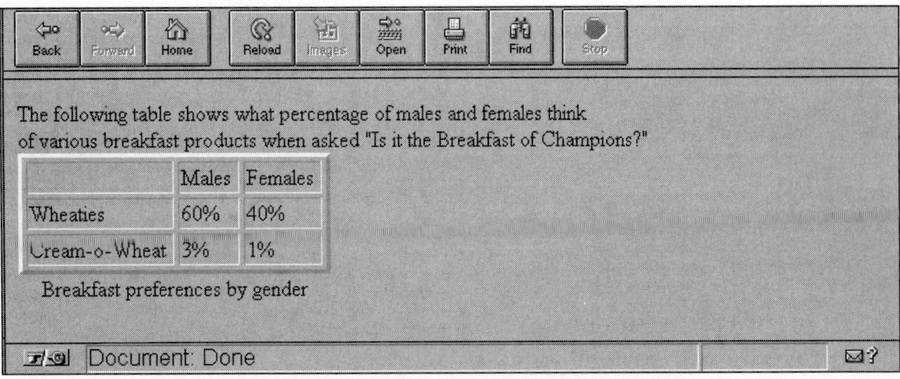

Figure 6.34 Netscape's presentation of <CAPTION>, ALIGN=BOTTOM.

Some Web weavers prefer to have captions above the tables, and others prefer to have them below. Unfortunately, until the browsers can agree, the best bet is to allow the caption to default to above the table and don't build your page dependent on the placement of the caption.

Exercises

6.1. Create a page that has three (2×3) tables on it, each table with six elements. The page should be filled with "words," demonstrating how a table can be aligned on the left, right, and center of the page. Use a nice border and background color for the table.

6.2. Add two additional tables to the page that explain and demonstrate the difference between VSPACE and HSPACE; CELLPADDING and CELLSPACING.

6.3. Create a three-row, two-column (3×2) table that demonstrates the alignments available on the <TR> tag. Also, use one of the same tables to demonstrate that the background color of the row takes precedence over the background color of the whole table. (Can you change the color of the border of the table by changing the color of the text?)

6.4. Create a table that demonstrates the four different VALIGN values for a table row.

6.5. Create a table that demonstrates (a) the difference between the <TH> and the <TD> containers and (b) how the color of each cell can be different (but not look horrible—use colors that work together, please!).

6.6. Create a table that demonstrates the use of the WIDTH attribute at the cell level. Make different cells in the same row different widths. Make different cells in the same column different widths.

6.7. Create an attractive table that presents the same data as those contained in the table shown here. The table should have headings that explain the data, like the ones shown here. Use good colors, proper padding and spacing, and good alignment. This table is your final table. It should demonstrate the absolute best you can do. Of course, there should be a proper caption on the page as well! Your table can look *much better* than this one, I am sure!

	Year	1998	1999	2000	2001	2002
Operating	Windoz 95	40%	30%	20%	10%	Ha!
System	Windoz NT	30%	40%	40%	45%	40%
	UNIX	30%	30%	40%	45%	60%

Percentage of the market share by OS by year, projections thanks to "Those Who Know."

CHAPTER **seven**

IMAGES ON THE PAGE

"A picture is worth a thousand words" is a large understatement in the world of the Web. Here a picture is worth many thousands of words, at least in terms of how much space a picture takes. It is not unusual for a picture to take up thousands and thousands of bytes. A text file takes up one byte per character. If we were to pick an arbitrary size for the "average" word, let's say a word of five characters, then any image that is larger than 5000 bytes (5 kilobytes) would be worth more than a thousand words!

Pictures and multimedia are what the Web is all about. Without pictures, a Web site becomes just a collection of text files, and you don't need a sophisticated package like a graphical browser to see text files. Properly used, images will enhance your Web pages, make them look more professional, and make it easier for your users to navigate through the information you provide. Of course, if the images you choose are overly large or if you use too many, they can clutter up your page and significantly increase the download time for your users. Images are a critical part of the Web, and it is important for you to learn how to use them, when to use them, and when *not* to use them.

What's an Image?

When an HTML author speaks of an image, he or she is talking about the whole range of picture-like elements that can appear on a Web page. Images include such diverse things as scanned photographs, icons, illustrations, drawings, and simple animation. We will discuss some of the various image formats in this chapter.

To Image or Not to Image

When you use images on your pages, you must bear in mind that a significant portion of the Net population will not or cannot use the information contained in images. These are the people who choose to use text-only browsers like Lynx to cruise the Web and those who turn off automatic image download on graphical browsers. They usually fall into one of three categories:

1. Users with slow modems who don't want to spend lots of time and/or money downloading images.
2. Users with a visual impairment. For a large number of Web cruisers, images are at best visually confusing and may be worthless. These users use text-to-speech software to gather information from the Net.
3. Users who want to access lots of information quickly and don't care about "pretty pictures," so they turn off the automatic image download function of their browser.

To accommodate these users, the wise Web weaver will never place information in an image that is available only in that image. It is really tempting to scan in a complex table, store the data as an image, and simply place the image of the table on the page. But then the information from that table is available only to those who use graphical browsers.

An additional problem with placing information only in images is that the majority of the search engines ignore all images. If you want the search engines to find the information you are providing to the world, that information must be in text form, not in an image.

However, the best argument for a judicious use of images on your pages is the time it takes to download images. Each image you include causes the browser to establish another download session with your page. Your users must wait until all the bytes from all the images are downloaded before they have the complete content of your page. Many times the page will not begin to paint up until the majority, or all, of the images are downloaded. Serious users do not want to wait for the pictures to show up. You, too, may have had the experience of waiting and waiting for a page to download, then finally clicking on the "stop" button and moving on to another page rather than waiting further. Wise Web weavers will not force their users to wait to see pictures.

Image Formats

Images can be stored in a number of different formats. The following are the most common.

GIF

Created by CompuServe, **GIF** stands for **Graphics Interchange Format**. It supports 8-bit color and is the most common format. All graphical Web browsers can display it. There are three forms of the GIF format:

1. Plain GIF, in which the picture looks like a snapshot.
2. Transparent GIF, in which the background is invisible so the image seems to be painted directly on the Web page.
3. Animated GIF, in which a series of still GIF images are quickly changed to create simple animation.

Figure 7.1 shows the difference between a plain GIF and a GIF with a transparent background.

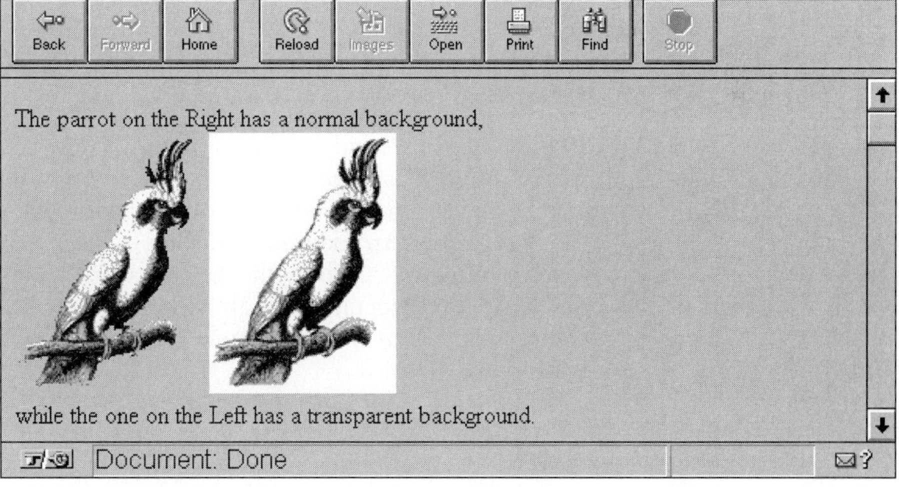

Figure 7.1 Netscape's presentation of two styles of GIF file.

GIF compression is considered **lossless** because the quality of the image does not change through many conversions to GIF format. Lossless compression keeps all the data bits in the image when the image is compressed. This results in a somewhat larger file, but the image quality does not degrade when it is compressed and then uncompressed many times.

JPEG

JPEG stands for **Joint Photographers Experts Group** and is a better choice for realistic color than GIF, because it can support either 8-bit or 24-bit color. There may be unwanted fuzzy edges on parts of the picture with JPEG formatting, though. JPEG is a **lossy compression** model, which means that each time the image is compressed into JPEG format, some of the pixels are discarded. The first few times this happens, it doesn't really detract from the image because the human eye cannot distinguish such a small loss of data. However if an image is repeatedly compressed into JPEG format, the image quality will discernibly degrade.

A JPEG file is smaller than a GIF file of the same image because JPEG uses a higher compression ratio. Like GIF, JPEG is supported by all the graphical browsers. A set of "progressive" JPEGs will create an effect similar to an animated GIF.

PNG

PNG stands for **Portable Network Graphics** and is a newer format that supports both 8-bit and 24-bit color. It uses a lossless compression algorithm. PNG is currently an **open standard**, which means that anyone is free to use it and no single body or organization has fixed all the parameters of the standard. In other words, an open standard is a standard that is still developing. PNG is supported by some of the most progressive browsers but not by all, the way GIF and JPEG are.

PDF

PDF stands for **Portable Data Format.** These images are created with a special software package from Adobe called Acrobat. PDF images cannot be read by any current browser without an additional software package called Acrobat Reader. An additional software package that works with a browser is called a **plug-in**. Currently the Acrobat Reader plug-in is available for free download. PDF documents look like a magazine page, with multiple columns. The PDF format supports "on page" searching. This format is not yet widely used.

TIFF

TIFF stands for **Tagged Image File Format,** which is commonly used to exchange documents between different computer platforms. There are six different "flavors" of TIFF files, so any one TIFF image may not be correctly displayed if the user's viewing software expects one of the other "flavors." TIFF supports 1, 4, 8, and 24 bits per pixel. It is an older formatting scheme but because of all its variants is not considered a standard.

BMP

BMP is a standard Microsoft Windows image format. It can support 1, 4, 8, and 24 bits per pixel. It is not compressed as a rule. These files are usually created using Microsoft's Paintbrush program and are used for the wallpaper in Windows. The standard browsers do not currently support this file type without invoking a program like Microsoft Paint.

PCX

PCX is an older image format that was developed by Zsoft for the PC Paintbrush program. In the early days, since there were no standards, this became a de facto standard. It will support 1, 4, 8, and 24 bits per pixel. It does not seem to support compression. If you encounter a PCX-formatted file, your browser will need to start an external application like Paintbrush to view it.

Generally it is best to use only GIF and JPEG image formats for your pages. They are the two standard formats that are supported by all the graphical browsers. Exotic formats (anything that is not GIF or JPEG) may result in wonderful images, but if your user cannot display them, they have no value. Most paint and drawing packages allow a file to be saved in any of several formats, so the aspiring artist can usually save a file in either GIF or JPEG format. In addition, many graphics programs will convert from one format to another.

If you are serious about building and maintaining Web pages, it would be a good idea to acquire software to create both GIF and JPEG images, as well as a software package to convert from one form of file format to another. Many of the more interesting images available on the Web were created on paper and then scanned into machine-readable form. The most serious Web weavers have a good color scanner to create images this way.

Image Sizes

It is important to understand how quickly an image can become a large, slow, troublesome impediment to your users. Let's do some simple math to see how large an image can become. We will use an image size of 500 × 300, or 150,000, pixels. This is a rather large image, but not a full-screen picture. If we were to use the GIF file format, with 8 bits per pixel, we would have a file of 1,200,000 bits. If the user is using a 28.8-kilobits-per-second modem connection, and if the modem actually connects at 28.8, it would take about 42 seconds to download that one image. That's not too bad if that is the only image we have; most users will wait 42 seconds to see it. But remember, this is at 28.8 kilobits per second! Many modems actually operate at a speed of only 9600 bits per second (**bps**) during the day, regardless of their speed capacity. The same image that took 42 seconds to download at 28.8 kilobits per second will take 125 seconds to download at 9600 bps. That is a little long for our user to sit staring at the screen!

And remember, that is just one image. If we have 10 or 12 images of the same large size on our page, we need to multiply the wait by the number of images. Then, too, this example is for an 8-bit (8 bits per pixel) image. Suppose instead we were to use a 24-bit image? You can see how images can really add to the download time for pages.

Bits per Pixel

In the preceding discussion of file format types, you saw that each file format supports a specific range of bits per pixel (**bpp**). This count determines how many colors an image can contain, as follows:

- 1 bpp allows an image to have two colors, usually black and white, with no gray scale.
- 4 bpp allows an image to have up to 16 colors. This is the old Windows palette. It is good enough for icons but not usually sufficient for pictures.
- 8 bpp allows an image to have up to 256 colors. This is the way GIF files are stored. This is an acceptable number of colors for most applications but does not provide the richness necessary for good rendering of photographs or scanned images.
- 16 bpp allows an image to have up to 32,768 colors. This is an older ratio and is not often supported since the next level is so much richer. Most applications skip this level.
- 24 bpp allows an image to have more than 16 million colors! Specifically, it allows 16,777,216 different colors. This is sufficient for a good rendering of photographs and other scanned images. The downside of the 24 bpp range is that our example image of 150,000 pixels would take more than 2 minutes to download at 28.8 kilobits per second. It would take more than 6 minutes to download at 9600 bps.

Graphics Tips

Following are some techniques for reducing download time for your user while still providing the visually rich environment you wish to create.

• **Simplify your graphics.** If you are building an image using a graphics package, keep the image simple. Use the fewest colors you can get away with, and save your image in either GIF or JPEG format. Avoid **dithering** (blending two colors among adjacent pixels to achieve a third color), because that can reduce the compressibility of the image. Large areas of a single color are best for compression.

• **Divide up large pages.** This is a general rule for Web pages, but it is especially important when dealing with pages that have many graphics. Users would rather flip from one quickly loading page to another than wait for one slowly loading, large page. A good rule of thumb is to keep pages under a 50-kilobyte maximum size, including all the graphics. That way the pages will be fairly quick to load even with very slow connection speeds. An absolute rule of thumb is to keep the page, and all the graphics associated with the page, at a size less than 720 kilobytes. An easy way to accomplish this is to store all the data for one page, both text and the associated graphics, on a single, low-density 3.5 inch floppy disk. If it won't fit on the disk, it is too large.

- **Keep large graphics on their own page.** If you must have a large image, put it on a page by itself and provide a link to it from the current page. You can either use a text link like, "I have enclosed a detailed picture of the part for you to examine; it is a 1.2 Meg image," or you can use a thumbnail image as the link. A **thumbnail image** is a very small version of the actual image. Figure 7.2 provides an example of a large graphic used on a home page. This single image is 18,900 bytes. It is a large image. Figure 7.3 shows how it would look as a thumbnail.

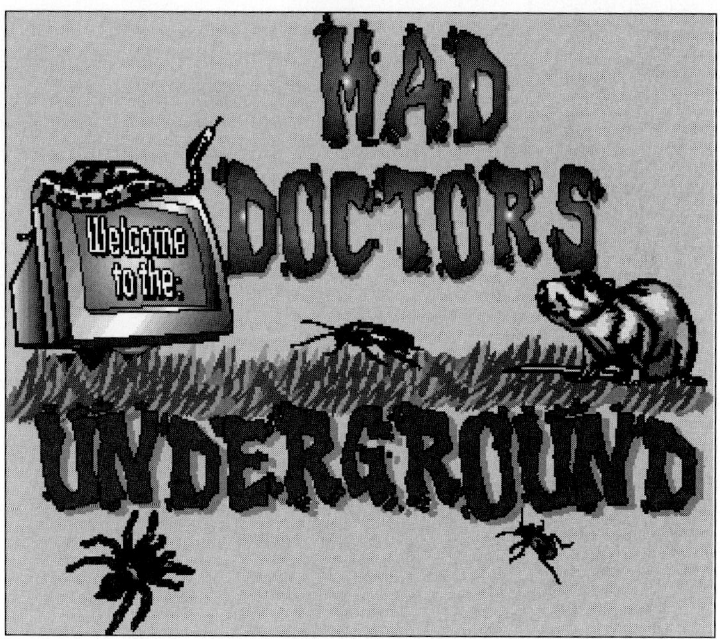

Figure 7.2 A large GIF file (18.9 kilobyes).

Figure 7.3 Thumbnail image of a larger GIF file.

In this example, the thumbnail is almost exactly half the size of the full GIF. That is a great savings for the user. Set up the page so that the user can click on the thumbnail image in order to see the full-size picture. It is also a good idea to tell the user how large that full size file will be. Then the user can decide if he wants to wait for it. If the "big picture" is an 18-megabyte file (1024 × 768 × 24 bpp), it could take several minutes to download!

- **Reuse the images on your page.** This is an especially important rule for icons; however, it is important for other images as well. Most browsers will **cache**, or store, images locally. That way, if you reuse the same image several times, the browser can take it from the local cache and not have to move it over the Net. While it might be nice, visually, to have a different icon for each item in a list, reusing the same icon could provide a substantial savings in download time for your users.

<IMG>

Images are inserted into a document using the **<IMG>** tag. This is an empty tag. There are several attributes available for this tag, some of them specific to one or the other of the two main graphical browsers, Netscape and Internet Explorer. Because the <IMG> tag doesn't force a line break, you can insert an image into the text line and it will simply appear along with the text.

The rendering of images is very browser-dependent. Nongraphical browsers will ignore image tags. Some browsers will force the images into specific size and color limitations. Some users will turn off automatic image loading, causing the browser to omit all the images unless the user specifically asks for one. So the pages you create must make sense even without their images. They must convey the same basic information whether the user uses a graphical browser or not.

Also, the browser will control the colors in the image. The actual hardware at the user site is involved here, too. If you have a wonderful image with 16,000,000 colors, and the user is displaying it on a monochrome monitor, it will appear as a black-and-white image. This is another example of the Web weaver supplying the *content* while the browser handles the *format*.

SRC

The **SRC** (source) attribute is the only required attribute of the <IMG> tag. This attribute tells the browser where to find the image that is to be inserted into your page. There are three schools of thought about where to keep your images. The first could be called the "minimize the server load" school. This school says that all the images should be on remote machines, and the SRC attribute should provide a link across the Net to the remote site. That way the load on the local server that is hosting the page is minimized. Generally, this is the very worst thing a Web weaver can do, because it causes the greatest load on the Net. In this model, each time a new image is requested, the browser must establish a link to another server where the picture is located and then download the picture before it can be displayed. Many Web sites that have pictures available for use will request that the images be copied rather than having a link pointing to their site.

The second school of thought could be summed up as the "put everything in the same directory" approach. These folks like to be able to minimize the paths coded in the SRC attribute. They want to make it as easy as possible to move a page from one site to another. This school has merit for small Web sites or for people who intend to move their pages from site to site. It is very easy to upload and maintain a page when all the links and all the images are local to the home page. But when the site is large, a third school of thought is preferred.

The third school could be described as the "a place for everything and everything in its place" approach. Here each type of file is kept in its own directory. Thus, the Web pages will be in a directory called "HTML," the pictures in a directory called "images," the sound files in a directory called sounds," and so forth. This approach can be taken to extremes, though, and become cumbersome for everybody involved. At some sites, for example, the "images" subdirectory is divided into "smallgif," "medumgif," "biggif," "smalljpg," "medumjpg," and "bigjpg."

It is usually necessary to create a directory structure when building a commercial site, because that type of site will have hundreds of files, and many times several different pages will use the same images. If images are put in common areas, then everybody can use them. Also, updating them is easy. For example, if 15 different pages all use an image of the corporate logo, and they are stored in 15 different locations, the Web weaver would have to update 15 different files in 15 different directories if a new version of the logo were created. On the other hand, if the logo is kept in a single directory, and all the pages use that one image, then it is easy to update the image.

For new users, it is usually easier to keep all the images, pages, and other files in one directory, the second school of thought. As you become more sophisticated and as your Web site grows, you will find it easier to collect related files into directories. This will make uploading a little more complex, as you may need to change the paths in the SRC attributes, but it is a small price to pay for organization and easy update. Never fall into the trap of linking across the Web to an image on a remote machine—that is the worst option available.

Following is an example of a link across the Net:

```
Here is the picture of a nice parrot: <BR>
<IMG SRC="http://fred.dc3d.edu/images/parrot3.gif">
```

In the next example, the image is located in the "images" subdirectory, possibly because the site has many images, and several of them are used across many different pages.

```
Here is the picture of a nice parrot: <BR>
<IMG SRC="images/parrot3.gif">
```

Now look at a snippet that shows the minimal <IMG> tag. Here all the files, both HTML and images, have been grouped into a single directory.

```
Here is the picture of a nice parrot: <BR>
<IMG SRC="parrot3.gif">
```

Notice that in all three cases, the actual filename is enclosed in quotation marks. Those quotation marks are required for the image to work correctly. Sometimes they can be omitted and the image will appear correctly anyway, but at a later time, the image may stop appearing. It is best, therefore, to always code the image, or the image and path, inside quotation marks. Then it will always work as long as the path is correct.

Figure 7.4 presents the code for bringing in an image. Each line ends in a line break, <BR>, to force the image onto a line of its own. Later we will see how the ALIGN attribute allows some control over where the image is placed on the screen.

```
<HTML>
<HEAD>
<TITLE> Image sample 1</TITLE>
</HEAD>
<BODY>
Here is the picture of a nice parrot:<BR>
<IMG SRC="parrot3.gif"> <BR>
Actually, it is a nice picture of a parrot, I don't really
know how nice the parrot is!
</BODY>
</HTML>
```

Figure 7.4 HTML code for putting an image on the page, using line breaks.

Figure 7.5 shows how the browser renders the code in Figure 7.4. We can see that the default alignment of the image is on the left margin. Figure 7.6 now presents the same code, but without the line breaks, and Figure 7.7 shows that the browser treats an image just like any other text element. Since there are no forced line breaks, an image appears like any other page element, in line with the text, and after the word "parrot," as we might expect. The first line of text is pushed down far enough to accommodate the image as well as the text. Notice how the bottom of the image is aligned with the bottom of the actual text. Soon we will see how to modify the alignment of the image.

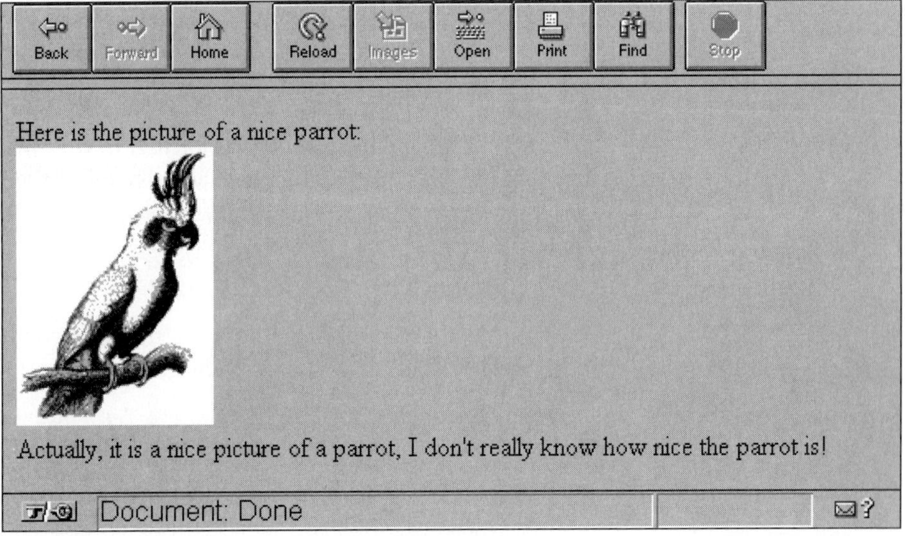

Figure 7.5 Netscape's presentation of the code for an image when line breaks are used.

```
<HTML>
<HEAD>
<TITLE> Image sample 1</TITLE>
</HEAD>
<BODY>
Here is the picture of a nice parrot:
<IMG SRC="parrot3.gif">
Actually, it is a nice picture of a parrot, I don't really
know how nice the parrot is!
</BODY>
</HTML>
```

Figure 7.6 HTML code for putting an image on the page, without using line breaks.

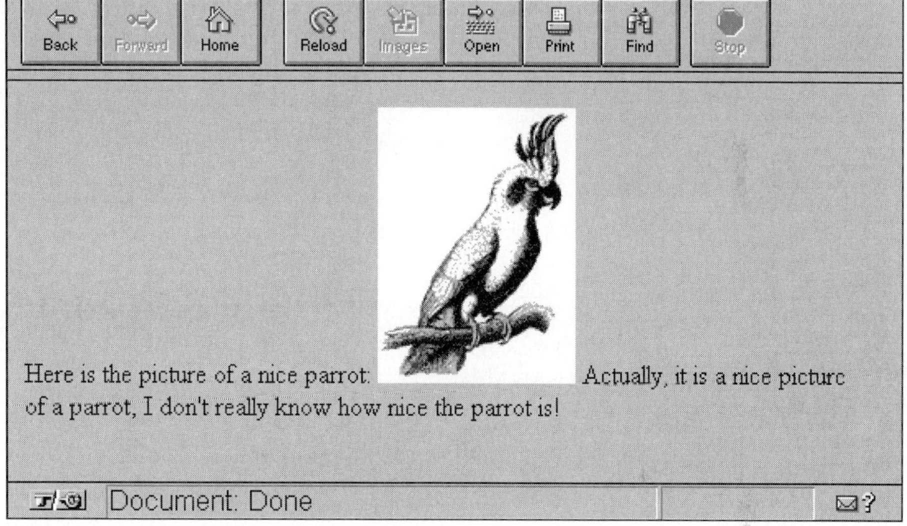

Figure 7.7 Netscape's presentation of the code for an image when no line breaks are used.

ALT

Although the SRC attribute is required by the browsers, the **ALT** (alternate) attribute is not—but it is nonetheless used by conscientious Web weavers. This attribute contains a text string that is displayed when the browser can't display the actual image, either because it is not a graphical browser or because the user has turned off image loading. This text string must be enclosed in quotation marks if it contains any punctuation or spaces. The string can be up to 1024 bytes long.

As mentioned earlier in this chapter, the careful Web weaver never places information in an image that is not available somewhere else on the page. The ALT attribute is one good way to present that information to users who cannot see the images. A good description of the image will also help those users who have turned off automatic image loading decide if they want to view the image.

In addition to providing content support for nongraphical users, the ALT attribute can serve as a substitute for icons. For example, suppose you had coded the following snippet in your page to indicate a new feature:

```
<H2>See the birdie <IMG SRC="hotnew.gif" ALT="**NEW**"> </H2>
```

Users with graphical browsers see the "hotnew.gif" image, but those with text-only browsers and those who have turned off automatic image loading will see the string "★★NEW★★" after the text "See the birdie."

Figure 7.8 presents the code for the parrot page in Figure 7.4 with the ALT attribute coded. The source filename is incorrect in this code, forcing Netscape to display the ALT text. Because the browser is graphically oriented, sometimes it will display the images even when the user has decided not to have them displayed, especially when the images are local and the browser doesn't have to load them from across the Net. In Figure 7.9 the alternative text is displayed because there is no image called "arrot3.gif" available.

```
<HTML>
<HEAD>
<TITLE> Image sample 1</TITLE>
</HEAD>
<BODY>
Here is the picture of a nice parrot:
<IMG SRC="arrot3.gif"
ALT="A black and white woodcut of a crested Cockatoo.">
Actually, it is a nice picture of a parrot, I don't really
know how nice the parrot is!
</BODY>
</HTML>
```

Figure 7.8 HTML code showing the ALT attribute.

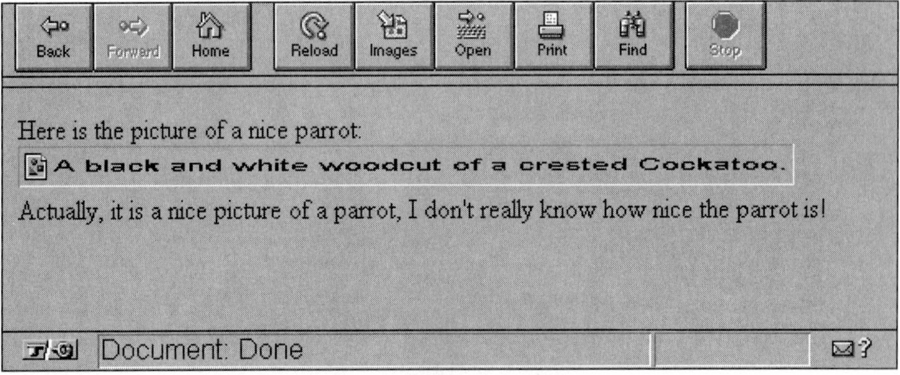

Figure 7.9 Netscape's presentation of the ALT attribute.

Using the ALT attribute should be standard procedure for any image you choose to add to your page.

LOWSRC

In addition to coding the ALT attribute, it is often helpful to include the **LOWSRC** (low-resolution source) attribute in the <IMG> tag. This attribute specifies a lower-resolution image that the browser can load first, before loading the final image. Usually (but not always) this first image is simply a lower-resolution version of the better image that will take its place.

Using LOWSRC will speed up the display of the document to the user, because the browser will display the LOWSRC image the first time it encounters the <IMG> tag. Then, after the rest of the page has been displayed, the browser will go back and display the image specified by the SRC attribute. That way the user doesn't have to wait for the high-resolution image to paint up before she can see the page.

Using both LOWSRC and SRC can provide some interesting effects. The browser reserves space for the LOWSRC image on the page. When it loads the SRC image, it forces that image to fit into the space reserved for the LOWSRC image. If the LOWSRC image is larger, smaller, wider, or taller than the final SRC image, the final image will be stretched or shrunk to fit the space. If the LOWSRC image is actually a lower-resolution version of the image, this process presents no problem, as the two images will be the same size. However, if the images are different and are of different sizes, then the wise Web weaver will use the HEIGHT and WIDTH attributes, discussed later in this chapter, to set the size of the display space.

Just because the attribute LOWSRC is intended to contain the URL of a lower-resolution version of an image doesn't mean it has to. An easy way to get an interesting effect is to code two different images that may complement each other as the SRC and the LOWSRC. Moreover, this is a simple way to get a one-frame animation. For example, in Figure 7.10 the LOWSRC attribute contains a URL that points to an upside-down image of a butterfly. The SRC attribute butterfly image is of the same butterfly, but right side up. As the document displays, the first image appears, in which the butterfly seems to be flying down the page. Then when the whole page has been displayed, the second image replaces the first, and the butterfly, turned around, seems to be flying up the page.

```
<HTML>
<HEAD>
<TITLE> Image sample 1</TITLE>
</HEAD>
<BODY>
At the "Fly Away Home" Web site you can experience <BR>
many of nature's pretty little creatures <BR>
as they frolic about the flowers of the pasture.<BR>
<IMG SRC="bflyhi.gif"
LOWSRC="bflyhiin.gif"
ALT="Images of a Painted Lady butterfly" WIDTH=210
HEIGHT=142> <BR>
Notice how the image seems to change right before your eyes!
</BODY>
</HTML>
```

Figure 7.10 HTML code for the LOWSRC attribute.

In Figure 7.10 both an SRC and a LOWSRC URL are coded. Figures 7.11 and 7.12 show the two different images as they appear when displayed by the browser. Since this book is static, it is impossible to show you how the effect works, but imagine the first image being replaced by the second after the text on the page has been displayed.

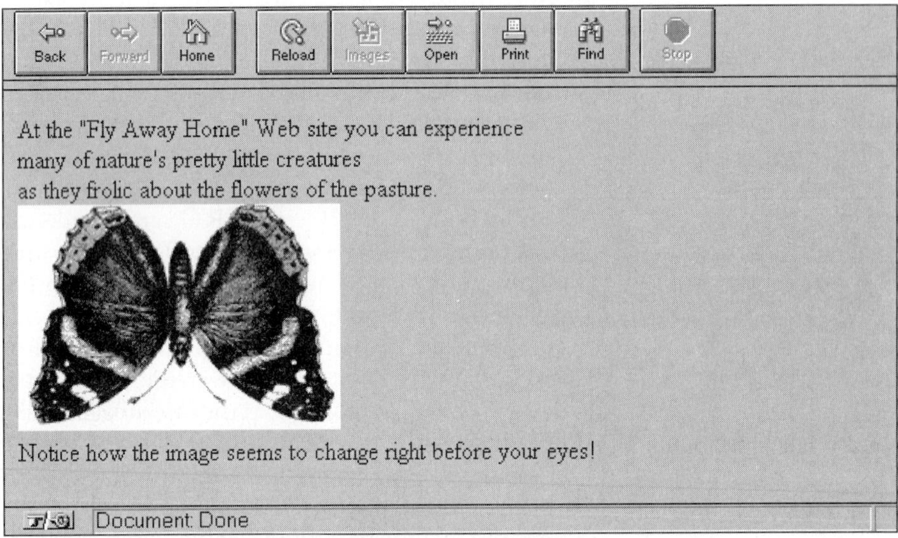

Figure 7.11 The first version of a page with the LOWSRC attribute.

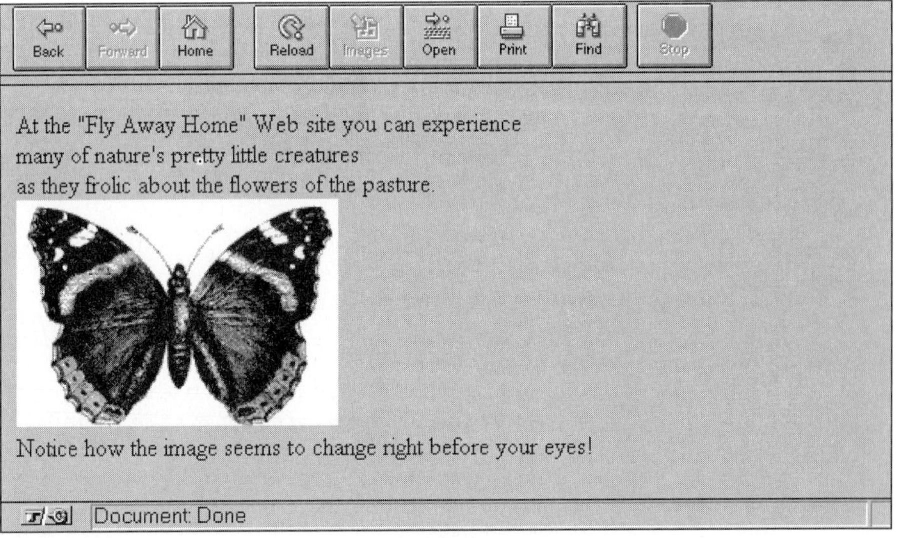

Figure 7.12 The final version of the page, after the SRC attribute has replaced the LOWSRC attribute.

Using the LOWSRC attribute can enhance your page while making it faster for the user to see the information. However, in the preceding example, both images are high-resolution images, so the LOWSRC attribute didn't make the page load faster—but it did provide an interesting effect.

Sizing the Image: HEIGHT and WIDTH

Another way to reduce the download time for the user is to tell the browser exactly how much screen real estate to reserve for the image. The **HEIGHT** and **WIDTH** attributes do this. They eliminate the need for the browser to spend time calculating how much space to allow for the image before it continues downloading and presenting the page.

As was mentioned in the previous section, using the HEIGHT and WIDTH attributes can simplify the way the LOWSRC and SRC images are displayed by making the two appear to be the same size. Since you can control the actual size of the image, using HEIGHT and WIDTH is an easy way to create the appearance of a thumbnail sketch of an image. Be careful with this—even though the image appears small on the screen, the browser must still download the whole image.

Besides creating thumbnail versions of images, you can use this feature to enlarge small images. Usually the larger version doesn't look as good as the original, but if you enlarge it only a small amount, the image quality usually doesn't suffer too much.

Another potential problem with coding image sizes is the effect created when the user has disabled the automatic image download. The browser still reserves space for the images, so the screen is filled with nearly empty frames containing only meaningless picture place-holder icons. The page looks very unfinished and may be of little use. Figure 7.13 shows how such a page would appear. If the Web weaver had not coded the HEIGHT and WIDTH, then the browser would have rendered the page as shown in Figure 7.14.

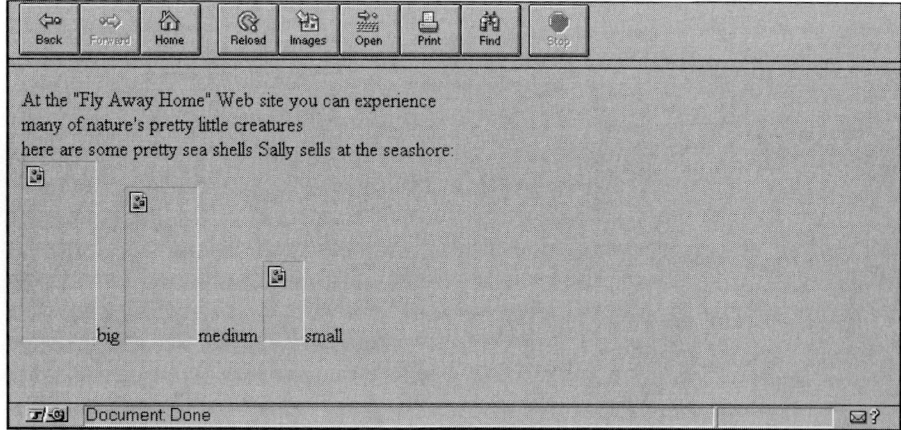

Figure 7.13 Netscape's presentation of images coded with HEIGHT and WIDTH attributes when there is no auto download.

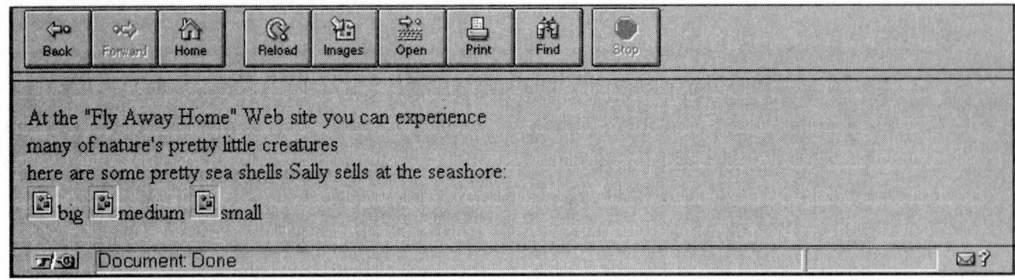

Figure 7.14 Netscape's presentation of the default size of images without HEIGHT and WIDTH attributes set.

Thus, if you don't set the HEIGHT and WIDTH attributes, and the user has the automatic download option turned off, the browser will display small placeholder icons inside the text block instead of creating the messy look of Figure 7.13.

Note that you must code the HEIGHT and WIDTH attributes in pixels. We have discussed earlier why it is not usually a good idea to code anything in pixels, as the number of pixels on your user's screen may differ from the number on your screen. However, in this case you have no choice. There is no other way to code HEIGHT and WIDTH than in pixels. Just remember that there are variations in users' screens, and take this into account as you set the number of pixels. For example, if you build an image that takes up the right third of your screen, and you have a 1024 × 1080 screen, but your user has a 600 × 400 screen, your image will be a lot larger on your user's screen. The difference in size can cause problems in presenting information and maintaining a reasonable screen layout.

It is important to keep the same proportions when you change the size of an image. If you don't retain the ratio of height to width, you can really distort an image. For example, if the WIDTH of the parrot image were decreased without decreasing the HEIGHT proportionally, the image would be distorted as shown in Figure 7.15.

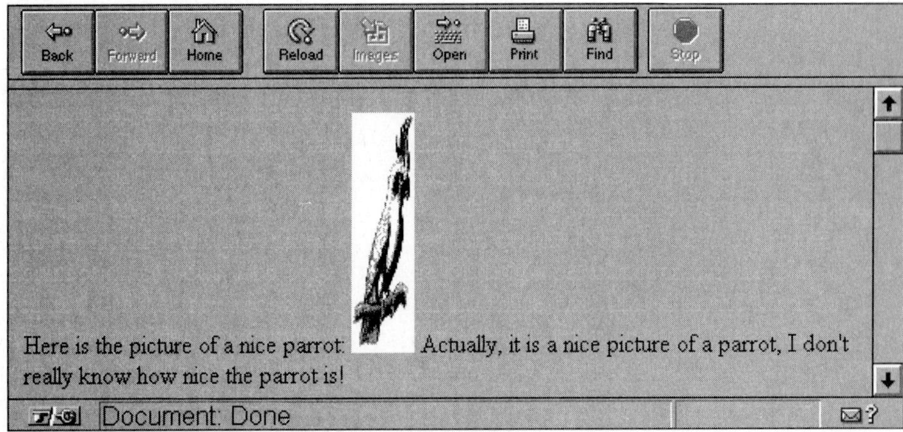

Figure 7.15 Netscape's presentation of an image distorted when the ratio of HEIGHT to WIDTH is changed.

A final trick you can do with images is called **flood filling,** or extreme image expansion. Here you create a large colored area by using the HEIGHT and WIDTH attributes to expand a very small image across the screen. For example, the code in Figure 7.16 creates a large line across the screen. The line is 450 pixels wide and 12 pixels tall. This single-pixel black GIF is used to fill all 5400 points. Figure 7.17 shows how it looks in the browser.

```
<HTML>
<HEAD>
<TITLE> Sneaky Expansion </TITLE>
</HEAD>
<BODY>
The following image is really only one pixel in size, <BR>
but by using HEIGHT and WIDTH, you can make it look like a <BR>
large bar across the screen!<BR>
<IMG SRC="onepixel.jpg" WIDTH=450 HEIGHT=12><BR>
Pretty neat, huh!<BR>
</BODY>
</HTML>
```

Figure 7.16 HTML code to expand a single-pixel GIF file into a line across the screen.

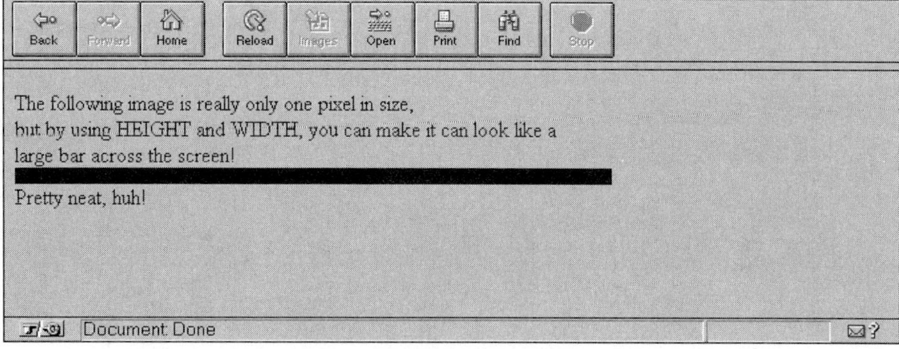

Figure 7.17 Netscape's presentation of the expansion of a single-pixel GIF into a line.

There are a couple of caveats about flood-fill imaging. First, browsers like Mosaic don't use the HEIGHT and WIDTH browser extensions, so in Mosaic all the user would see is a single black pixel. Second, there is always a risk when using absolute pixel counts. If the user has a very high-resolution screen, this line might extend across only a small part of the screen. On the other hand, if the user has a low-resolution screen, the line might extend nearly the width of the whole screen. In either case, the user's browser and hardware will determine how the screen appears.

ALIGN

The browsers don't specify a default alignment across the page for images because images are treated like any other text object. As you have seen, if you insert an image in the middle of a text block, it will simply appear there, with the line of text on either side of it. In most cases the browser will align the bottom of the image with the bottom of the text line, but browsers vary, so a wise Web weaver will always specify where the image is to align if it makes a difference in the presentation of the information.

There are nine different values to control the placement of the image on the page, and within the text line. The three standard **ALIGN** values of TOP, MIDDLE, and BOTTOM, along with their extended values, control how the image lines up with the text line in which it is embedded.

TOP

The ALIGN value of TOP aligns the top of the image with the top of the tallest item in the current text line. If the tallest item is an image, TOP will align its image with the preceding one. If there are no other images in the current line, TOP will align its image with the top of the text. Figure 7.18 gives an example of a top alignment when there are no other images in the current text line.

Figure 7.18 Netscape's presentation of top alignment when there are no other images in the current text line.

MIDDLE

The ALIGN value of MIDDLE aligns the middle of the image with the bottom, or baseline, of the text (not the middle of the text). The **baseline** of the text is the imaginary line that runs across the bottom of the letters, like the point of the v and the bottom of the x, not counting the descenders, like the tail of y or g. Figure 7.19 gives an example of a middle alignment.

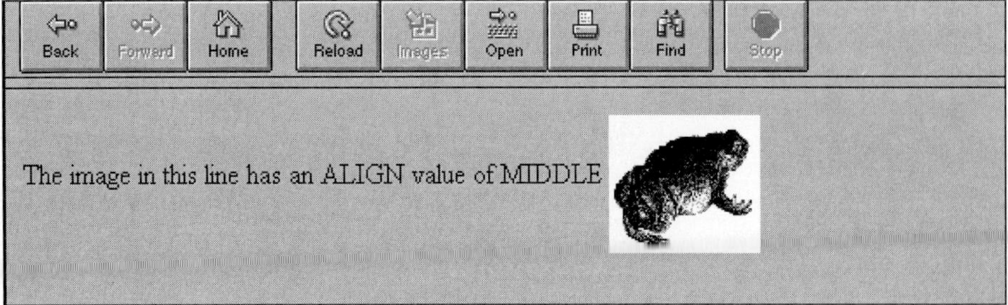

Figure 7.19 Netscape's presentation of middle alignment.

BOTTOM or BASELINE

The ALIGN value of BOTTOM aligns the bottom of the image with the bottom, or baseline, of the text. BOTTOM is usually the default value for Netscape, but the wise Web weaver will not count on a browser default value, but rather will code a value if it is important. This alignment is useful for putting special symbols like dingbats into the text line. The BASELINE value generates exactly the same code as the BOTTOM value. The term was chosen by Netscape because it is more descriptive of the actual functioning of this alignment. Figure 7.20 gives an example of bottom alignment.

Figure 7.20 Netscape's presentation of bottom alignment.

ABSBOTTOM

The ABSBOTTOM (absolute bottom) value of the ALIGN attribute is an extension to the basic value of BOTTOM. It allows the Web weaver to shift the bottom of the image to the true bottom of the text line, as defined by an imaginary line that connects the bottoms of the descenders. In Figure 7.21 you can see that the BOTTOM value aligns the image with the base of the letters—the "v" part of the "y", for example—whereas the ABSBOTTOM value aligns the same image with the bottom of the descenders, as shown by the "y" next to the image.

Figure 7.21 Netscape's presentation of the alignments of BOTTOM and ABSBOTTOM.

TEXTTOP

The TEXTTOP value for the ALIGN attribute is an extension to the basic value of TOP. The difference between TOP and TEXTTOP is obvious in Figure 7.22. The TOP alignment aligns the image with the tallest preceding element anywhere in the line. Here the first toad image, which was aligned MIDDLE, is the tallest text element in the line, so the TOP-aligned image is even with it. In contrast, an alignment value of TEXTTOP does exactly what it says—it aligns the image with the top of the text, not with the tallest element in the current line. The last image here is aligned TEXTTOP, so it ignores the taller elements and aligns with the top of the actual text line.

Figure 7.22 Netscape's presentation of the alignments TOP and TEXTTOP.

ABSMIDDLE

The ABSMIDDLE (absolute middle) value of the ALIGN attribute is an extension to the basic value of MIDDLE. As seen in Figure 7.23, ABSMIDDLE aligns the middle of the image with the *middle* of the text line. As explained earlier, and as shown in the figure, MIDDLE aligns the middle of the image with the *bottom* of the text line. The underlines following each alignment value in the figure provide a consistent visual cue. The middle of the first image is slightly above the underline, and the middle of the second image is lined up with the middle of the text line.

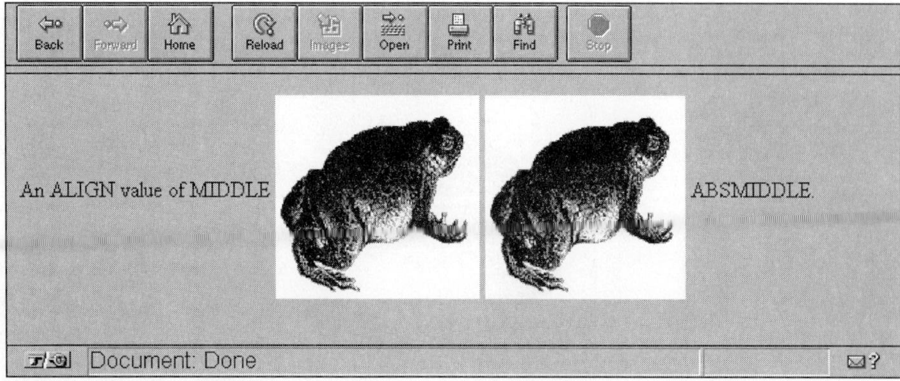

Figure 7.23 Netscape's presentation of the alignments MIDDLE and ABSMIDDLE.

LEFT

In addition to positioning the image vertically in the line, the extended browsers will also recognize codes to place images in either margin. Some Web weavers refer to these as **floating images.** It is often handy to be able to place a larger image in the margin and then flow the text next to the image, rather than imbedding the image in a single line. Figure 7.24 presents the code for a typical line-embedded image with text describing it. Figure 7.25 shows how the browser will render this image. As you can see, the text does lie to the right of the image, but only on the line that contains the image. The "white space" on the right of the image is wasted space.

```
<HTML>
<HEAD>
<TITLE> Floating Images </TITLE>
</HEAD>
<BODY>
<IMG SRC="file:///d|/book1/images/toad1.gif" ALT="Image of a
nice toad used to illustrate floating images." WIDTH=175
HEIGHT=154>
The toad is a very valuable helper in most gardens. They eat
many harmful insects including mosquitos, grubs, ants, and
flies. There are at least 11 species of toad that live in
North America. Almost all toads are nocturnal, so you will
have to wait until late evening or nightfall to see them out
and about. Although they are usually covered with wart-like
bumps, you cannot catch warts from a toad.
</BODY>
</HTML>
```

Figure 7.24 HTML code for an image on the left margin of the page, with no special alignment.

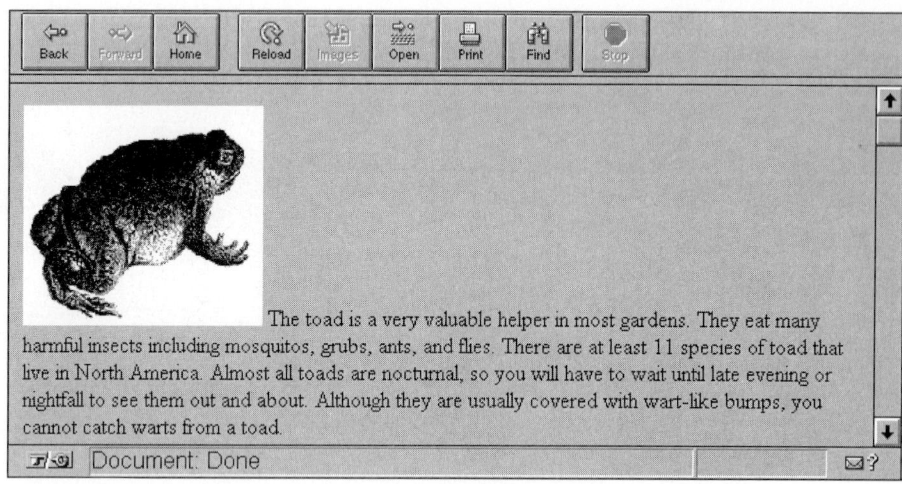

Figure 7.25 Netscape's presentation of an image in the left margin of the page, with no special alignment.

Now Figure 7.26 presents the code to create a floating image that is tied to the left margin. Notice that the only change in the code is the addition of an **ALIGN=LEFT** attribute. See the result in Figure 7.27. By simply adding the ALIGN value, we have changed the whole look of the screen. Now the text flows along the right side of the image, so the information takes up much less space on the page. This is a nice option for images that are folded into the text stream.

```
<HTML>
<HEAD>
<TITLE> Floating Images </TITLE>
</HEAD>
<BODY>
<IMG SRC="file:///d|/book1/images/toad1.gif" ALT="Image of a
nice toad used to illustrate floating images." WIDTH=175
HEIGHT=154  ALIGN=LEFT>
The toad is a very valuable helper in most gardens.  They eat
many harmful insects including mosquitos, grubs, ants, and
flies.  There are at least 11 species of toad that live in
North America.  Almost all toads are nocturnal, so you will
have to wait until late evening or nightfall to see them out
and about.  Although they are usually covered with wart-like
bumps, you cannot catch warts from a toad.
</BODY>
</HTML>
```

Figure 7.26 HTML code for a floating image on the LEFT margin.

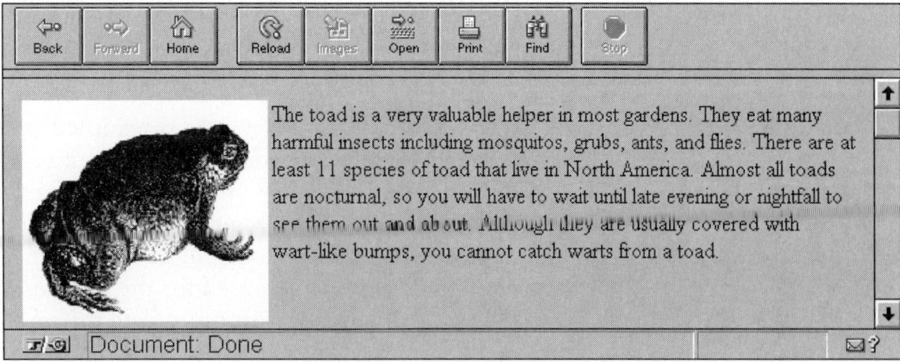

Figure 7.27 Netscape's presentation of an image aligned on the LEFT margin.

RIGHT

The **ALIGN=RIGHT** option works just like the left alignment except that it places the image in the right margin, with the text flowing around its left side. The choice of left or right image placement is determined by the aesthetic taste of the Web weaver. Figure 7.28 shows the same image from Figure 7.27, now located on the right margin.

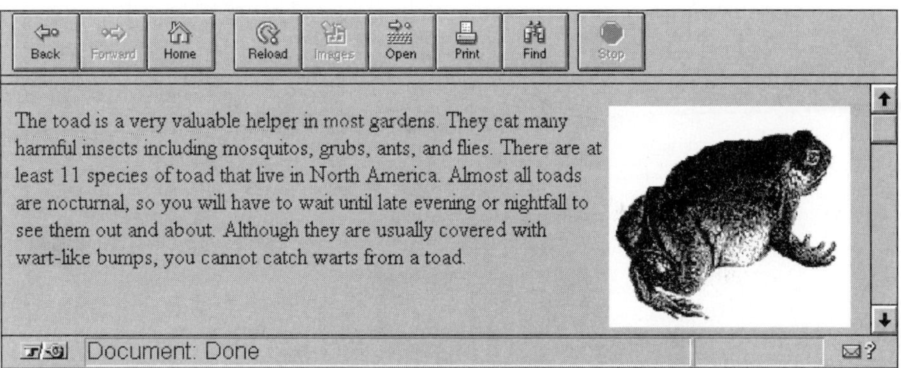

Figure 7.28 Netscape's presentation of an image aligned on the RIGHT margin.

Image placement in the margin is often the best choice for layouts with larger images. However, sometimes it is necessary, especially with small images or icons, to imbed the images inside the line. The use to which the image is put will usually dictate where it should be placed on the page.

CENTER?

Right and left alignments are nice, but what about centering an image? Ideally we should be able to place an image in the center of the screen and flow text on both sides of it. Unfortunately, this option has not yet been created. It no doubt will be in the future, but for now, although there are two ways to get an image centered on the page, the text cannot be made to flow around it. The image will be isolated from the text. Let's look at these two ways of centering an image.

Centering an Image: <CENTER> or <P> with ALIGN=CENTER

One way of centering an image is to place it within a **<CENTER>** container. The image will be separate from the text, but it will be centered on the page. In Figure 7.29 the <CENTER> option is coded for the first image. Notice, in Figure 7.30, how the text is closer to the top and bottom of the first image than to the second. Although the <CENTER> container was used for the first image, a different method was used for the second. When you want more space above and below the image, you can isolate the image in a paragraph container, **<P>,** that has an alignment of **CENTER.** This technique was used to code the second image.

```
<HTML>
<HEAD>
<TITLE> Floating Images </TITLE>
</HEAD>
<BODY>

The toads are  very valuable helpers in most gardens. <BR>
<CENTER>
<IMG SRC="file:///d|/book1/images/toad1.gif" ALT="Image of a
nice toad used to illustrate the use of images." WIDTH=90
HEIGHT=77>
</CENTER>
They eat many harmful insects including mosquitos, grubs,
ants, and flies. There are at least 11 species of toad that
live in North America. <BR>
<P ALIGN=CENTER>
<IMG SRC="file:///d|/book1/images/toad1.gif" ALT="Image of a
nice toad used to illustrate the use of images."
WIDTH=90 HEIGHT=77>
</P>
Almost all toads are nocturnal, so you will have to wait
until late evening or nightfall to see them out and about.
Although they are usually covered with wart-like bumps, you
cannot catch warts from a toad.
</BODY>
</HTML>
```

Figure 7.29 HTML code for two techniques of centering an image.

From the code in Figure 7.29, you can see that the two techniques are easy to use. Notice again how the first image is very close to the text above and below it, whereas the second image is separated from the text by a blank line. While it is not currently possible to imbed an image into a paragraph of text and have the text flow on both sides of the image, these two options for centering an image, along with the two floating options of LEFT and RIGHT, will give the Web weaver sufficient control over the placement of images on a page.

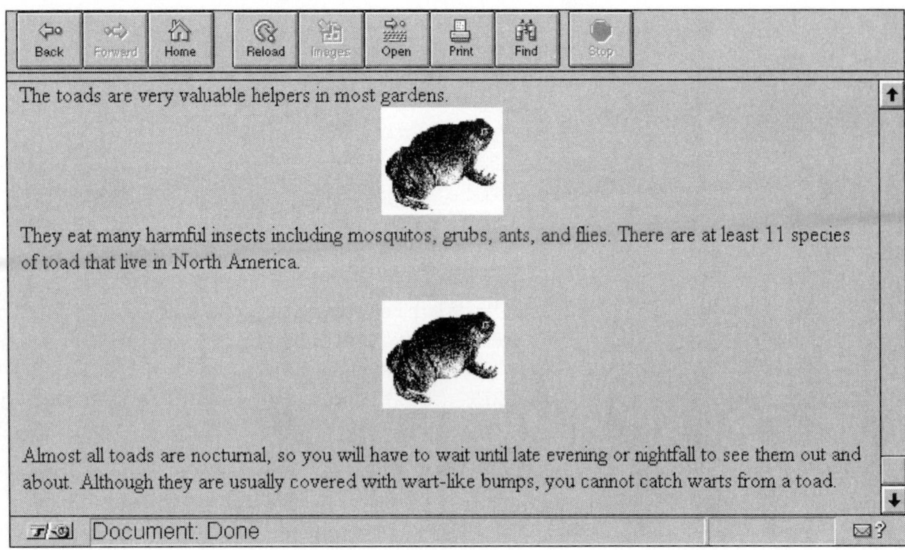

Figure 7.30 Netscape's presentation of two differently centered images.

BORDER and Image Links

Normally a browser will indicate text that is a link by making it a different color and underlining it, as you have seen in previous sections. It has become chic to replace textual links with icons or images. If the image is included within an anchor container, the image becomes a link to the URL specified in the anchor. For example, today it is common to have the link to the home page appear as a little house, and most Web pages have fancy buttons or arrows indicating forward and backward links from the page.

It is easy to fill a page with images, each a link somewhere, but try to resist the mountain-climber mind-set. Don't put images on your page just because they can be there. As we discussed at the beginning of the chapter, each image you place on your page should have a definite purpose. Its purpose should justify the space it is taking up on the page and the time it takes to download.

If an image defines a link, the browsers usually surround the image with a 2-pixel border that is the same color as has been set for link text. The default color is blue for unvisited links and purple for links that have been visited. Some images don't look good when surrounded by a colored border. The **BORDER** attribute on the <IMG> tag controls the width of the border on link-images.

Figure 7.31 presents the code for changing the size of the border on four images. Figure 7.32 shows the rendering of that code by the Netscape browser. Notice that the border can become large enough to be distracting. Also notice the first image. It is actually a link, but there is no border around it to clue the user that it is a link.

```
<HTML>
<HEAD>
<TITLE> Image borders </TITLE>
</HEAD>
<BODY>
The following four images have the border set to 0, 2, 4, and
8 pixels respectively:<BR>
<A HREF="test.html"><IMG SRC="goldfish.gif" ALT="A pretty
little fishie picture" WIDTH=90 HEIGHT=72 BORDER=0></A>
<A HREF="test.html"><IMG SRC="goldfish.gif" ALT="A pretty
little fishie picture" WIDTH=90 HEIGHT=72 BORDER=2></A>
<A HREF="test.html"><IMG SRC="goldfish.gif" ALT="A pretty
little fishie picture" WIDTH=90 HEIGHT=72 BORDER=4></A>
<A HREF="test.html"><IMG SRC="goldfish.gif" ALT="A pretty
little fishie picture" WIDTH=90 HEIGHT=72 BORDER=8></A>
</BODY>
</HTML>
```

Figure 7.31 HTML code showing four different border widths.

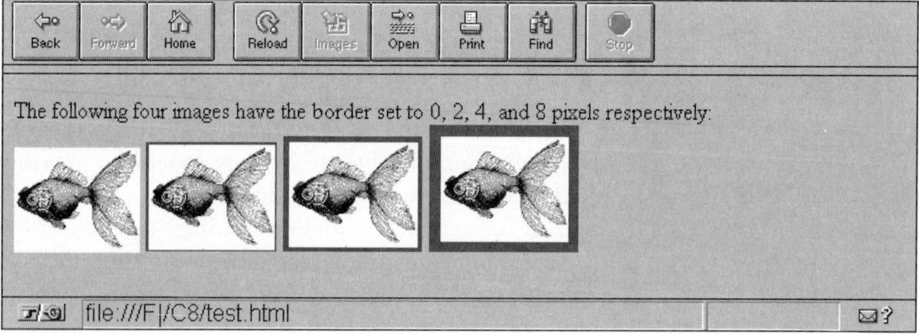

Figure 7.32 Netscape's presentation of four different border widths.

All four of these images are the same size, and they align on the bottom edge, but the border actually controls the vertical placement on the line. The wide border image is much closer to the preceding line than the borderless image is.

As pointed out, a too-large border around an image can be distracting. Figure 7.33 shows another example of how a border can be distracting. Here the border around the image with a transparent background defeats the purpose of the transparent background by defining a rectangle on the screen. Both images in this figure are links. The difference between the two is that the one on the left has the BORDER attribute set to zero.

Figure 7.33 Netscape's presentation of a transparent background image with and without a border.

The image on the left is clearly floating on the background. If you choose to use a borderless image like this as a link, you must tell your user that the image is a link. Without a border, the only way the user can tell that an image is a link is if she happens to pass her pointer over it and notices the way the pointer changes when it passes over the link. Since you can't count on this, in most cases you should tell the user that the image is a link with simple text instructions.

VSPACE and HSPACE

Many Web weavers find that browsers leave too little room between the images and the text. Such close quarters are even more obvious when the image is a link, with a border around it. The browsers that support extensions have two attributes that control the horizontal and vertical space around images: **VSPACE** and **HSPACE**. The code in Figure 7.34 shows how the space around images can be manipulated. The three images in this code have different values for HSPACE and VSPACE. The double line breaks are necessary to push the text line down below the image to provide a consistent look.

```
<HTML>
<HEAD>
<TITLE> Image borders </TITLE>
</HEAD>
<BODY>
The image below has no VSPACE and HSPACE attributes coded.<BR>
<IMG SRC="goldfish.gif" WIDTH=90 HEIGHT=80 ALIGN=left>
Notice how close the text lies to the image. The goldfish has
a long and interesting past as a pet. Ancient Oriental
civilizations kept goldfish in ponds, and valued them for
their color and graceful movements. Modern people find that a
couple of goldfish add a necessary touch of life to an
otherwise dull and drab existence.<BR><BR>
The image below has both VSPACE and HSPACE attributes set to
10.<BR>
<IMG SRC="goldfish.gif" WIDTH=90 HEIGHT=80 ALIGN=left
VSPACE=10 HSPACE=10>
Notice how close the text lies to the image. The goldfish has
a long and interesting past as a pet. Ancient Oriental
civilizations kept goldfish in ponds, and valued them for
their color and graceful movements. Modern people find that a
couple of goldfish add a necessary touch of life to an
otherwise dull and drab existence.<BR><BR>
<BR>
The image below has both VSPACE and HSPACE attributes set to
20.<BR>
<IMG SRC="goldfish.gif" WIDTH=90 HEIGHT=80 ALIGN=left
VSPACE=20 HSPACE=20>
Notice how close the text lies to the image. The goldfish has
a long and interesting past as a pet. Ancient Oriental
civilizations kept goldfish in ponds, and valued them for
their color and graceful movements. Modern people find that a
couple of goldfish add a necessary touch of life to an
otherwise dull and drab existence.<BR>
</BODY>
</HTML>
```

Figure 7.34 HTML code for different VSPACE and HSPACE values.

Figure 7.35 shows how the Netscape browser renders the code. The vertical and horizontal spaces set the image off from the text more and more as the values for VSPACE and HSPACE increase. Since these values are measured in pixels, monitors of different resolutions will either increase the distance between the text and the image or decrease it. The higher the resolution of the monitor, the smaller will be the distance between the image and the text. For that reason, larger values for VSPACE and HSPACE, say over 10 or 12, usually should be avoided.

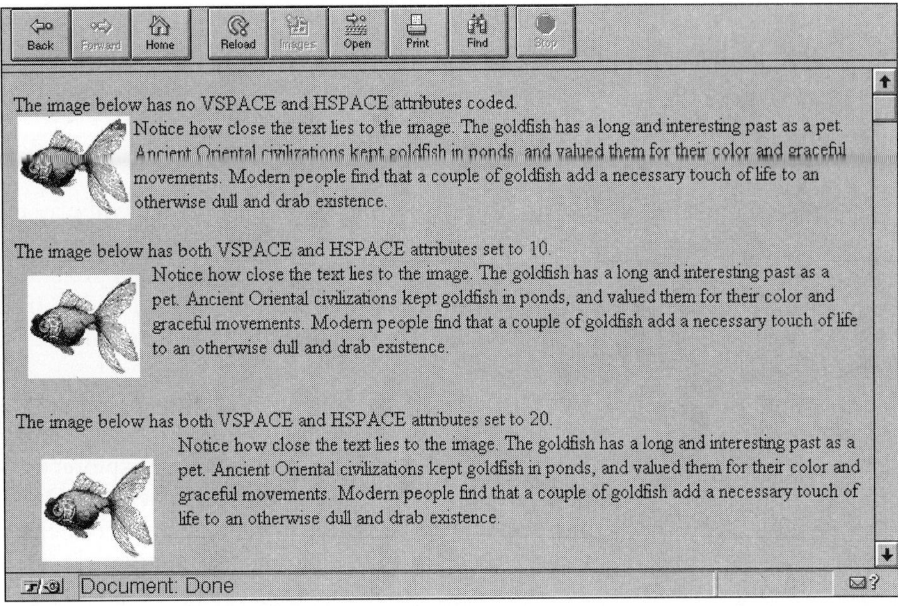

Figure 7.35 Netscape's presentation of different values for the VSPACE and HSPACE attributes.

Special Video Options

Only the Internet Explorer allows the Web weaver to incorporate an inline movie as an image. This set of attributes enables **AVI (Audio Video Interleave)** movies for users who reach the page through the Internet Explorer browser running on a Windows 95 or Windows NT machine. **Java applets**, a special type of small program that serves as an extension to an HTML document, provide better visual and other effects than AVI. Therefore, the use of the Internet Explorer video control extensions is expected to decrease. Many HTML specialists support this prediction because the <IMG> tag is already overloaded with options, and limiting this type of video to just AVI format is very restrictive. The subject is included here for completeness.

Obviously, because a book is a static medium, we can only describe the use of these video attributes, not show how they work. Following are the four attributes used to establish and control a video.

DYNSRC

The **DYNSRC** (dynamic source) attribute identifies the video to be loaded and played by the browser. The value for this attribute is the URL of the movie. It is coded just like the SRC attribute. Since only Internet Explorer can use this option, it is a good idea to also code a SRC attribute in the <IMG> tag. If users are not using Internet Explorer, their browsers will display the still image coded in the SRC attribute rather than having nothing on the page. To code a simple video clip in your document, you could include the following line:

```
<IMG DYNSRC="movies/video.avi" SRC="pics/vidstill.gif">
```

If the user is running Internet Explorer, the video will start as soon as the page is downloaded. With any other graphical browser the user will see the still image.

CONTROLS

Normally the Internet Explorer browser will play the selected video one time, as soon as the page is downloaded. However, there are options to vary this behavior. The **CONTROLS** attribute will present a VCR-like control panel that allows the user to control playing the video. If there is an audio track, CONTROLS also provides a volume control.

LOOP

Without special attributes, the Internet Explorer browser plays the video once, as soon as the page is loaded. If you code the **LOOP** attribute and give it an integer value, the browser will play the video the number of times you specify. For example, the following code would play the video five times:

```
<IMG DYNSRC="movies/video.avi" SRC="pics/vidstill.gif" LOOP=5>
```

When you want the video to repeat continuously, the value INFINITE can be assigned to LOOP. Be careful, though. If you forget to code the CONTROL attribute, the only way the user can stop the video is to exit from the page.

START

When the browser finishes loading a page with a video, it plays the video. Sometimes the Web weaver wants to delay playing the video until the user asks for it. Or the Web weaver may want the video to play when the page is first loaded, and then again when the user moves the mouse over the video window or view port. There are two possible values for the **START** attribute: FILEOPEN and MOUSEOVER. The default value is FILEOPEN. If START has a value of MOUSEOVER, then the video will play when the user moves the mouse over the video window or view port. If the video is to be played both times, then the START attribute can be assigned the value "FILEOPEN, MOUSEOVER". Notice that the two values are separated by a comma and enclosed in quotation marks.

According to several HTML pundits, this type of video is not an up-and-coming technology. Usually it is wise to use only features that are supported by the "big two" graphical browsers. Java applets may well be the next dynamic image tool, and it won't add to the burden on the <IMG> tag.

Image Maps

It is easy to create a set of individual images that are links, but some applications call for more sophisticated imagery that will enable the image to react to the position of the mouse *within* the image. In that way, different parts of one image can represent several different links. For example, some home pages provide an

image map of an area—either a state, city, or building—and allow the user to click on different parts of the image to retrieve information. Another nice image is a bookshelf, with each book representing a different HTML document that the user can click on to view.

Although image maps are a nice feature, they require a significant amount of labor to set up and code. Before we look at building an image map, we need to examine the two different image-mapping scenarios. One requires the server to intervene; the other is complete on the client side.

Server-Side Mapping

The original image-mapping scheme required the client (browser) to capture the position of the mouse when the left mouse button was clicked and then send those coordinates back to the server for processing. This is called **server-side mapping** because the server controls the map of the image and decides what the browser (client) is supposed to do. There are several disadvantages to server-side map processing.

- **Increased Net traffic.** Each time the user clicks on any part of a server-side image map, the browser must send the coordinates of the mouse to the server. This process increases the traffic on the Net, because the browser doesn't know if the coordinates selected will map to an actual URL or not, and each mouse click causes another transaction over the Net.
- **Confusion for the user.** Normally when the user moves the mouse pointer over a link, the URL is displayed on the screen. In a server-side model, the browser has no idea what URL, if any, is associated with any part of the image. Therefore, the browser displays either the URL of the image-map program or the X and Y coordinates of the mouse location. Neither are very helpful for the user.
- **Much slower response for the user.** In a server-side model, each response for the user must be generated by the server. That means that the browser has to send a signal to the server requesting that the server process the information about a mouse click. Then the client has to wait until the server returns the information before it can continue processing. If there is much congestion on the Net, that response can take significant time to reach the client. The user has to wait for the request from the client to reach the server, then for the server to process the request and reply to the client.
- **Local testing is impossible.** To test a server-side image map, the Web server must run a special image-mapping program and process the X and Y coordinates sent from the client. This means that it is impossible to test the functionality of an image map without being connected to a Web server. This is a big hindrance for many Web weavers who work "off-line" at home or in the office.
- **There are several different server-side mapping packages.** If the Web weaver chooses to use server-side image mapping, he must decide which type of image mapping software is run on his server. Two of the most common are the W3C (CERN) httpd server and the NCSA (National Center for Supercomputing Applications) httpd server. Each requires different, incompatible coding from the browser. An image map that works on one server may fail on another if the server-side mapping packages are different.

• **Often a system administrator must set up the server code.** Although it is possible in some circumstances for the Web weaver to also maintain the Web server, in most cases the Web weaver doesn't control the server. That means that the software necessary to receive, process, and reply to the image must be written and loaded on the server. The system administrator usually is in charge of those aspects of the server.

For all these reasons, server-side image mapping is falling from favor in the Net community. Client-side image mapping poses none of these problems. Following historical order, we will first consider the processes necessary to establish and use the older server-side images, then we will examine the more recent—and more favored—client-side image process.

Server-Side Image; Client Duties: ISMAP

The **ISMAP** attribute tells the browser that the image included in the <IMG> tag is a server-side image map. The browser must send the coordinates of any mouse click within that area to the server address specified in the anchor tag that also contains the image.

For example, the following code would present the image called navtool.gif to the user, record where in the image the user clicked the left mouse button, and then send those data to the server. The server would then use navtool.map to determine what the user wanted to do. Sounds complicated, doesn't it? But for its time it gave the Web weaver a really powerful tool to create dynamic images. Here is the code necessary to establish the server-side image map in this example:

```
<A HREF="/cgi-bin/image-maps/navtool.map">
<IMG ISMAP SRC="images/navtool.gif">
```

This code tells the client that when the user clicks the left mouse button inside the area described by the "navtool.gif" image, the mouse coordinates will be sent to the server hosting that page. Here is an example of what the client would send:

```
/cgi-bin/image-maps/navtool.map?24,61
```

This code tells the server to run its image-map processing software using the map called navtool.map and return the link address, if there is one, associated with a point 61 pixels down and 24 pixels to the right of the top left corner of the image. The top left corner of the image has coordinates of 0,0. Once the data are passed to the server, the client waits for the address of the selected document.

Server-Side Image; Server Duties

When the server gets the request from the client, it must first start the image-map software, then consult a file called an "image map." This filename ends in **.map.** It lists the URL of each link that any location in the image is mapped to.

Figure 7.36 shows a simple navigational tool for a document. It has three mapable areas, the Hither arrow, the Yon arrow, and anything outside the two arrows but still within the image boundaries. This image was created with Microsoft's Paintbrush program. It is a simple GIF file. All sorts of images can be used as image maps, but most of the time simple images with easily definable areas are best.

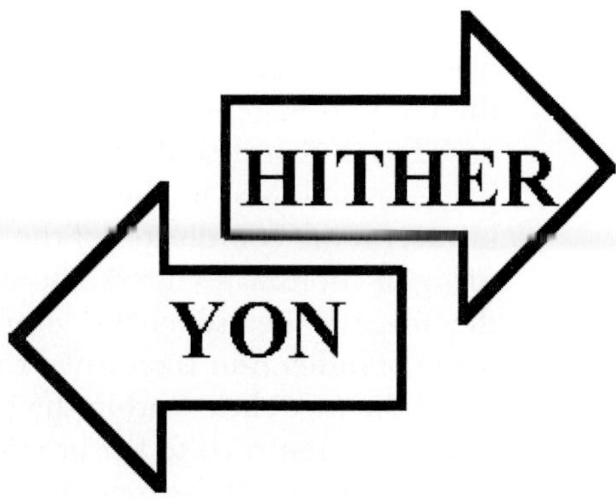

Figure 7.36 A simple, mapable image.

In the parlance of image mapping, areas that can be selected and have an associated HTML document are called **hot spots.** In the case of the image in Figure 7.36, both arrows are hot spots, as is the background. Complex pictures, like a work of art, can be used as image maps, but they are difficult for the user to understand because usually they don't have clearly delineated areas. It is best to use simple images with easily defined areas.

Figure 7.37 shows how the image from Figure 7.36 would look as an image map on a page. If the user moves her cursor anywhere in this image and clicks the mouse, the browser will send the coordinates of the mouse click to the server. The server needs to have an image-map file to decide which HTML document to display for the user.

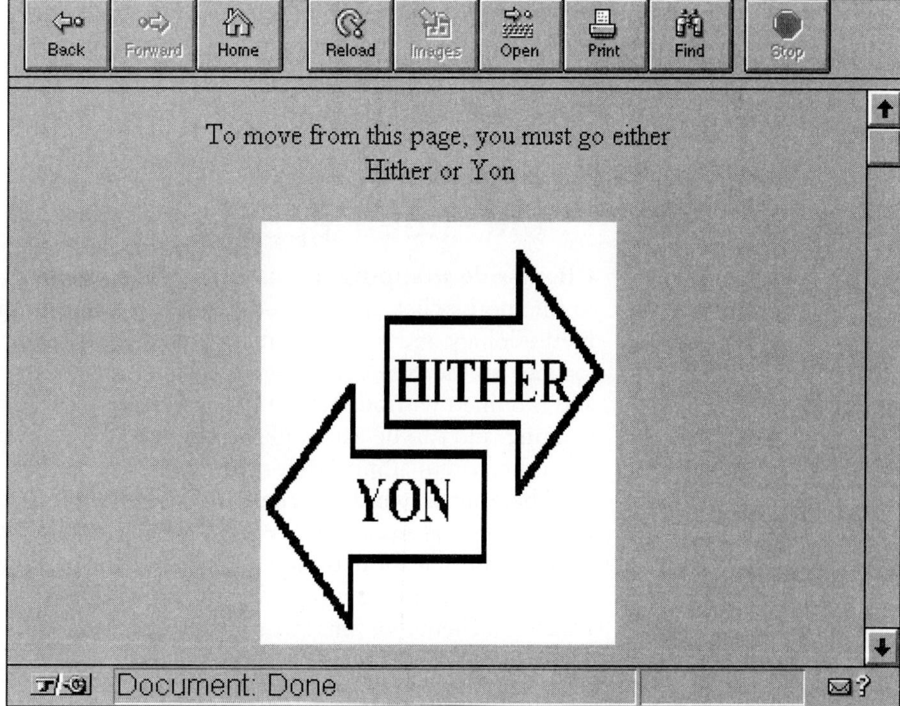

Figure 7.37 Netscape's presentation of a simple image map.

Figure 7.38 presents an image-map file built for the NCSA type of image-mapping software. The layout of the image-map file is the shape of the hot spot, the URL to be returned if the mouse click is within that hot spot, and the coordinates that describe the outline of the hot spot. In this case, there are two polygons, followed by the name of the HTML file to be sent back to the browser if the coordinates of the mouse click are within the area defined by the string of coordinates listed. Those coordinates are the corners of the arrows in the image. If the user clicks within the borders of the HITHER arrow, the file name of hither.htm is returned to the browser, and the browser then loads that file. If the user clicks within the borders of the YON arrow, the filename of Yon.htm is returned to the browser. There is a third region described, the default hot spot. If the user clicks somewhere on the image but outside either of the arrows, the filename of missed.htm is returned to the browser. Although coding a default hot spot is not required, most Web weavers recommend doing so to help the user understand how to use the image.

```
poly hither.htm 87,48 181,46 181,16 238,73 183,130 179,97
86,97 86,46
poly Yon.htm 155,114 62,114 62,83 7,137 61,193 61,164 157,163
155,113
default missed.htm
```

Figure 7.38 An NCSA type of server image map.

Software packages like the Mapedit package by Boutell.Com Inc. make it relatively painless to create the map file. Mapedit will create a map file for either the CERN or NCSA server-side programs, or even a client-side map. The most difficult part of creating a server-side image map is coordinating the software and the files necessary to enable the server to process the image data when they are sent from the browser. Usually this involves working with the system administrator at the server site.

Client-Side Mapping

Client-side mapping means that the client does all the work, and the reaction to the mouse click is processed locally, by the browser. This is a newer methodology, and it is preferred by most Web weavers because it decreases loading on the Net, generally allows faster response to the user, can be tested and modified without having a connection to the server already up and running, and can be accomplished by the Web weaver with no outside help from the system administrator.

The only drawback to client-side mapping is that it is supported only by the newer browsers like Netscape 2.0. But with most of the industry moving to new browsers as soon as they are released, this is a small price to pay for all the benefits that client-side mapping provides. The only time-consuming task when creating a client-side image map is creating the actual hot spots. Software like

Mapedit make the creation of client-side maps very simple. Refer again to Figure 7.37, the Web page with our Hither and Yon image. Now let's look at what must be added to our simple page to make the image a client-side image map.

USEMAP

Rather than the ISMAP attribute, which tells the browser to use a server-side map, we code the **USEMAP** attribute to specify a client-side image map. This attribute is assigned the name of the URL that contains the actual mapping information, the <MAP> container and the <AREA> tags inside the <MAP>. Usually this URL is within the current HTML document, so the URL is simply the internal target name preceded by an octothorp (#).

In Figure 7.39 our MAP tag is located at the target name "arrow" in the HTML code for the client-side version of the page in Figure 7.37. Notice that all the code necessary to process the image map is contained within this page. When the user clicks anywhere on the image, the browser doesn't have to send information across the Net and then wait for another computer to respond. If the user clicks within the boundaries defined by the first polygon, the hither.htm document is displayed. If the user clicks inside the area defined by the second polygon, the Yon.htm document is displayed. If the user clicks anywhere within the rectangle of the image that has not been defined by either of the two preceding polygons, the missed.htm document is displayed.

```
<HTML>
<HEAD>
<TITLE> Demo Image Map </TITLE>
</HEAD>
<BODY>
<P ALIGN=CENTER>
To move from this page, you must go either<BR>
Hither or Yon<BR><BR>
<IMG SRC="arrow.gif" WIDTH="200" HEIGHT="230" usemap="#arrow"
BORDER=0></P>
</P>
<map name="arrow">
<area shape="polygon"    coords="87,49,181,46,181,17,239,74,
       182,131,179,100,86,99,86,47, "
       href="hither.htm">
<area shape="polygon"
       coords="154,113,155,162,62,162,60,195,5,139,62,82,62,
       113,153,112, "
       href="Yon.htm">
<area shape="rect" href="missed.htm" coords="0,0,251,204">
</map>
</BODY>
</HTML>
```

Figure 7.39 HTML code showing client-side mapping and map data.

Notice that the third hot spot is a rectangle that encloses every point in the whole image. This shows that we can define an area more than once, and the first mapping will take precedence. There are two new tags shown in Figure 7.39. Let's look at them.

<MAP>

The **<MAP>** container encloses all the HTML code to define a client-side image map. There is one required attribute, **NAME**, that defines the name for that container. The browser uses the NAME value to associate a particular set of mapping instructions with an image. The value of the NAME attribute must be the same as the value of the USEMAP attribute in the <IMG> tag. Of course, the leading octothorp (#) in the USEMAP attribute value signifies that the name is local to the document. This octothorp would be omitted from the NAME attribute of the <MAP> container.

In addition to the NAME attribute, the <MAP> container holds a set of <AREA> tags, one for each hot spot in the image.

<AREA>

The real work of a client-side image is described by the **<AREA>** tag. This empty tag defines each mouse-sensitive region in the document and tells the browser what to do if the user clicks on them. When the user moves the mouse pointer over any area that has been defined by an <AREA> tag, the pointer changes to a pointing finger, and the browser displays the URL of the related link at the bottom of the screen. There are four attributes to this tag, as follows.

SHAPE

The **SHAPE** attribute works with the COORDS attribute (discussed next) to define the hot spots on the page. SHAPE tells the browser how to process the coordinates. It also describes the general shape of the hot spot. There are three valid shapes: circle, rectangle, and polygon.

COORDS

The **COORDS** attribute is required. It describes the boundaries of the hot spot being described. Each entry in this list is an X,Y coordinate pair. All coordinates are measured in pixels. COORDS can be the vertices of polygons, or the X and Y coordinates of the center of a circle and the radius of the circle. Following are the three types of shapes with the required COORDS information for each:

- **Circle**—requires the X and Y coordinates of the center of the circle and of the radius.
- **Polygon**—requires the X and Y coordinates for each vertex or corner. As you can see from Figure 7.39, there can be several pairs.
- **Rectangle**—requires two sets of coordinates. The first is the X and Y coordinates for the top left corner, and the second is the X and Y coordinates for the lower right corner of the rectangle. The rectangle is a specialized form of polygon. You need specify only two points to define it.

HREF

Each <AREA> must have an associated **HREF** or have the NOHREF attribute (discussed next) coded. Usually the HREF attribute describes the URL of the HTML document to be displayed if the user clicks within the defined area of that <AREA>. We will discuss how to create links across the Internet in a later chapter. If you are using the identified area to link to a local HTML document, or to target within the existing document, simply code the URL of the document as the value for this attribute.

NOHREF

Each <AREA> must have either the HREF or the NOHREF attribute coded. The **NOHREF** attribute defines an area that the user can click on but that contains no link. Thus, the user can click on the hot spot described by the <AREA>, but nothing will happen. There are only two reasons for using this attribute. If you are building a large image map and want to define all the areas in the beginning but don't have URLs created for some of the hot spots, you could bring up the page and fill in the HREFs later. The other reason for using this attribute would be if you want to annoy your users. This attribute creates hot spots that the user can click with no response. That could be very frustrating.

Making It Easy

It is fairly simple to use a software package like Mapedit by Boutell.Com, Inc., that is designed to create the <MAP> container for you. It is a WYSIWYG package that takes as input an HTML file that has the image(s) to be mapped already coded in one or more <IMG> tags. The software asks which image you wish to map. It then displays that image. You simply outline each region you want to be a hot spot. The software next prompts you for the URL to be associated with that hot spot, and it creates the <MAP> container for you, right in the HTML document specified.

If you don't have access to a mapping program, then you can usually use a drawing package to determine the required points of reference on any figure. Most drawing packages provide the option of having all the corners and points labeled with their X and Y coordinates. In that case you will need to record those coordinates and create your own <MAP> container.

Other Considerations

Not all browsers support client-side images, and not all browsers even support image mapping. To make your pages as friendly as possible for the whole range of potential users, you could include your image map within an anchor tag. That way if the user cannot use image maps, she would at least have the option of linking to a page that provides her with more useful options.

Figure 7.40 presents the code from Figure 7.39, modified to make it more widely accessible. If the user doesn't have a browser that supports client-side image mapping, he can click anywhere on the image and see the document called choices.htm, which should contain a set of links to all of the documents available from the image map. Hence, a majority of users will be able to access the information from the page.

```
<HTML>
<HEAD>
<TITLE> Demo Image Map </TITLE>
</HEAD>
<BODY>
<P ALIGN=CENTER>
To move from this page, you must go either<BR>
Hither or Yon<BR><BR>
<A HREF="choices.htm" >
<IMG SRC="arrow.gif" WIDTH="200" HEIGHT="230" usemap="#arrow"
BORDER=0>
</P>
</A>
<map name="arrow">
<area shape="polygon" coords="87,49,181,46,181,17,239,74,182,
131,179,100,86,99,86,47" href="hither.htm">
<area shape="polygon" coords="154,113,155,162,62,162,60,195,
5,139,62,82,62,113,153,112"href="Yon.htm">
<area shape="rect" href="missed.htm" coords="0,0,251,204">
</map>
</BODY>
</HTML>
```

Figure 7.40 HTML code showing client-side mapping with the map enclosed in an anchor.

There is another important consideration if you choose to build a graphics-dependent page using image maps. You should build a parallel page that is designed for the text-only browser. Most major sites—and all conscientious Web weavers—allow the user the choice of seeing a graphical rendering or a text-only page right from the home page. This is a technique that will win you the gratitude of the text-only users on the Net.

Using inline images or an image map is also a great way to provide simple navigation tools for your user. A set of images that are links provides a consistent, reliable way to allow your user to move forward, backward, or back to the home page for your Web site. Remember to always create a set of text links to perform the same tasks so the nongraphical users can navigate easily too.

Exercises

Putting together some of our previous labs and adding pictures makes a really dynamic page. We will start small and work up to some fancy pages.

7.1. Go get some images. Surf the Web and find at least five nice, small (1–3 K) images, GIFs that are in the public domain and therefore available. Make sure at least one is transparent. Download them to your diskette. Copy them (ftp) to your /GIF subdirectory on your server or PC.

7.2. Create a page with one of the images you have harvested. Put text on the page explaining where you found the image. Create a link to the site where the image was found so that your user can go harvest other images from that site. Demonstrate how the image can be placed by itself with no text around it, and how it can be aligned with text on either the right or left. Can the image be imbedded directly in the text? Demonstrate.

7.3. Create another page. Put an image in the center of the line, with text below it. Make sure you have an ALT description that does the image justice. Turn off auto-loading of images on your browser, or use a text-only browser to verify that your ALT description works. *All* your images should have good ALT descriptions!

7.4. On the same page as Exercise 7.3, create an image pair with one image as a LOWSRC. Notice how the pseudo-animation works. If you can, find a pair of images designed to be used this way and demonstrate them with <BR>.

7.5. On a new page, create a text block that explains the use of the image-size attributes (HEIGHT and WIDTH). Play with these attributes, explaining what you are doing. Make one image very tall and thin and one very wide low. Also create a thumbnail image. Does it shorten the download time if you size the image smaller than normal?

7.6. Create a set of images on the same page that demonstrate each of the possible alignments (TOP, MIDDLE, BOTTOM, ABSBOTTOM, TEXTTOP, ABSMIDDLE, LEFT, RIGHT). Make sure the text present allows you to demonstrate the alignments correctly.

7.7. Create a new page that contains different images that are links back to the previous pages in this lab. Use different borders on the images, from a wide border of 10 pixels to a border of zero. Also include a couple of links from transparent images. Notice how the border defeats the purpose of the transparent link! Explain how your user will know the image is a link if there is no border.

7.8. Create a nice table with at least five images. Make them all the same size, and provide descriptions of the images. For extra credit, have each image act as a thumbnail. When the user clicks on the image, send him to a page that contains the full-sized version of the image.

CHAPTER eight

MULTIMEDIA

Multimedia—the use of sound, video, and other special effects—is currently the "rage" on the Web. That has an unfortunate effect on the load on the Net. Multimedia files are BIG! They download slowly because of the great amount of information that must be transferred. To give you some idea, consider sound files on the Net. The most common are the WAVE files, discussed under "RIFF WAVE" in this chapter. These files require about 10 *megabytes* of storage for each *minute* of sound. Ten million bytes of storage per minute! So a sound is worth a whole lot of words—660 times more words than a picture. Considering the expense of multimedia files in terms of download time and Net traffic, they have to be of great significance before you can justify using them. Let's look at the different types of media that comprise the HTML multimedia suite.

What Is Multimedia?

According to the 1990 edition of *The New Lexicon Webster's Dictionary of the English Language,* multimedia refers to "a means of communication involving several media, e.g., film and sculpture, print matter, and voices." That's not quite the definition we use when talking about multimedia on the Net. Rather, we take the spirit of the *Webster*'s definition and add what could be called a multisensory aspect. When Web weavers speak of multimedia they are usually referring to sounds, video, animation, or other elements of a page besides static images and text. We will examine each of these different features in this chapter.

Considerations When Using Multimedia

As noted, multimedia is very expensive in terms of time to download and the amount of data transferred across the Net. The first consideration, then, in using multimedia is the delay it imposes on your page's users—and on all the other Net users, because multimedia data will replace other data as they traverse the Net. Thus, you should have a compelling reason to include multimedia objects on a Web page. Just to be cute, just because it can be done, just for the "oh wow" value—none of these are good reasons to include large multimedia files.

If your site discusses birds of a particular region and then includes the song of each bird, good information is conveyed. On the other hand, if you include bird calls simply because they are fun, not because they are related to any information on the page, they are of little value to the users. The first question the Web weaver must answer about multimedia is, will the user gain enough information from the multimedia object to justify the wait and increased load on the Net?

We have already examined a second consideration when we discussed adding images to Web pages. Like images, multimedia objects are not available to all users of a site. Unlike images, most multimedia objects require the user to have additional hardware, some sort of sound card, and speakers. Besides the sound card, the user must have loaded and configured an additional software package, called a **plug-in,** to display the multimedia object. If the user hasn't installed the plug-in, or if her browser doesn't support such a plug-in, the information available in the multimedia object is lost to her. If the multimedia object contains essential information, or information that is only available in that format, then those data on the page are not available to the widest audience. Since the purpose of placing a page on the Net is to provide information, heavy reliance on multimedia can reduce the effectiveness of your page.

Pictures are, of course, multimedia objects, but they were discussed in detail in Chapter 7, so in this chapter we will discuss the other common types of multimedia objects: sounds, animated GIFs, and video.

Adding Sound

Next to images, sound is the most common type of multimedia data added to Web pages. The sound you normally hear is a continuous series of different tones and noises. A continuous series of the normal sounds is called an **analog**

series because the values flow from one to another continuously. Computers don't handle analog data well; they want their data in a **digital format.** Digital data is **discrete,** meaning the values are represented by numbers, not by a continuous stream. To convert analog sound to a digital format, it must be captured and encoded as a number. The more samples taken, the better the sound reproduction, but also the bigger the file that contains the sound will be. By the same token, the larger the space used to encode the sound value, the more exactly that number will represent the true sound.

Usually sound files are recorded at sampling rates of either 11 kHz, 22 kHz, or 44 kHz. A **kilohertz (kHz)** is roughly a thousand samples per second. The more samplings per second, the better the sound quality will be. Sound can also be stored as either an 8-bit or 16-bit number. A 16-bit sound file will be much more accurate than an 8-bit sound file.

There is a price we have to pay for quality, however, and that is in size. An 8-bit, 8 kHz sample is about the quality of a standard telephone—not very good for audio on a Web page. A 16-bit, 44 kHz sample is nearly the audio quality of a compact disk (CD) player. A minute of 8-bit, 8 kHz sound takes about a meg and a half (1½ megabytes) of file space. A minute of 16-bit, 44 kHz sound takes 10 megabytes. If you want to add stereo, you have to double these numbers! Before we examine how to add sound, it is important to look at the different types of sound files available.

Types of Sound Files

Audio files can be found in several different formats. Usually each different format requires a different player, or plug-in, so it is a good idea to limit the format of the sound files on your page to one of the more common types. That way the user needs only one plug-in to play all of the sounds you present.

Software packages exist that can convert one type or format of sound file to another. For example, a program called SOX, for PC-compatible machines and UNIX boxes (written by Lance Norskog), can convert between most of the common formats and do some simple processing like filtering as well. WAVany, also a PC package (written by Bill Neisius) can also convert most formats to the WAV format. SoundApp (written by Norman Franke) is a similar program for the Macintosh. These products or others like them are often available for downloading from the Internet.

µ-law (mu-law)

The most widely supported, most commonly used type of sound file on the Net is the **µ-law** file. Originally developed for the UNIX operating system, it uses a 2:1 compression ratio and is an international standard for compressing voice-quality audio. These files are supported by almost all operating systems. They usually end in the extension **.au.** This type of file supports only **monaural** (single-channel) sound, not stereo (multiple-channel) sound. There is a library of sounds in .au format located at **http://sunsite.unc.edu/pub/multimedia/sun-sounds/.**

RIFF WAVE

Resource Interchange File Format Waveform Audio Format (RIFF WAVE), or **WAVE,** is a proprietary format sponsored jointly by Microsoft and IBM. It is the audio file format most commonly used on Microsoft Windows products. This audio format is also supported by most operating systems. The RIFF WAVE file usually has a file extension of **.wav.**

Normally this sound format takes about 10 megabytes of file data to produce a single minute of audio. It is an uncompressed format, so a given WAVE sound file is roughly twice the size of the same sound encoded in μ-law format. There are other encoding methods, for example using 8 bits rather than 16 bits to store the sounds, that can be employed in WAVE files to reduce the amount of storage required. But these methods degrade the quality of the sound. The RIFF WAVE format can support both monaural (single-channel) and stereo (multichannel) audio. There is a large collection of sounds in this format at **http://sunsite.unc.edu/pub/multimedia/pc-sounds/.**

AIFF and AIFC

Audio Interchange File Format (AIFF) is used to store high-end audio data. It is uncompressed and takes about the same amount of space as WAVE files, 10 megabytes per minute of audio. This recording format can support both monaural and stereo recordings. It was developed by Apple and is most often used by Macintosh and Silicon Graphics software. Because it takes so much space to store audio data in AIFF, Apple developed AIFF-C, better known as **AIFC** for **AIFF Compressed Format.** This compression algorithm can compress sounds up to 6:1, but it is a lossy form of compression. **Lossy** means that some of the data are discarded or lost during compression. As in the JPEG image compression, some of the data bits are removed from the sound file as it is compressed in the AIFC format. The result is a deterioration of the sound. Nevertheless, usually the reduction in quality is not sufficient to outweigh the saving of space.

MPEG Audio

The International Standard Organization's **Moving Picture Experts Group (MPEG)** has defined a standard for audio, but it is usually used with video. This format has the best compression algorithms. They can compress to a ratio of 4:1 with almost no loss of signal quality. MPEG-compressed audio is the best format for distributing high-quality sound files online. MPEG files are usually designated with an extension of **.mp2.** Since MPEG is also used to store, transmit, and display video, make sure the files you collect are just audio files, not small videos.

Other Formats

Many other formats can be used to move sound files across the Internet; however, the ones just discussed are by far the most common. One of the other formats is Creative Voice (**.voc**) files, used by Creative Lab's Sound Blaster audio cards. Another format, used by Sun/NeXT computers, usually with an extension of **.snd,** is far less common than the other types of sound files although it does show up occasionally.

Which Format to Use?

With all these choices, which format should the wise Web weaver choose? Sometimes the choice is made for you. If you find a sound you like, and it is in one of the common formats or it is in a format your browser has a plug-in for, you will be tempted to simply use that format. Usually this is a fine strategy. Problems result only if your user doesn't have the same software you chose to use.

Most Web weavers will agree that **.au** and **.wav** are the two most useful types of sound files. If you keep all your sounds in one of these two formats, you can be assured that the vast majority of the graphical browsers will have plug-ins able to use them. Remember to do your best to limit all the sounds to a single format on a Web site. That reduces the work the browser has to do, and could speed up your user's work as well.

Regardless of the format, you should describe the sounds you have included so your user will know what he is downloading. It would be a shame to have a user spend several minutes downloading a sound file in a format he cannot listen to. Also, as we discussed when talking about large images, you should give your user an idea about the size of the file. That way he can decide if he wants to spend the time necessary to download it.

If you have audio processing and editing software available, you may consider creating a very short sound bite that can serve as a lead-in to the larger sound file you have available for download. Then the user can download the smaller sound byte first and, based on that, decide if she wants to spend the time necessary to download the actual, large file. It is also common courtesy to use a special, easily recognizable icon to indicate sound files. Politeness is always in fashion, and describing the file a user can download in terms of content, format, and size is indeed polite.

Ethical Questions

It is very easy to collect sound files from sites all across the Net. All you need to do is look at the URL of the sound site and ftp the sound to your own computer. In addition, many people have built pages that contain a large number of links to sound files that enable you to quickly download the sounds. But sounds can be copyrighted, just like images, so before you download sounds to use on your page, make sure they are free, or get permission from the owner of the sound you wish to use.

Be careful, because the fact that a sound appears on XYZ page does not necessarily mean that the owner of XYZ page has the authority to give you permission to use it. For example, if you were to go to the "Sounds-Do-Be-Do-Us" Web page, and download a 3-minute cut of a Beatles song with the permission of the Web weaver of that page, you could well be in violation of the copyright on the song. You probably need to obtain permission from the Beatles themselves!

Show tunes, theme songs, and popular music are all available on the Web, but most of them are copyrighted works, and you can get into trouble for using them without permission. Another common mistake Web weavers make is downloading and using short audio snippets from television-program dialog. These, too, are usually copyrighted works.

If you are going to use sound that you have not created yourself, make sure that the sounds you use are in the **public domain,** meaning you can use them without permission. If they are not in the public domain, you will need to obtain permission for their use from the copyright holder, who may or may not be the Web weaver of the site where you find the sounds.

Adding Video

Digital video is another new tool that is being incorporated into some Web sites to add interest and provide an additional medium for transferring information. As we saw in the previous section, adding audio to a Web page increases the download time because audio objects are large compared with text or even pictures. Video files are a collection of images plus, usually, a related sound file, so they are larger then either pictures or audio! Digital video clips are created by capturing analog video at regular intervals and saving each capture as a distinct image called a **frame.** Frames are played back at a particular speed, the **frame rate,** the number of frames per minute, to give the appearance of motion. As the frame rate approaches 60 frames per second, the video becomes smooth and actually like a videotape. A digital video file, or **movie,** may also have an audio track associated with the frames. Then the video display software has to display the images and play the sound at the same rate to keep the two together.

MPEG Video

The MPEG format, devised by the Motion Picture Experts Group, is the most common format for digital video files, or movies, because all the graphical browsers support it and viewers exist for all the platforms. Unlike the case with AVI, anyone with a graphical browser can either download a plug-in or use a browser to play MPEG movies. Although this is the most common type of movie on the Net, it has three disadvantages:

First, MPEG files are very slow to decompress. Often this decompression is handled by a special, separate expansion card that assists in preparing the file for viewing. If the user's machine cannot decode the frames quickly enough, the MPEG player will drop some frames from the playback. This results in a jerky or choppy motion.

Second, MPEG files require a fast processor for software decompression. Again, the user needs a powerful, fast computer to keep up a pleasing frame rate in decompression. If the processor is too slow, the resulting video is choppy. Normally MPEG video does not have an associated sound track, because just the video takes most of the processor's capability.

Third, MPEG files are very expensive to create. MPEG encoders are expensive, requiring equipment costing several thousand dollars. That is beyond the range of most users. Creating MPEG files is not usually an option for the casual Web weaver, but using these files is easy, and all the graphical browsers support an MPEG viewer.

MPEG files usually have the file extensions of **.mpg** on Intel platforms and **.mpeg** on systems that support longer file names.

QuickTime

QuickTime was developed for the Apple Macintosh. It is nearly as common as MPEG, (some of the Macintosh folks say it is more common) and is another Net standard. QuickTime movies can be played on PCs using the QuickTime for Windows (QTfW) software. They can be played using the Xanim program on UNIX machines. Usually QuickTime movies have an extension of **.qt** or **.mov** on all platforms.

Video for Windows (VfW)

Video for Windows was developed for the PC by Microsoft. It is the nominal standard for PC video, and a large number of files exist on PC platforms. However, there are few players outside the PC platform, so it is far less suitable for use across the Net. It is not, nor is it expected to become, a Net standard. Video for Windows files usually have a file extension of **.avi,** which stands for Audio/Video Interleave.

Streaming Audio/Video

One of the newer forms of multimedia is the Shocked movie created with Macromedia's Director program. These multimedia movie presentations feature **streaming audio and video,** which means that the movie or audio clip starts as soon as the browser plug-in begins to receive the file. As the frames are downloaded from the Net, they are displayed. Ideally, the frames are downloading more quickly than they are being displayed, so the download stays ahead of the presentation. Consequently, the multimedia event begins more quickly, because the user doesn't have to wait for the whole file to download.

The drawback to streaming presentations is that a slow Net connection can produce a choppy presentation in which the audio seems to fade in and out. Some early streaming audio presentations, like RealAudio, a live Net radio broadcast site, had the characteristics of old AM radio. The signal would wax and wane, with interference and garbled sound occurring.

Although streaming audio and video is exciting, it places a huge demand on the Net. Other forms of multimedia that require the user to download and store the presentation before it is played affect the Net only while the file is being downloaded. In contrast, streaming technology places a high demand on the Net all through the presentation. As modems become faster and compression becomes better, more and more streaming audio and video will probably appear on the Net. Their presence may have a serious impact on connect speeds.

Applets for Multimedia

The newest form of multimedia presentation, **Java applets,** are small programs that run within a window inside a browser. They are the "latest thing" in Web page design. You will learn how to install and use applets later in this book. Java applets are another way to provide your user with audio, video, and animation as well as making your page interactive. For example, one applet will allow the user to change the background color of your page. Others will elicit information from the user and produce changes based on that information.

Java applets are very powerful. They provide a wonderful set of additional features for users of those browsers that can support them. Unfortunately, older browsers, and some platforms, cannot display Java applets, so they are restricted to users with newer technology.

Linking Across the Web

In Chapter 3 you learned how to create interpage and intrapage links on the same machine. Now we need to examine links that bring data from distant machines. Linking across the World Wide Web is as easy as linking down into the same document, but it consumes Net resources and can lead to some problems that are outside the control of the Web weaver. For example, if we link to a site to bring in an audio file, that site may be down, preventing our users from hearing the audio clip. Or perhaps the site that has the clip is working just fine, but between our site and the Net a problem occurs, preventing our users from getting onto that path. Still another possibility is that the site we are linking to may change its address.

For all these reasons, a wise Web weaver will regularly check to ensure that the links from his page are valid. There are some software packages that will do this, but the conscientious Web weaver will try each link on his page at regular intervals to ensure that they still work.

To Link or to Copy

When using multimedia, there is a temptation to simply link to a large file on another server rather than store that file on your own server. Indeed, some authors of multimedia ask that you link to their site rather than copying the files to your own server. The advantages of saving space as well as having a current copy of an event make the idea of linking to another server appealing. However, this practice increases congestion on the Net. When users make a connection to your Web page, they are putting a certain load on the Net. If you require another connection, to another machine, that increases the load. In addition, making your users wait to retrieve data from another machine adds to the delay. So the idea of linking to resources on another machine is not as good as it first appears. It is best to copy a resource from a remote site and store it on the same server that hosts your page, unless, of course, the resource is copyrighted and you cannot obtain permission to use it. In any case, it is considered proper to put a small credit line on your page indicating where the resource came from, even if it is in the public domain.

Linking Considerations

When you create a link to a page on another machine, you are giving the user's browser a different address from which to download data. Often this process is referred to as "sending the user across the Net." Naturally, this is only a figure of speech, as your user stays exactly where she was but simply begins to use a different server. In most cases, when the user finishes accessing the distant server, she can return to your server using the "Back" button.

If you are using a framed document, consider using a **TARGET="TOP"** attribute to give your user a full-sized browser window to display the new page. If you don't include this target value, the data from the new page will be constrained in the frame that contains the link, or in the frame pointed to by the TARGET attribute of the link. As we will see in Chapter 9, using frames is sometimes done to give the user a navigation frame, but it is usually considered a bad design practice.

Domain Name or IP Address

You can specify a link address, or URL (the value of the HREF attribute to the <A> container), by either the IP or the domain name. As explained earlier, an IP address is a set of four numbers separated by periods or dots. For example, **204.151.55.44** is an IP address. Each device connected to the Internet has a unique IP address. The domain name describes the path to the server by giving the server's actual name and the other names of the computers that constitute the domain of the server. For example, www.McGraw-Hill.com is a domain name. Some domain names are short, and others can be quite long. The parts of domain names were discussed in Chapter 1.

If you choose to use a domain name, the browser must access a Domain Name Service (DNS) to translate the domain name into an IP address. Some Web weavers think that this extra step is best avoided, so they code the domain as an IP address. Although this does save a little time when the browser takes the link, it is not a good practice.

For example, one company decided that it needed a firewall to protect its systems from attack across the Net. This company had an extensive Web site and used IP addressing throughout, even to link to other pages on its own site. When it implemented the firewall computer, it had to change the IP address of its Web server. This meant going into dozens of pages and finding and changing all the addresses. (After making the change, the company started using a domain name instead of an IP address.)

In addition to being more stable, domain names can give the user, as well as the Web weaver, an idea of where the link will go. When the user moves the mouse pointer over a link, most browsers indicate the address to which the link points. If the user sees **http://204.151.55.44/,** he has little idea where the link will take him, unless he memorizes IP addresses! However, if he sees **http://www.McGraw-Hill.com/,** he has some idea of the kind of information he will be seeing.

In addition, the Web weaver herself, in maintaining her page, will be more likely to remember where the **www.McGraw-Hill.com** HREF points to than she would the **204.151.55.44** IP address. All things considered, it is best to use domain names rather than IP addresses as targets for links.

Paths to Files

As we learned in Chapter 1, the third part of a URL is the **path** to the file. Usually this is a set of directory names that allows the browser to find the actual HTML document referenced by the link. There are a few important considerations when building a path name. First, since the vast majority of the computers that run Web servers use the UNIX operating system, and UNIX is case-sensitive, you need to be careful with the case of your path names. If the file you want is in the path **Wilbur.pages.stuff,** and you code **wilbur.pages.stuff** as part of your link address, the link will fail. Wilbur and wilbur are two different directories on a UNIX computer.

Second, if there is no path, or if the path is simply a forward slash (/), the document you will retrieve is the highest level HTML index document on that server. This is called the **home page.** It represents the highest level page for that hierarchy. Sometimes it is called **public_html, public.htm.** On UNIX computers it is usually called **index.html.** This document normally provides the doorway into the rest of the HTML files on that site.

Third, the shorthand use of the tilde (~) symbol is used to specify a path name from a personal HTML directory in the home directory of the individual specified. For example, the URL **http://SomeCompany.Somewhere.com/~clyde/** would bring up the highest level HTML document in Clyde's subdirectory structure. Usually this would be Clyde's **index.html file,** or Clyde's home page.

This raises an interesting point. There can be a home page on **SomeCompany.Somewhere.com** that is the gateway into all the HTML documents on that server. Usually a well-constructed home page will provide links to all the other pages, or at least the index to each set of pages on that server. The exact location of that **index.html** file depends on (1) the actual server software and (2) the Web weaver that set up the site. The main index page for the whole server is obviously a home page. However, in the parlance of the Web, the index into Clyde's collection of HTML pages is also considered to be a home page. Generally avoid coding the file name **index.html** when linking to a home page; let the browser pick the name.

Sample URLs

The following are all examples of URLs that point to different Web pages. The comments following the URL explain the particular features of the URL being referenced.

- **http://www.yahoo.com/.** This link assumes that there is a home page or index page on the root directory of the **www.yahoo.com** Web server. (This is actually the yahoo search engine home page.) Notice that there is no "index.html" coded, as it is inferred by the browser.
- **http://www.mcgraw-hill.com/books.html.** In this case, the link points to an actual page on the McGraw-Hill Web server. Rather than

retrieving the main page (index.html), this link will cause the browser to retrieve a particular page. You need to be careful with this sort of link, as it can lose the user. In this case, if the user doesn't know that she can just change the address (location) of the link to **www.mcgraw-hill.com,** she may not know how to get to the main page, and the "Back" button will send her back to your page, not the main page of McGraw-Hill. That means you need to be careful in constructing your linkages to various sites.

- **http://www.server.com/subpage.html#frag.** This is a fictitious site, but the URL shows how a particular anchor within a page may appear as part of the URL. In this case, the browser will retrieve the subpage.html from the server.com site. When it begins displaying the document, it will start at the internal hyperlink target, "frag." This allows direct access into a longer document, allowing the user to go directly to information of interest rather than having to either jump again, to the internal target, or scroll down through the document to the information he wants. To establish this sort of linkage, the Web weaver must know the target document and how it is constructed.
- **http://www.otherserver.com:80/subpage.html#frag.** This is also a fictitious site, but demonstrates the use of a **port number.** Port numbers are necessary only if the server is set up to receive http traffic on a network port other than the default port, 21. In this example, the server, "otherserver," expects WWW requests to come into port 80. If you need to code a port number, it must follow the actual server name and be preceded by a colon, as in the example.

We have already examined the considerations involved in creating good links in your documents. When you create links across the Web, you should apply the same rules of good structure that you use for internal links. In addition, you should ensure that the links you create actually work! Think how frustrating it is for your user to try to take a link to a site you recommend only to see, "Unable to locate the server . . . The server does not have a DNS entry," or the even more deadly message, "404 Not Found The requested URL . . . was not found on this server."

One of the most important functions you will perform for your users is to ensure that the links you provide are valid links. This means you will need to check them at regular intervals. There are some software packages that will check your links for you, but the best practice is for you to regularly check the links on your own pages.

Exercises

The following exercises assume you have the plug-ins you need installed in your browser. If you don't have the plug-ins, you will need to download them and install them before you can begin to explore these multimedia sites.

These sites were valid when this book was written but may have subsequently changed. Use a search tool to search for the name of the multimedia tool if the site is no longer valid. In each case notice not only the "gee whiz" of the multimedia but also the time it takes to download the material and how long it plays. It may be interesting to compare the download time as a function of the playing time.

8.1. Visit the ShockWave site, **www.macromedia.com** and some of the sites it recommends.

8.2. Visit the Real Audio/Video site at www.real.com and some of the sites it recommends.

8.3. Explore the Web to find three other examples of true multimedia. Share them with your classmates.

CHAPTER nine

FRAMES

9

Using **frames** to divide the browser page into smaller "pagelets" is a popular way to control the layout of the screen while giving the user a consistent navigational tool and a common "look and feel" to Web pages. Each frame is, in essence, a separate HTML document, and you can change the content of each frame individually. However, frames can easily be overdone, creating an unstructured mess that renders the information presented difficult, if not impossible, for the user to find and use. If you need to use frames, and there are some good uses of them, you should use them judiciously, bearing in mind the following caveats.

Considerations When Using Frames

Frames are a relatively new extension to HTML, so older browsers (before Netscape 2.0 and Internet Explorer 3.0) will not support them. For that reason, you should *always* use the **<NOFRAMES>** container to accommodate browsers that don't support frames.

To make matters more "interesting," you can build a framed document that appears *within the frame* of another framed document! This brings to mind the ancient Oriental curse, "May you live in interesting times." Although frames within frames—and, by extension, frames within frames contained in frames—can show the logical prowess of the Web weaver, they are of little use in most circumstances and can leave the user totally confused.

By the same token, the proper use of frames can build an outstanding tool for your users. You will need to exercise careful construction and consideration for your users' navigational needs. For example, you can build a narrow frame along one of the margins, left, right, top, or bottom that contains a table of contents to your site. As the user selects different choices from the table of contents, the text and graphics for the chosen pages appear in the main frame. That way the user always has her navigational tools available, and she doesn't have to link forward and backward to peruse your site.

Another factor you need to consider is the way the "Back" and Forward" buttons on the browser work or rather, in the case of frames, don't work. Instead of moving the user from page to page as usual, "Back" and "Forward" have a different effect in a framed document. Sometimes they will change the contents of the most recent, active frame. Using these buttons may result in errors very upsetting for your users.

Another major difference for your users is the way the "view source" works in a framed document. If your user asks to "view source," he will see the source of the main frame document, with <FRAMESET> tag, and so on. To view the source of the document displayed within the frame, he must choose instead the "view frame source" option. This can be very confusing for users.

To add even more interest to the life of your users, the URL of the framed document doesn't change, regardless of how many pages you load. That defeats the bookmarking tools most users have come to depend upon. They may have difficulty finding their way back to a specific part of your site. To try to help them, you could put the URL of each page that is displayed in a frame somewhere on that page. Then the user could at least copy and paste the URL into another document. In addition, you need to ensure that each page that is presented in a frame has a way to link to the main page. That way your user always has a good navigational tool available. Let's look at a simple framed document as Netscape displays it to see exactly what we are talking about.

Rather than being able to show you the dynamic document, the print medium forces this to be a series of "still" frames. Figure 9.1 shows the first screen. Notice the two frames, one with three navigation links and the second, larger frame taking up the lower 85 percent of the screen.

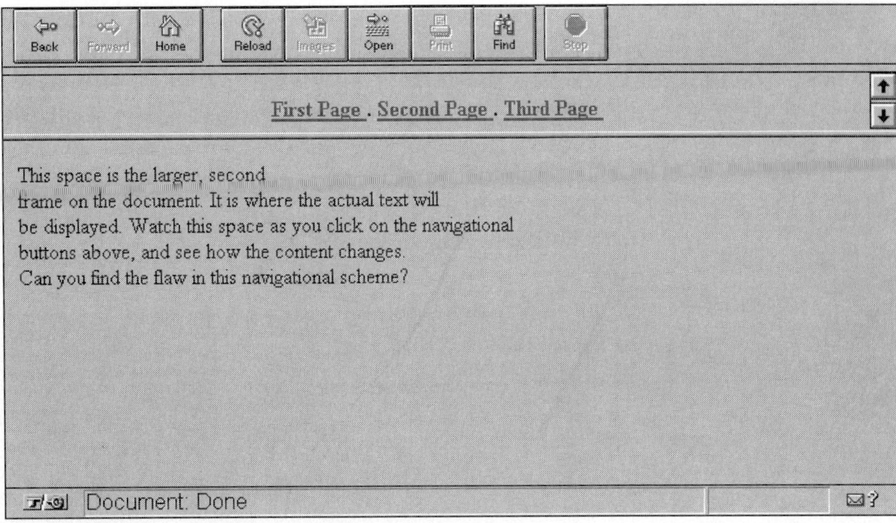

Figure 9.1 Netscape's presentation of the first of a series of frames.

In Figure 9.2, look at what happens when the user clicks on the first link, "First Page." The larger, "text" window now displays a second document, called FP1.htm for simplicity. Even though the larger window changed, the smaller, navigation window did not. That is one feature of frames that make them useful. The user can change the text without losing the control given by the navigation window.

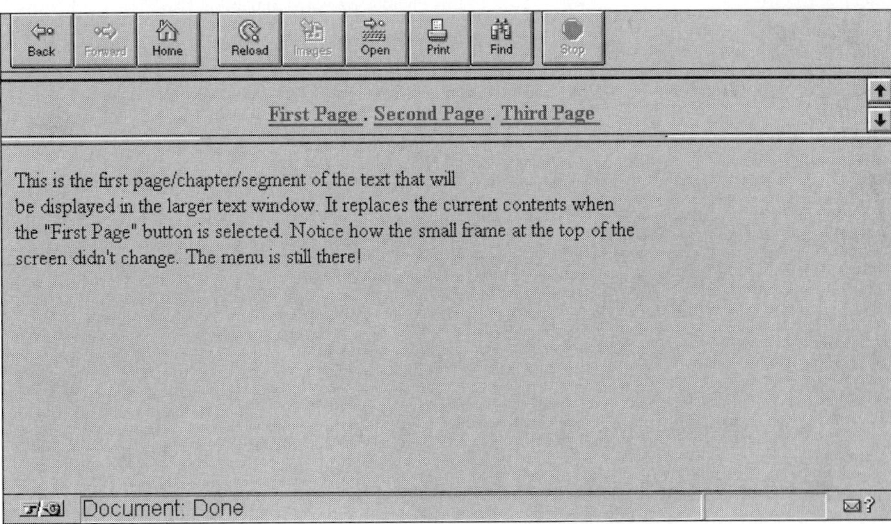

Figure 9.2 Netscape's presentation of the "First Page" in a frame.

Now let's see what happens when the user clicks on the "Second Page" link. As Figure 9.3 shows, the contents of the "text" window changed again. It now displays the contents of the document FP2.htm. The HTML documents that are displayed in the frame can be any HTML document or any graphic that the browser can display. Using this type of "table of contents" and large display window can be very effective when trying to display a series of pictures. Use the small frame to allow the user to choose among the images and the larger window to display them.

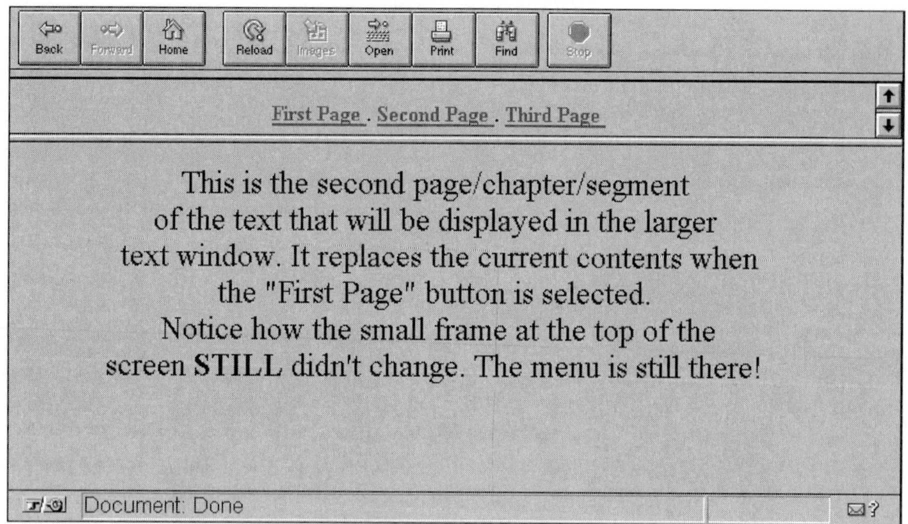

Figure 9.3 Netscape's presentation of the "Second Page" in a frame.

Figure 9.4 shows what happens when the user clicks on the "Third Page" link. Notice the scroll bar that suddenly appeared on the right side of the frame. That is another feature you can control, or allow the browser to control for you. In this case, the browser detected that the contents of the document were larger than could be displayed in the frame window, so it added the scroll bar to allow the user to see the complete contents of the document.

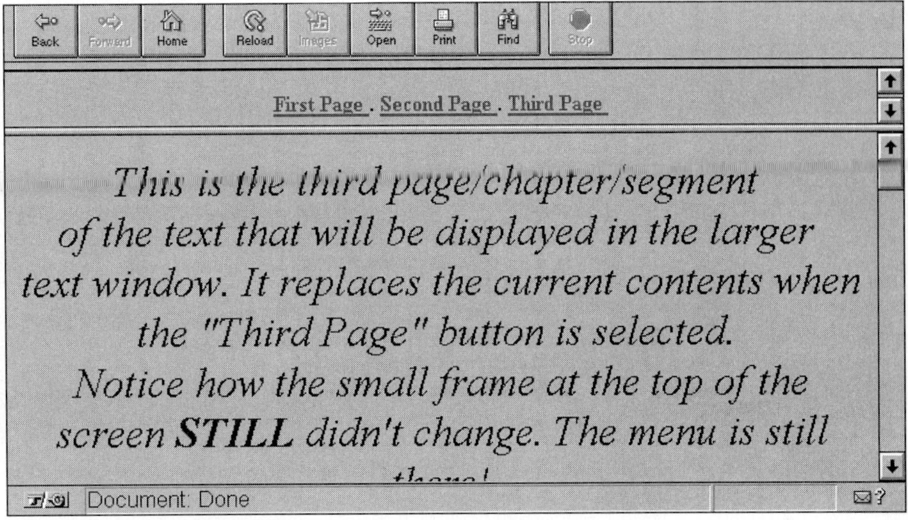

Figure 9.4 Netscape's presentation of the "Third Page" in a frame.

Figure 9.5 presents the code that generates these four documents. This is the **driver,** or master document, that builds the frames, which are then filled by various other documents. This is also what the user sees if he clicks on "view source." We will explore each of the tags and attributes in detail, but for now, just look at the overall structure of the frame document. Notice that there is no <BODY> container. The <FRAMESET> container replaces the <BODY> container.

```
<HTML>
<HEAD>
<TITLE>Frame Sample 1 </TITLE>
</HEAD>
<FRAMESET ROWS="15%,*">
     <FRAME SRC="FMenu.htm" >
     <FRAME SRC="FIntro.htm" NAME="BODY">
</FRAMESET>
</HTML>
```

Figure 9.5 HTML code for frames.

Figure 9.6 presents the code for the menu in our frames example. Figure 9.7 presents the code for the introductory screen, and Figures 9.8–9.10 for the three pages. One of the important things to note is that the pages that are placed into the frames look like the documents we have seen all through our experience with HTML. That is an important realization. The documents that fill frames are simply HTML documents that are placed within frames. They need no special formatting to appear in a frame.

```
<HTML>
<HEAD>
<TITLE> It doesn't matter </TITLE>
</HEAD>
<BODY>
<CENTER>
<B>
<A HREF="FP1.htm" TARGET="BODY">First Page  </A>  .
<A HREF="FP2.htm" TARGET="BODY"> Second Page  </A> .
<A HREF="FP3.htm" TARGET="BODY"> Third Page </A>
</B>
</CENTER>
</BODY>
</HTML>
```

Figure 9.6 HTML code for the menu that appears across the top of the frames example in Figures 9.1–9.4.

```
<HTML>
<HEAD>
<TITLE> Mox-Nix </TITLE>
</HEAD>
<BODY>
This space is the larger, second<BR>
frame on the document. It is where the actual text will<BR>
be displayed. Watch this space as you click on the
navigational<BR>
buttons above, and see how the content changes.<BR>
Can you find the flaw in this navigational scheme?
</BODY>
</HTML>
```

Figure 9.7 HTML code for the Intro screen from the frames example in Figure 9.1. Notice that it looks like any HTML page.

```
<HTML>
<HEAD>
<TITLE> No one will ever see it </TITLE>
</HEAD>
<BODY>
This is the first page/chapter/segment of the text that will<BR>
be displayed in the larger text window. It replaces the
current contents when<BR>
the "First Page" button is selected.  Notice how the small
frame at the top of the<BR>
screen didn't change.  The menu is still there!
</BODY>
</HTML>
```

Figure 9.8 HTML code for the first page that will move into the main frame, shown in Figure 9.2.

```
<HTML>
<HEAD>
<TITLE> I'm Invisible </TITLE>
</HEAD>
<BODY>
<CENTER>
<FONT SIZE=+2>
This is the second page/chapter/segment <BR>
of the text that will be displayed in the larger <BR>
text window.  It replaces the current contents when<BR>
the "Second Page" button is selected. <BR>
 Notice how the small frame at the top of the<BR>
screen <B>STILL</B> didn't change.  The menu is still there!
</FONT>
</CENTER>
</BODY>
</HTML>
```

Figure 9.9 HTML code for the second page that will move into the main frame, shown in Figure 9.3.

```
<HTML>
<HEAD>
<TITLE> I'm Invisible </TITLE>
</HEAD>
<BODY>
<CENTER>
<FONT SIZE=+3>
<I>
This is the third page/chapter/segment <BR>
of the text that will be displayed in the larger <BR>
text window. It replaces the current contents when<BR>
the "Third Page" button is selected. <BR>
 Notice how the small frame at the top of the<BR>
screen <B>STILL</B> didn't change.  The menu is still there!
</I>
</FONT>
</CENTER>
</BODY>
</HTML>
```

Figure 9.10 HTML code for the third page that will move into the main frame, shown in Figure 9.4.

Formatting Frames

The most important thing to remember about frames is that they are just like the frame on a picture. They are there to hold some other content. If there is no content, there is no need for a frame. Netscape seems to understand this, because if you define a set of frames but have no content for them, the browser will not even display them. The exception to this rule is the case where, for example, four frames are defined and three of them have content. Obviously, the fourth frame will be shown, because the other three force the appearance of the fourth by their presence.

Although the documents that *fill* frames are just like any other HTML document, the document that *has* frames must be constructed differently than any HTML document we have seen so far. In a framed document, there is no <BODY> container. As you may have noticed in our example, the <FRAMESET> container replaces the <BODY> container for a framed document. This distinction is important, because if a browser encounters a <BODY> tag before the <FRAMESET> tag, it will ignore the <FRAMESET> all together. Thus, you can have a traditional HTML document with a <BODY>, or you can have a framed document with a <FRAMESET>, but not both.

<FRAMESET>

The **<FRAMESET>** container defines a page that contains frames. Although it is possible to have a page with a single frame, most of the time a Web weaver will have at least two different frames within the same page. It is also possible to have nearly an unlimited number of frames defined, but with more than four or five, the user could get lost, and the content will be difficult to find. The <FRAMESET> container defines the physical layout of the page, determining how much of the real estate of the screen is given to each of the different frames.

The </FRAMESET> tag must never be omitted. Some browsers will not even build the page if this closing tag is left out. All you will see is an empty gray screen. There are only two attributes for the current <FRAMESET> container, ROWS and COLS, discussed next.

ROWS and COLS

Together ROWS and/or COLS define how many frames are on the screen. You can use either attribute alone, or you can use both attributes together to define a more complex layout. At least one of these attributes must be coded in the <FRAMESET> open tag. Both have values expressed either in absolute pixels or as a percentage of the screen. You know what is coming next. It is considered better to define sections of the screen as percentage values rather than using absolute pixel sizes, because all screens are not of the same resolution as the one you use to build the document.

To make it easier for you to figure out the relative percentages, you can use the asterisk (*) for one of the values, and the browser will fill in the asterisk with whatever is left over when your exact percentages are subtracted from 100. For example, given the code `COLS="30%,*,18%"`, the browser will replace the * with 52%. This is an aid to those of us who need a calculator to do simple math. This feature is also available if you choose to code your ROWS and COLS in pixels.

The browser can help you further with your math: If you were to code `COLS="25%,60%,25"`, the browser would actually build three columns that added up to 100%, with roughly the proportions you asked for.

Bear in mind that the browsers will also allow the user to resize the frames by dragging on the frame dividers, unless you specifically prevent it. That means that all your careful calculation of frame sizes can be reset by a savvy user.

Nested <FRAMESET> Containers

"Like a circle in a spiral, like a wheel within a wheel," you can include one or more <FRAMESET> containers within an outer <FRAMESET> container. This allows the creation of some fancy formatting, with different numbers of rows or columns across the page. For an example, examine the code in Figure 9.11. The left column (of size 40%), contains only one frame. It displays the document called Frame1.htm. The second column contains the nested <FRAMESET> with three rows, occupying 33%, 40%, and 27%, respectively. The three documents—Frame2.htm, Frame3.htm, and Frame4.htm—are displayed from the top to the bottom of that column. Figure 9.12 shows how the browser displays this HTML code. You need to be very careful as you construct your nested <FRAMESET>s, because skipping something as simple as a closing angle bracket may have very strange results.

```
<HTML>
<HEAD>
<TITLE>Frame Sample 1 </TITLE>
</HEAD>
<FRAMESET COLS="40%,*">
                    <!--This is the first (leftmost) column -->
     <FRAME SRC="Frame1.htm">
<FRAMESET ROWS="40%,33%,*" >
                    <!-- All this is in the second
                    (rightmost) column -->
           <FRAME SRC="Frame2.htm">
           <FRAME SRC="Frame3.htm">
           <FRAME SRC="Frame4.htm">
</FRAMESET>
</FRAMESET>
</HTML>
```

Figure 9.11 HTML code for a more complex framed document, showing one level of nested frames.

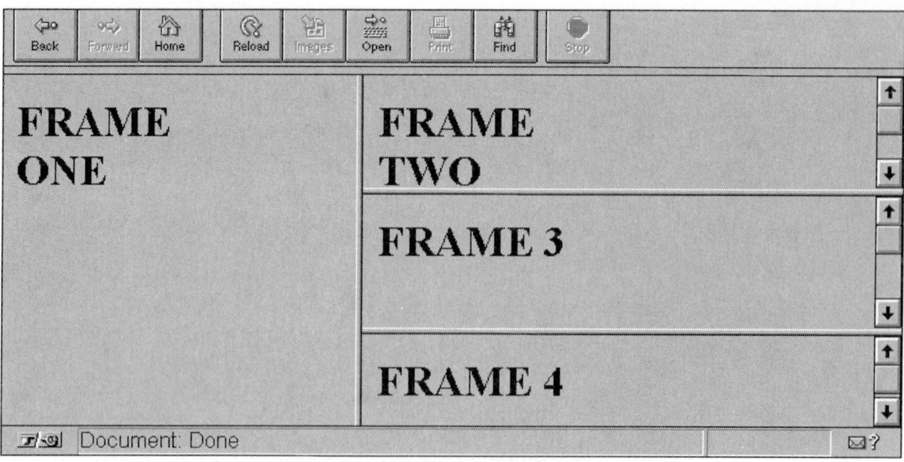

Figure 9.12 Netscape's presentation of a single nested <FRAMESET>.

Now let's consider a slightly more complex nesting situation. Figure 9.13 presents the code for two nested <FRAMESET>s, the left one with two rows, and the right with three. The placement of the </FRAMESET> tag in this example is critical. Although one frameset can be enclosed within another, the end of one frameset cannot occur after the beginning of another. In other words, you cannot overlap framesets as shown in Figure 9.13.

```
<HTML>
<HEAD>
<TITLE>Frame Sample 1 </TITLE>
</HEAD>
<FRAMESET COLS="40%,*">
     <!--  This is the first (leftmost) column -->
     <FRAMESET ROWS="50%,*">
     <FRAME SRC="Frame1.htm" >
     <FRAME SRC="Frame2.htm">

<FRAMESET ROWS="20%,40%,*" >
     <!--  This is the second (rightmost) column -->
     </FRAMESET>
           <FRAME SRC="Frame3.htm">
           <FRAME SRC="Frame4.htm">
           <FRAME SRC="Frame5.htm">
</FRAMESET>
</FRAMESET>
</HTML>
```

Figure 9.13 HTML code with overlapping framesets.

Note that the third frameset is started before the second is closed, causing an overlapping of framesets. The frameset that has two rows, each 50%, is still open when the frameset that has three rows, 20%, 40%, and 40%, is opened. The very next line of code closes the second frameset.

Figure 9.14 shows how Netscape handles this situation. When the browser becomes confused, it takes the simple course of not doing anything until it again understands what to do. In this case, since the browser cannot infer a close to the frameset, it ignores the new open <FRAMESET> tag. When it finds the closing tag, since it doesn't understand how <FRAME> tags can exist within a <FRAMESET> tag, it ignores the closing tag as well. The result is the large, empty column on the right.

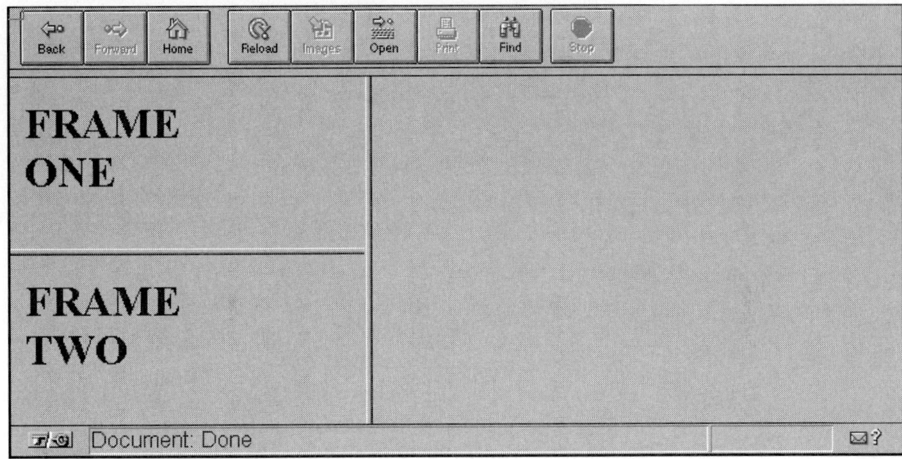

Figure 9.14 Netscape's presentation of overlapping framesets.

Figure 9.15 presents the same code, fixed so the framesets don't overlap. But this code contains another little problem. Look at the rendering in Figure 9.16, and try to find the error in the code.

```
<HTML>
<HEAD>
<TITLE>Frame Sample 1 </TITLE>
</HEAD>
<FRAMESET COLS="40%,*">
  <FRAMESET ROWS="50%,*">
      <FRAME SRC="Frame1.htm" >
      <FRAME SRC="Frame2.htm">
  </FRAMESET>
  <FRAMESET ROWS="20%,40%,*"
            <FRAME SRC="Frame3.htm">
            <FRAME SRC="Frame4.htm">
            <FRAME SRC="Frame5.htm">
  </FRAMESET>
</FRAMESET>
</HTML>
```

Figure 9.15 HTML code in which the overlapping framesets have been fixed, but there is another error.

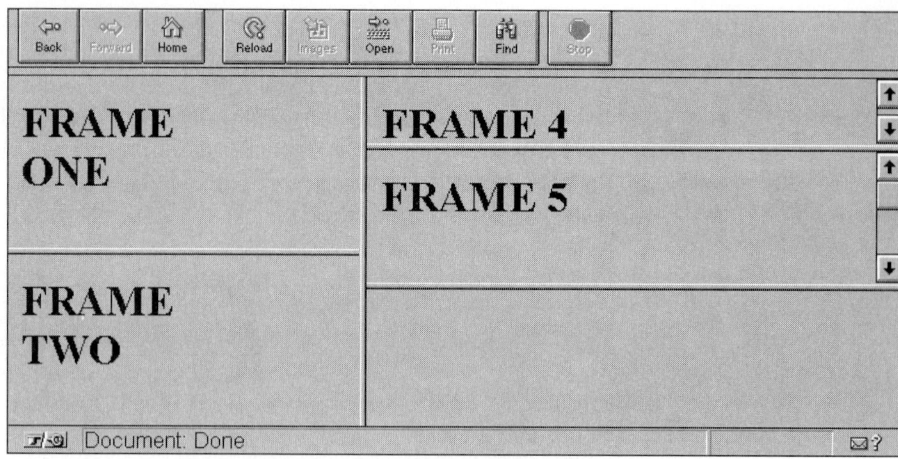

Figure 9.16 Netscape's presentation of a framed document with one small error.

For some reason, Frame 3 is not displayed. Look closely at the code. Notice that the close tag bracket (>) is missing from the <FRAMESET> tag for the right column. Because there is no closing bracket, the browser continues to look for one, ignoring anything that shouldn't be part of the <FRAMESET> tag, until it finds a closing bracket. In this case, it finds the closing bracket at the end of the first <FRAME> tag. Since the browser ignored everything up to that closing bracket, the first <FRAME> was ignored, and Frame 3 did not display. This is an example of how a subtle error can cause very strange results.

Figure 9.17 presents the corrected code. Figure 9.18 shows how Netscape renders that code. The frames now appear as intended in the first place. This example may have too many frames to be functional. It was designed to illustrate nested framesets, not to show proper coding or good page layout.

```
<HTML>
<HEAD>
<TITLE>Frame Sample 1 </TITLE>
</HEAD>
<FRAMESET COLS="40%,*">
     <FRAMESET ROWS="50%,*">
     <FRAME SRC="Frame1.htm" >
     <FRAME SRC="Frame2.htm">
</FRAMESET>
<FRAMESET ROWS="20%,40%,*" >
            <FRAME SRC="Frame3.htm">
            <FRAME SRC="Frame4.htm">
            <FRAME SRC="Frame5.htm">
</FRAMESET>
</FRAMESET>
</HTML>
```

Figure 9.17 Corrected HTML code for the nested-frameset document.

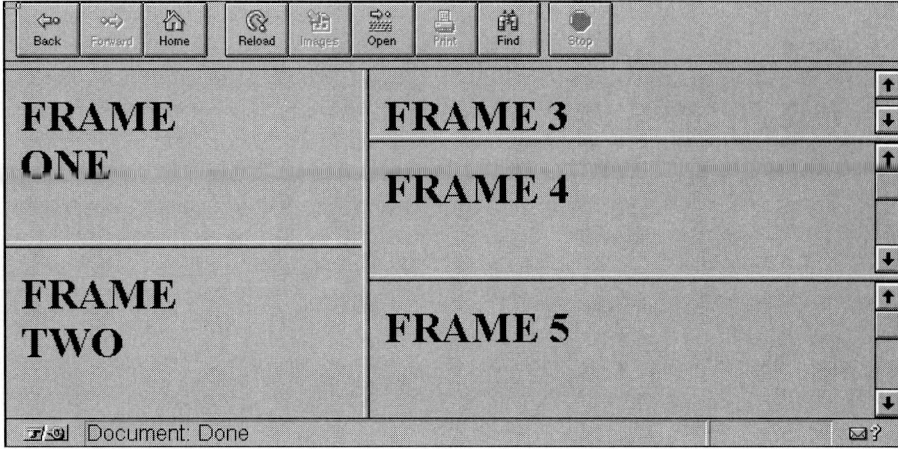

Figure 9.18 Netscape's presentation of a correctly coded nested frame.

<FRAME>

The <FRAMESET> container is not designed to display any information, just to format or structure a page with frames. Only containers coded within the <FRAMESET> can present data. There are two types of containers in this class, <FRAME> and <NOFRAMES>. The latter will be discussed at the end of this chapter.

The **<FRAME>** tag allows presentation of one or more HTML documents within a specific frame on the page. Each <FRAME> container is controlled by a series of attributes that define the properties of the frame as well as specifying the initial content. Some experts advise that the closing tag, </FRAME>, can be omitted in much the same way the </LI> tag was omitted in lists. Since the <FRAME> container can only exist within the confines of a <FRAMESET>, and since any other tag within the <FRAMESET> will cause the browser to infer a close to the <FRAME>, you can treat the <FRAME> as an empty tag for now. Remember, however, that as frames become more powerful, this may create a maintenance problem in later generations of HTML.

SRC

The value coded for the **SRC** attribute is the URL of the document, image, multimedia presentation, or any other displayable object that initially appears in the frame. If you want to create a very complex page, you can even use the URL of another framed document in one of the frames. This may well be the most important attribute for the <FRAME> tag, because *if there is no SRC and associated value coded in any particular <FRAME>, that frame can* ***never*** *have any content,* even if it has a NAME attribute.

Figures 9.19 and 9.20 provide an example. We will examine how the NAME attribute works next, so for now just look at the example, noticing that the <FRAME> descriptor for the second frame has no SRC attribute, but it does have a NAME attribute. In Figure 9.20, Frame Two seems to be missing its content. The link in Frame 3 would supply content to the area where Frame Two is missing because it has a NAME—in this case, "Wilbur." However, since that frame did not have initial content, trying to push another document into the frame is impossible. Netscape starts another browser when the link is taken.

```
<HTML>
<HEAD>
<TITLE>Frame Sample 1 </TITLE>
</HEAD>
<FRAMESET COLS="40%,*">
     <FRAMESET ROWS="50%,*">
     <FRAME SRC="Frame1.htm" >
     <FRAME NAME="Wilbur">
</FRAMESET>
<FRAMESET ROWS="40%,30%,*" >
            <FRAME SRC="Frame3a.htm">
            <FRAME SRC="Frame4.htm">
            <FRAME SRC="Frame5.htm">
</FRAMESET>
</FRAMESET>
</HTML>
```

Figure 9.19 HTML code for a frame with no SRC but with a NAME.

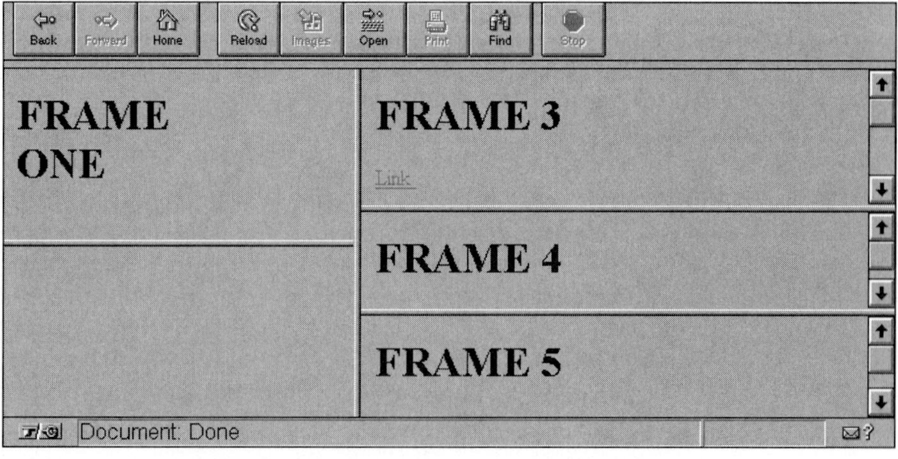

Figure 9.20 Netscape's presentation of a frame with no SRC but wih a NAME.

Figure 9.21 shows the code for the new contents for Frame 3. If you are going to try to place content into a targeted frame, that frame *must* have an initial SRC document declared when it is defined.

```
<HTML>
<HEAD>
<TITLE> Frame 3 example </TITLE>
</HEAD>
<BODY>
<H1>FRAME 3</H1>
<A HREF="Frame6.htm"  TARGET="Wilbur">Link</A>
</BODY>
</HTML>
```

Figure 9.21 HTML code for a sample document with a target.

NAME

The **NAME** attribute allows the named frame to be the target of other links, so other frames can influence the content of a specific frame. For example, if you were to use a framed document to create a table of contents and a text page, the table of contents would use the name of text page in each link, replacing the contents of the text page rather than changing the table of contents.

Look at the example in Figure 9.22. The narrow column on the right is the table of contents, and the larger frame on the left is the actual content of the selected section. As the user clicks on the various options from the menu on the right, the text that corresponds to that option appears in the frame on the left. For example, if the user clicks on the SRC choice, the screen will look like Figure 9.23. As you can see, the contents of the right frame, the menu, have not changed, but the information on the SRC option has appeared in the left frame. This is an excellent example of the navigational power of frames.

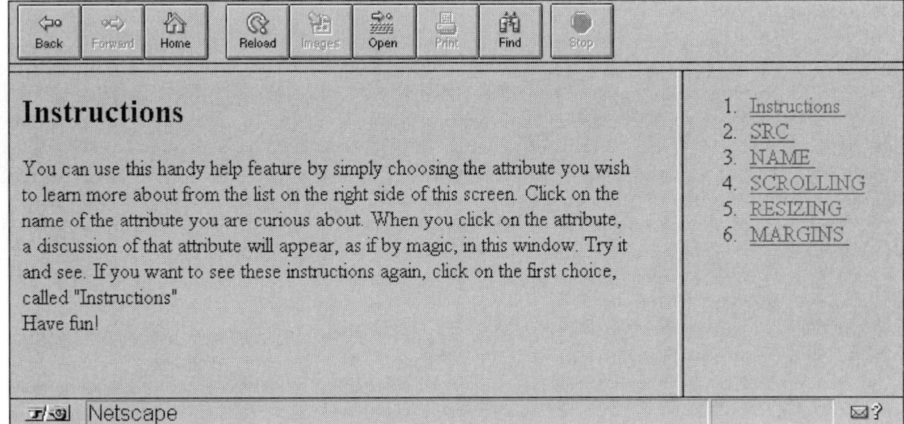

Figure 9.22 Netscape's presentation of a sample document with frames.

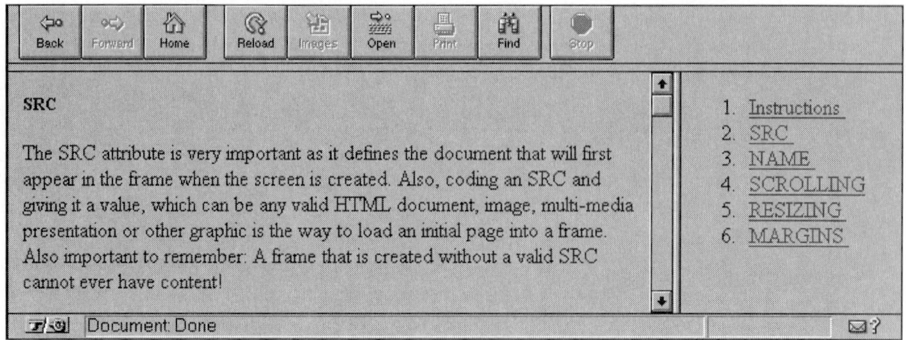

Figure 9.23 Netscape's presentation of a sample document showing the result of selecting the SRC menu option.

If the user selects the scrolling option, the screen will look like Figure 9.24. A new feature appears here—the scroll bar on the right side of the large frame. Unless you (1) force a scroll bar on every frame or (2) prevent scroll bars from being created, the browser will create a scroll bar if the contents of the document to be displayed extend beyond the boundaries of the window. You can prevent the generation of scroll bars by using the SCROLLING="NO" option with the <FRAME> tag. Figure 9.25 shows how the same page looks with the SCROLLING="NO" option set.

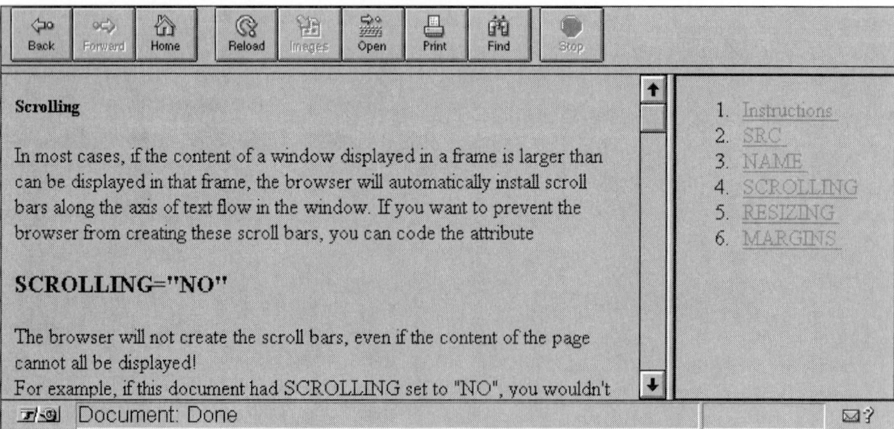

Figure 9.24 Netscape's presentation of a sample document showing the result of selecting the scrolling menu option.

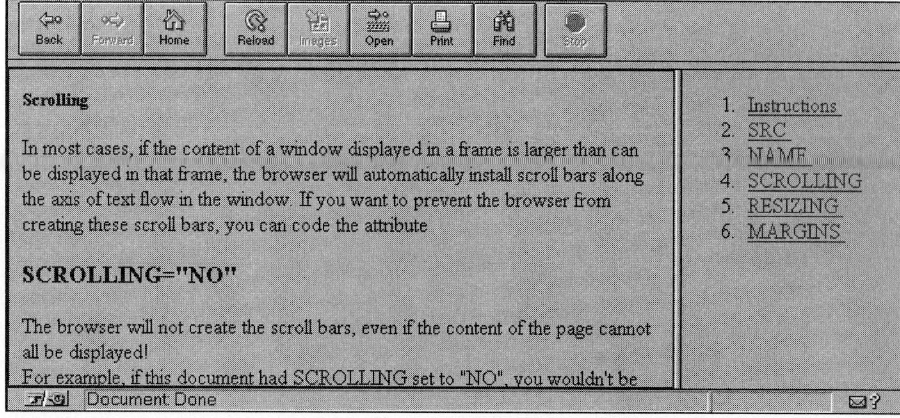

Figure 9.25 Netscape's presentation of a sample page showing the result of selecting the scrolling menu option when the scroll bars are turned off.

Now that you see what the browser can provide, let's look at the code for a couple of these pages. The first page, coded in Figure 9.26, is the actual frame document. It has only two frames defined. The one for the content is first, because the frames are built left to right, top to bottom. The first frame takes up 75 percent of the whole area of the frames, and it is named "Data". The second frame gets what is left (roughly 25 percent) and contains the document that is the menu.

```
<HTML>
<HEAD>
<TITLE> Sample Menu </TITLE>
</HEAD>
<FRAMESET COLS="75%,*">
     <FRAME SRC="fig0924.htm" NAME="Data">
     <FRAME SRC="fig0923.htm"  >
</FRAMESET>
</HTML>
```

Figure 9.26 HTML code for the frame document showing data area and menu area.

Figure 9.27 shows the code for the menu document. The menu document is nothing more than a list containing the references to the different HTML files that present the data. In each, the TARGET attribute is defined. That attribute directs the browser to place the contents of the HTML file listed in the anchor—for example, "Fig0924.htm"—into the frame or window with the name of "Data". This is how one frame, in this case the menu, can affect another frame, in this example the "Data" frame. We will examine this subject in detail later in the chapter.

```
<HTML>
<HEAD>
<TITLE> Sample Menu </TITLE>
</HEAD>
<BODY>
<OL>
      <LI> <A HREF="Fig0924.htm" TARGET="Data">Instructions</A>
      <LI> <A HREF="Fig0924a.htm" TARGET="Data">SRC</A>
      <LI> <A HREF="Fig0924b.htm" TARGET="Data">NAME</A>
      <LI> <A HREF="Fig0924c.htm" TARGET="Data">SCROLLING</A>
      <LI> <A HREF="Fig0924d.htm" TARGET="Data">RESIZING</A>
      <LI> <A HREF="Fig0924e.htm" TARGET="Data">MARGINS</A>
</OL>
</BODY>
</HTML>
```

Figure 9.27 HTML code for the menu document.

Figure 9.28 presents the code for the first actual content page. This code looks like any of the other HTML documents we have already examined. An HTML document that appears as the content of a frame requires no special formatting or special attributes. It is simply a regular HTML document placed within a subdivision (frame) of the screen.

```
<HTML>
<HEAD>
<TITLE> SRC info </TITLE>
</HEAD>
<BODY>
<H5>SRC</H5>
The SRC attribute is very important as it defines the
document that will first appear in the frame when the screen
is created.  Also, coding an SRC and giving it a value, which
can be any valid HTML document, image, multi-media
presentation or other graphic is the way to load an initial
page into a frame.  <BR>
Also important to remember:  A frame that is created without
a valid SRC cannot ever have content!
</BODY>
</HTML>
```

Figure 9.28 HTML code for a sample text document from the frame example.

Now we can examine some of the special attributes available to control how the frame is handled and how it looks on the screen.

SCROLLING

As shown in the previous example, you can control whether the browser puts scroll bars on the frames you build. If you don't code this **SCROLLING** option, the browser defaults to SCROLLING="AUTO", which allows the browser to add scroll bars if the document's content is larger than the frame space allowed to display it. If the whole content of the document can be displayed, then no scroll bar is created. If SCROLLING="YES" is coded, the browser will always create a scroll bar on the frame, whether the contents extend beyond the boundaries of the frame or not.

In the previous example, the frame was created with a SCROLLING="NO" option. That prevented scroll bars from being added by the browser, even though the content of the document was larger than the frame space. As you can see in the example, some of that content was unavailable. Text outside the frame will always be unavailable if there is no scroll bar to bring it into the visible part of the frame.

Figure 9.29 shows how the frame document would look coded to prevent scrolling. Note that the scrolling option is turned off for the entire life of the frame. If any document exceeds the size of the browser window, the content outside the window area will be lost. For example, selecting the SCROLLING option from the menu for this frame document would give us the screen in Figure 9.30. Note that there is no scroll bar in the data window. The text beyond the words "wouldn't be" are lost to the user and cannot be recovered unless the screen is made larger. In most cases, therefore, the data are just lost.

```
<HTML>
<HEAD>
<TITLE> Sample Menu </TITLE>
</HEAD>
<FRAMESET COLS="75%,*">
     <FRAME SRC="fig0924.htm" NAME="Data" SCROLLING="NO">
     <FRAME SRC="fig0923.htm"  >
</FRAMESET>
</HTML>
```

Figure 9.29 HTML code for a frame that disables scrolling.

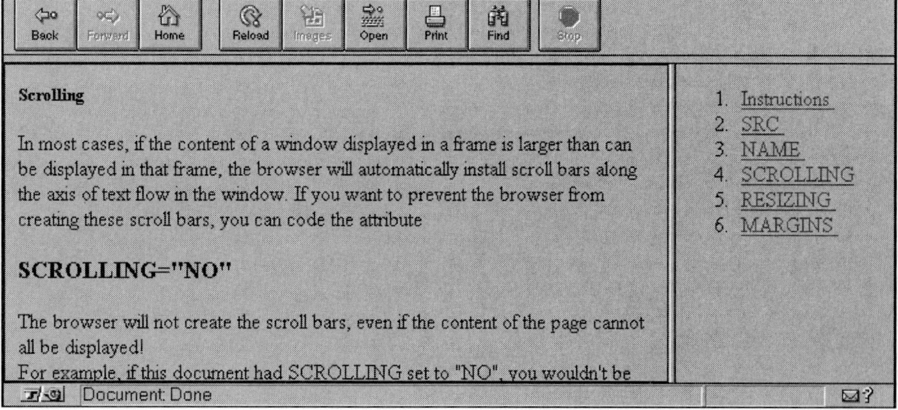

Figure 9.30 Netscape's presentation of the effect of NOSCROLL on a long document.

Usually it is best to allow the browser to use the default, AUTO, mode and place scroll bars on the frame when necessary. There appears to be no good reason to turn off scrolling.

NORESIZE

In most cases, the user can control the size of the windows on his screen by simply clicking and dragging on the dividers. This allows the user to compensate for any errors in your "guess" as to the best size for a frame for his hardware. If you use the Netscape news reader, you know all about dragging dividers to change the size of frames. With the news reader, you drag the frame dividers around the newsgroups box to see the different newsgroups. Once you find a group you want to stay with, you drag the horizontal divider up to maximize its content space. That is very handy.

Your users have that same option in your framed document by default. However, if you have an image that must fit exactly in a specific size space, and you have placed it in a frame of that exact size, you may wish to restrict the user from playing with the size of that frame. You can do that by coding the **NORESIZE** attribute to the <FRAME> tag.

Bear in mind, the NORESIZE option is set for the whole frame, and for the life of the frame. And like the SCROLLING option we discussed in the last section, this attribute sets the characteristics of the frame, not of a specific document shown in the frame. If you code the NORESIZE attribute, the frame will *never* be resizable.

Another point on that same thought process: if you have only a few frames on your document, let's say three columns, and you code NORESIZE on the center frame, you have effectively locked the horizontal size of all three frames. The two center dividers cannot be moved, so the size of all three frames is fixed. Use this option very judiciously. It is occasionally necessary, but most of the time the user can benefit from being able to resize the frame.

MARGINHEIGHT and MARGINWIDTH

The browsers usually place a minimum amount of space between the frame edges and the text within the frame. In some cases this space is so small that parts of the letters may be lost along the margins. To create a better visual effect, especially in a tight frame, use the **MARGINHEIGHT** and **MARGINWIDTH** attributes to add spacing along the edges of the frame.

Figure 9.31 presents the code for setting margins in our frame document. The margins are excessively large, chosen to illustrate how the presentation of the document can differ based on these attributes. Normally a margin of 5 to 10 pixels is sufficient to visually separate the contents from the frame. Here the margins are coded for 50 pixels.

```
<HTML>
<HEAD>
<TITLE> Sample Menu </TITLE>
</HEAD>
<FRAMESET COLS="75%,*">
    <FRAME SRC="Fig0924.htm" NAME="Data"  MARGINHEIGHT=50
    MARGINWIDTH=50>
    <FRAME SRC="Fig0923.htm"  >
</FRAMESET>
</HTML>
```

Figure 9.31 HTML code for MARGINHEIGHT and MARGINWIDTH.

Figure 9.32 shows how these very wide margins look in the browser. Obviously, they are too wide, and they constrain the amount of text the user can see without scrolling. When you design frames, it is important to minimize the amount of work the user has to do to glean information. Putting a large document into a small frame requires users to scroll excessively, frustrating them.

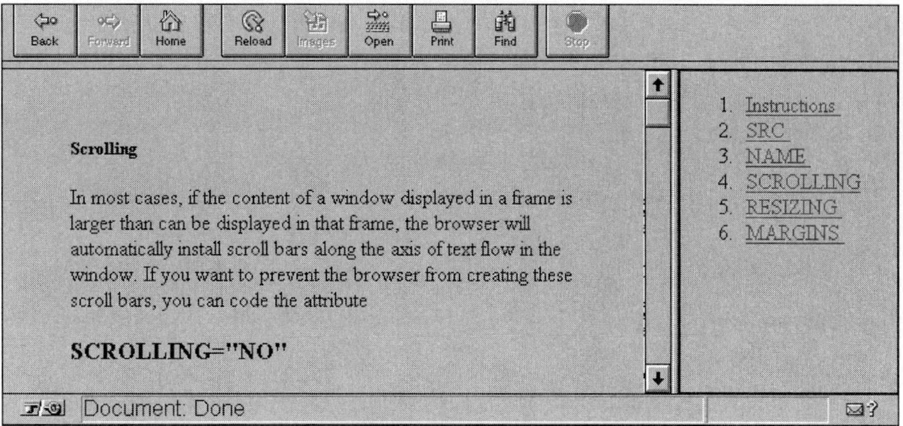

Figure 9.32 Netscape's presentation of a wide margin.

Whenever you design a page, bear in mind the central tenet that a Web page is designed to transfer information as efficiently as possible. Slick designs with lots of "bells and whistles" don't always accomplish this goal. A less fancy page that is easy to use is better for the user than one that has lots of fancy features but is inefficient.

Help for the Frameless: <NOFRAMES>

Not all browsers support frames. Early versions of Netscape and Internet Explorer do not support this extension to the HTML language, and some other browsers still don't have the capability to support frames. For users with those browsers, HTML has the **<NOFRAMES> . . . </NOFRAMES>** container.

Even though the use of this tag is not required by the syntax of HTML, you should always code it within your framed document. Otherwise your page will be worthless for users with browsers that don't support frames. Whenever you design a set of documents, always try to make the contents available to the widest audience.

You can code any HTML tag set within the <NOFRAMES> container, even a <BODY> tag. A frame-compliant browser will ignore the contents of the <NOFRAMES> container, while a browser that doesn't support frames will usually display them.

The way <NOFRAMES> works takes advantage of the flexibility of the browsers. When a browser encounters a tag it doesn't know, it ignores that tag. Since a nonframe browser ignores all the frame tags, including the

<NOFRAMES> tag, all it finds to display are the contents of the <NOFRAMES> container. There are a few, very strict browsers that will not even display the contents of a <NOFRAMES> container and will generate an error message instead, but they are in the distinct minority.

Figure 9.33 shows how a <NOFRAMES> container would be coded in a frame document. Figure 9.34 shows how a non-frame-compliant browser would show this page. To produce the output in Figure 9.34 the <NOFRAMES> tag was forced to work by misspelling the <FRAMESET> container and thereby disabling it. The misspelling caused the frame to break, triggering the <NOFRAMES> message.

```
<HTML>
<HEAD>
<TITLE> Sample Menu </TITLE>
</HEAD>
<FRAMESET COLS="75%,*">
      <FRAME SRC="fig0924.htm" NAME="Data" >
      <FRAME SRC="fig0923.htm"  >
<NOFRAMES>
I am sorry, but this document is designed to be read by a
frame compliant browser.<BR>
If you see this message, your browser doesn't support
frames.<BR>
You can either update your current browser to one that
supports framing, or you can see the same content, page by
page, using the <A HREF="fig0924.htm">index</A> and the
"BACK" button. Sorry for the inconvenience.<BR>
The Management<BR>
</NOFRAMES>
</FRAMESET>
</HTML>
```

Figure 9.33 HTML code for <NOFRAMES> container.

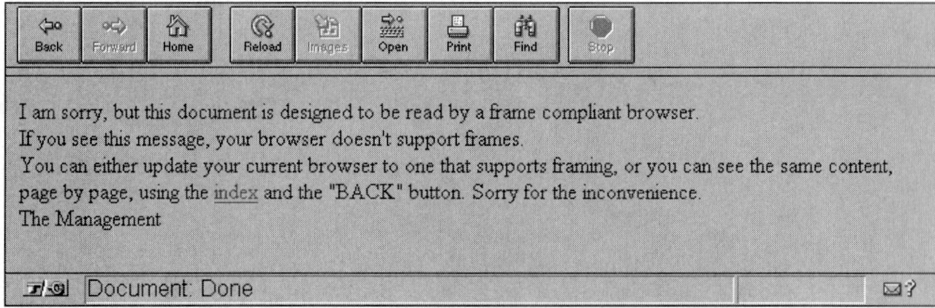

Figure 9.34 Netscape's presentation of the <NOFRAMES> message.

This message explains to users with non-frame-compliant browsers that they need to either upgrade their browser or link to index. The link will take them to the same index document that appeared in the right frame. When invoked this way, the index takes up the whole browser window, as shown in Figure 9.35.

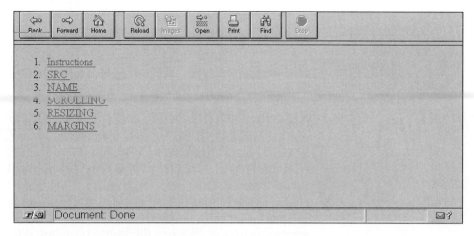

Figure 9.35 Netscape's presentation of the index document as it appears when called from the <NOFRAMES> link.

When the user clicks on one of the links, the browser ignores the TARGET attribute. Why? Because the target doesn't exist, since there is no frame with that name. So the browser loads the image onto the current screen, replacing the index. To get back to the index, the user merely clicks on the "Back" button. However, there should be a link back to the index from the SRC document, as shown in Figure 9.36, to make it easier for the user to navigate.

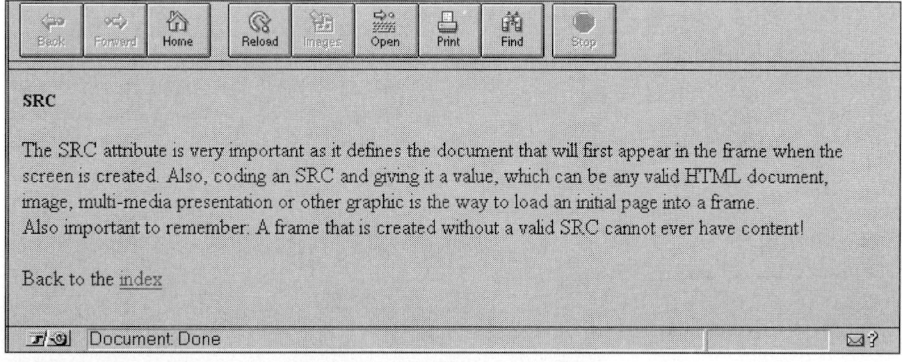

Figure 9.36 Netscape's presentation of a page called from the index, showing an explicit link back to the index.

Using the technique shown in Figure 9.36 is very important because your users may bookmark this page for later use. If you rely on their using the "Back" button on the browser, they will be unable to return to the index page after using their bookmark for this page. A good Web weaver will always make navigation as simple as possible for users.

TARGET for Frames or Windows

As we saw in the example of the framed window, you can specify a label, or **TARGET** attribute, in an anchor, <A>, tag and thus direct the browser to load the document referenced in the HREF into the window or frame specified. For example, the line

```
<A HREF="Fig0924.htm" TARGET="Data">Instructions</A>
```

will load the HTML document called Fig0924.htm into the window or frame labeled "Data" when the user clicks on the Instructions link. If there is no frame with the NAME attribute of "Data", the browser will create a new window and call it "Data."

Let's suppose the Web weaver makes a mistake coding the anchor, and calling the target "Daat," as shown in Figure 9.37. The browser will produce the screen in Figure 9.38 when the Instructions link is taken. The browser cannot put the document into the frame specified in the anchor, because the name, "Daat", doesn't match any known TARGET name. Therefore, the browser opens a new window and places the document there.

```
<HTML>
<HEAD>
<TITLE> Sample Menu </TITLE>
</HEAD>
<BODY>
<OL>
      <LI> <A HREF="Fig0924.htm" TARGET="Daat"> Instructions </A>
      <LI> <A HREF="Fig0924a.htm" TARGET="Data"> SRC </A>
      <LI> <A HREF="Fig0924b.htm" TARGET="Data"> NAME </A>
      <LI> <A HREF="Fig0924c.htm" TARGET="Data"> SCROLLING </A>
      <LI> <A HREF="Fig0924d.htm" TARGET="Data"> RESIZING </A>
      <LI> <A HREF="Fig0924e.htm" TARGET="Data"> MARGINS </A>
</OL>
</BODY>
</HTML>
```

Figure 9.37 HTML code showing an incorrect TARGET in an anchor.

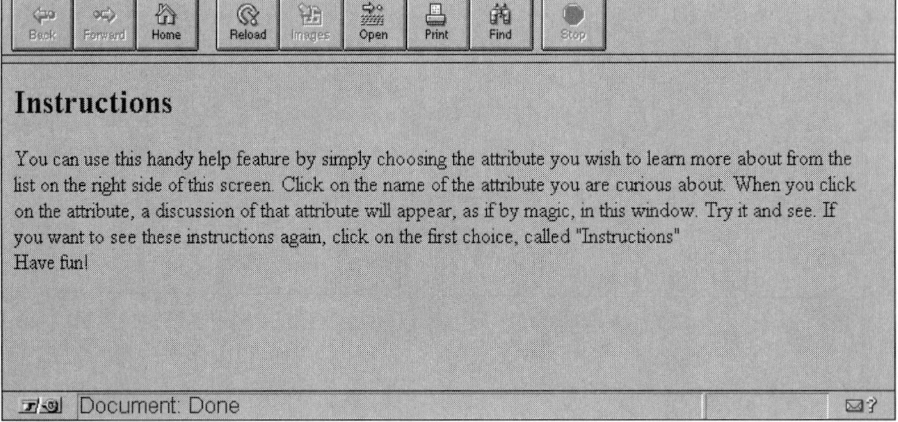

Figure 9.38 Netscape's presentation when the instructions link is chosen from the code in Figure 9.37.

In some cases a mistake like this may even cause the operating system to create a second browser session. It is very important that you code correct and accurate tags when you choose to use targets from a link.

Another common mistake is to forget to include the target with the link, as shown in Figure 9.39. If the user chooses the instructions link from this menu, the framed document will be overlaid by a standard window containing only the data found in the Fig0924.htm document. Figure 9.40 shows how it would look. When the browser encounters a document that has no target, it will create a new window for that new document. That sounds almost like a rule, so there must be an exception to it. The exception is that you can specify a default target for each link that has a specified target by coding the **<BASE>** tag. We could change the code in the index page as shown in Figure 9.41. Notice that the individual links no longer specify a target, yet the page behaves exactly the same as when they did. The <BASE> tag with the TARGET attribute sets the target for any link that is not explicitly specified. This default target only works on the page that has the <BASE> tag, but it will save us some typing time and ensure that we have a consistent presentation.

```
<HTML>
<HEAD>
<TITLE> Sample Menu </TITLE>
</HEAD>
<BODY>
<OL>
     <LI> <A HREF="Fig0924.htm" >Instructions</A>
     <LI> <A HREF="Fig0924a.htm" TARGET="Data">SRC</A>
     <LI> <A HREF="Fig0924b.htm" TARGET="Data">NAME</A>
     <LI> <A HREF="Fig0924c.htm" TARGET="Data">SCROLLING</A>
     <LI> <A HREF="Fig0924d.htm" TARGET="Data">RESIZING</A>
     <LI> <A HREF="Fig0924e.htm" TARGET="Data">MARGINS</A>
</BODY>
</HTML>
```

Figure 9.39 HTML code showing an anchor without a target.

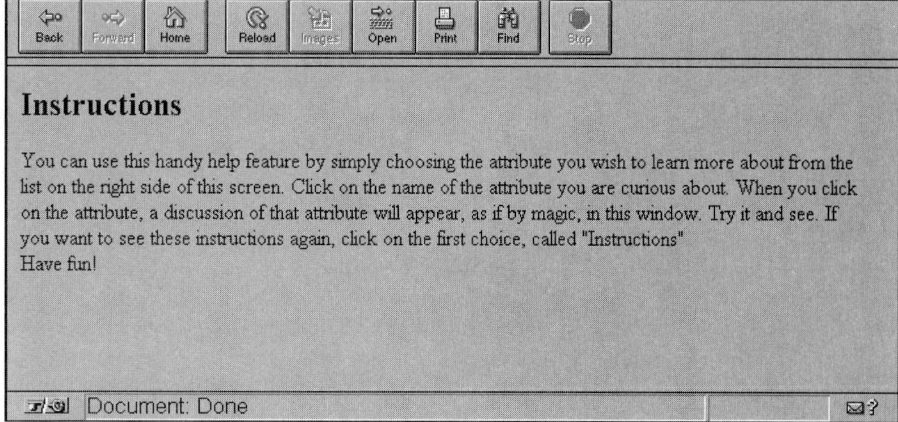

Figure 9.40 Netscape's presentation when the instructions link is chosen from the code in Figure 9.39.

```
<HTML>
<HEAD>
<TITLE> Sample Menu </TITLE>
<BASE TARGET="Data">
</HEAD>
<BODY>
<OL>
      <LI> <A HREF="Fig0924.htm" >Instructions</A>
      <LI> <A HREF="Fig0924a.htm" >SRC</A>
      <LI> <A HREF="Fig0924b.htm" >NAME</A>
      <LI> <A HREF="Fig0924c.htm" >SCROLLING</A>
      <LI> <A HREF="Fig0924d.htm" >RESIZING</A>
      <LI> <A HREF="Fig0924e.htm" >MARGINS</A>
</OL>
</BODY>
</HTML>
```

Figure 9.41 HTML code showing the use of the <BASE> tag with the TARGET attribute.

Special Targets

The browsers support four special targets that serve particular needs. All of these targets start with an underscore. Only these targets may start with an underscore. Any other target coded with an underscore will be ignored by the browser.

_blank

The **_blank** target is used by the browser to initiate a newly opened window. It is usually used for unnamed windows. There is no real use for this target by most Web weavers; it is included here for completeness.

_self

If an anchor tag, <A>, does not specify a target value, the **_self** target is the default target. This target points to the current frame or window, that is, the frame or window that contains the document that is the source for the anchor, <A>. The _self tag is useful when the Web weaver wants to place a particular document into the frame or window that called it but has a <BASE> target defined. Otherwise this tag is redundant and unnecessary.

_parent

The **_parent** target causes the document to be loaded into the **parent window** (the window containing the frameset that has the actual hypertext reference.) If there is only one level of frame structure, then this is the same as the target of _top.

_top

The most important special target is **_top.** It causes the browser to load the document into a window without any frames, that is, the top, or initial, window. If you are going to send your user off your Web site to a remote page (one that is not part of your Web site) you probably won't want to keep your menu on the screen. It would make little sense to your user. As a general rule, when using frames or special formatting, you should always code a target of _top for a link to a remote document. That way, the new document will be loaded into the entire contents of the browser window, not just the portion allocated by your formatting.

Recommendations

Although frames provide some nice navigation features, they often cause problems, depending on the type of browser used. Use them only if you must.

Exercises

There is great controversy surrounding the use of frames in HTML. This lab will give you the chance to look at both sides of that issue.

9.1. Build a framed document. It should have four frames: two vertical frames that are also each divided into two horizontal frames. Yes, frames within frames. The first window should display a document that tells about an image in the corresponding horizontal frame for each of the two divisions. It will go something like this:

description ----> picture
description ----> picture

9.2. Build a second framed document that demonstrates the use of links that change the content of the document. Create a small table of contents that lists four or five HTML tags. When the user clicks on the tag name in that frame, the description and usage of that tag should appear in the left, larger frame. The right frame (with the list) should occupy only about 20 percent of the browser plane.

9.3. Build a third page that demonstrates the misuse of frames. Divide the browser plane into three columns. Create a table document for the first column with four rows and four columns. Put different contents in each of the cells. Create a second framed document (like the one you did for the first item), and load it into the second column. Create a third document that changes the contents of the first two columns, and load it into the third column. Set the links so that clicking on different links will move the contents of the columns around. This should create a very confusing page.

9.4. Create a fourth page that is also a framed document. This document should replace your current main lab page and contain links to all the main pages from each lab. The lab pages should load into the large frame on the document. Use good style and format for this page. Oh, and one little extra: this lab's main page should give the user the option of seeing it in an unframed window. :-)

CHAPTER ten

FORMS AND CGI

10

Everything we have discussed up to this point involves what are known as a **static Web page** design elements. Even animated GIFs are static from the users' point of view in the sense that although they can watch the pretty pictures, they cannot interact with them. The only interaction the user has with most pages is to enter or leave them via a mouse click. In this chapter we will explore some ways the Web weaver has of allowing the user to do more than that—to interact with a page by providing information and then receiving a response. Usually this is done by the user filling out a form, then either touching the enter key (on a very simple form) or clicking on some sort of "submit" button that sends the data from the form to the server that hosts the page. That server processes the information using a program called a **script** program and sends response information back to the user. The response is generally an HTML document that either requests more information or simply thanks the user for her input. All pages don't need this capability, but well-designed forms with good scripts to process the data provided can give the Web weaver a tool for collecting and processing information from his users.

How Forms Work

Before we get into the nitty-gritty details of building forms, we need to have an idea how the forms and their data are actually processed. A **form** is simply another type of HTML document, or part of an existing HTML document, that allows users to provide input by performing any of several actions: they can click on one of a set of radio buttons, click to mark one or more check boxes, use a pull-down menu to select an element from a predefined list, or even simply enter free-flowing text in a text field. After entering all their data, they click on a submission button (such as "Submit Query") to send those data to the server that is hosting the Web page.

At this point the server must run a program called a **CGI (Common Gateway Interface)** program to do something with the data sent in from the form. The CGI program is usually written in a language like Perl, C, or even in a shell script on UNIX machines. Because there are so many UNIX machines out there working as servers, we will present some examples of these simple shell scripts. The **Perl** programming language, written by Larry Wall, is emerging as one of the standards in CGI scripting. The wise Web weaver should learn at least simple Perl programming if she wants to build powerful CGI scripts. CGI scripts can be very long and complex, and we cannot deal with all their intricacies in this text.

Java is becoming a popular way to build interactive Web pages. Indeed, some Web weavers believe that Java is going to replace CGI as the interactive scripting methodology of choice. But the two tools have different uses and purposes. Java is an excellent programming tool for allowing the user to manipulate the page, and Java applets can perform outstanding animation of both text and graphics. CGI is better for handling forms processing, because it is more universal across the browsers and because it is designed specifically for the purpose of forms processing. Therefore, we will focus our forms-processing discussion on CGI scripting and the other interactive programming on Java, later in this book.

A Simple Example Form

Figure 10.1 presents a simple form designed to allow users to input three fields: their name, gender, and e-mail address. After entering their name, users click on one of the two radio buttons (radio buttons are explained later) indicating their gender and then enter their e-mail address. Finally, they click on the "Submit Query" button to send the data to the server for processing. Obviously, this is a trivial form, but it will serve as an example to start our exploration. When the server processes the information, it sends back the response shown in Figure 10.2 to the user, indicating that the data have been processed.

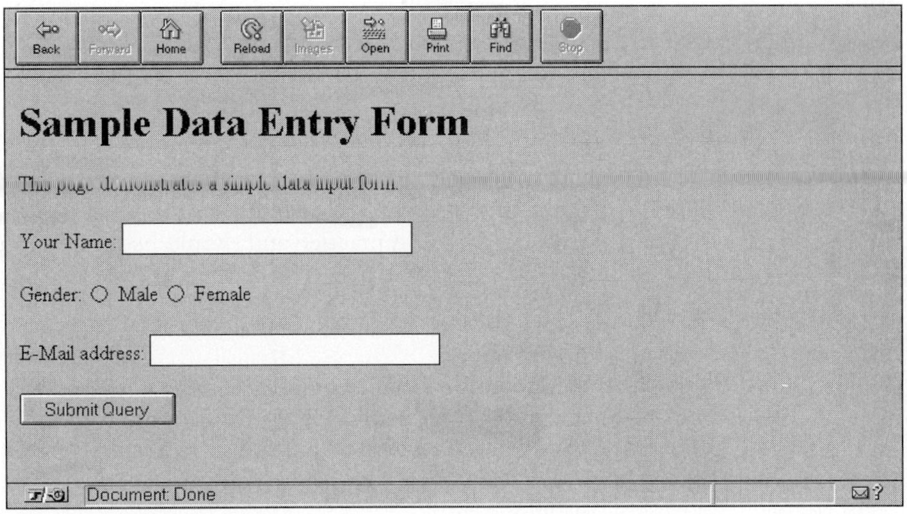

Figure 10.1 Netscape's presentation of a simple form.

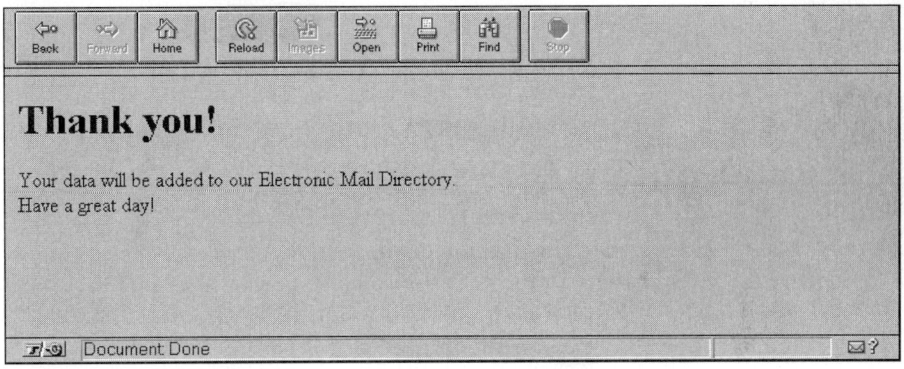

Figure 10.2 Netscape's presentation of the response to the simple form in Figure 10.1.

Building a form is easy, so we will tackle that part first. Then we can look at building a CGI script to process the information and perform the actual work.

<FORM>

The **<FORM>** container holds all the other contents of the form. The ending tag of **</FORM>** is never omitted. This container has three attributes: ACTION, METHOD, and ENCTYPE. The first two are required. Browsers treat the form as if it were an image embedded in the text, flowing the rest of the text around it.

There are no special layout rules for forms, other than that they should be easy to read and use. You can use most of the standard HTML elements within a form, so you can control the placement of the fields and text within the body of the form to the same degree as in the rest of the document. You cannot embed one form within another, but it is possible to have more than one form on a page as long as each form has its own submission button. That means that if you have two forms on the same page, and users need to fill out both, they would fill in the data for the first form, submit it with a submission button, then go back to the same page and fill in and submit the second form. That could be confusing for your users, because they would return to the page they just left. While it is indeed possible to code more then one form on a page, it is not considered a good practice and should be limited to cases where the user needs to fill out only one of the forms on the page.

ACTION

The **ACTION** attribute points to the application that is going to process the data captured by the form. You can have the data sent to the server and processed by a CGI script, or you can have the data e-mailed directly to your mailbox.

Common Gateway Interface (CGI)

If you choose to use the CGI method (described in detail later), the URL of the CGI script should specify not only the path but also the filename of the receiving program. Usually the program is in a directory called **cgi-bin** because it is a CGI script. An example of an ACTION attribute follows:

```
<FORM ACTION="http://www.wilbur.com/cgi-bin/emailer">
```

In this example, the data the user entered would be sent to the server **www.wilbur.com,** and the program or script called **emailer** would be started, with the data passed to that program. Most Web site administrators keep all the CGI programs and scripts in a common directory called something like **cgi-bin** or **cgibin** so that all the Web weavers will know where to point the ACTION attributes of their pages.

Electronic Mail

If you are collecting a small amount of data from only a few users, you may not want to go through the exercise of building a program to handle the data. You can have the form simply send you an e-mail containing the data that were collected by the form. In this case the action would look a little different:

```
<FORM ACTION="mailto:me@my.mailserver.com" METHOD=POST>
```

In this example, the data will be sent to you (**me**) at your e-mail address **(my.mailserver.com)** rather than being sent to a program you have written. *Note: You should always use the POST method rather than the GET method for sending mail.* These methods will be explained later in this chapter.

You will need to **parse**—that is, divide up the data—and do your own processing if you choose the e-mail method instead of the CGI method. If you are simply requesting input on your page and don't expect more than a few responses, this e-mail method could be a good choice. But if your page becomes popular, and lots of users are sending information to your mailbox, the e-mail method could pose some problems.

Figure 10.3 shows how our simple form would look when filled out by a user. The following data string is what would show up in your mailbox shortly after the user touched the "Submit Query" button:

```
name=Patti+Toad&gender=F&email=patti@ToadHall.com
```

Notice that there are no spaces in the data string. The space between Patti and Toad is replaced by the plus sign (+). The three variable names, **name, gender,** and **email** were set by the form itself. Those are the variable names the Web weaver chose when building the form. These form data were processed by sending them to the browser's mail utility which passed them on to the address specified in the action, in this case **me@my.mailserver.com.** You will need to decide what to do with these data now, because there is no more automatic processing done.

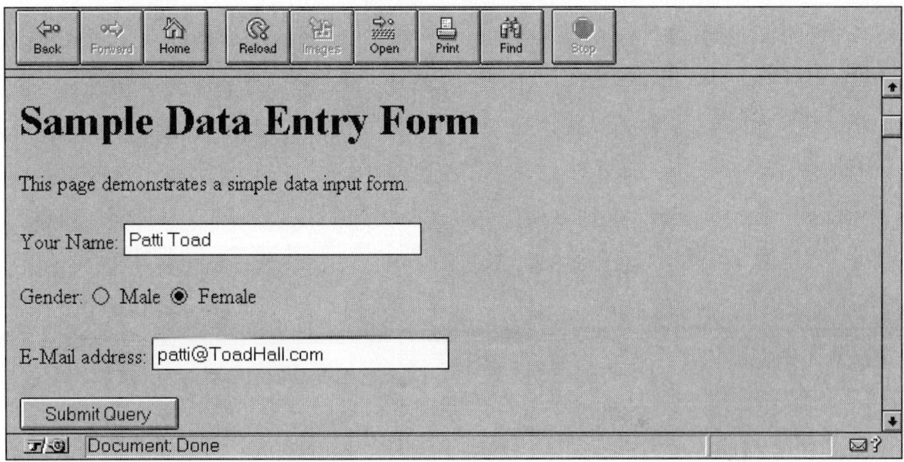

Figure 10.3 Netscape's presentation of data to be sent via the simple form in Figure 10.1.

For a Web site with small number of users and only a few data elements, this is a fine way to gather data. However, if you expect more than a few postings a day, you probably want to consider using a CGI script rather than e-mail. There are a couple of caveats that you need to take into account before using the e-mail method. First, the user must have her browser correctly set up to send electronic mail. This means that in Netscape, for example, the user will have had to identify herself as well as correctly configuring her browser to use the mail server on her ISP. If her electronic mail is not correctly configured, she will get an error message and will not be able to send you her data.

Second, the user will expose his e-mail address when he sends you a message. If he wants to remain anonymous, therefore, he will decide against sending the e-mail. Thus, using e-mail may result in your form collecting fewer responses than it would have with automatic data retrieval using a script.

Third, any data the user sends will be sent as ASCII text, easily readable by others on the Net. Don't use this method for collecting and transmitting secure data like credit card numbers or other data that is very personal, as it may be intercepted by unethical users.

Finally, if the user uses special characters, like the exclamation point (!), the browsers will usually code it as its hexadecimal value. The string "Hi there!" would look like this:

Hi+there%21

The space between **Hi** and **there** would be replaced by the plus sign, and the exclamation point would be coded as hexadecimal 21.

Because the **mailto** action generates one or more additional screens for users, you should warn them about what will happen before they submit their data. Figure 10.4 shows the warning screen generated by Netscape.

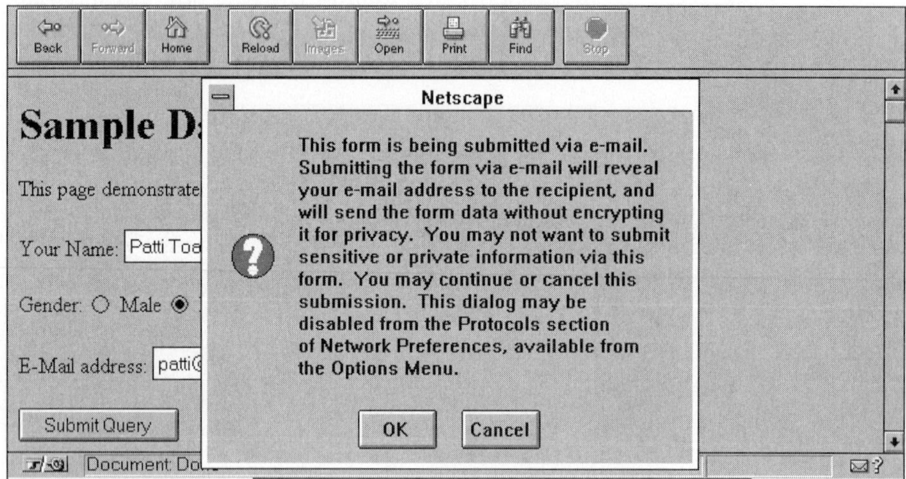

Figure 10.4 The mail warning message generated by Netscape.

METHOD

The **METHOD** attribute tells the browser how to send the data to the server. There are two ways the data can be sent: **GET** or **POST**. These two methods place very different demands on both the server and the Net. GET and POST are named after the http commands that the browser uses to communicate with the server.

GET

GET is the least complex way to pass information back to the server. The GET method creates a long string that contains all the data the user entered. It sends those data back to the server, where they are placed into a single environmental variable and made available in that form to the CGI application. The form of the data is in a series of NAME=VALUE pairs. The name is specified in the form, and the value is that which was typed in by the user. A sample of this sort of string follows:

```
variable1=data+for+1&variable2=data+for+2
```

Notice there are no intervening spaces. All the spaces in the data are replaced by plus signs. Also, the different variable names after the first are preceded by an ampersand (&). The CGI application must parse, or divide, the long string into different variable values before they can be processed by the program. All the processing of the data is the responsibility of the program written by the Web weaver and running on the server.

The application on the server will receive all the data in a single environmental variable called **QUERY_STRING.** This is one important limitation of the GET method. On many machines environmental variables are limited to a specific size, often 256 bytes. This means that if your data and variable names together total more than 256 characters, some data will most likely be chopped off and lost. GET is an excellent method for sending short variable lists to the server, but POST is better for more substantial data.

POST

POSTing data allows you to send much more information to the server. However, it entails a second transmission across the Net to establish communication before the data are sent. Some of the visionaries feel that POST is the proper method for future development, while others see value in both GET and POST methods.

As we saw with regard to the mailto action, there are times when the method is dictated by the ACTION. When data are posted to the server, they are sent to the application from a source called **standard input,** or **STDIN** in UNIX parlance. STDIN is the default input file given to all UNIX applications. You will need to decode the data, and there are standard tools to perform the decoding. Once the data are decoded into variables, usually the variable is the same as the NAME part of the NAME=VALUE pair, and the variable created is assigned the VALUE part of the pair. The program you write can process them like any other environmental variable. When we look at building simple CGI scripts, we will examine how the data from the user needs to be processed.

GET versus POST Considerations

In deciding whether to send the data to the server via GET or POST, your first consideration must be the types of forms processing the Web server supports. If your system administrator supports only the POST type of CGI programs, you have no choice. On the other hand, if your server supports both GET and POST, then the following considerations may also come into play:

- If you are sending just a few bytes of data, use GET. That method is fine for short data streams and is easy to process.
- When your form processes more data, or if it has a potentially long text field, use the POST method to ensure that data won't be truncated (chopped off) and lost.
- It is easier to build a CGI script to support GET than POST because you don't need to do the extra steps of decoding POST parameters.
- POST can be a more secure method of transmission than GET. With GET the data are appended to the URL of the CGI program and sent as

plain ASCII text. POST can encrypt the data, and the actual data stream is not part of the history buffer. The history buffer is where the browser stores previous location lines. In Netscape you can access the history buffer by clicking on the down arrow at the right end of the Location field.

- As we saw with the mailto action, sometimes the program you choose to run will dictate which method must be used. Mailto expects a POST method, but some other script may want the data sent via GET.
- If you want to be able to create an anchor that invokes a CGI script without involving a form, you should use the GET method of sending data.

Let's discuss this last point further. For example, if you have a series of small CGI programs that return different pages to the user depending on their selection, you can explicitly code values to send to the script without your user having to fill out any part of the form. Suppose you had a CGI script that took as input a number between 1 and 5, and depending on the value of that number would perform some different action, returning different data to the user. You could explicitly code the value in the anchor tag that invoked the script rather than having the user fill in a form.

Let's say the variable to be passed is NUM. You could invoke the CGI script with a simple anchor tag like the following:

```
<A HREF=//www.cgiserver.com/cgi-bin/myscript?num=4>
```

This code would invoke the script called **myscript** on the server **www.cgiserver.com,** passing a value of **4** for the variable **num.** This method is also handy for testing, but you must use GET.

There is a caveat about this method. It works fine if you have only one variable, but if you have two or more, you need to precede each variable name after the first with an ampersand (&). Unfortunately, that same ampersand could be considered a character insertion character when it is within an HREF. Therefore, you must use the HTML equivalent, either **&** or **&** as a substitute for the literal ampersand.

ENCTYPE

The **ENCTYPE** attribute allows you to specify a different encoding format for the data sent from the form to the CGI script. It is very unlikely that you will ever need to use this attribute, and it is of value only when you are sending binary data or non-ASCII data, usually part of a file.

The normal coding type is called **application/x-www-form-encoded.** This coding is necessary to prevent the data from becoming corrupted during transmission from the browser to the server. We saw an example of this standard encoding when we discussed the GET method of data transmission. **Application/x-www-form-encoded** data use the following conventions:

1. All spaces are converted to plus signs (+).
2. Nonalphameric characters are represented by their ASCII code, represented as a two-digit hexadecimal number preceded by a percent sign (%).
3. Each field name except the first is preceded by an ampersand (&).

These conventions are important to remember if you choose to use the mailto action rather than the CGI script action. They are also important to remember in debugging scripts.

There is a second type of encoding, called **multipart/form-data encoding,** which encloses the data in a form as several parts of a single document. Each field's data are preceded by a line of 30 minus signs (–) followed by a large random number. The minus signs and the random number serve as dividers between the different data fields. Each field is represented by at least one line of header information, then the actual data. The actual data are not encoded, so there is no possibility of corruption of binary data. **Multipart/form-data encoding** is normally used to send binary file data, so your forms processing will most likely not need to handle them.

<INPUT>

The **<INPUT>** tag is the tool most often used to create the actual input areas of a form. Using <INPUT> allows the Web weaver to create text fields, multiple-choice lists, clickable images, submission and reset buttons, and radio buttons. With the exception of submission and reset buttons, all the different forms of input require the use of the NAME attribute, and all the <INPUT> forms require the TYPE attribute. Each different type of input form requires different attributes. After looking at some guidelines for forming names, we will explore each type of input form, along with the applicable attributes for each.

Name

The **NAME** attribute is required by every form of input except the immediate buttons (submission and reset). The NAME attribute specifies the label, or name, that makes up the left half of the NAME=VALUE pair. The name, then, is the tag, or label, with which the data will be associated when passed back to the server. The selection of a good, useful name is very important. The rules for forming a name are very flexible, but common practice in programming has provided a few guidelines that will make your work with NAME=VALUE pairs less confusing.

1. Make the name meaningful. While it is acceptable to the browser and script to use names like "a," "n," and "e" they usually make little sense. Names like "age," "name," and "email" tell you and anyone else who is reading your form or script what data you are processing. The few extra keystrokes will be more than justified by the ease of understanding that meaningful names provide.

2. Use lowercase letters for the name. Some operating systems, like DOS, don't recognize uppercase and lowercase letters as being different, but other operating systems, like UNIX and Windows NT, do. That means that the variable name of "Email" is different from the variable name of "email." UNIX programmers usually use lowercase for their variable names because (a) it is slightly easier to read, (b) will not usually conflict with system variables, which are usually all uppercase, and (c) is easier to type because there is no need to use the shift key. Try to always use lowercase variable names.

3. Start the name with an alphabetic character. It is possible to start the name with nearly any character, but if you limit your names to alphabetic characters, there is less chance of either browser or CGI script problems. Although special characters like the ampersand and asterisk may look nice, they can cause problems and so should be avoided.

4. Make the name continuous. With some systems it is possible to embed blanks in variable names. This may work on your machine, but it is generally considered poor programming practice. To create multi-word names, use an underscore rather than an embedded blank. For example, the variable name of "first name" describes the content, starts with an alphabetic character, and is lowercase. It is a good name except for the fact that it contains a space. Some operating systems may try to make it into two different names, "first" and "name." A better name would be "first_name," in which the underscore holds the place between the two words.

A properly formed name will make life easier for you and anyone else who chooses to use your form or your script. Take a few minutes to select variable names that make sense and are well formed.

TYPE=TEXT

Text-entry fields, **TYPE=TEXT,** are probably the most common type of <INPUT> field on most forms. They require little from the Web weaver other than assigning a NAME. However, some of the other attributes can provide additional features. Figure 10.5 presents a very simple form with a text-entry field that uses all default values. This form takes in any length of text the user wants to enter, scrolling the window to the left as the user keeps typing. The figure shows that the default text window is 20 characters wide, but the maximum size of the field was not specified, so the user can just keep typing and the most recent 20 characters will show.

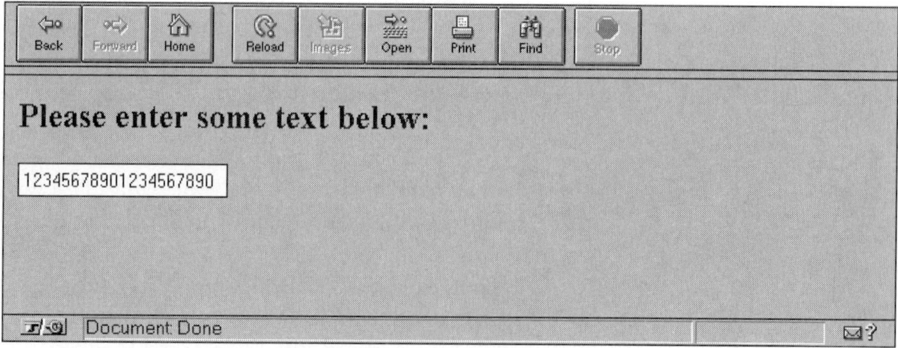

Figure 10.5 Netscape's presentation of a very simple text-entry form using default values.

Figure 10.6 presents the code for this simple form. Note that the only attributes for the <INPUT> tag in this code are TYPE and NAME. All the rest of the layout of the form is the default for this browser. Using all default values is not a good idea, because the layout will vary among the various browsers. Let's look at some attributes that should be specified.

```
<HTML>
<HEAD>
<TITLE> Text entry form </TITLE>
</HEAD>
<BODY>
<FORM>
<H2>Please enter some text below:</H2>
<INPUT
     TYPE=TEXT
     NAME=INPUT1>
</FORM>
</BODY>
</HTML>
```

Figure 10.6 HTML code for a simple text-entry form using default values.

SIZE

The **SIZE** attribute specifies the size of the text-entry field. Figure 10.7 shows the same form, as in Figure 10.5, but with a SIZE=15 attribute added. Now the text-entry area is only 15 characters wide. The user can enter as many characters as the browser will allow, but only the rightmost 15 will show in the window.

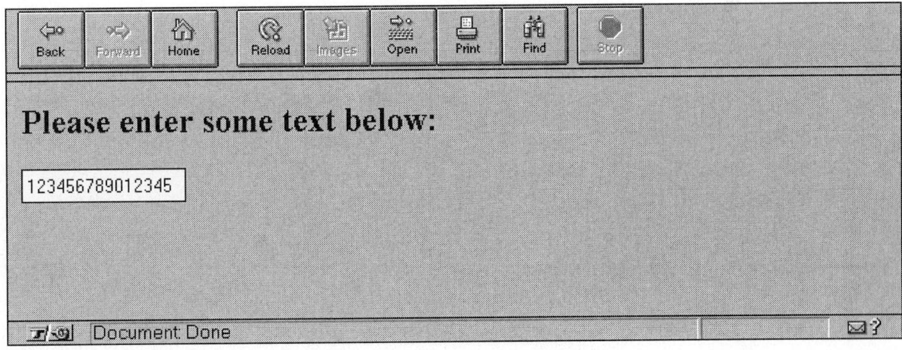

Figure 10.7 The browser representation of a simple text entry form with a SIZE=15.

MAXLENGTH

The **MAXLENGTH** attribute limits the actual number of characters the user can enter. Figure 10.8 shows how the form looks with a MAXLENGTH=10 coded. Only 10 characters fit in the form, even though it has a size of 15, because the MAXLENGTH value was set to 10. This may be somewhat confusing for the user; and the browser will usually issue a warning sound each time the user tries to type beyond the MAXLENGTH, so it can be distracting as well. Usually it is best to have the SIZE of the text input field no larger than the MAXLENGTH of that field.

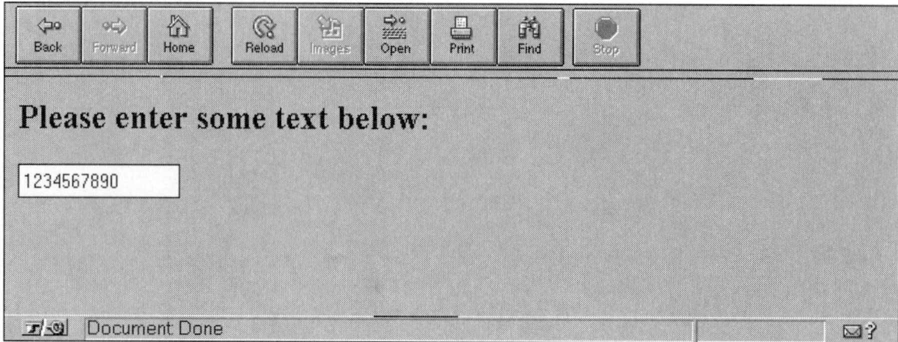

Figure 10.8 Netscape's presentation of a simple text-entry form with SIZE=15 and MAXLENGTH=10.

VALUE

The Web weaver can assign a default **VALUE** to the field, so the user need only submit the form if he wishes to use the default value. Figure 10.9 shows the simple form with a VALUE="Default" coded. If the user types anything in the field, it is appended to whatever was specified by the VALUE attribute. The user must delete the data placed in the field before he can enter his own data.

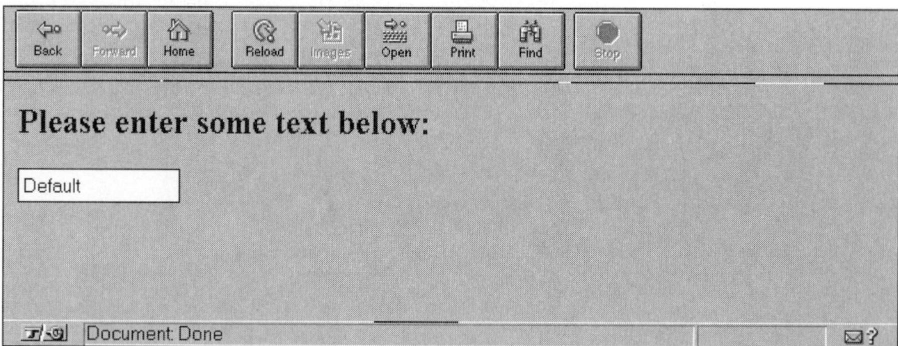

Figure 10.9 Netscape's presentation of a simple text-entry form with SIZE=15, MAXLENGTH=10, and VALUE="Default."

Use the VALUE attribute sparingly, and only when you think that the user will most likely take the default value you have provided, because it takes significantly more work for the user to replace your VALUE than to simply type in her own data.

Regardless of what type of prompt you use, the user can type anything that fits into a text line. So if, for example, you want to have the user type a number between 5 and 9, she could as well type any single letter or character. There is no way to validate the user's input in the form. Your application must do the validation. The validation can be a long, complex process, so the best bet is to give your user excellent instructions as to your expectations for her input.

Hidden Input: TYPE=PASSWORD

There are times when you want to help users protect the data they are typing from prying eyes at their site. If you set the TYPE to PASSWORD, anything the user types will appear as special characters, like asterisks. Obviously, this is most often used to hide passwords, hence the name, but it can also be used to hide other selection data.

Figure 10.10 shows our simple input form with the TYPE changed to PASSWORD. As you can see, even the default value was changed to asterisks. Although the data in a field of type PASSWORD are protected from people looking at the browser screen, they are not protected when sent to the server. When the data are sent across to the server, the data can be intercepted and read electronically.

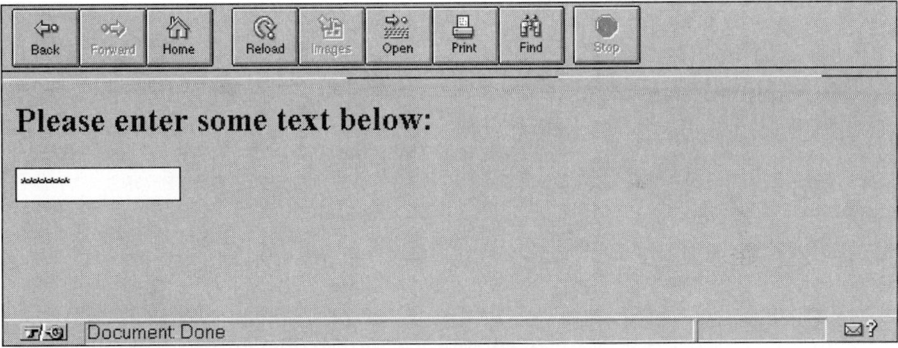

Figure 10.10 Netscape's presentation of a PASSWORD text-entry form with SIZE=15, MAXLENGTH=10, and VALUE="Default".

TYPE=CHECKBOX

Using a **checkbox,** or a set of checkboxes is an easy, fast way for your user to enter data is to select and deselect different items. If you lay out your form efficiently, setting TYPE to CHECKBOX will allow your users to quickly enter the data you are requesting, and you will be able to accurately retrieve those data with less need for data validation. Unlike radio buttons, several checkboxes from a series can be selected.

Figure 10.11 shows a form with a set of checkboxes allowing the user to select all the operating systems he uses. Figure 10.12 shows the code that creates the checkboxes for this form. Notice that each line of code ends in a break (<BR>) to force the different selections to appear on individual lines. Leaving out the breaks would cause the checkboxes to appear in a line across the browser window. The layout of the form is the job of the Web weaver, and some careful thought can make the form much more easily understood.

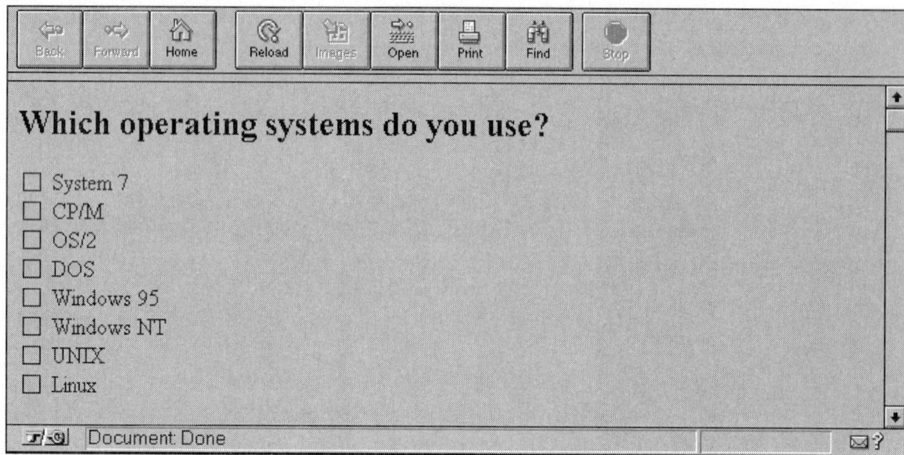

Figure 10.11 Netscape's presentation of a set of checkboxes.

```
<H2>Which operating systems do you use?</H2>
<INPUT   TYPE=CHECKBOX  NAME=OPS  VALUE="sys7"> System 7 <BR>
<INPUT   TYPE=CHECKBOX  NAME=OPS  VALUE="cpm"> CP/M <BR>
<INPUT   TYPE=CHECKBOX  NAME=OPS  VALUE="os2"> OS/2 <BR>
<INPUT   TYPE=CHECKBOX  NAME=OPS  VALUE="dos"> DOS <BR>
<INPUT   TYPE=CHECKBOX  NAME=OPS  VALUE="w95"> Windows 95 <BR>
<INPUT   TYPE=CHECKBOX  NAME=OPS  VALUE="nt"> Windows NT <BR>
<INPUT   TYPE=CHECKBOX  NAME=OPS  VALUE="unx"> UNIX <BR>
<INPUT   TYPE=CHECKBOX  NAME=OPS  VALUE="lnx"> Linux <BR>
```

Figure 10.12 HTML code for a set of checkboxes.

In the code, all of the checkboxes have the NAME set to OPS. Checkboxes can be collected into a group by giving all of them the same name. In this case, all of the values the user marks will be sent back to the server as a string of comma-separated data. Notice that the values for the different checkboxes are short, and all are coded in lowercase letters. These features will make the code easier to process on the server.

Figure 10.13 shows the form as it might be filled out by a typical user. When the user clicks on the box (checkbox) in front of an operating system, the browser marks the selected box with an X. Here the user has selected four different operating systems. Because the Web weaver has designed the form using the same NAME for all the different boxes, the browser will send the following data stream back to the server:

```
OPS=dos,nt,unx,lnx
```

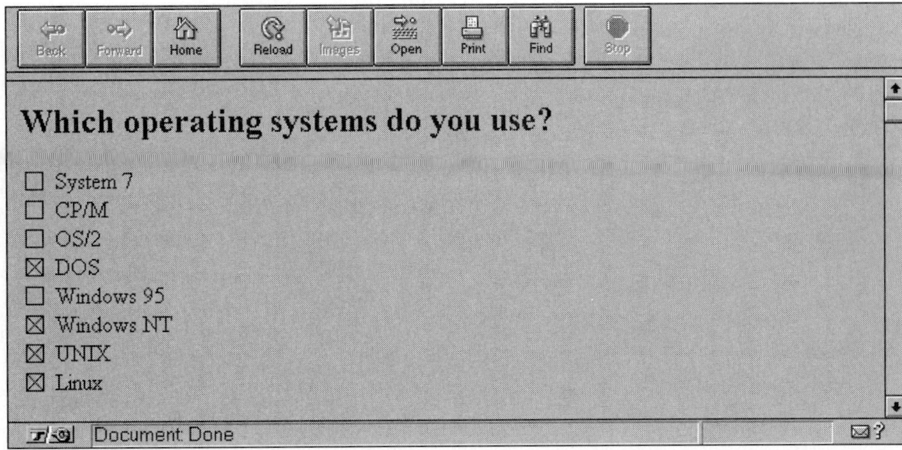

Figure 10.13 Netscape's presentation in which four checkboxes have been selected by user.

Checkboxes are a very efficient way to transmit the data, and they are also very efficient for the user. On the other hand, using this example, if the user is using an operating system that is not listed, like MVS, the form will not represent his choice. Probably a text field called "other" should be added.

As with the text field, you can set one or more of the checkboxes as default values. Figure 10.14 shows how this works: When the user brings up the form, one of the checkboxes is already marked. This is done using the **CHECKED** attribute. The user must click on that checkbox to turn it off. This may cause the user extra work, and it may give you invalid data if the user doesn't bother to turn off your preselected choice(s).

Back
Forward
Home
Reload
Images
Open
Print
Find
Stop
Which operating systems do you use?
System 7
CP/M
OS/2
DOS
Windows 95
Windows NT
UNIX
Linux
Document: Done

Figure 10.14 Netscape's presentation of one checkbox as a preselected value.

Checkboxes are a very useful tool when you want the user to be able to select one or more elements from a set. Be careful to provide some order to your choices when possible, and lay out the form in a way that makes it easy for your user to determine what you want her to do.

TYPE=RADIO

As just explained, checkboxes are good when you want the user to be able to select more than one option from the form. But radio buttons are best when you want to ensure that the user selects only one option. The term **radio button** needs a little explanation. Not all that long ago, car and console radios had a series of mechanical buttons for selecting the radio station. Pushing one button in would cause the previously pressed button to pop out. In that way only one selection could be made at a time. It was a somewhat complex, mechanical way of ensuring that only a single button was depressed at any one time. Likewise, the radio-button type of input item ensures that only one of a series of choices can be selected.

There are many uses for the radio type of input form: salary ranges, age, and gender, to name a few. As with checkboxes, you can group a set of radio buttons by giving all of them the same NAME attribute. Also like checkboxes, each radio button must have a VALUE assigned. The VALUE assigned should be different for each button, so that the CGI script can figure out the user's selection.

Figure 10.15 shows a set of radio buttons that allow the user to select his favorite operating system. Unlike the checkboxes in the examples in the previous section, the user can select only one from this series. When he clicks on one of the selections, the "button" changes from a plain circle to one with a dot inside it, as shown in Figure 10.16. If he selects another button, the browser deselects the first choice. That button goes back to the simple circle, and the button for the new selection is changed.

As with checkboxes, you can preselect a choice for your user. Indeed, some browsers will preselect for you, usually the first button in the series. Others don't preselect. It is always a good idea to preselect one of the radio buttons so you are assured of having a value sent to the server. Unlike checkboxes, with radio buttons, the user can deselect your choice simply by clicking on another button. Preselection creates no more work for the user.

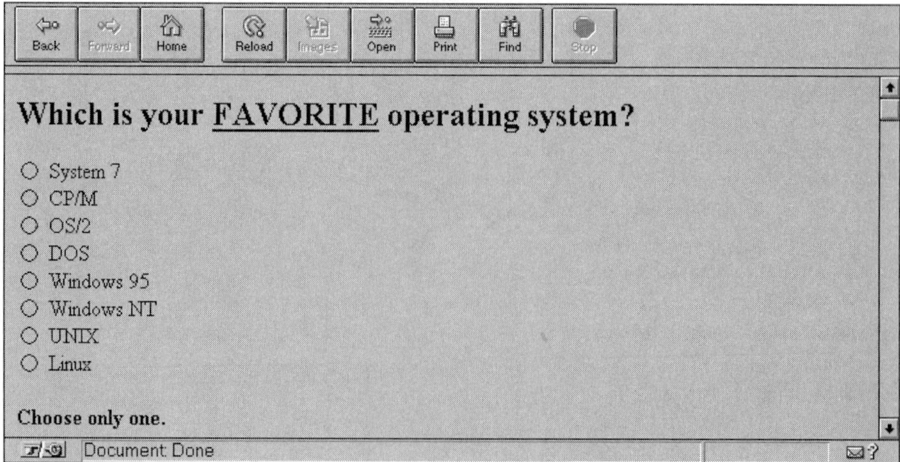

Figure 10.15 Netscape's presentation of a series of radio buttons.

Figure 10.16 shows the screen from Figure 10.15, but with the Linux operating system preselected. Figure 10.17 presents the code used to generate this screen. Notice that only the Linux option has the CHECKED attribute, marking it as preselected. After executing this code, the browser will return the variable FAVOPS with one of the values specified. Since one of the radio buttons should always be preselected, always have more than one radio button on a form. Radio buttons should be used when the user is making a selection that is exclusive of the others in the list.

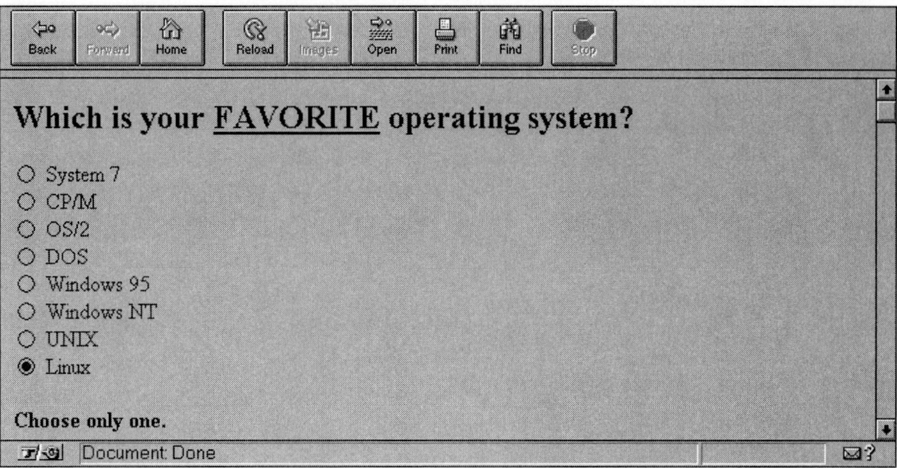

Figure 10.16 Netscape's presentation of a series of radio buttons with one preselected.

```
<H2>Which is your <U>FAVORITE</U> operating system?</H2>

<INPUT  TYPE=RADIO NAME=FAVOPS VALUE="sys7"> System 7 <BR>
<INPUT  TYPE=RADIO NAME=FAVOPS VALUE="cpm"> CP/M <BR>
<INPUT  TYPE=RADIO NAME=FAVOPS VALUE="os2"> OS/2 <BR>
<INPUT  TYPE=RADIO NAME=FAVOPS VALUE="dos"> DOS <BR>
<INPUT  TYPE=RADIO NAME=FAVOPS VALUE="w95"> Windows 95 <BR>
<INPUT  TYPE=RADIO NAME=FAVOPS VALUE="nt"> Windows NT <BR>
<INPUT  TYPE=RADIO NAME=FAVOPS VALUE="unx"> UNIX <BR>
<INPUT  TYPE=RADIO NAME=FAVOPS CHECKED VALUE="lnx"> Linux <BR>
<H4>Choose only one.</H4>
```

Figure 10.17 HTML code creating a series of radio buttons with the last one preselected.

One easy way to cause problems for the script parsing the form data—and to confuse your user as well—is to misspell one of the names. For example, in the code in Figure 10.18 the name in the Windows NT line is misspelled. Figure 10.19 shows that when the user has clicked on that button, the Linux button is also selected. It is critical that you check your code for this kind of sneaky error.

```
<H2>Which is your <U>FAVORITE</U> operating system?</H2>

<INPUT   TYPE=RADIO    NAME=FAVOPS    VALUE="sys7"> System 7
<BR>
<INPUT   TYPE=RADIO    NAME=FAVOPS    VALUE="cpm"> CP/M <BR>
<INPUT   TYPE=RADIO    NAME=FAVOPS    VALUE="os2"> OS/2 <BR>
<INPUT   TYPE=RADIO    NAME=FAVOPS    VALUE="dos"> DOS <BR>
<INPUT   TYPE=RADIO    NAME=FAVOPS    VALUE="w95"> Windows 95
<BR>
<INPUT   TYPE=RADIO    NAME=FAOVPS    VALUE="nt"> Windows NT
<BR>
<INPUT   TYPE=RADIO    NAME=FAVOPS    VALUE="unx"> UNIX <BR>
<INPUT   TYPE=RADIO    NAME=FAVOPS    CHECKED VALUE="lnx">
Linux <BR>
<H4>Choose only one.</H4>
```

Figure 10.18 HTML code creating a series of radio buttons containing an error.

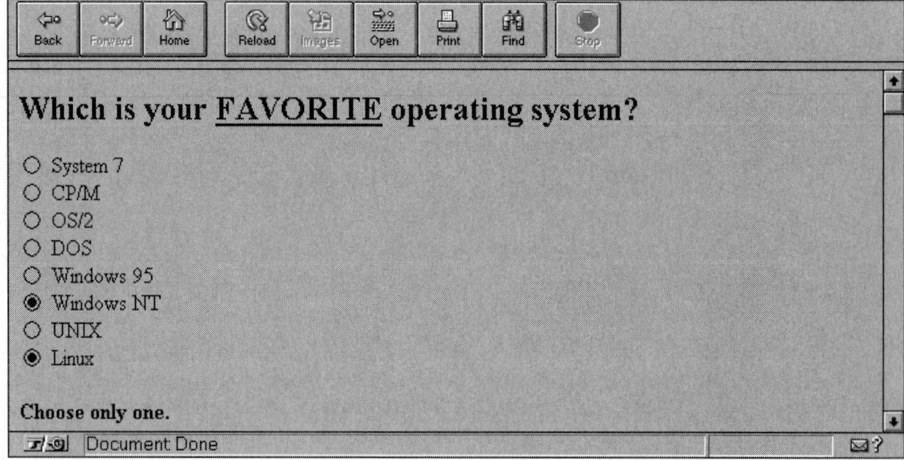

Figure 10.19 Netscape's presentation of the code for a series of radio buttons containing a NAME spelling error.

Local Action Buttons

All of the input fields we have examined so far set up data to be processed by the CGI script on the server. The next two buttons cause the *browser* to perform specific actions, and so are called **local action buttons.**

TYPE=RESET

TYPE=RESET provides a button that causes the browser to reset, or change, all the input areas back to the way they were when the user entered the page. Any CHECKED buttons will again be set, and any that the user had selected will be deselected. Always include a reset button on any form you create. It will enable a user to quickly undo errors she has made or easily change her mind.

Figure 10.20 shows our simple form, reformatted to better fit on the page, with some input from the user. Notice that the user has selected five different operating systems in the first set, and Windows NT in the second set. The reset button is labeled "UnDo Selections" to give the user a good idea of its function. If you assign a VALUE to the <INPUT> field, that VALUE will replace the default name of RESET. Sophisticated users will understand the function of RESET, but for less Web-wise users, a more explicit label may help.

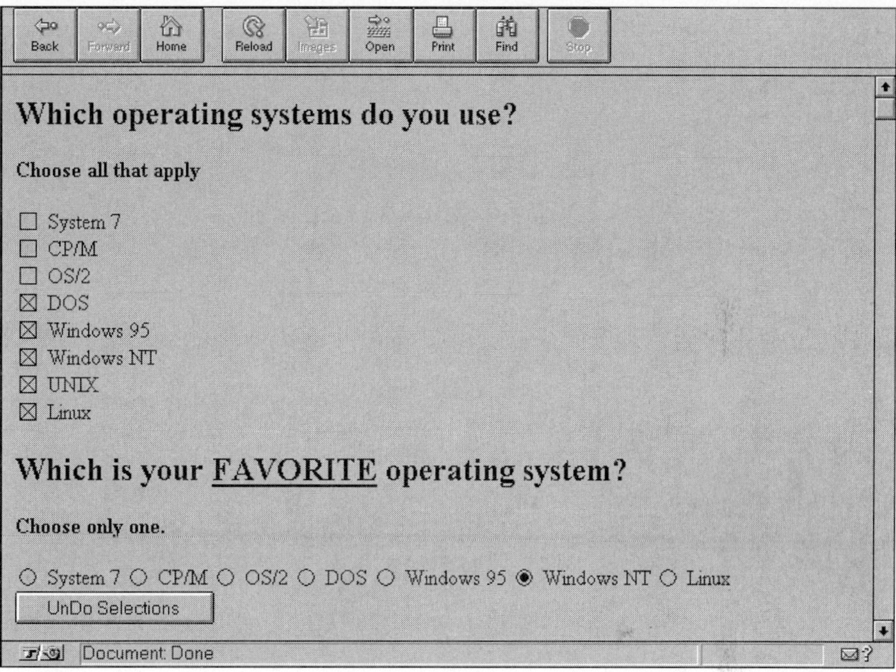

Figure 10.20 Netscape's presentation of a simple form showing some user input.

By clicking the "UnDo Selections" button, the user will see the screen in Figure 10.21, which was the screen shown before the user had made any selections. In one click the user can undo everything she had selected. The Web weaver has no control over what is reset when this button is clicked. It is not currently possible to simply undo part of a form. A RESET button resets all the fields on the form.

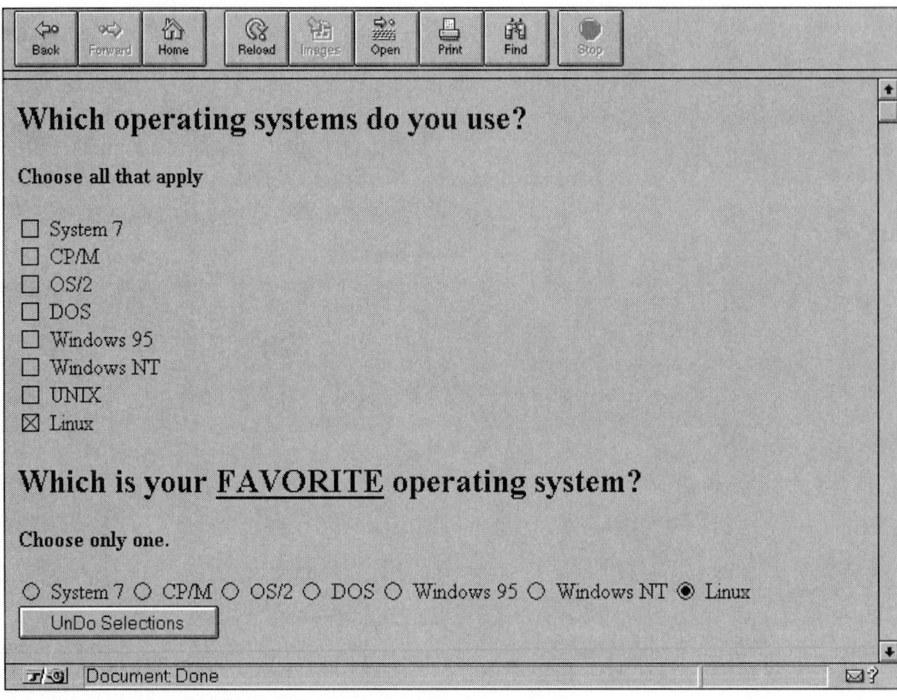

Figure 10.21 Netscape's presentation of the simple form in Figure 10.20 after the user clicks on the "UnDo Selections" button.

TYPE=SUBMIT

The **TYPE=SUBMIT** button does what it implies—it starts the process of the browser encoding and sending the information to the server. Like the RESET type, if you just use a TYPE=SUBMIT, the browser creates a small button for the user, in this case labeled "Submit Query." As with the reset button, if you want to change the label on the submit, or submission, button, you need to give the input field a VALUE attribute.

One clever way to handle layout of the submit and reset buttons is to use a table. Figure 10.22 shows our simple form, but with both the reset and submit buttons on the bottom of the form. Notice how one is on the left and the other on the right to help the user avoid clicking one by mistake. The two <INPUT> fields are put into a table to control their placement on the form. Figure 10.23 presents the code used to generate that portion of the form. WIDTH attributes are used to force the size of the table elements. Align attributes are set to right and left to justify the input fields.

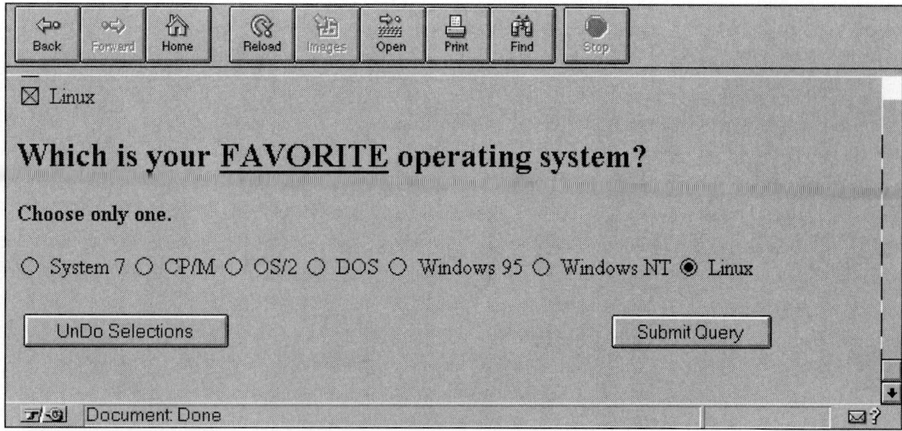

Figure 10.22 Netscape's presentation of SUBMIT and RESET fields.

```
 <TABLE WIDTH="90%">
<TR><TD WIDTH="50%" ALIGN=LEFT><INPUT   TYPE=RESET
     VALUE="UnDo Selections" ></TD>
<TD  ALIGN=RIGHT><INPUT TYPE=SUBMIT ></TD>
</TR>
</TABLE>
```

Figure 10.23 HTML code used to lay out SUBMIT and RESET fields.

You can also supply a NAME attribute, and the browser will add the NAME=VALUE pair to the information sent to the server. This allows you to set up multiple submit buttons, each with a different NAME and VALUE, and the browser will add those data to the data stream. Each submit button can signal a different processing step within the CGI script.

For example, you could create a form that allows the user to learn about your product line by requesting information about any of several different products. Or you could create a form that allows the user to order one of several different products by choosing different submit buttons. Figure 10.24 shows a form that lets the user choose the color of the product she wants by using different submit buttons. When she clicks on any of these color selections, the form is sent to the server. These are all submit buttons. This is a simple example of using a submit button to send additional information.

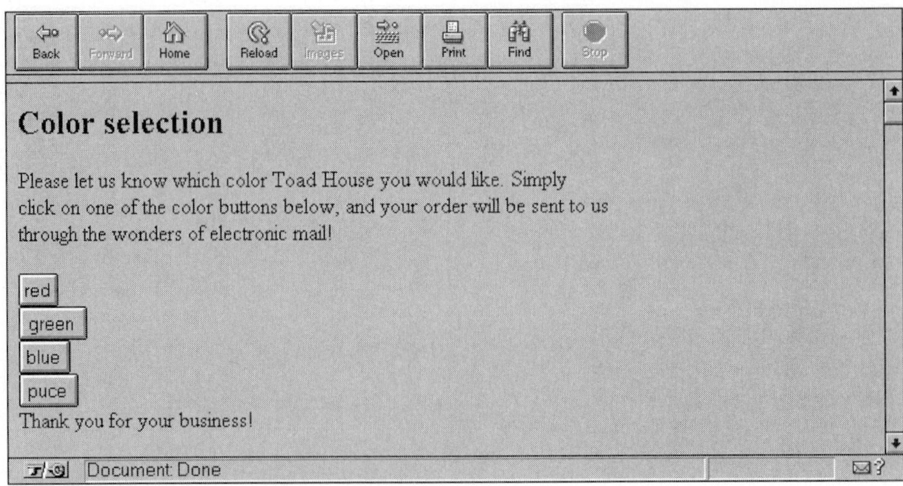

Figure 10.24 Netscape's presentation of multiple submit buttons.

Figure 10.25 presents the code that created the screen in Figure 10.24. Notice that all four buttons have a TYPE of SUBMIT, all have the same NAME, and each has a different VALUE, reflected in its name on the form, that signifies its relative contents, or value. Using multiple submit buttons can simplify processing for your user. In addition, multiple submit buttons provide an easy way of creating an additional variable that can give direction to your CGI scripting or, if you are using e-mail, provide more data in the mail sent to you.

```
<H2>Color selection</H2>
Please let us know which color Toad House you would like.
Simply<BR>
click on one of the color buttons below, and your order will
be sent to us<BR>
through the wonders of electronic mail!<BR>
<FORM METHOD=GET>
<INPUT TYPE=SUBMIT NAME="Color" VALUE="red"><BR>
<INPUT TYPE=SUBMIT NAME="Color" VALUE="green"><BR>
<INPUT TYPE=SUBMIT NAME="Color" VALUE="blue"><BR>
<INPUT TYPE=SUBMIT NAME="Color" VALUE="puce"><BR>
Thank you for your business!
</FORM>
```

Figure 10.25 HTML code with multiple SUBMIT buttons.

Graphical Buttons

You will recall that when you built anchors that were links, it was possible to include a graphic or image that served as part of the link. It is also possible to do that with the <INPUT> tag. However, the processing done by the browser is very different in these two cases. In the case of the anchor link, when the user clicks on the image, the browser takes the associated link. If the Web weaver adds an image to an <INPUT> tag, a graphical browser treats it like a mouse-sensitive image map rather than a simple link.

When the Web weaver has coded an <INPUT> tag with a TYPE=IMAGE, the user sees a picture that she can click on. Rather than simply sending the preset value for the name of the input field, the browser sends an X,Y coordinate pair associated with the NAME attribute. The script needs to process the X,Y pair to determine just where in the image the user clicked.

Figure 10.26 shows a simple example of an image used as a button to send in an order. A naive Web weaver might think that the browser will simply submit the order, but when the user clicks on the "ORDER" button, the browser will also send the X,Y coordinates of the actual mouse position within the graphic in the following form:

```
orderme.41&orderme.22
```

Here **41** represents the number of pixels in from the left edge of the image, and **22** represents the number of pixels down from the top edge of the image.

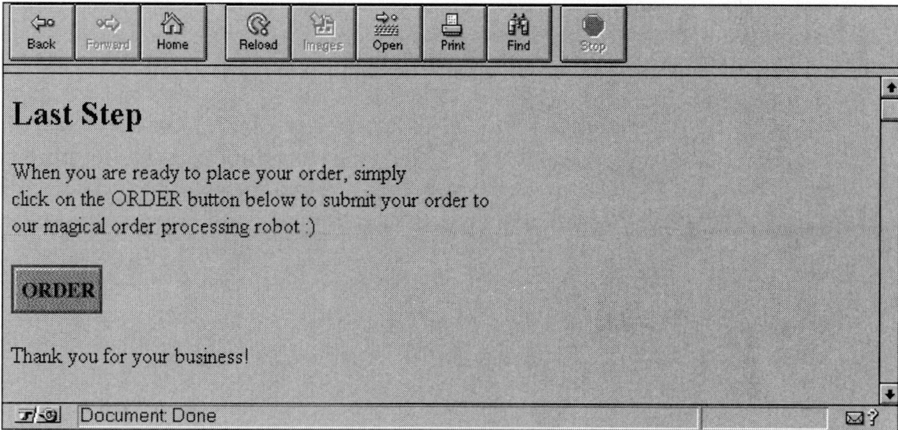

Figure 10.26 Netscape's presentation of a graphical submit button.

Figure 10.27 presents the code used to generate this screen. Notice that the image, **"order1.gif"**, is in the same directory as the page, so it is not necessary to code the path to that image. Since the graphic functions like a link, some browsers will put a frame around the image, as we saw earlier with images used as links. Most browsers also allow the Web weaver to control the alignment of the image just as the <IMG> tag allows.

```
<HTML>
<HEAD>
<TITLE> Multi-submit example </TITLE>
</HEAD>
<BODY>
<H2>Last Step</H2>
When you are ready to place your order, simply<BR>
click on the ORDER button below to submit your order to<BR>
our magical order processing robot :)<BR>
<FORM
ACTION="http://phred.dcccd.edu/cgi-bin/demo1"
METHOD=GET>
<INPUT TYPE=IMAGE NAME="orderme"  SRC="order1.gif"><BR><BR>

Thank you for your business!
</FORM>
</BODY>
</HTML>
```

Figure 10.27 HTML code for a graphical submit button.

There may be some specialized need to create a graphical button, but the code in Figure 10.28 seems to achieve the same general effect as the code in Figure 10.27. Compare Figure 10.29 with Figure 10.26. Although the submit button is not quite so pretty, the screen in Figure 10.29 has the same "look and feel" as the screen that uses a graphical button, and it requires less processing. Although it is less elegant, this code works just fine to submit the order. An important principle is to use only the HTML tools you need to do the job, avoiding the trap of creating fancy code just because you can. In this example, a text-only browser can do no more than submit the form, as there is no mouse pointer to return the coordinates from.

```
<HTML>
<HEAD>
<TITLE> Multi-submit example </TITLE>
</HEAD>
<BODY>
<H2>Last Step</H2>
When you are ready to place your order, simply<BR>
click on the ORDER button below to submit your order to<BR>
our magical order processing robot :)<BR>
<FORM
ACTION="http://phred.dcccd.edu/cgi-bin/demo1"
METHOD=GET>
<STRONG><INPUT TYPE=SUBMIT NAME="orderme"  VALUE=ORDER >
</STRONG>  <BR><BR>

Thank you for your business!
</FORM>
</BODY>
</HTML>
```

Figure 10.28 HTML code that simulates the graphical submit button.

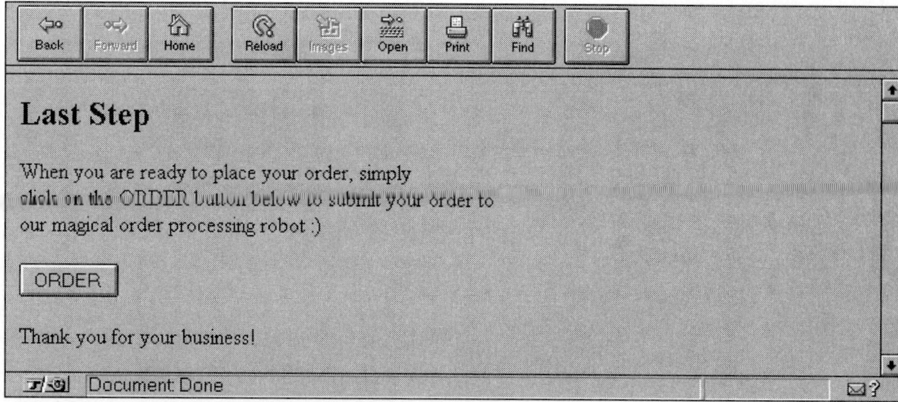

Figure 10.29 Netscape's presentation of a page that looks like the graphical page.

Hidden Data Fields: TYPE=HIDDEN

Sometimes you will want to send CGI script data that you don't want the user to be able to manipulate or even see. For example, if part of the processing involves sending you a mail message about some of the contents of the data stream, you would want to send the script your e-mail address in such a way that the user could not modify the address. Another example would be special coding that tells the server exactly which form was used to send the information. Those data, too, could be coded in a hidden field and sent to the server so as to prevent any action or interference by the user.

This type of <INPUT> field requires only three attributes: NAME, VALUE, and **TYPE=HIDDEN.** Here is a sample line from a form that sends some hidden data to the server:

```
<INPUT TYPE=HIDDEN NAME="mailto" VALUE="me@ToadHall.com" >
```

Neither the user nor the browser sees this field. It is passed exactly as coded to the server for processing at that end. Hidden fields are not a common feature of Web pages, but they provide a very useful way to handle some specialized situations.

<TEXTAREA>

All of the input tools discussed thus far limit the user to a single line of input. Even the TYPE=TEXT input tool shows the user only a single line for input. Users can type an unlimited number of characters if the Web weaver has not set a MAXLENGTH attribute, but the input happens on only one line, and only part of a large input string is visible. The **<TEXTAREA>** container (**</TEXTAREA>** is never omitted) sets the user free from the single-line restriction by creating an area for textual input.

It is possible, and even advisable, to include default text in a <TEXTAREA> field to give the user instructions. When the form is submitted to the server, the browser takes all the lines of text that have been entered, each line separated by a carriage-return line feed (%0D%0A), called a **newline** in UNIX. That long text stream is the value of the variable specified by the NAME attribute.

Figure 10.30 shows a form that provides the user with a text area for input. Gee, what a wonderful place to enter expansive text passages! What is shown here is the standard, default text-area box. It has scroll bars, but it shows only one line of text. Browsers don't seem to understand the need for size that prompts us to use a <TEXTAREA>, so they build a minimal area for text input. Fortunately, there are a couple of attributes that allow us to build a better looking, more useful text area.

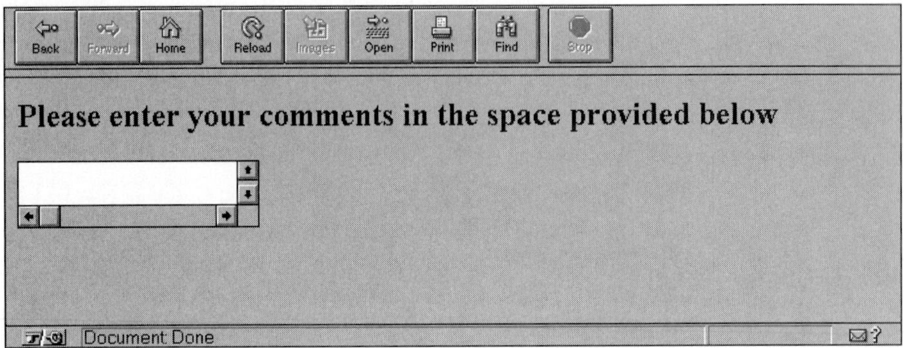

Figure 10.30 Netscape's presentation of a form showing the use of <TEXTAREA>.

ROWS and COLS

The **ROWS** and **COLS** attributes define the initial size of the text-input area. Not surprisingly, ROWS specifies the number of lines in the input block, and COLS is a count of the number of columns (characters) across each line. Together they define a rectangular region on the screen that is set aside for user input. Good HTML practice is to always code ROWS and COLS in text areas.

Figure 10.31 shows a new version of our form, with ROWS=7 and COLS=60. As you can see, this is a much more appealing place to enter text. Notice that it is exactly 60 characters wide. There are still scroll bars, because the user can enter more than seven lines, and each line can be as long as the user wants. Remember that the browser and the form merely supply a place for the user to enter text. At this point they do not restrict or control how the text looks. Users who type long lines can still lose sight of what they have typed.

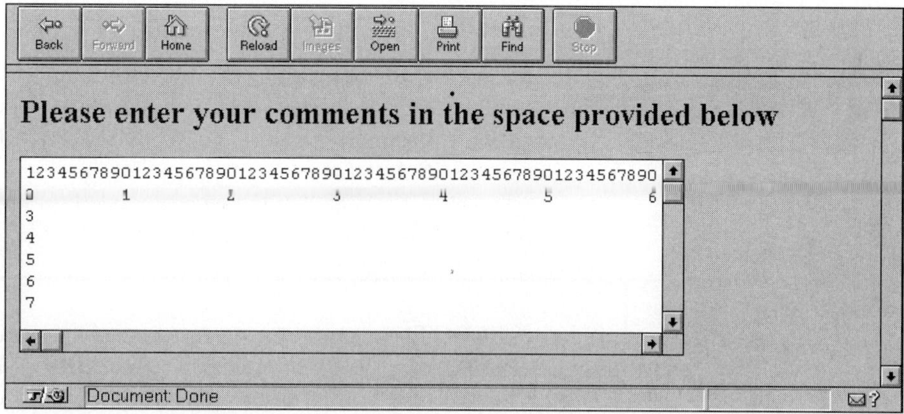

Figure 10.31 Netscape's presentation of a form showing the use of <TEXTAREA> with ROWS=7 and COLS=60.

Because users have become used to the wordwrap feature of most word-processing packages, it may seem cumbersome to them to have to keep touching the return key to move down to the next line. Again, the designers of HTML have taken that into account, as explained next.

WRAP

The **WRAP** attribute causes the browser to break lines, on word boundaries, as close to the right margin as possible and continue the text on the next line. This is like the wordwrap feature of most word processors. Coding WRAP can make your <TEXTAREA> a friendlier place for your users. And, indeed, they will expect this feature from a sophisticated Web page. There are three different values for the WRAP attribute, as follows.

WRAP=VIRTUAL

WRAP=VIRTUAL will cause the text to break at word boundaries on the user's screen, but when the text is transmitted to the server, only those **carriage-return line feeds (CrLfs)** that the user actually entered will be in the text stream. Most of the time the text will be passed as a continuous stream with no CrLfs. Usually this is not the ideal choice.

WRAP=PHYSICAL

With the **WRAP=PHYSICAL** option, the word breaks happen at the browser just as they do with a VIRTUAL wrap, but the actual CrLfs are added to the text the user enters as if the user had actually coded them. This is the preferred option on the WRAP attribute because it creates a more readable copy. However, it must be noted that using this attribute with this option will cause the browser to add data, albeit just CrLfs, to the data the user enters.

WRAP=OFF

The **WRAP=OFF** option sets the browser to the standard default processing where the only CrLfs are those actually entered by the user and the text can scroll to the right nearly infinitely. Usually WRAP=PHYSICAL is a better option than WRAP=OFF.

<SELECT>

The **<SELECT>** container is a very powerful yet easy-to-use tool. Use it to create a pull-down menu of selections. Normally <SELECT> acts like a radio button in that only one of the options can be selected. However, with an attribute you can cause <SELECT> to act like checkboxes instead, allowing the return of multiple data elements.

Figure 10.32 shows a screen created with code including a <SELECT> container. When the user looks at this screen, the arrows on the scroll bar tell him that there are more options available. When he clicks on one of the selections, that option is highlighted and that value is sent back to the CGI script. Figure 10.33 presents the code for the menu used here. The code shows a nearly generic pull-down <SELECT> menu. When the user selects one of the options, the form sends the actual option as the value in the FAVOS=*value* string. For example, if the user selects Linux (smart user!), then the form sends **FAVOS=Linux** back to the CGI script.

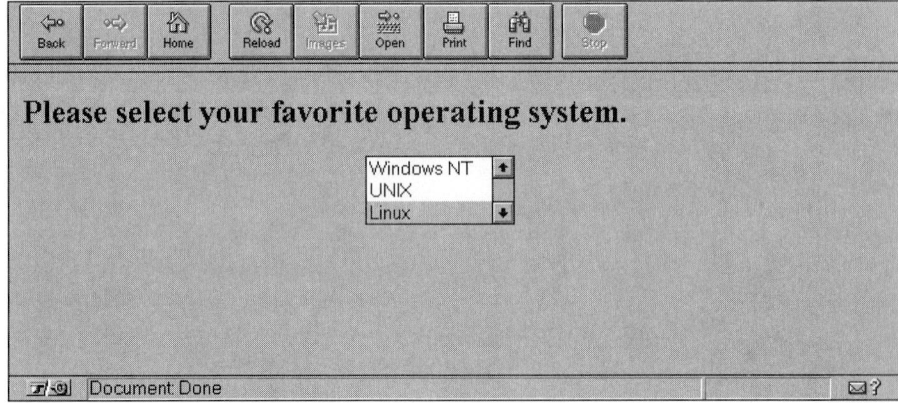

Figure 10.32 Netscape's presentation of a form showing the use of <SELECT>.

```
<HTML>
<HEAD>
<TITLE> SELECT example </TITLE>
</HEAD>
<BODY>
<FORM>
<H2>Please select your favorite operating system.</H2>
<CENTER>
<SELECT  NAME="FAVOS"  SIZE=3 >
      <OPTION> CP/M
      <OPTION> OS/2
      <OPTION> DOS
      <OPTION> Windows 95
      <OPTION> Windows NT
      <OPTION> UNIX
      <OPTION> Linux
</SELECT>
</CENTER>
</FORM>
</BODY>
</HTML>
```

Figure 10.33 HTML code showing the use of <SELECT>.

Unlike the case with the other elements we have discussed, if the user does not select an option here, the value of the NAME attribute is null. Look back to our previous examples. The value returned in those elements was different. If the Web weaver doesn't want to use the whole prompt, for example "Linux", she can code the VALUE attribute to specify a value other than the prompt. This attribute is discussed later. There are three attributes to the <SELECT> container, as follows.

NAME

Like all the other elements in a form (except RESET and SUBMIT), a <SELECT> container must have a **NAME** attribute coded. The name should be unique on the form so the CGI script will know where that particular data stream is coming from.

SIZE

The **SIZE** attribute, which should be a positive integer, determines how many of the choices are shown in the pull-down menu window. The default (when this option is not coded) is a single entry with a downward scroll arrow next to it. Figure 10.34 shows how that looks on the screen. Only one element, the first in the list, is shown. However, if the user clicks on the down arrow next to the selection, the whole list of options appears as a drop-down menu like that shown in Figure 10.35.

Figure 10.34 Netscape's presentation of the default SIZE attribute used in a <SELECT> list.

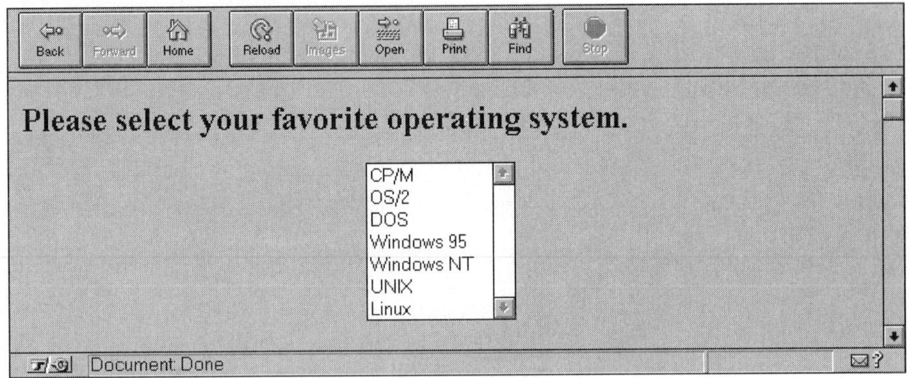

Figure 10.35 Netscape's presentation of the screen in Figure 10.34 after the user clicks on the downward arrow to show the whole list of options.

This is a very handy option. When the user clicks on her choice, the list contracts back to a single entry, with her choice highlighted and shown in the window. If you want your user to see a fixed number of options and be able to scroll among them, then set the SIZE to that number. However, the default for the SIZE attribute is often the most effective choice.

MULTIPLE

The **MULTIPLE** option allows the <SELECT> element to accept multiple inputs. This is the "check all that apply" rather than "check only one" option. Used this way, the <SELECT> option works something like checkboxes rather than radio buttons. MULTIPLE takes no value; it is just coded as an attribute. There are three ways for the user to select multiple entries. The first way is to hold down the shift key and click on two different values, in which case all the values between the first and second are highlighted and chosen. The second way is to hold down the right mouse button and move the pointer, covering several different contiguous values, all of which are chosen when the user lifts the mouse button. The third way is to hold down the Control key and then click on any of the selections. Each one that has been clicked will appear highlighted. If the user simply clicks on one selection, then another, only the most recent selection will be chosen.

<OPTION>

The **<OPTION>** container has a closing tag, but it is no longer used, because the next <OPTION> tag or the closing </SELECT> tag acts as a closing tag for <OPTION> as well. This tag has only two possible attributes. The text that follows <OPTION> is displayed in the pull-down selection box. Usually the text should be short, only a word or two rather than a phrase. The choices should be distinct from one another so that the user clearly knows what she is choosing.

VALUE

Normally the <SELECT> tag returns as a value the text string that follows the <OPTION>. For example, if the user selected the third <OPTION> from the set that follows, the browser would return the string **SEARCH=HotBot** to the CGI script.

```
<SELECT>
<OPTION>Lycos
<OPTION>Magellan
<OPTION>HotBot
<OPTION>Yahoo
<OPTION>AltaVista
</SELECT>
```

The CGI script has to have exactly that same string, with the H and B in uppercase. In the code that follows, if the user makes the same choice, it will cause the browser to return the string **SEARCH=hb** to the selected script.

```
<SELECT>
<OPTION VALUE="ly">Lycos
<OPTION VALUE="mg">Magellan
<OPTION VALUE="hb">HotBot
<OPTION VALUE="ya">Yahoo
<OPTION VALUE="av">AltaVista
</SELECT>
```

Usually it is worth the small effort to set the **VALUE** attributes because they make the script that much easier to code.

SELECTED

Just like the CHECKED attributes on the radio buttons and checkboxes, the **SELECTED** attribute causes the <OPTION> it is coded with to be preselected. The SELECTED attribute has no value associated with it. You can preselect only one option if SELECTED is coded without the MULTIPLE value. If you try to preselect more than one option, none of them will be preselected. If you don't specify a SIZE attribute, and do preselect one of the options, then that option will appear in the selection box regardless of its position in the list. When the user opens the list, that selection will be highlighted. If the MULTIPLE attribute has been coded, then you can use SELECTED to preselect several of the options, and each will appear highlighted.

Introducing Common Gateway Interface (CGI)

We have looked at forms from the perspective of the browser, but the real work with forms occurs at the server. Remember, the form is a tool for collecting data from the user. After the data are collected, the browser packages them up, then ships them to the server. The server runs a program that takes the data from the browser, processes them, and passes them to a user program that does something with the data. Exactly what is done can range from simply thanking the users for their input to running a sophisticated search program, retrieving some set of data from a database, and creating an HTML document to present those data back to the users. The Web-based package-tracking program used by a major package-delivery company is an example of how complex this type of program can become.

CGI (Common Gateway Interface) provides the standards and format that browsers use to send data to the server, as well as the format the server uses to hand the data off to an application program. That application program, usually called the CGI script, is often written by the Web weaver. It does whatever is necessary to process the data and send something back to the user. There are three ways to obtain a CGI script:

1. You can write your own, usually in either the Perl or C programming languages or as a shell script on your UNIX machine. While Perl and C are the most common high-level languages used for CGI scripting, theoretically any high-level language can be used for this purpose.
2. If you are not a programmer, you can have a programmer write the script for you.
3. You can search across the Net, find a script that will work for you, download it to your server, and use it.

If you choose this last course, respect the **intellectual property** of others. Copy only software that is presented as public-domain software, or freeware. The problem with this third choice of obtaining a CGI script is that you must use the tools available from your source on the Net rather than having a tool crafted to your exact needs. This is fine for simple applications and for testing, but if you are contemplating a complex response to the user, you will usually need to find a way to create your own, specialized CGI script.

Teaching programming is outside the scope of this text. Instead, examples of programs that provide simple applications will be presented. These examples are useful in learning how to build and use forms but are not intended to be used without modification. If you already know how to program in a high-level language, you can use the introduction to CGI in this chapter to help you create your own CGI scripts on your server. Even if you are not a programmer, you can use these simple scripts to see if your form is working correctly, then have a programmer build a specialized script for you.

CGI is becoming very popular as a forms-processing tool. It is considered better than Java for this purpose.

How CGI Works

CGI is the application of a Web server that communicates with other programs on the server. The most common use of CGI is processing forms, but there are other, more sophisticated ways to use CGI to run programs on a server. However, we will direct our attention here to the use of CGI to process data from forms.

Following are the steps for using a CGI script on a server to process a form:

1. The browser requests a form from the server.
2. The user fills out the form and clicks the SUBMIT button.
3. The browser sends the form to the server.
4. The server recognizes the CGI call and passes the program name and the associated data to the CGI application.
5. The CGI application massages the data and creates a set of environmental variables, then calls the requested program, called a CGI script.
6. The CGI script runs, usually generating a response to the user along with the other processing.
7. The program passes the response back to the server.
8. The server passes the processed data and response back to the browser.
9. The browser displays the processed data and response to the user.

The only parts of this process that the Web weaver is concerned with are the form the user fills out and the CGI script that processes the data and sends it back, along with a proper response, to the user. The rest can be considered part of the "magic of http." When a server gets a request for a CGI script, the server handles it differently than the request for any other Web page. Rather than posting the requested document back to the browser, the server looks for the script, or program, specified in the request, or **call,** and tries to run that CGI script.

Part of setting up the CGI script to run is passing the data from the client to the script. Different platforms and different operating systems dictate different ways that the CGI scripts get their data. On UNIX systems a CGI script will get data from either standard input, the input file given to all processes created on a UNIX system, and/or from a set of special environmental variables. If you choose the POST method, the CGI script will need to read the data from the standard input file. If you choose the GET method, all the data will be stored in the environmental variable $QUERY_STRING. Because this is a UNIX example, the fact that the variable name is uppercase is important.

Following is an example of a simple Perl script that will process data sent with either method and create a small HTML page to be sent back to the user. The page will list all the data sent from the form. This script has little value for users except as a testing and debugging tool. It serves here only to illustrate the necessary input and output processing.

Figures 10.36 and 10.37 show two different pages that send data using either GET or POST methods (look at the submit button). In either of these versions, data sent to the CGI script shown in Figure 10.38 will return the screen shown in Figure 10.39. The script that does the processing is written in the Perl scripting language. If you are serious about building scripts, learning Perl is almost a must. It is a very powerful language that is an excellent choice for CGI scripting.

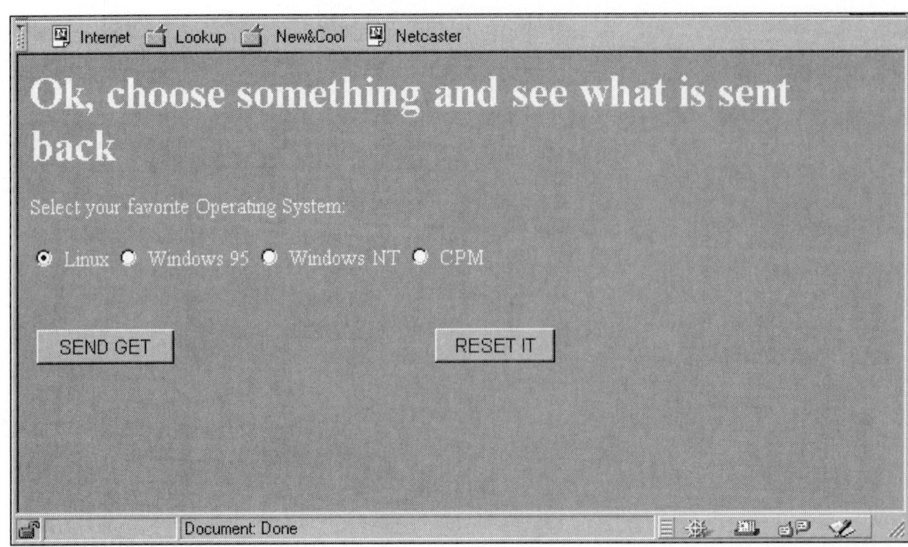

Figure 10.36 Netscape's presentation of the GET form of the submission screen.

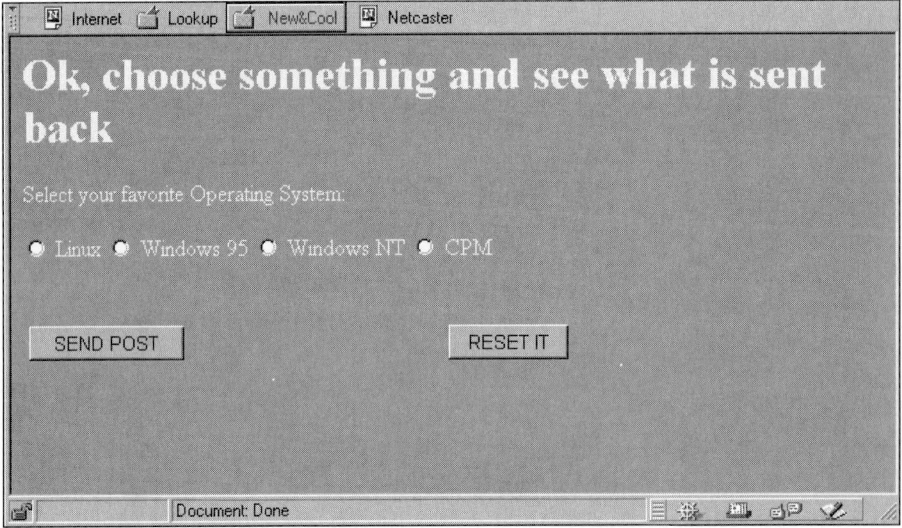

Figure 10.37 Netscape's presentation of the POST version of the submission screen.

The code in Figure 10.38 will create a Web page that simply shows the name and value of the variable sent to it—nothing fancy, but it does illustrate the concept. The script is available on the CD that accompanies this textbook. You might want to install it and play with it at this point.

```
#!/usr/bin/perl
#           This perl script will take a single variable, in
#           either GET or POST however it was sent, and
#           report back to users a small HTML page showing
#           the data they sent. To actually process the data
#           would require further processing at the end of
#           this script.
#
$how = $ENV{'REQUEST_METHOD'};
if ($how eq "GET") {
      $form_data = $ENV{'QUERY_STRING'}
#           with a GET, all data are in QUERY_STRING
                  }
else              {
      $form_size = $ENV{'CONTENT_LENGTH'};
      read (STDIN,$form_data,$form_size);
#           with POST I need to read from standard input
                 }
#           the data are now collected into the variable
#           $form_data
#           let's parse it apart into name and value.
#
($nameis,$valueis)=split (/=/, $form_data);
#
#           the data are now stored in the variables $nameis
and $valueis
#
#           Let's create the HTML code
print "Content-type: text/html\n\n";
print "<BODY BGCOLOR=\"FFFFFF\">\n";
print "<H1>Your data </H1>\n";
print "<H2>Variable name      $nameis </H2>\n\n";
print "<H2>Variable value     $valueis </H2>\n\n";
print "Isn\'t that nifty";
exit (0);
```

Figure 10.38 The Perl script that does either GET or POST processing.

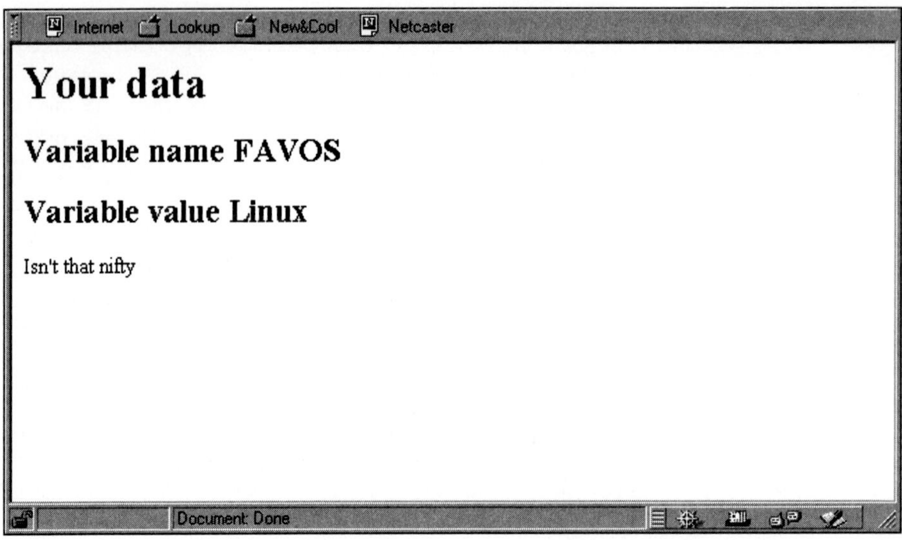

Figure 10.39 Netscape's presentation of the screen returned after the user makes a selection in either of the screens shown in Figures 10.36 and 10.37.

Header Information

When the CGI script prepares the data to return to the browser through the server, it must conform to some rules. First, the return data must begin with either (1) some http header data telling the receiving system what type of file is being passed or (2) the URL of another HTML document. Second, the header *must* end with a blank line. That is how the browser and the server know where the end of the header is, by the blank line. Everything following the blank line is considered part of the body of the returned document.

There are several other header data you can code, but we will let the server handle most of those for us. If you return a partial header to the server, it will fill in the missing information before sending it on to the browser. For now we will allow the server to help us out like that. If you want to explore creating your own complete http headers, read one of the several books on the market that deal exclusively with CGI. One is *CGI Programming on the World Wide Web* by Shishir Gundavaram, published by O'Reilly & Associates, Inc. For purposes of this overview, we will focus on the least complex header information. The two most common first header lines are discussed next.

Content-type:

The **Content-type:** header specifies the MIME content type of the data being sent back to the browser. **MIME** stands for **Multipurpose Internet Mail Extensions.** It was originally developed to send different types of files through the Net using electronic mail. The browser needs to know what type of information is being sent so that it will be able to decipher it. Some of the more common content types are **"text/plain"**, **"text/html"**, **"image/gif"**, **"image/jpeg."** A complete description of the different MIME types is available on the Net at **http://www.w3.org/.** This site has a wealth of information on HTML, including new HTML specifications. It is a site well worth checking out.

Location:

As opposed to sending back a dynamically created HTML document, the **Location:** header line specifies the URL of a different HTML page that is to be sent in response to the user's request. This header line allows you to build very dynamic pages on your site. When the user submits a form, the browser will display one of many different pages depending on the choices specified in the form.

Let's suppose you were selling homes and had pages for different price ranges and different general locations. One way of presenting your information would be to create a large table with links to each of the different pages. But that could be very confusing for your user. It would be better to create a simple form asking users to select a price range and an area of your city, using, for example, radio buttons. The CGI script would look at their selections and return the correct page. Figure 10.40 shows what that kind of form would look like. This simple form, requiring the user to simply click on two buttons, replaces a complex 15-element table. When the user clicks on the "Show Me Stuff" button, the browser submits the form to the server, and the server runs the CGI script to select the correct page to return to the user.

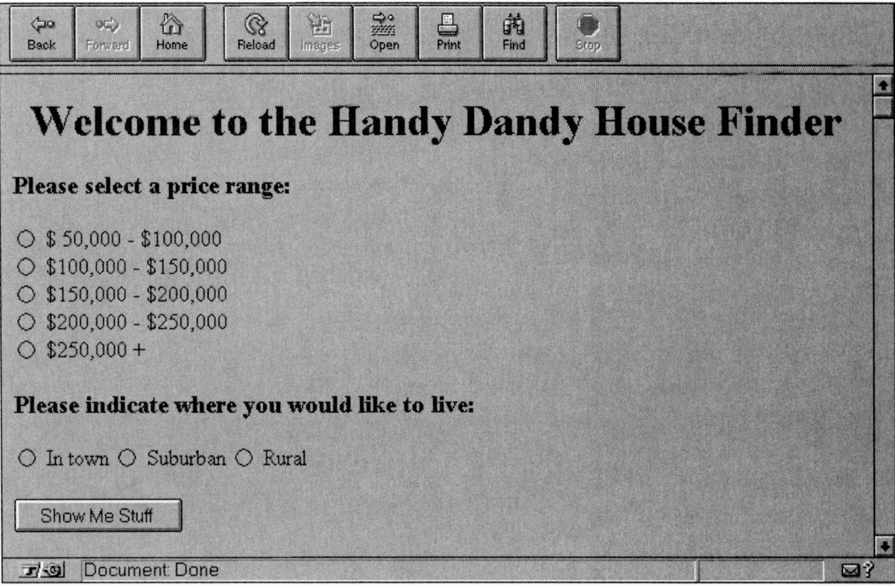

Figure 10.40 Netscape's presentation of a simple real-estate form.

Figure 10.41 presents the code for the page in Figure 10.40. The code will pass two parameters to the CGI script, the cost and the location (loc). Figure 10.42 presents a shell script to process the data and return one of 15 different pages to the user. Note, this is a condensed version of the script. Each of the 15 choices actually returns a small HTML screen, rather than a complete listing.

```
<HTML>
<HEAD>
<TITLE> SELECT example </TITLE>
</HEAD>
<BODY>
<FORM METHOD=GET ACTION="cgi-bin/house.cgi">
<H1 ALIGN=CENTER>Welcome to the Handy Dandy House Finder</H1>
<H3>Please select a price range:</H3>
<INPUT TYPE=RADIO name=cost value=1> $ 50,000 - $100,000 <BR>
<INPUT TYPE=RADIO name=cost value=2> $100,000 - $150,000 <BR>
<INPUT TYPE=RADIO name=cost value=3> $150,000 - $200,000 <BR>
<INPUT TYPE=RADIO name=cost value=4> $200,000 - $250,000 <BR>
<INPUT TYPE=RADIO name=cost value=5> $250,000 + <BR>
<H3>Please indicate where you would like to live:</H3>
<INPUT TYPE=RADIO name=loc value=1> In town
<INPUT TYPE=RADIO name=loc value=2> Suburban
<INPUT TYPE=RADIO name=loc value=3> Rural <BR><BR>
<INPUT TYPE=SUBMIT VALUE="Show Me Stuff">
</FORM>
</BODY>
</HTML>
```

Figure 10.41 HTML code for a simple real-estate form.

Actually, rather than returning a script with a content-type of text/html, you could use a technique called **server redirection.** That is, rather than using a content-type assignment in the header, you could simply code

```
Location: URL-to-transfer-to
```

as a return to the browser, and the new URL would be loaded into the browser. For example, rather than the two headings in Figure 10.42 that show the location and the dollar amount the user requested, each heading pair could be replaced by a location tag, and the browser would load the page (in this case, the page that had the houses in that price range and in that location). This is a very powerful technique to let the user see different pages based on her choices.

```
#!/bin/sh
#
#     The following code sets the correct header
information..gotta have it
#
echo Content-type: text/html
echo
echo '<BODY BGCOLOR=\#FDFFCC\>'
echo '<CENTER>'
echo '<H1>Handy Dandy House Finder</H1>'
echo '<H1>RESULTS !</H1>'
echo '</CENTER>'
#
#     Ok, so much for the easy stuff...now let's parse out
#     those variables so we can use them...
#
echo $QUERY_STRING | awk -f parse2.awk
#
```

The following is the awk script, called from the shell script above

```
#
#     This script will parse out the variables from
      $QUERY_STRING
#
#     It was passed as a command line variable using the syntax:
#     echo $QUERY_STRING | awk -f parse2.awk
#     Where parse2.awk is this script.
#
{
num=split($0,vars,"&")

stfx=split(vars[1],costx,"=")
stfx=split(vars[2],wherex,"=")
cost=costx[2]
where=wherex[2]
#print "<H2> Debug values Cost = "cost" Location = "where"
</H2>"

print " <BR><BR>"
#     Now we figure out where they want to live
#
if (cost == 1) {
      if (where == 1 ) {
           print "<H2> I am the In town, $50,000 page </H2>"
           print "<H2> Imagination is wonderful! </H2>" }
     if (where == 2 ) {
           print "<H2> I am the Suburban, $50,000 page </H2>"
           print "<H2> Imagination is wonderful! </H2>" }
     if (where == 3 ) {
           print "<H2> I am the Rural, $50,000 page </H2>"
           print "<H2> Imagination is wonderful! </H2>" }
           }
```

Figure 10.42 A shell script to select one of 15 pages to return to the user.

Continued.

```
#
#
if (cost == 2) {
     if (where == 1 ) {
          print "<H2> I am the In town, $100,000 page </H2>"
          print "<H2> Imagination is wonderful! </H2>" }
     if (where == 2 ) {
          print "<H2> I am the Suburban, $100,000 page </H2>"
          print "<H2> Imagination is wonderful! </H2>" }
     if (where == 3 ) {
          print "<H2> I am the Rural, $100,000 page </H2>"
          print "<H2> Imagination is wonderful! </H2>" }
       }
#
#
if (cost == 3) {
     if (where == 1 ) {
          print "<H2> I am the In town, $150,000 page </H2>"
          print "<H2> Imagination is wonderful! </H2>" }
     if (where == 2 ) {
          print "<H2> I am the Suburban, $150,000 page </H2>"
          print "<H2> Imagination is wonderful! </H2>" }
     if (where == 3 ) {
          print "<H2> I am the Rural, $150,000 page </H2>"
          print "<H2> Imagination is wonderful! </H2>" }
       }
#
#
if (cost == 4) {
     if (where == 1 ) {
          print "<H2> I am the In town, $200,000 page </H2>"
          print "<H2> Imagination is wonderful! </H2>" }
     if (where == 2 ) {
          print "<H2> I am the Suburban, $200,000 page </H2>"
          print "<H2> Imagination is wonderful! </H2>" }
     if (where == 3 ) {
          print "<H2> I am the Rural, $200,000 page </H2>"
          print "<H2> Imagination is wonderful! </H2>" }
       }
#
#
if (cost == 5) {
     if (where == 1 ) {
          print "<H2> I am the In town, $250,000 page </H2>"
          print "<H2> Imagination is wonderful! </H2>" }
     if (where == 2 ) {
          print "<H2> I am the Suburban, $250,000 page </H2>"
          print "<H2> Imagination is wonderful! </H2>" }
     if (where == 3 ) {
          print "<H2> I am the Rural, $250,000 page </H2>"
          print "<H2> Imagination is wonderful! </H2>" }
       }
}
```

Figure 10.42 (*continued*).

This script is actually very simple. It does not do any error checking. If for some reason the browser sends data that don't fit the pattern, the script simply generates a "there were no files found, try again" page. Not very helpful. However, using this shell as a model, you can create more complex and useful scripts.

Pragma: or Expires:

A very valuable albeit infrequently used pair of header tags is **Pragma:** and **Expires:** This pair of tags can be used to (1) prevent the browser from caching the page in the case of Pragma: or (2) force the browser to reload the page after a specified date in the case of Expires.

Suppose you are creating a page that supplies different information to your user over and over, such as a count of some ongoing action or the results of different mathematical operations. In this case, you don't want the browser to reload a previous version of the page from cache memory; rather, you want it to download the new page from the server. To prevent the browser from caching the page, include the following line in the header information:

```
Pragma: no-cache
```

Pragma, according to the *Princeton Online Dictionary,* stands for pragmatic information. This is a standardized form of comment that has special meaning to a program, usually a **compiler.** A pragma usually conveys information that is nonessential but helps optimize the program. "No-cache" is the only value currently defined for pragma in HTML.

Expires defines a date after which the page should be considered outdated. You can use this header information to force the browser to always reload a page if you specify the expiration date as being before the current date. For example, you could code the following in a heading:

```
Expires: Monday, 01-Jan-90 00:00:00 GMT
```

This code would cause the browser to reload the page each time it was referenced because the existing page, in cache, would be marked as expired.

Decoding the Response

The CGI script must perform the following tasks when passed data from the server:

1. Figure out the type of request method, either GET or POST, by looking at the REQUEST_METHOD variable. This task is important because even though you know how your form is initially arranged, having your script able to process data from either method gives you the flexibility to use either method. Once you write or obtain the code that will split up the variables depending on method, you can use it in all your scripts.
   a. If the method is POST, figure out how many bytes were sent by looking at CONTENT_LENGTH, then read that many bytes from standard input.
   b. If the method is GET, the data will be in QUERY_STRING.

2. Divide the data stream on the ampersand (&) to isolate the NAME=VALUE pairs.
3. Change the special characters from hexadecimal back to ASCII, and replace the plus signs with spaces.

Once the data are restored to their original condition, you can begin processing. This series works for either GET or POST, and it creates a set of variables that contain the data passed from the user.

A Sample Application

Paulette's Primer Publications Palace deals in rare and wonderful books, like this one, and has only a few in stock at any one time. She wants her customers to be able to find the exact book they want and then request that she hold it for them until they can pick it up. After searching her Web site, if the customer finds a book he wants, he requests the "hold for me" form. Figure 10.43 shows what that form looks like. Figure 10.44 shows the HTML code that generates Paulette's page and invokes the CGI script to process it.

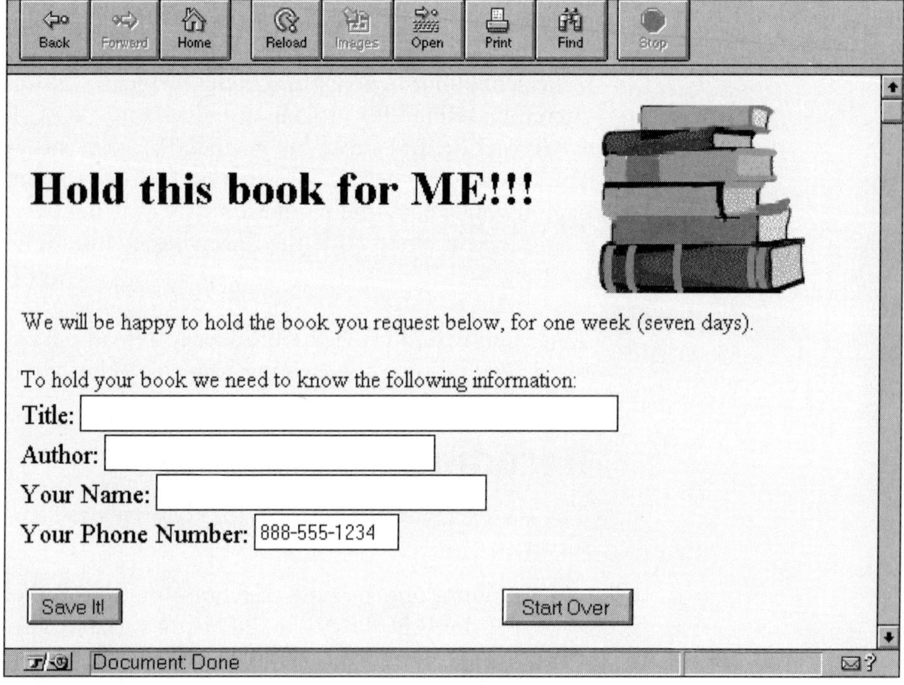

Figure 10.43 Netscape's presentation of a "hold for me" form.

```
<HTML>
<HEAD>
<TITLE> Paulette's Primer Publications Palace </TITLE>
</HEAD>
<BODY  BGCOLOR="CCFFFF">
<TABLE WIDTH="95%">
<TR>
<TD>
<H1>Hold this book for ME!!!</H1>
</TD>
<TD ALIGN=RIGHT >
<IMG SRC="books.gif" WIDTH=139 HEIGHT=123>
</TD>
</TR>
</TABLE>
We will be happy to hold the book you request below, for
one week (seven days).  <BR>
<FORM ACTION="/cgi-bin/bookhold.cgi" METHOD="POST" >
To hold your book we need to know the following
information:<BR>
 <BIG>Title:</BIG>
<INPUT TYPE="text" NAME="title" SIZE=50, MAXSIZE=100 ><BR>
<BIG>Author:</BIG>
<INPUT TYPE="text" NAME="auth" SIZE=30, MAXSIZE=100 ><BR>
<BIG>Your Name:</BIG>
<INPUT TYPE="text" NAME="cust" SIZE=30, MAXSIZE=100 ><BR>
<BIG>Your Phone Number:</BIG>
<INPUT TYPE="text" NAME="phon" SIZE=12, MAXSIZE=12
VALUE="888-555-1234" ><BR><BR>
<TABLE WIDTH="75%">
<TR>
<TD>
<INPUT TYPE="submit" VALUE="Save It!" >
</TD>
<TD ALIGN="right">
<INPUT TYPE="reset" VALUE="Start Over">
</TD>
</TR>
</TABLE>
</CENTER>
</FORM>
</BODY>
</HTML>
```

Figure 10.44 HTML code for a "hold for me" form.

Notice the use of tables to format the screen. The first table causes the image to appear next to the text, and the second table aligns the reset and submit buttons at the end of the form. Because there is a default phone number listed, which cannot match the customer's phone number, the CGI script can check to see if the customer input a phone number. If the default number is still assigned to that variable, the customer failed to input his own number. Figure 10.45 shows an example of Paulette's screen filled out by a customer with excellent taste.

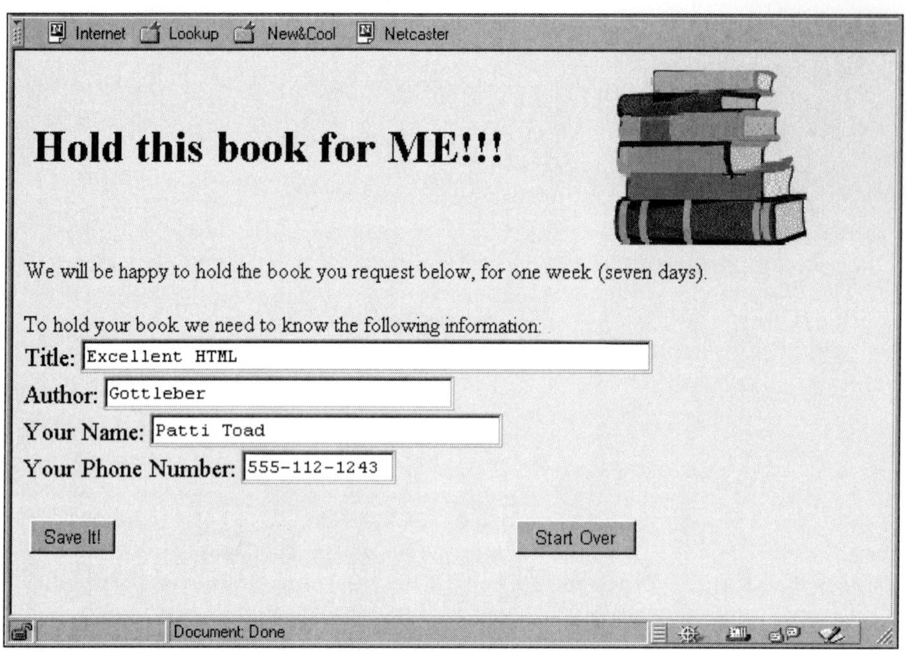

Figure 10.45 Netscape's presentation of the "hold for me" form filled out by a customer.

Once the customer requests the book, the CGI script checks to make sure that all the fields have been filled out, then sends the confirmation shown in Figure 10.46 back to the customer. This screen tells the user that she has successfully requested Paulette to hold the book for her.

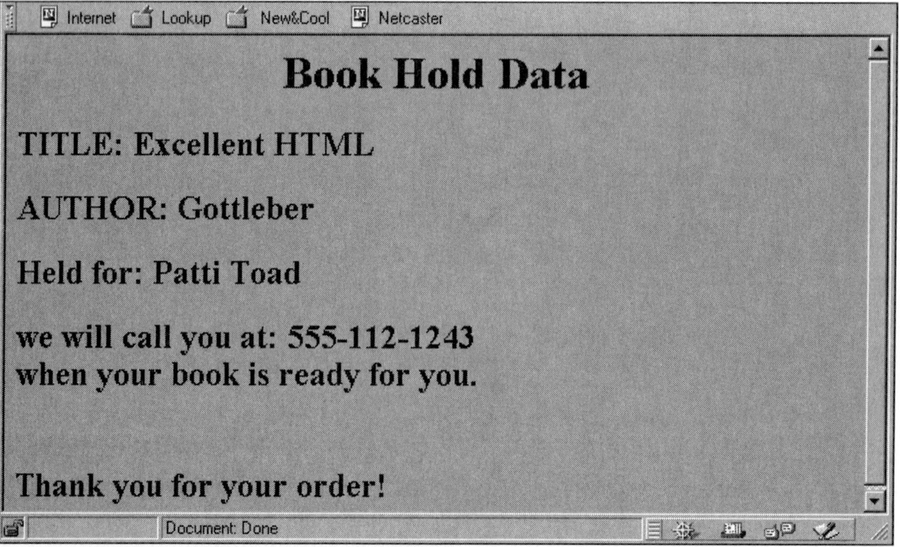

Figure 10.46 Netscape's presentation of the screen returned to the customer who successfully filled out the "hold for me" form.

Figure 10.47 presents a shell script to process data and send the user a thank-you screen.

```
#!/bin/sh
#
#   The following code sets the correct header
information..gotta have it
#
echo Content-type: text/html
echo
echo '<BODY BGCOLOR=\#CCDDEE\>'
echo '<CENTER>'
echo '<H1>Book Hold Data</H1>'
echo '</CENTER>'
#
#      Ok, so much for the easy stuff...now let's parse out
#      those variables so we can use them ...
#
echo $QUERY_STRING | awk -f parse3.awk
#

The code below is the awk script that is invoked above.

#
#      This script will parse out the variables from
       $QUERY_STRING
#
#      It was passed as a command line variable using the
       syntax:
#       echo $QUERY_STRING | awk -f parse3.awk
#   Where parse3.awk is this script.
#
{
num=split($0,vars,"&")

stfx=split(vars[1],titlex,"=")
stfx=split(vars[2],authorx,"=")
stfx=split(vars[3],custx,"=")
stfx=split(vars[4],phonex,"=")
#
title=titlex[2]
author=authorx[2]
cust=custx[2]
phone=phonex[2]
#   Get rid of the +s
for (x=1;x<=10;x++)
    stfx=sub("+"," ",title)
for (x=1;x<=5;x++)
    stfx=sub("+"," ",author)
for (x=1;x<=5;x++)
    stfx=sub("+"," ",cust)
#
```

Figure 10.47 The CGI script that processes the "hold for me" form.

Continued.

```
error=0
#
if (length(title) < 1) {
     print "<H2> You need to enter a TITLE, please </H2>"
     error=1
                  }
else
     print "<H2>TITLE: "title"</H2>"
#
if (length(author) < 1) {
     print "<H2> Please enter the AUTHOR's name </H2>"
     error=1
                  }
else
    print "<H2>AUTHOR: "author "</H2>"
#
if (length(cust) < 1)   {
    print "<H2> Please tell us who you are...</H2>"
    error=1
                  }
else
    print "<H2>Held for: "cust "</H2>"
#
if (phone == "888-555-1234")   {
    print "<H2> We need your phone number, please </H2>"
    error=1
                  }
else       {
    print "<H2> we will call you at: "phone "<BR>"
    print "when your book is ready for you.<BR>"
    }
if (error > 0) {
    print "<BR><BR>Oops, looks like a little problem here.
<BR>"
    print "Please "
    print "<A HREF=\"fig1042.html\">resubmit</A> your order"
           }
else
    print "<BR><BR>Thank you for your order! "
}
```

Figure 10.47 (*continued*).

If this were an actual commercial form, the script would also either add the customer to a database or send Paulette an e-mail telling her what book to hold for whom. As this is an exercise, that part of the code is left to the student.

Exercises

10.1. Create a form that uses one of the CGI scripts shown in this chapter. They are all available on the CD that accompanies this textbook. Make sure that your page works.

10.2. Modify the house-finder script to return different pages using server redirection.

10.3. Create a form like the one for Paulette's shop, only make it a record shop. Then modify the CGI script to process those data.

CHAPTER eleven

OTHER INTERESTING FEATURES

11

Several HTML techniques that can bring added life to your pages are somewhat outside the realm of "standard" HTML. Some, like searchable documents or dynamic documents, may require close work with your Webmaster or whomever administers your Web server.

Searchable Documents: <ISINDEX>

A document that runs a search on your Web site, called a **searchable document,** can be a great feature for your users. However, it can present a very dangerous security concern for your Web server administrator. As mentioned in the preceding chapter in regard to CGI scripting, you need to be very aware of the presence of unethical users. Just as you should carefully review your CGI scripts with your Web server administrator, likewise you should consult with your Web server administrator when you are going to set up a searchable document.

You should also be aware that a document that asks for a search can cause a problem for the server. The server normally expects to return an HTML document to the browser rather than running a search program and sending back the results. As with a document that executes a CGI script, a searchable document invokes a user-written search script. In this chapter we will consider how to prevent problems with the server.

The **<ISINDEX>** tag is another way to link to the browser. This tag is much like the <A> and <SUBMIT> tags. The difference is that <ISINDEX> passes only one or more keywords to the server to be matched by the search script. The search script may look at the contents of a single file or database, or it may search across one or more directories. It may even search every file on the server to locate specific data requested by the user. If you are designing the script to search more than a single file, be sure to check with your Web site administrator to ensure that any sensitive files are protected from the script.

The Calling Document

You can include a search element on one of your Web pages, but it is often more useful for your users, and easier to code, if you create a separate page to serve as the search-form page. A **calling document** is then needed to bring the search page up. An example of a calling document is shown in Figure 11.1. Here the user can click on the link that acts as a request for information, and a new screen will pop up to allow him to perform the search. He can enter the data he wants on the search page, touch the enter key, and see another screen that gives him the results of his search.

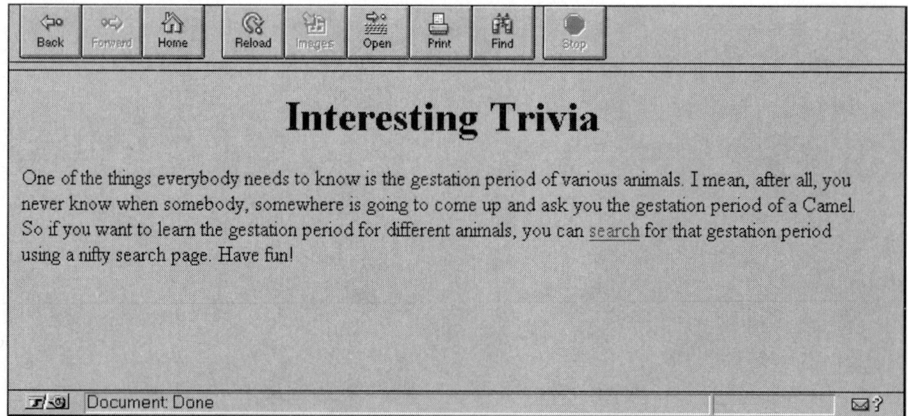

Figure 11.1 Netscape's presentation of the initial page that calls the search page.

Figure 11.2 presents the code for the simple calling page in Figure 11.1. When the user clicks on the link "search," the link invokes a CGI script on the server called **search1.cgi.** This script, shown later in this section, looks at the request and determines if the user has asked for a particular animal or not.

```
<HTML>
<HEAD>
<TITLE> Interesting Trivia </TITLE>
</HEAD>
<BODY >
<CENTER><H1>Interesting Trivia</H1></CENTER>
One of the things everybody needs to know is the gestation
period of various animals.  I mean, after all, you never know
when somebody, somewhere is going to come up and ask you the
gestation period of a Camel.  So if you want to learn the
gestation period for different animals, you can
<A HREF="http://phred.dcccd.edu/cgi-bin/search1.cgi">
search</A> for that gestation period using a nifty search
page.
Have fun!
</BODY>
</HTML>
```

Figure 11.2 HTML code for the initial page that calls the search page.

The Search Page

In this case, since there are no data passed to the script, the script assumes the user wants to see the **search page,** that is, form for entering data as shown in Figure 11.3. The browser displays the Web page that was generated by the search script and waits for the user to type in an animal name and touch the enter key. In our example here, the user has asked for the gestation period of a camel. Smart user! She will be ready when asked! The browser sends the requested word, "Camel," back to the same address as that of a data element in the URL.

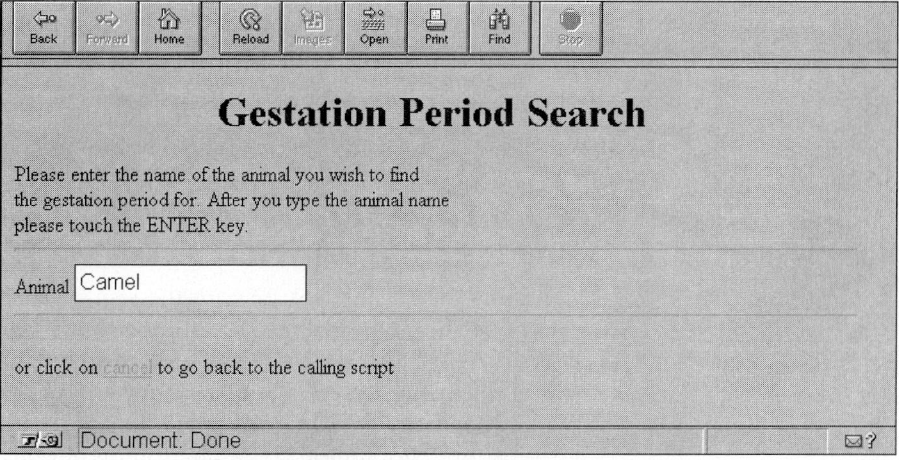

Figure 11.3 Netscape's presentation of the page returned to users when they ask for a search.

This step works like the CGI examples you saw in the previous chapter. The differences are that (1) there is no submit button and (2) the code that creates the CGI call is not inside a <FORM> container. Recall that with a form that contained only one text area for input, the user could simply touch enter to submit the form. That is the case here as well. The address to which the browser sends the data is the address of the search script, so this works just fine.

Beware, however, if you use the <ISINDEX> tag from within a regular HTML document. There could be a problem with your document handling the return data. The <ISINDEX> tag will send the data back to the URL of the page that contains it. That means that the URL of the page that contains the <ISINDEX> must be able to process the data returned to it. The <BASE> tag, discussed later in this chapter, is very useful, as it modifies the URL of the document to the one specified in the tag.

The Success Page

After the user sends her choice to the server, the script that created the page for the user to enter her choice builds another, different HTML page (a **success page**) containing the requested data and sends it back to the user. Notice that the user has the option of canceling the search by clicking on the "cancel" button on the search page (Figure 11.3). Figure 11.4 shows the document generated by the search1.cgi script that is returned when the browser finds one or more matches in the database.

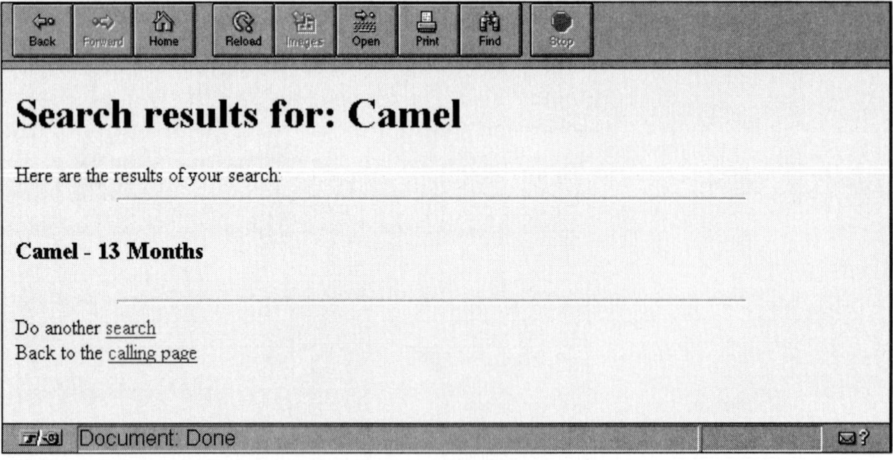

Figure 11.4 Netscape's presentation of the results of a successful search.

Besides presenting the user with the results of her search, this document also gives her some additional navigation tools. If she wants to search again, for a different animal, she can click on the "search" link and go back to the search page. If she is finished searching, she can click on the "calling page" link and go back to the document that originally offered the search link.

If the user chooses the "Back" button on her browser, she will go back to the search page as well, but the additional navigation tools are essential, as she may have bookmarked this page and then come back to it. In that case she would be sent to the search engine with the word requested, and the search script would return the same results page. The URL stored in the bookmark file would be **http://a.server.somewhere/cgi-bin/search1.cgi?camel.** (Note that this looks suspiciously like the CGI calls we saw before. Actually, the <ISINDEX> tag allows some different formatting and restricts the user to a single text field, but otherwise it works remarkably like the CGI we have already studied.)

If the user had only this screen bookmarked, and there were no navigation links on the screen, she would be unable to return to either the search itself or to the page that called the search. Neither of those URLs would be available in their cache, that is, in the memory of the browser. Navigation links are essential on *all* the pages you create!

The "Miss" Page

Now let's look at the case when the search script doesn't find a match—that is, when the search was a "miss." If the user requests the name of an animal that is not in the database, he is politely told that there is no entry for that animal and is allowed to either start a new search or go back to the page that sent him to the search in the first place. This kind of navigation tool is critical.

Figure 11.5 shows the screen the user sees (the **miss page**) if he asks for the gestation period of a toad. (Note: Toads are amphibians, so they lay eggs. The time it takes an egg to hatch is usually called the incubation period not the gestation period.) The user is given the same navigation choices after he is told there was no match. The screen looks similar to the screen that gives the results if the search is successful. It is important to keep some consistency of style, or similarity of layout, across related screens in a series.

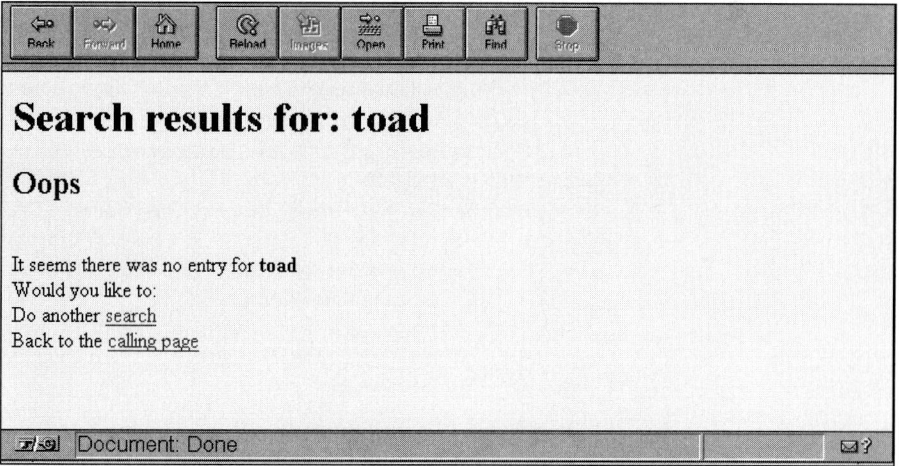

Figure 11.5 Netscape's presentation of the results of an unsuccessful search.

The Search Script

Now, without further ado, we present in Figure 11.6 the CGI shell script that does all these wonderful things. The script is a Bourne shell script, which should run on most UNIX machines with little or no modification. The following discussion is not intended to teach you UNIX scripting—that is far too grand a topic for this book. Rather, we will provide an overview of this particular script. This script can be used "as is" or modified to generate many different HTML pages. It can be logically divided into three different areas: the code to generate the search page, the code to report on successful hits, and the page to report a miss. Areas that are common to one or more pages are coded only once to increase efficiency and reduce maintenance time and effort.

```
#!/bin/sh
# This shell script will do a simple search of a document to
# demonstrate how the <ISINDEX> tool can be used. It allows
# the user to submit a request for the search form by calling
# this script w/ no arguments, or to cause a search by
# calling the document w/ an argument. The script will check
# first and generate different HTML documents depending upon
# the presence or absence of command line parameters. This
# script is based on work done by Ian Graham.
#
echo "Content-type: text/html"
echo
#     Put out the standard header info...
#
if test $# -lt 1
then
#           Ok, so they didn't give us any parameters...give-em
#           the form so they will do it right!  :)
echo "<HTML>"
echo "<HEAD>"
      echo "<TITLE>Gestation Period Search </TITLE> "
      echo "</HEAD> "
      echo "<BODY BGCOLOR=lightblue> "
      echo " <CENTER><H1>Gestation Period Search
</H1></CENTER>"
      echo " Please enter the name of the animal you wish to
      find<BR> "
      echo " the gestation period for. After you type the
      animal name <BR>"
      echo " please touch the ENTER key. <BR>"
      echo " <ISINDEX PROMPT=\"Animal \" >"
      echo "<BR>"
```

Figure 11.6 CGI shell script to either build a search page or report success or failure of the search.

```
            echo "or click on "
            echo "<A HREF=\"/test-search.html\">cancel</A>"
            echo "to go back to the calling script"
            echo " </BODY>"
            echo "</HTML>"
else
#                Great, they gave us a word to look for...build
#                the basis for the results page...
            echo " <HTML>"
            echo " <HEAD>"
            echo " <TITLE> Search results for:  $* </TITLE>"
            echo " </HEAD>"
            echo " <BODY BGCOLOR=\"#DDFFFF\">"
            echo " <H1>Search results for: $* </H1>"
            lost=`grep -i "$*" /etc/httpd/cgi-bin/Gestlist.txt 2>&1
            /dev/null`
#                do the grep, to see if it gets a hit...
            if test $? -ne 0
            then
#                     OK, if the previous command (grep) returned
#                     non-zero then we got no hit...so the search
#                     failed, tell user.
                 echo " <H2>Oops </H2> <BR>"
                 echo " It seems there was no entry for <B>$* </B>
                 <BR>"
                 echo " Would you like to: <BR>"
            else
#                     The previous grep worked, do it again but
#                     let the output happen
                 echo " Here are the results of your search: <BR>"
                 echo " <HR WIDTH=\"75%\" ALIGN=\"CENTER\">"
                 grep -i "$*" /etc/httpd/cgi-bin/Gestlist.txt
                 echo " <HR WIDTH=\"75%\" ALIGN=\"CENTER\">"
            fi
            echo " Do another <A HREF=\"/cgi-bin/search1.cgi\">
            search</A> <BR>"
            echo " Back to the <A HREF=\"/test-search.html\">
            calling page</A> <BR>"
            echo " </BODY>"
            echo "</HTML>"
            fi
```

Figure 11.6 (continued).

Initial Search Page

The initial search page is generated by the code that starts with the four **echo** lines that output the **Content-type,** a trailing blank line, and the <HTML> and <HEAD> lines, as they are standard for any page this script will generate. It is more efficient to put them in this script once, rather than doing the same thing in each of the three scripts that will be created.

There must be a blank line after the required header line to tell the browser where the header information ends. The **echo** command causes the information following it to be sent to standard output, and the server will send that output back to the browser. Next the script checks to see if the user has included any data. In this case the data are sent as command line parameters. The Bourne shell variable **$#** contains the count of those command line parameters. If that count is less than 1 (i.e., zero), then the user didn't send any word to search for. To the script, that is a sign that the user didn't know how to use the search, so the script generates the lines of code to build a <TITLE> and the rest of the lines of code that are unique to the code for the search page.

Figure 11.7 presents the actual code generated by this option of the script. Notice the first two lines of the generated code. The first line is all we are putting in the header; the server builds the rest of the header for us. The second line is the required blank line that closes the header information for the browser and server. (We keep talking about this blank line, because one of the most common errors new writers of CGI scripts make is forgetting the required blank line after the header.)

```
Content-type: text/html

<HTML>
<HEAD>
<TITLE>Gestation Period Search </TITLE>
</HEAD>
<BODY BGCOLOR=lightblue>
<CENTER><H1>Gestation Period Search </H1></CENTER>
Please enter the name of the animal you wish to find<BR>
the gestation period for.  After you type the animal name
<BR>
please touch the ENTER key. <BR>
<ISINDEX PROMPT="Animal " >
<BR>
or click on
<A HREF="/test-search.html">cancel</A>
to go back to the calling script
</BODY>
</HTML>
```

Figure 11.7 The generated HTML code for the search page.

The lines starting with <HTML> and ending with </HTML> are also generated by the script and probably look just like the HTML code you have been writing so far. If you look back at the figure with the whole script, you will see the lines that generate this code after the first **if.**

The last two lines of the script are also common across all the scripts that will be generated, so the script will create them in only one place, after all the other processing has been done. This kind of efficiency makes the script short and sweet and easy to understand and maintain. Well, okay, *easier* to understand.

If the script detects a command line parameter (there can really be only one because the <ISINDEX> tag sends back just one variable), it performs the search on the file specified in the search (**grep**) line. In this code the grep is done twice. The first time the results are deliberately thrown away, because we don't want an error reported to the user if the word she is looking for is not in our file and the script isn't ready to have the results reported at that point.

```
lost=`grep -i "$*" /etc/httpd/cgi-bin/Gestlist.txt 2>&1
/dev/null` if test $? -ne 0
```

Immediately after we do the grep (which searches the specified file for the string specified by the user, stored in **$*** in this case), we check the return status of that command, stored in **$?.** If the results from the grep are zero, then the word occurs at least once in the file, and we have success. If the grep returns any other value, we know the word does not exist in the file, so we have a miss. Following the order of the script, we will first look at the miss code.

The "Miss" Page

If the first grep failed, there is no reason to go on with the searching. The word the user specified does not exist in the data file. All we have to do is report the "miss" to the user and ask him what to do next. The code generated to do that is very simple. The header and first two lines of the HTML code have already been generated, so all we need to do is add the code to tell the user about the miss.

After telling the user that the word isn't on the list, the generated code will give him two choices: either to do another search, going back to the search script, or to go back to the calling program. That URL of the calling program must be hard-coded into the document. In this case it is the **test-search.html** document.

In Figure 11.8, notice the search term **toad** has been inserted into the actual code. What you are seeing is the generated HTML. Each time the script misses, it will generate a different page based on the user's input. In this case the user was looking for the word "toad," and it doesn't seem to be in the file. Figure 11.8 shows the actual code generated for a miss on the word "toad."

```
Content-type: text/html

<HTML>
<HEAD>
<TITLE> Search results for:  toad </TITLE>
</HEAD>
<BODY BGCOLOR="#DDFFFF">
<H1>Search results for: toad </H1>
<H2>Oops </H2>
It seems there was no entry for <B>toad </B> <BR>
Would you like to: <BR>
Do another <A HREF="/cgi-bin/search1.cgi">search</A> <BR>
Back to the <A HREF="/test-search.html">calling page</A> <BR>
</BODY>
</HTML>
```

Figure 11.8 The generated HTML code for the page reporting a miss.

The Success Page

If the initial grep returns a zero, that indicates that the word or words the user specified occur at least once in the file. In this case we will have good data to return to the user, so instead of the "miss" page, we will return a success page. The initial part of the success page looks just like the preceding pages. The Content-type, <HTML>, <HEAD>, and <TITLE> are all the same. But from there on the code is different for the success page. There is an <H1> header, a horizontal rule, and then the results of the actual grep command. The <H3> header is the actual line from the file. It contains the word "camel," so grep returns it. (The **-i** option on grep tells it to ignore the case of the word, so "Camel", "CAMEL", and "camel" would all match.) This illustrates the importance of the design of the data file. The data file actually contains the <H3> heading lines that appear in the HTML document. Part of the file follows the generated code in Figure 11.9.

Following the line or lines drawn from the data file by grep is another horizontal rule to act as a visual bottom for the data section. The closing lines of the generated document are the same that were on the "miss" document, so they were added outside the IF-THEN-ELSE structure.

```
Content-type: text/html

<HTML>
<HEAD>
<TITLE> Search results for:  camel </TITLE>
</HEAD>
<BODY BGCOLOR="#DDFFFF">
<H1>Search results for: camel </H1>
Here are the results of your search: <BR>
<HR WIDTH="75%" ALIGN="CENTER">
<H3>  Camel - 13 Months</H3>
<HR WIDTH="75%" ALIGN="CENTER">
Do another <A HREF="/cgi-bin/search1.cgi">search</A> <BR>
Back to the <A HREF="/test-search.html">calling page</A> <BR>
</BODY>
</HTML>
```

Figure 11.9 The generated HTML code for the page reporting one or more hits.

The Data File

It was easy to write the code for this search because the data file was correctly designed. Each entry in the file was a heading (<H3>) line, so when the grep retrieved the line or lines from the file, they were already formatted for use in the document. In an alternate form of this code, the data file could be composed of list <LI> entries, and the list structure could be generated to surround the elements and make them into a list. Figure 11.10 shows the first ten lines from the data file. Notice how each is a heading, so no matter how many are retrieved, they stand out one from another and produce an attractive screen.

```
<H3>  Anteater - 6 months</H3>
<H3>  Ardwolf - 3 months</H3>
<H3>  Aardvark - 7 months</H3>
<H3>  Bear - 7-9 months</H3>
<H3>  Bison - 9 months</H3>
<H3>  Bobcat - 2 months</H3>
<H3>  Bow Head Whale - 12 months</H3>
<H3>  Bush Baby - 4 months</H3>
<H3>  California Sea Lion - 12 months</H3>
<H3>  Camel - 13 Months</H3>
```

Figure 11.10 The first ten lines of the data file.

Correctly designing the data file is a very important part of setting up for almost any searchable structure or set of files. If your user is going to select data from several different files, it may be necessary to add code to your script to format the data. That kind of additional formatting was not necessary in our example here, because the data file was designed to work with the script.

<BASE>

There are two ways to refer to an address (URL) within a page. It can be specified as an absolute URL, with all the parts of the address coded as follows:

http://www.myserver.edu/mydir/neatpage.html

Or it can be specified as a relative address, based on the address of the page, like this:

pagetwo.html

With the second method, the browser would supply all the additional necessary data to the left of the data we supplied. In this example, the browser would fill in the address of the server hosting the current document. Suppose **neatpage.html** is the current page, and we are using a link to **pagetwo.html.** The browser would complete the address for the link as follows:

http://www.myserver.edu/mydir/pagetwo.html

We are able to use relative—that is, partial—addresses because the browser will complete them.

Sometimes it would be handy to be able to tell the browser to use a different path than the one to the current page. For example, if we wanted a series of documents in a subdirectory different from the one housing the current page, we would have to code the absolute address for each document—if the authors of HTML had not anticipated this need. The <**BASE**> tag allows the Web weaver to specify a different base address to the browser. The browser uses the address specified in the <BASE> tag when completing relative URLs instead of using the address of the current page.

The <BASE> tag is an empty tag and must be coded inside the <HEAD> container. It changes the way relative addresses are specified for all the <A>, <IMG>, <LINK>, and <FORM> tags in the document. It also specifies a searchable document for the <ISINDEX> tag if you want to have the user queries posted to a document other than the host document.

<BASE> is a very powerful and useful tag. Be careful with it, though. If you insert it into an existing document that is already using relative addressing, the additional data necessary to complete the relative URL will be taken from the tag instead of from the actual URL of the page. Therefore, you need to either (1) change all relative addresses to absolute URL or (2) move the items being relatively addressed.

HREF

The **HREF** attribute is the only required attribute for the <BASE> tag. It is used to specify the address of the URL that is to become the new base address. The specified URL can be an absolute address or a relative address. For example, we can code

<BASE HREF="/docs/">

for the previous example, and the brower would then complete the relative URL, making it appear as the absolute URL where the documents would be stored:

http://www.myserver.edu/docs/

TARGET

The progressive browsers also support **TARGET** as a second attribute to the <BASE> tag. As we saw in the chapter on frames, the TARGET attribute can specify a particular named frame as the default frame where the browser will display redirected documents. In addition, if the Web weaver sets a TARGET-TOP in the base tag, any framed document will be forced out of frames and displayed in a full browser window. You will not need to code <BASE> in most of the documents you build, but when you need it, it is a most handy tag.

Dynamic Documents

In the previous section, the CGI search script we wrote actually created a Web page to do the search and another to return the results of the search. In a similar fashion you can create a script that will build a page for a specific user based on information that user supplies in a CGI script. The actual coding of this type of script is just a bit beyond the scope of this book, but if you have the need for this type of HTML code generation, you can write or have written very sophisticated scripts that can build HTML code on the fly. As we discussed in the last chapter, you need to consult your Web page administrator before you create powerful HTML generators or other types of software that are accessed from the Net, because that type of script can pose a dangerous security risk if it enables outside users to access files or commands on the host machine.

Dynamic HTML generation is on the cutting edge of the Web. They can be as complex or simple as you want them to be. Each different server has some idiosyncrasies that make installing and running scripts like these an "interesting" experience. It will be of great help to have your Web site administrator working with you. If you are also the Web site administrator, we must assume you know what you are doing, right? When the script for this example was set up, two different machines at the college handled the code slightly differently, requiring that the actual script be put in different directories. Please consult with your Web site administrator when you start this process; it will make things much easier!

Document Relationships

Up until now we have not been concerned with the relationships among different documents or pages except for supplying a direct link to send users back to the URL of the page they need. But, in addition to this, there are several tags that can establish relationships among different pages. For example, suppose you had a document with several pages that the user could read in any order but that had a logical order, like the chapters in a book. You could use document relationships to establish a "next" and "previous" page for the user. These relationships may seem to provide more documentation than actual change in the document, but they are important in working with a set of pages that comprise one large, related document. Some pundits envision changes to the browsers that use this type of data to create browser-generated buttons that will go forward and back using the data coded in the document-relationship tags. There are two places to code the relationship among several documents: the <A> tag and the <LINK> tag.

<A>

We have explored most of the attributes for the anchor, **<A>,** container. Now we will look at the two that define document relationships: REL and REV. Both specify the relationship between the source document and the target of the link. **REL** goes forward, from source to target, and **REV** goes backward, from target to source. There are four possible values for REL and REV:

- **NEXT**—indicates that the URL referenced in the HREF is the next in the series. This is usually used only with the REL attribute.
- **PREVIOUS**—shows that link pointed to by the HREF is the previous element in a series. That is, the element is the one that precedes the URL in the HREF. Normally this is used with the REV attribute.
- **PARENT**—indicates that the document listed as the URL for the HREF is the original source, or parent, of the file that points to it.

<LINK>

The **<LINK>** tag occurs inside the <HEAD> tag because it links an entire document to another object, rather than linking some part of a document to some other object. Users do not see this element (unless they view the source, of course), so its only purpose is to provide additional data to the browser—or to some other Web tool that can search the header. Some search engines and some indexing programs are smart enough to read the header data and parse out information like <LINK>. A number of different attributes are associated with <LINK>. Some of the more common are discussed next. At this time <LINK> tags are usually ignored, but they will most likely become very important in future releases of the HTML standard.

CLASS

The **CLASS** attribute usually indicates either style information or, more commonly, subdivides a common REL or REV attribute. For example, if a user could go three different places with a REL=NEXT attribute, depending on her level of expertise, the following set of links could appear in a document head:

```
<LINK REL=NEXT CLASS=BEGINNER HREF="http://...">
<LINK REL=NEXT CLASS=EXPERT HREF="http://...">
<LINK REL=NEXT CLASS=WIZARD HREF="http://...">
```

Depending on the expertise of the user, she can take different paths through the document. At present the acceptable list of CLASS values is very open-ended; some set of standard values needs to be devised.

HREF

The **HREF (Hypertext Reference)** is a required attribute of the <LINK> tag. There can be only one HREF attribute per <LINK>. It should point to some valid http address, either internal or external to the document that contains it. When HREF is used with the <A> container, some browsers may display its value when the user moves the pointer over the associated link.

TITLE

The **TITLE** attribute usually describes the object pointed to by the HREF attribute. A browser may choose to display the value of the TITLE attribute rather than the HREF when the user moves the mouse pointer over an <A> tag, or it may use the TITLE attribute in an e-mail **SUBJECT: field** when the **mailto:** option is selected.

REL and REV

The list of possible values for the REL and REV attributes is still open and growing. Some specialized HTML agents use these relationship attributes already. SCO (Santa Cruz Operation) has a browser that uses a subset of these tags in its online documentation project. Various groups are building specialized browsers to handle large online document projects. After all, HTML is an offshoot of SGML, which was designed to enable people with different machines to see documents formatted for their screens. This sort of project suggests a "return to the roots" of HTML trend. The attributes supported by most of these specialized browsers, added to the standard in May of 1995, follow:

- **MADE**—indicates the author, or "maker," of an HTML page. Usually the HREF associated with this attribute is the mailto: address of the author of the page. Most often this value is used with the REV attribute.
- **NEXT**—indicates an author-defined relationship, like the pages or chapters of a book. REL=NEXT indicates that the document pointed to by the HREF is the next document or page in the series. REV=NEXT indicates that the current page should follow the page specified in the HREF. NEXT is the inverse of PREVIOUS.
- **PREVIOUS**—indicates an author-defined relationship that is the inverse of NEXT. REL=PREVIOUS indicates that the target document or page should precede the current page. REV=PREVIOUS indicates that the current document should precede the target document.
- **CONTENTS**—indicates a table of contents and can also be coded TOC. REL=CONTENTS identifies a document pointed to by the link as the table of contents for the current document or for the collection of documents. REV=CONTENTS identifies the current document as the table of contents.
- **INDEX**—indicates an index to either the current document or to the collection of documents. REL=INDEX identifies the document pointed to by the link as an index. REV=INDEX identifies the current document as the index.
- **NAVIGATE**—the least well-defined of this set of values. Anything that helps the user navigate around the document or document set is considered a navigation tool. For example, the HREF may be part of a table of contents, a list of documents, or a page that describes the current set of documents.

Some of the possible values for the REL and REV attributes are specifically disallowed. Three that are never allowed are HOME, BACK, and FORWARD, because these are always to be defined by the browser itself and not reset by the code. REL and REV are among the more dynamic attributes in the current release of HTML. There are many other suggested and proposed values for these two attributes that will define other, more complex relationships.

<META>

As if there weren't enough HTML tags to learn about already, we will now look at the **<META>** tag. The use of the <META> header element is growing and will become more important in the future. This empty tag is always located in the <HEAD>...</HEAD> container. It provides some interesting options to Web weavers. Many of the <META> attribute values are still under discussion, and not all browsers and search or indexing engines use the same ones, or use them the same way. Much debate exists at the present time, but the use of these will become standardized in the future, and then they will be very important and valuable.

Some of the <META> attribute values are already useful. One of the emerging standards is called the **Dublin Metadata Core Element Set** (or **Dublin Core**), proposed by the March 1995 Meta Data Workshop. It specifically addresses information stored in documents as opposed to other forms of data like image or sound files. You can find a great deal of information on these values by searching the Web for "Dublin Core" or "OCLC/NCSA Meta Data Workshop Report".

The <META> tag is an empty container with up to four different attributes: HTTP-EQUIV, CONTENT, NAME, and URL. Two of these attributes, HTTP-EQUIV and NAME, are mutually exclusive; and one, URL, is currently not supported by all the browsers. Each <META> tag has this form:

```
<META HTTP-EQUIV="name" CONTENT="value">
```

or

```
<META NAME="name" CONTENT="value">
```

The "name" in this code is the name of one of the special attributes, and the "value" is the content, or value, assigned to that name. Following is a discussion of the attributes for the <META> tag.

HTTP-EQUIV

Coding an **HTTP-EQUIV**="name" is the same as including that "name" in the http header. We saw a simple http header when we looked at the procedure for returning generated Web pages from CGI scripts. These values are often used by browsers, search engines, and spiders to perform specialized actions. Let's look at the more commonly used HTTP-EQUIV names. This list is not exhaustive, and it will change and grow over time.

EXPIRES

The **EXPIRES** value for the HTTP-EQUIV attribute sets a date and time after which a document is said to have expired. When some of the browsers pull a document from cache rather than requesting the document from the Net, they will check to see if there is an EXPIRES value. If the document has "expired," then the browser will generate a Net request and download a new copy of the document.

An example of this <META> attribute follows:

```
<META HTTP-EQUIV="EXPIRES" CONTENT="Wed, 31 Dec 1997 00:00:00 GMT">
```

This code will mark the page that contains it to expire at midnight on the 31st of December, 1997. The format of the date field must be exactly correct, or the browser will consider it an invalid date. When the browser encounters an invalid expiration date, it considers the date to be *now* and reloads the page. If the EXPIRES value is zero, the browser will never use the page in cache but will consider the page expired and reload it from the source.

CONTENT-TYPE

CONTENT-TYPE value can be used to direct the browser to load a specific character set before it displays the page. This is a little used value, but it can be important if the page contains special text characters or is designed to be displayed in a nonstandard character set. This value will probably take on greater significance in the next HTML standard, indicating the scripting language and the style-sheet language for the document.

CONTENT-LANGUAGE

If you are designing a page to be read in a specific language, like British English rather than whatever the browser defaults to, you can use the **CONTENT-LANGUAGE** value. The language must be specified as a "language-dialect" paired value, for example, CONTENT="en-GB", which signifies that the language to be used is **en** (English) with the **GB** (Great Britain) dialect.

WINDOW-TARGET

The most common use for the **WINDOW-TARGET** value is to stop a document from appearing in a frame. Specifying the following <META> tag, attribute, and value will normally cause the document to appear in a full window rather than being displayed inside a frame.

```
<META HTTP-EQUIV="WINDOW-TARGET" CONTENT="_TOP">
```

This value works much like the NAME attribute we have already discussed in relationship to the <FORM> and <FRAME> tags. WINDOW-TARGET works with some browsers but not all, so don't depend upon it.

PICS-LABEL

PICS-LABEL stands for Platform-Independent Content rating Scale or System. This value is a way to specify the type of content for the document or page. Some legislators want to require ratings on all Web pages as a way to get around the Supreme Court's rejection of the Exxon amendment as unconstitutional. The scheme of PICS-LABEL is flexible and intended for other purposes as well as censorship, but some are concerned that this rating scale might eventually be imposed on Web weavers by an outside agency. As a Web professional, you need to become aware of the ways PICS can be used or abused. Then you should educate others about your findings.

REFRESH

The **REFRESH** value provides one of the most dynamic and exciting uses currently available for the <META> tag. REFRESH allows the Web weaver to specify when a page should be reloaded from the server ("refreshed"). This is very handy when the contents of a page change at regular intervals. For example, if you have the ultimate "fish-tank camera" page, and the camera puts out a new picture every 30 seconds, you can have your Web page refresh each 30 seconds as well. This way the user will always get the newest picture.

REFRESH enables Web-potatoes to watch the scene on the screen change without even having to click their mouse to update the page: the ultimate in convenience. REFRESH is also handy if your page is driven from a CGI script that updates data on a regular basis. You can force your page to reload at regular intervals to capture the new, updated information.

REFRESH allows the skillful Web weaver to mimic **push technologies** as well. To the users, this reload attribute is invisible. All the users know is that at specific intervals the page refreshes itself with new data. It is really a **pull technology,** but it looks like push.

The most exciting way this attribute can be used, though, is to display a series of pages without the user having to do anything. This is very handy if you are creating a kiosk or other Web-driven attention-getting display. It is also handy to cycle among a set of pages in one small frame on a page. For example, if you have a business selling fruit, you can create a framed Web page with one of the frames containing a set of "REFRESHing" documents, each of which presents a picture of your orchards at different seasons. Thus, one corner of your Web page will have a pretty, attractive frame of small pictures to attract your customers. The following pages will produce a loop of pages, with each pointing to the next in the series.

Assume you have four pages, the first of which is shown in Figure 11.11. The fourth page points back to the first page to start the cycle over again. These pages have very fast REFRESH, so it is easy to see them work. They are available on the Web site for this book. Notice the <META> line. It is the only new code in this page; you have seen the rest many times before. The HTTP-EQUIV is assigned the value of REFRESH, and the content is allocated both (1) the time to wait before the screen is refreshed (3 seconds), and (2) the address of the new file to refresh from after that time interval. Look closely at the syntax for the CONTENT attribute. The time and the URL are both contained within the same set of quotation marks, and the URL is separated from the time by a semicolon. In addition, the URL must always be specified as an **absolute path;** this tag will not use relative path names.

```
<HTML>
<HEAD>
<TITLE> A refresh series page 1 </TITLE>
<META HTTP-EQUIV="REFRESH" CONTENT="3;
URL=FILE:///F|/C11/FIG1112.HTM" >
<!--This screen will wait for 3 seconds, then refresh with
the second screen in the set...-->
</HEAD>
<BODY BGCOLOR="#AA0000">
<H1>First screen in a refresh series</H1>
This screen will display for 3 seconds<BR>
then it will be replaced by the second screen in the
series.<BR>
The background color will change too, to make it obvious that
the<BR>
screens are changing.
</BODY>
```

Figure 11.11 HTML code for the first of the four-page set of reloading REFRESH pages.

If you make a mistake in coding this tag, the results can be very interesting. For example, if you use two sets of quotation marks at the beginning of the CONTENT value, the screen will begin to refresh at once, reloading the same page that contains the <META> tag with an interval of close to zero. If there are any mistakes in coding the URL, such as using a relative path, the browser will simply ignore the URL and refresh the current page at the interval specified. Correctly coding the value for the CONTENT is critical, but REFRESH is well worth the effort, for when it works, it is really a neat procedure.

```
<HTML>
<HEAD>
<TITLE> A refresh series page 2 </TITLE>
<META HTTP-EQUIV="REFRESH" CONTENT="5;
URL=FILE:///F|/C11/FIG1113.HTM" >
<!--This screen will wait for 5 seconds, then refresh with
the third screen in the set...-->
</HEAD>
<BODY BGCOLOR="#558800">
<H1>Second screen in a refresh series</H1>
This screen will display for 5 seconds<BR>
then it will be replaced by the third screen in the
series.<BR>
The background color will change too, to make it obvious that
the<BR>
screens are changing.
</BODY>
```

Figure 11.12 HTML code for the second of the four-page set of reloading REFRESH pages.

In the code in Figure 11.12, the only changes involve the URL of the new target (now it points to the next page), the duration (which changes to 5 seconds), and the color of the background. If you use a stopwatch to time the screens, you will see that the REFRESH values are not exact measures of time. Rather, the intervals specified are guidelines, or "relative" time intervals. A window that refreshes after 10 seconds will change more slowly than one that refreshes after 8 seconds. Don't try to create a time-sensitive series with this sort of REFRESH. As with FORMAT, you are a bit at the mercy of the browser with timing.

```
<HTML>
<HEAD>
<TITLE> A refresh series page 3 </TITLE>
<META HTTP-EQUIV="REFRESH" CONTENT="7;
URL=FILE:///F|/C11/FIG1114.HTM" >
<!--This screen will wait for 7 seconds, then refresh with
the third screen in the set...-->
</HEAD>
<BODY BGCOLOR="#5588AA">
<H1>Third screen in a refresh series</H1>
This screen will display for 7 seconds<BR>
then it will be replaced by the fourth screen in the
series.<BR>
The background color will change too, to make it obvious that
the<BR>
screens are changing.
</BODY>
```

Figure 11.13 HTML code for the third of the four-page set of reloading REFRESH pages.

Again, as shown in Figure 11.13, only the URL, the delay time, and the color change. If you go to the Web site for the book and look at this series, or if you code them yourself, you will notice that the delay is getting progressively longer on each screen—3, 5, and now 7 seconds.

```
<HTML>
<HEAD>
<TITLE> A refresh series page 4 </TITLE>
<META HTTP-EQUIV="REFRESH" CONTENT="3;
URL=FILE:///F|/C11/FIG1111.HTM" >
<!--This screen will wait for 3 seconds, then refresh by
going back to the first screen in the set...-->
</HEAD>
<BODY BGCOLOR="#AABBAA">
<H1>Last screen in a refresh series</H1>
This screen will display for 3 seconds<BR>
then it will be replaced by the first screen in the
series.<BR>
The background color will change too, to make it obvious that
the<BR>
screens are changing.
</BODY>
```

Figure 11.14 The last of the four-page set of reloading REFRESH pages.

Like the other screens of the series, the one coded in Figure 11.14 has a different duration, color, and URL. In this screen we send the user back to the first screen to start the whole process over again. It has a short duration of only 3 seconds.

This set of four screens is designed to illustrate the looping that can be accomplished with the REFRESH value. Another interesting way to use this feature is to automatically redirect the user to a new URL when a page or Web site moves. Code a page at the old URL that says something like the message in Figure 11.15 to automatically send the user to the new page. But always give users the option of clicking on the new URL rather than waiting for your code, and give them enough time to read the screen before you send them off.

If the user clicks on a link within the page, the browser will interrupt the REFRESH timer and go to the link the user chose. User input always has precedence over automatic REFRESH. For that reason, you should give your users a link to click, rather than forcing them to endure the series you have created. The code in Figure 11.14 has no such link, so it locks the user into the series. That is an error of design. Notice that the screen in Figure 11.15 allows the user to manually go to the new site as well.

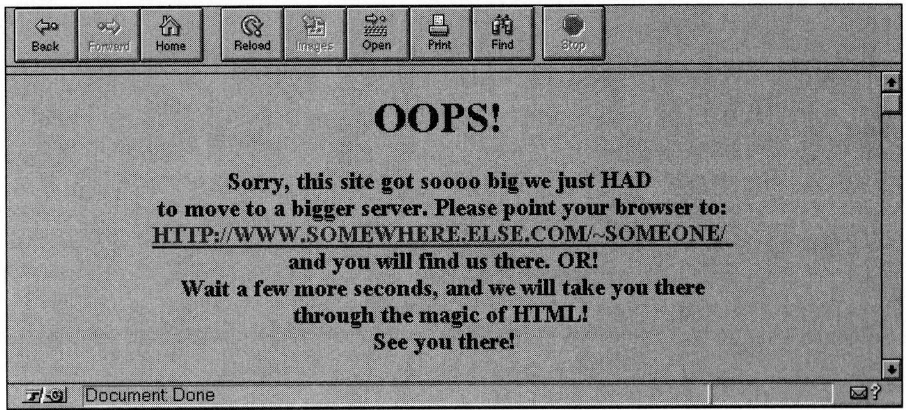

Figure 11.15 Netscape's presentation of a redirection screen.

The screen in Figure 11.15 is a nice, polite, "I'm sorry to inconvenience you" screen to tell the users that you have moved your site. The new address is shown so that they can write it down, cut and paste it, or click on it and then bookmark the site. After about 20 seconds, the browser will refresh the screen with the data from the new URL. The first screen the users see at the new location should remind them to bookmark the new site and edit their list of bookmarks to remove the old URL.

Figure 11.16 presents the code for the screen in Figure 11.15. Notice that in the <META> tag, the absolute URL is typed out and the refresh time is a reasonable one for allowing the user to read the screen. Remember, however, that the older browsers don't recognize this <META> tag. Therefore, you should always give your users the option of clicking to go to the address the REFRESH will send them to. This is true even if you are simply refreshing the current screen to update the information.

```
<HTML>
<HEAD>
<TITLE> OOPS, we moved </TITLE>
<META HTTP-EQUIV="REFRESH" CONTENT="20;
URL=http://www.somewhere.else.com/">
</HEAD>
<BODY>
<CENTER>
<H1>OOPS! </H1>
<H3>Sorry, this site got soooo big we just HAD <BR>
to move to a bigger server. Please point your browser to:
<A HREF="http://www.somewhere.else.com/~someone/">
HTTP://WWW.SOMEWHERE.ELSE.COM/~SOMEONE/ </A><BR>
and you will find us there.  OR!<BR>
Wait a few more seconds, and we will take you there<BR>
through the magic of HTML!  <BR>
See you there!</H3>
</CENTER>
</BODY>
</HTML>
```

Figure 11.16 HTML code for a redirection screen.

Guidelines for REFRESH Like all the other "neat" tools we have discovered, REFRESH can be abused. There are a few rules of thumb that should be followed so as not to abuse your user. First, give the user enough time to read the contents of the screen before you refresh it. As the Web weaver, you probably wrote the page you are refreshing, so you know the content. When you read the page, you are really just skimming it because you already know what it says. You are reading it *much* faster than the average reader will. Give your reader ample time to read the wonderful content you have provided before you send her to a new page.

If you are concerned that a fast reader will be bored, give that reader a link to the new page as well. Thus, if she finishes the page, she can click on a Next Page link to go on to the next page in the series rather than waiting for your page to refresh and send her there.

Second rule of thumb: use pages that paint up quickly. The whole purpose of this technique is to provide some action or activity for the user. Don't have pages in your set that contain lots of graphics and are many screens long, as that will violate the first guideline and this one as well. The pages you set up in this sort of series should be small and contain few graphics that are also small, so the pages will paint up quickly.

Third rule of thumb: provide a way for your user to stop the series. As was noted above, the browser will always take user input over a REFRESH. If the user clicks on any tag in the page, the browser will take him there rather than loading the new page or reloading the existing page. Usually this type of automatic sequence is used to provide some dynamics to an otherwise static Web kiosk or unattended browser. Give the user a way out of the series.

URL

The **URL** value is used, as we have seen, with the REFRESH value. It specifies the URL of the page to which control is given when the REFRESH time expires. In this context the URL must be a complete URL. The browser will not supply any portion of the URL, so relative URLs will not work. The URL itself should be enclosed in quotation marks and be separated from the time value by a semicolon. The syntax of the CONTENT for REFRESH is very critical; any mistake may cause the REFRESH to fail, possibly refreshing only the current screen.

NAME

The **NAME** attribute is used for other data that do not correspond to the standard http header tags. You can declare additional data for use by your own software using the different values of the NAME attribute. Some of the NAME values will move into HTTP-EQUIV as the browsers become more sophisticated. For example, the KEYWORDS value is almost universally recognized and will most likely move into HTTP-EQUIV in the near future.

DESCRIPTION

The **DESCRIPTION** value will allow some search engines to capture a description of your page. Normally the search engine takes the first few lines from the page content as the description, but if you have a framed document, or one with extensive formatting, those lines may not tell what your page is about. You can code the following to give the search engines a better idea of the content of your site:

```
<META NAME="DESCRIPTION" CONTENT="A collection of great...">
```

KEYWORDS

Just as the DESCRIPTION content value helps the search engines display the true content of your site, the **KEYWORDS** value allows the index-based search engines to have a better idea of the topics available on your site. Usually the index-based search engines take the keywords from the title of the document. Using this <META> tag attribute value of KEYWORDS will give those search engines a better set of words for referencing the content of your site. Code the tag like this:

```
<META NAME="KEYWORDS" CONTENT="UNIX, Ferengi, HTML">
```

Notice that the CONTENT is a list of keywords, separated by commas and enclosed in quotation marks. This is one of the more important tags if you want the index-based search engines to accurately represent the content of your site.

AUTHOR

The CONTENT of the **AUTHOR** value should be self-explanatory . . . but if not, it is the name of that wonderful individual who wove the page. This is a nice feature to include.

COPYRIGHT

The **COPYRIGHT** value has as its CONTENT a copyright statement about the site or about those parts of the site that are copyrighted. This value does not replace nor should it be substituted for a copyright symbol (©) and copyright notice at the bottom of each page you wish copyrighted.

Other Attribute Values

There are a large number of additional attribute values, most of them specific to a particular application or browser. New values will be incorporated into the standard, and the <META> tag will take on additional importance in future versions of the HTML standard.

Custom Bullets

As we learned long ago—gee, it sure seems a long time ago—there are usually three different bullet types in an unordered list. Sometimes it is necessary, or at least pretty, to have a list that contains special images rather than circles, disks, or squares. Okay, we did say the Web weaver is to control content and the browser the format, but we can bend the rules just a little here to create a page with some fancy bullets. Figure 11.17 shows an example.

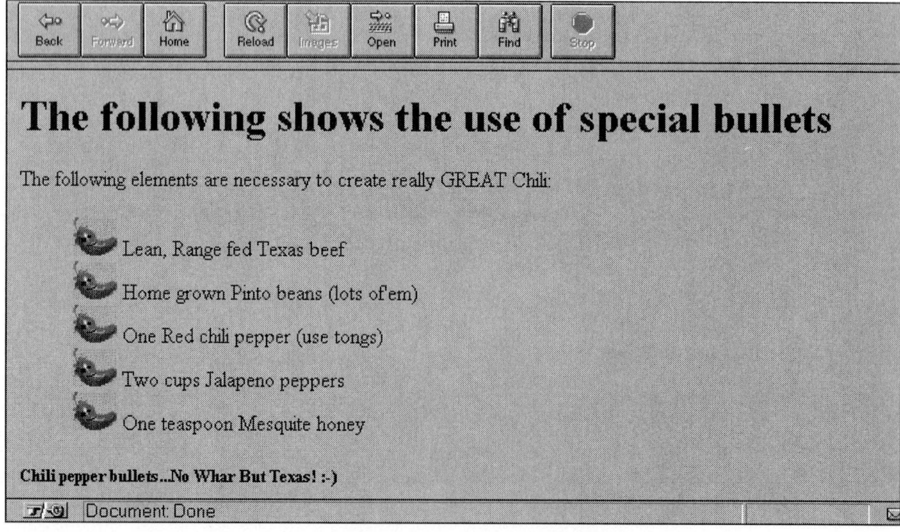

Figure 11.17 Netscape's presentation of special graphics as bullets.

The custom bullets are a nice little addition, as long as the images aren't too big. Remember, pictures take time to download. In this case, however, the little pepper is only a 1.22 K file, and it needs to be downloaded only once, because the browser will reuse the cached version on each of the five lines of the page.

Figure 11.18 presents the code for the page with the fancy bullets. As you can see, we used the definition list (<DL>) and inserted an image into each line of the definition. It isn't a real bulleted list, but it looks like one. This is a way to bend the rules, just a little, to create some interest without loading up the page with big graphics. The technique works fine for very short lines. When the lines are long enough to wrap, the text will align with the left edge of the graphic, not the left edge of the previous text line as you might want. Figure 11.19 shows what happens when we add a line that is a bit too long. Because the image is embedded within the actual definition, the text wraps to the edge of the image, not to the edge of the text.

```
<HTML>
<HEAD>
<TITLE>Special Bullets </TITLE>
</HEAD>
<BODY>
<H1>The following shows the use of special bullets</H1>
The following elements are necessary to create really GREAT
Chili:
<DL>
<DT><DD><IMG SRC="chili.gif" WIDTH=35 HEIGHT=28> Lean, Range
fed Texas beef
<DT><DD><IMG SRC="chili.gif" WIDTH-35 HEIGHT=28> Home grown
Pinto beans (lots of 'em)
<DT><DD><IMG SRC="chili.gif" WIDTH=35 HEIGHT=28> One Red
chili pepper (use tongs)
<DT><DD><IMG SRC="chili.gif" WIDTH=35 HEIGHT=28> Two cups
Jalapeno peppers
<DT><DD><IMG SRC="chili.gif" WIDTH=35 HEIGHT=28> One teaspoon
Mesquite honey
</DL>
<FONT  SIZE=-1><B>Chili pepper bullets...No Whar But Texas!
:-)</B></FONT>
</BODY>
```

Figure 11.18 HTML code to use custom bullets.

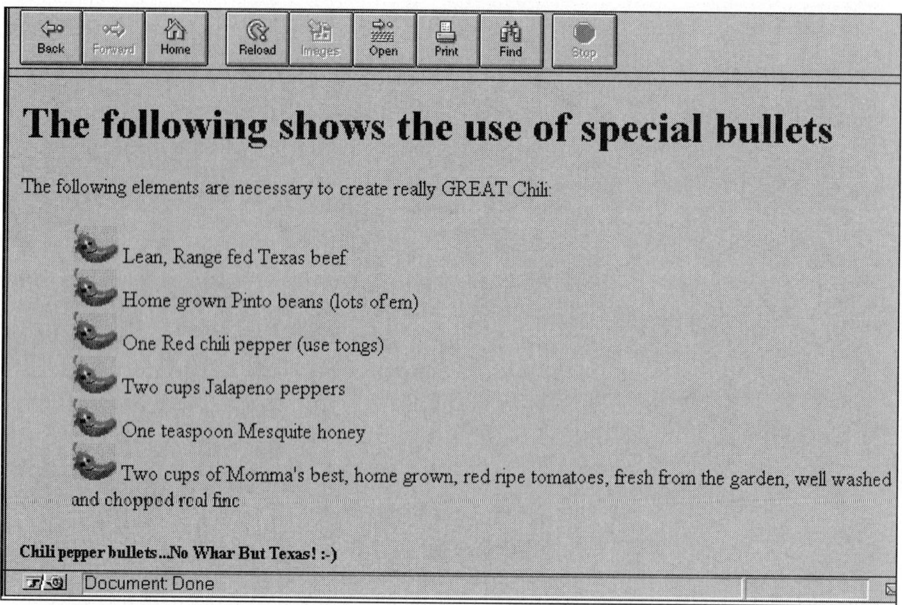

Figure 11.19 Netscape's presentation of special graphics as bullets, showing how the text wraps in a <DD> list element.

You could put the image in the <DT> container, but then the image wouldn't align with the text. Figure 11.20 shows how that would look. The bullets' placement is not as attractive, although the text will be aligned.

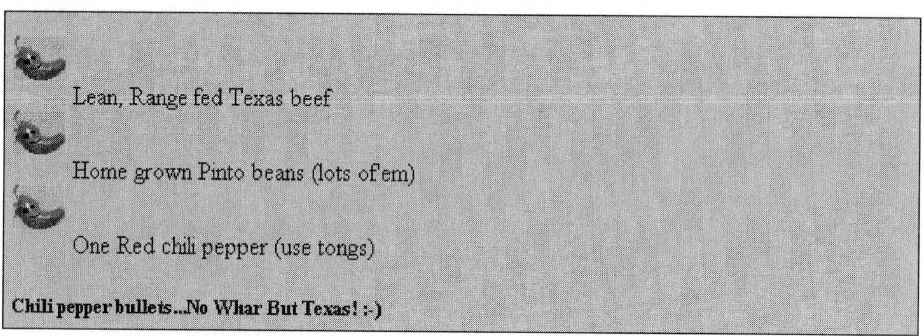

Figure 11.20 Netscape's presentation of special graphics as bullets, showing how the images align when coded in the <DT> tag.

This technique of creating fancy bullets is not one to use with impunity, but it will serve in those special occasions when you need to make your list look outstanding. It may be a good technique for your home page, but probably not for all the pages on your site. On the other hand, used carefully, this technique can provide a consistent look across several pages. Remember, the browser will need to download the image file only once. Later pages will not be affected, as the GIF will be cached.

Multicolumn Pages

If you want your page to look like a magazine or newspaper, you will need to construct multicolumn pages. Currently there is no HTML code designed specifically to create the multicolumn layout, but as we saw in the last example, we can use an existing container to perform tasks other than that for which it was specifically designed. We will use a table to create our multicolumn page. Figure 11.21 shows how it looks in the browser. Although it looks like a simple columnar text, when we look at the source code in Figure 11.22, it becomes obvious what was done to force the text into this format. HTML code works differently than a word processor, which simply creates columns and then flows the text into them. In HTML code, the text needs to be manually placed into the columns. If one of the columns contains more text than the other, the results look most strange, as we can see Figure 11.23.

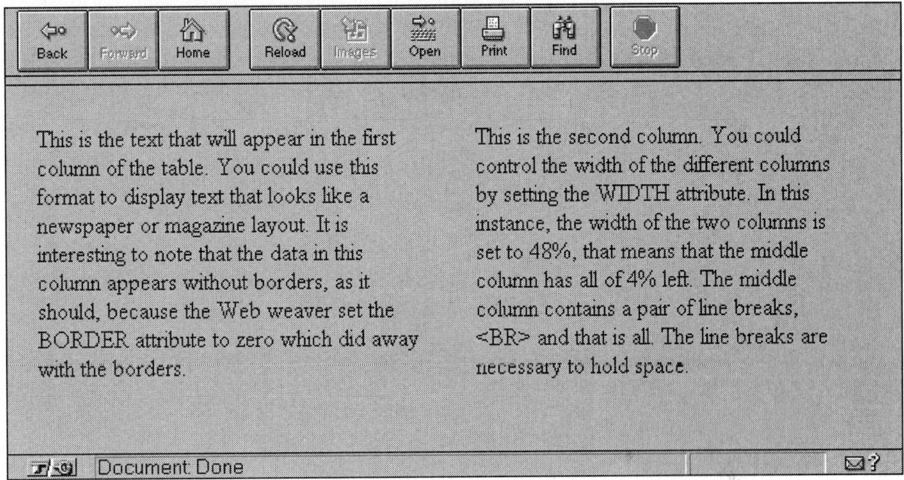

Figure 11.21 The way multicolumn text looks in the browser.

```
<HTML>
<HEAD>
<TITLE> Showing off a three column page </TITLE>
</HEAD>
<BODY>
<TABLE BORDER=0 CELLSPACING=10 >
      <TR>
            <TD WIDTH="48%"> This is the text that will
appear in the first column of the table.  You could use this
format to display text that looks like a newspaper or
magazine layout.  It is interesting to note that the data in
this column appears without borders, as it should, because
the Web weaver set the BORDER attribute to zero
which did away with the borders.
            <TD> <BR><BR>
            <TD WIDTH="48%">This is the second column.  You
could control the width of the different columns by setting
the WIDTH attribute.  In this instance, the width of the two
columns is set to 48%, that means that the middle column has
all of 4% left.  The middle column contains a pair of line
breaks, &lt;BR&gt; and that is all.  The line breaks are
necessary to hold space.
      </TR>
</TABLE>
</BODY>
```

Figure 11.22 HTML code for putting out text in columns.

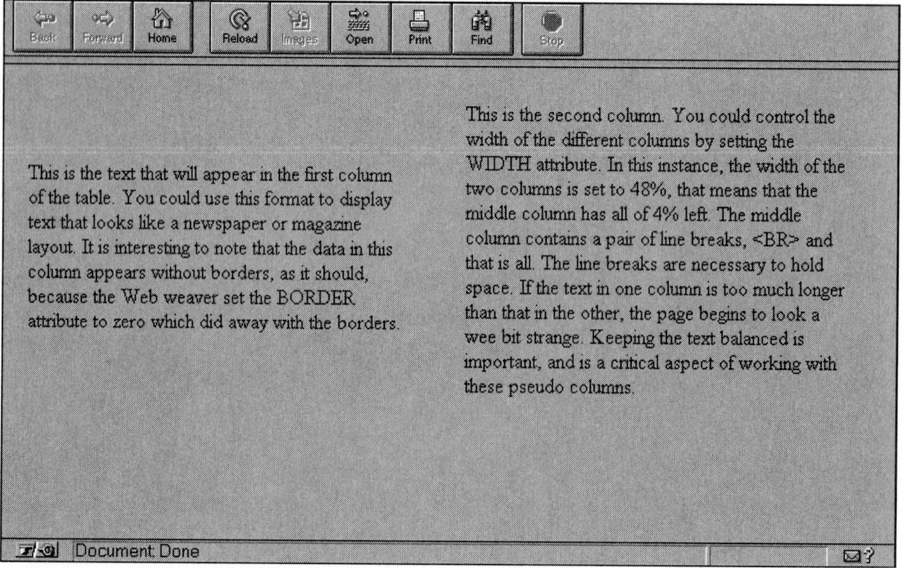

Figure 11.23 Netscape's presentation of columns of unequal length.

The text in the left column seems to float, somewhat suspended, whereas the text fills the right column. If you are going to try to present text using this technique, it is best done after all the text has been written, so you can balance the two columns, keeping approximately the same number of lines in each. Obviously the task becomes more difficult as the number of columns grows. This technique is valuable, but it is somewhat more difficult to apply than other text presentations.

By using the COLSPAN attribute and changing the font, you can create headline-like text. Figure 11.24 provides an example. Several tags were used to create this headline-like text. Figure 11.25 presents the code. Notice that we added a new row to handle the headline, and we forced alignment, increased the font size, and bolded the text. The result looks like a headline, and that is what we were shooting for. If you find your code causes you to use a lot of tags, like the code in Figure 11.25, you might consider better utilizing the HTML you know. The following line will produce the same output as the code for the headline in Figure 11.25, but with fewer tags:

```
<TH COLSPAN=3 ><FONT SIZE=+3>EXTRA !!! NEAT HEADLINES </FONT>
```

Using the Table Header <TH> tag rather than <TD> took care of the bolding and the centering. This code is more efficient and much more readable as well. It represents much better HTML!

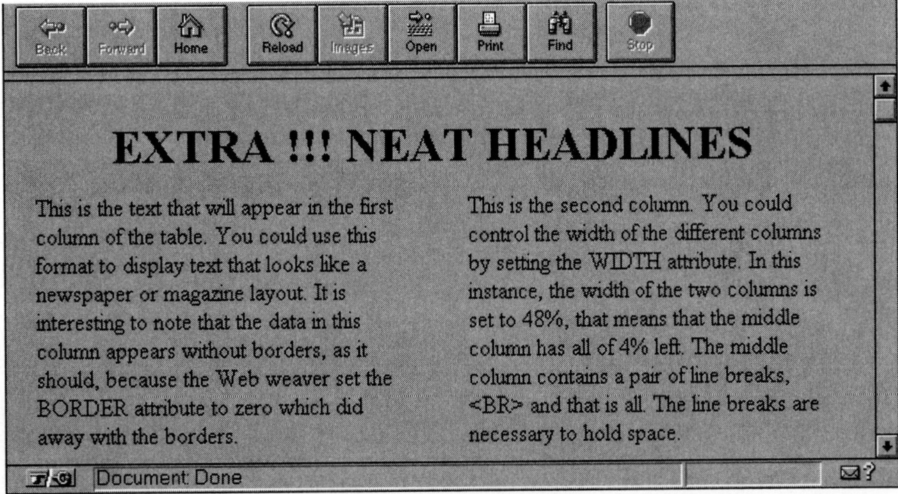

Figure 11.24 Netscape's presentation of headlines created with COLSPAN.

```
<HTML>
<HEAD>
<TITLE> Showing off a three column page </TITLE>
</HEAD>
<BODY>
<TABLE BORDER=0 CELLSPACING=10 >
      <TR>
      <TD COLSPAN=3><FONT SIZE=+3><B><CENTER>EXTRA !!! NEAT
      HEADLINES </CENTER></B></FONT></TD>
      </TR>
      <TR>
            <TD WIDTH="48%"> This is the text that will
appear in the first column of the table.  You could use this
format to display text that looks like a newspaper or
magazine layout.  It is interesting to note that the data in
this column appears without borders, as it should, because
the Web weaver set the BORDER attribute to zero which did
away with the borders.
            <TD> <BR><BR>
            <TD WIDTH="48%">This is the second column.  You
could control the width of the different columns by setting
the WIDTH attribute.  In this instance, the width of the two
columns is set to 48%, that means that the middle column has
all of 4% left.  The middle column contains a pair of line
breaks, &lt;BR&gt; and that is all.  The line breaks are
necessary to hold space.
      </TR>
</TABLE>
</BODY>
</HTML>
```

Figure 11.25 HTML code for headline-like text.

Sidebars

Sometimes it is handy to have a **sidebar,** or side head, to set the heading off from the rest of the text of the document. Figure 11.26 shows what sidebars look like. They take up a lot of space but make a nice visual division of the page. In addition, they can help your user find things more easily on your page. While they are not a good idea for long pages, because you need to put all the text into a table, they are a very powerful tool for smaller pages where the content is divided into specific thoughts.

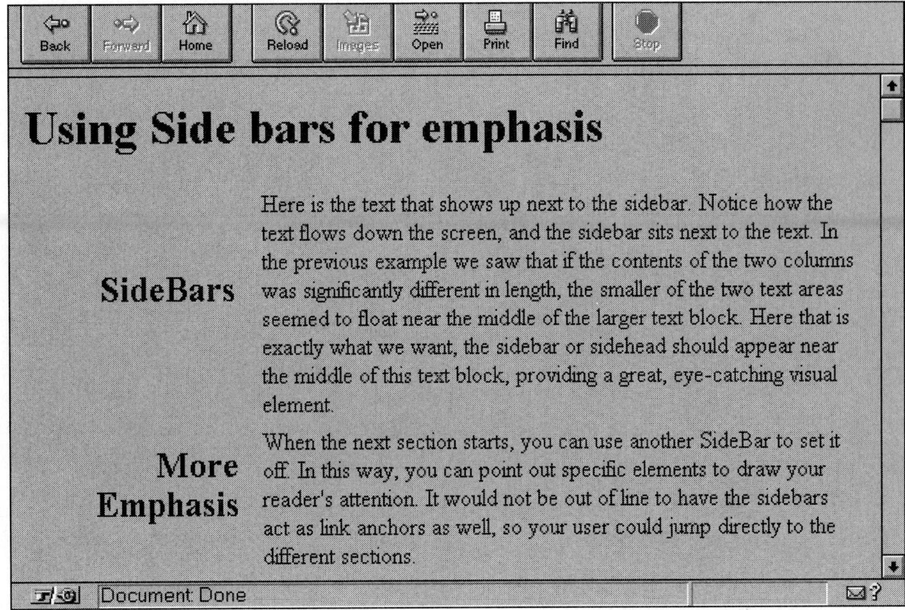

Figure 11.26 Netscape's presentation of sidebars, or side heads.

Figure 11.27 presents the code for the sidebars in Figure 11.26. As you can see, the way the text is coded, the sidebar takes up 10 percent of the screen's width. That is a significant amount of space in a long document. This technique is best used for shorter pages and only when it is needed to draw the reader's attention.

```
<HTML>
<HEAD>
<TITLE> Side bars </TITLE>
</HEAD>
<BODY>
<H1>Using Side bars for emphasis</H1>
<TABLE>
<TR>
      <TH WIDTH="10%" ALIGN=RIGHT> <H2> SideBars</H2>
      <TD> <BR>
      <TD>
          Here is the text that shows up next to the sidebar.
          Notice how the text flows down the screen, and the
          sidebar sits next to the text.  In the previous
          example we saw that if the contents of the two
          columns was significantly different in length, the
          smaller of the two text areas seemed to float near
          the middle of the larger text block.  Here that is
          exactly what we want, the sidebar or sidehead
          should appear near the middle of this text block,
          providing a great, eye-catching visual element.
</TR>
<TR>
<TH WIDTH="10%" ALIGN=RIGHT> <H2>More Emphasis</H2>
      <TD> <BR>
      <TD>
          When the next section starts, you can use another
          SideBar to set it off.  In this way, you can point
          out specific elements to draw your reader's
          attention.  It would not be out of line to have the
          sidebars act as link anchors as well, so your user
          could jump directly to the different sections.
</TR>
</TABLE>
</BODY>
</HTML>
```

Figure 11.27 HTML code for sidebars, or side heads.

Exercises

Now that you have all of these great techniques in your repertoire, it is time to put them to use.

11.1. Experiment with the different types of document relationships. Create a set of documents (small documents), and use the document relationship tags to show interrelationships.

11.2. Experiment with the EXPIRES <META> element. See if you can create a document that will be not be cached.

11.3. Create a set of five small Web pages that invoke each other, one after the other, using the REFRESH <META> element.

11.4. Build a framed document with four sections, the top left section measuring only 10% by 10% of the page. In that top left frame, create a set of five image documents that REFRESH on a 10-second interval. Explain in one of the other frames how this type of document could be used in a commercial environment.

11.5. Try to create the same type of situation as you did in Exercise 11.4 but with tables instead of frames.

11.6. Build a page that shows how to use custom bullets. On the same page create a section with three columns of text. Each column should have close to the same amount of text. Notice the complications multiple columns add to the maintenance of the page.

11.7. Create a page that demonstrates the use of sidebars. Top bars might be nice, too.

CHAPTER **twelve**

What Is Java?

The official definition of **Java** from the company that invented it, Sun Microsystems, is "a simple, object-oriented, distributed, interpreted, robust, secure, architecture-neutral, portable, high-performance, multithreaded, and dynamic language." That is a great collection of buzzwords. What it means is that Java is a programming language that uses object-oriented techniques, works across the Internet, is translated line by line, is safe and hard to crash, runs on many different computer platforms, does powerful things quickly, seems to do more than one thing at a time, and is changing even as we speak.

In other words, Java is the hot new language used to write applications that are used over the Internet, as well as programs used in a stand-alone mode. A **stand-alone program** is one like your word processor or a computer game you play on your computer. It runs on a single, local machine and is complete on that machine. In contrast, a **distributed program** is one that runs on computers across the Internet. An example is an HTML browser. The HTML code is transferred across the Internet to the browser. In the same way, Java applet code is transferred across the Net to the Java interpreter on the local machine. That way the Java program can run across the Net.

With Java you can add dynamic action to your Web page. This dynamic action can be a simple scrolling marquee, an intricate form or spreadsheet the user fills out, or a sophisticated interactive game for the user to play. Nearly anything you can imagine your page doing can be done in Java.

Java Terminology

Before we start looking at Java programs, some terms need defining:

- **Java**—a programming language with the features described earlier. The name does not stand for anything. Some say it stands for "Just Another Veritable Acronym" or "Jeepers Another Virtual Acronym," but the truth is, Java stands for Java, nothing more.
- **Object-oriented approach**—one of two ways to design and develop a program. The other approach is the traditional approach, called a **procedural approach,** in which the programmer lists the actual steps the computer needs to take to solve the problem. The data are separate from the instructions, and the whole system is designed and developed based on the idea that the programs exist only in the special environment of a computer. Object-oriented languages are designed to build programs that act like objects in the real world. Objects in our world have a state and a behavior. For example, the state of a dog may be its location and whether it is awake or asleep. The dog's behavior would be what it is currently doing, barking at the moon or chasing its tail.

Another feature of objects is that they are **modular**, or self-contained. Each object contains both the instructions and the data those instructions will process. Each object performs a specialized task, which is part of the overall objective for a program. Objects also have the property of being **hierarchical**, meaning they can be composed of smaller parts and can be part of a larger object as well. A house is an excellent example of a hierarchical object. The plumbing system, the electrical system, and the heating system all are objects within the house. Each of those objects—for example, the heating system-object—is composed of smaller objects, like the furnace-object and the ductwork-object. The furnace-object can be further divided into still smaller objects, like the burner, the fan, and the chimney. Moving the other way, the house-object can be considered part of the neighborhood-object, and so on.

- **Applet**—a small Java program that requires a browser or other support environment to run. Applets are the Java tools Web weavers use to bring animation and other Java features to their Web pages. Applets are usually small, and they are considered safe because they cannot modify the system upon which they are running. Applets cannot access memory out of the range specified and reserved for the browser, nor can they modify the contents of the secondary storage on the host computer. Consequently, they cannot be used to implant a **virus** (destructive software).

Applets are downloaded just like any other HTML object, and the Java Virtual Machine, running inside the browser, executes the applet to perform the specified task. We will get into the specific steps necessary to build an applet later.

- **Bytecode**—is an intermediate step between the Java source code and actual executable code that can be run by a specific processor, like a Pentium 300 MMX. Bytecode is generated by the Java compiler.

Most computer languages are **compiled,** meaning that a translator program changes the people-readable source code into a machine-readable binary code created for a specific computer chip or chip set. A **binary file** is also called an **executable file**. When a program is compiled, all of the source code is translated into binary code, and the binary code is saved in a separate file.

Some programming languages, like BASIC (Beginners All-purpose Symbolic Instruction Code), are interpreted instead of compiled. An **interpreter** translates the source code into binary code, one line at a time, as it is needed, just before the binary code is executed by the computer. This is usually a slower process than compiling. It is slower because the binary is not saved, so if the program executes the same code more than once, the source code has to be translated more than once.

Java takes advantage of both these techniques—compiling and interpreting—and works a little differently than any other programming language. The Java compiler translates the Java source code into the intermediate code called *bytecode*. Bytecode is universal. All Java interpreters will translate bytecode into the binary data needed by the computer on which the Java program is running.

The Java interpreter is also called a **Java Virtual Machine**. The virtual machine is designed for a specific platform, like a UNIX computer, an Intel processor running Windows 95, or an Apple Powerbook running System 7. The Java Virtual Machine takes care of the specifics necessary for the particular computer and translates bytecode into machine language for execution on that machine. In this way Java is portable across any computer on the Net that supports the Java Virtual Machine. The only requirement to keep this concept working is that all the developers of browsers agree to use the same standard set of bytecodes. If any of the players in this drama decide to go off and use a specialized set of instructions that generate nonstandard bytecodes, the true beauty and functionality of the pure Java environment will be damaged.

- **Just-in-time**—a new idea in programming. Traditionally all of a program had to be loaded into a computer before it could be run. You have experienced this when downloading traditional, non-Java programs from the Net. You need to have all of the program on your computer before it can start working. Java, however, can support **multithreading**, which means that while the program is waiting for the user to do something, like type a response on the keyboard, it can do something else, like download part of the Java applet from the Web. That means that as soon as a critical minimum of the applet's code has been downloaded, it can begin running. As it waits for the user to take some action or for some other event to occur, it can continue to download more of the applet. As the applet needs more code, it is available, just in time. This makes some Java programs very fast to begin executing. They don't have to wait for the whole application to be downloaded before they start.

Java and the World Wide Web

HTML allows the Web weaver to present information in an excellent, hyperlinked environment, augmented by pictures, sounds, and other multimedia. However, Web designers have realized that they need ways to enable the user to execute more dynamic programs than are possible with HTML, even with advanced CGI scripting. There is a need for more multimedia and real-time (or close to real-time) data input. Java fits this niche very well. It gives Web developers a tool that is fast, efficient, portable, and supportive of distributed computing. In addition to adding features, Java also makes animations run much more efficiently, because with Java they don't require constant refreshing from the server. A Java applet can be downloaded and then run locally, at the speed of the PC running the applet rather than at the speed of the download stream. For all these reasons, Java has become an important force in the development of commerce and interactivity on the Net.

History of Java

The powerful and sophisticated programming language of Java started life as a programming language for a universal remote control for TV, stereo systems, VCRs, and the like. It was invented a long time ago, way back in 1990, when the Web had yet to explode and PCs weren't exactly everywhere as they are today. Java was designed by a team from Sun Microsystems, but it was a team with a very different direction than the rest of that company. These team members had been assembled by a group of farsighted Sun executives for the task of creating a simple, small, intuitive consumer tool, a computer for the people. They were called the Green Team.

In the spring of 1991 the Green Team set up shop in Menlo Park and began doing everything possible as different as possible from the way Sun did things. Two software specialists, Patrick Naughton and Jim Gosling, and two hardware engineers, Mike Sheridan and Ed Frank, composed the team. They began building their device with parts of Nintendo Gameboys and Sharp TV sets. The hardware was coming together, but the programming language was the sticking point. Existing languages had been designed from the computer point of view, with speed the issue and reliability less important. Since reliability is a critical issue, existing languages just wouldn't work.

Naughton was working on a graphical user interface, and Gosling was developing a new language to replace C++. When they brought their respective parts together, in August 1991, a new language was born. They called it Oak, because there was an oak tree outside Gosling's window.

The next year, the Green Team was demonstrating its new toy for Sun management. It was a handheld device that had no buttons at all, not even an on/off switch. The user interacted with the device graphically. To turn on the device, the user tapped on a screen. A cartoon house was drawn on the screen, and a little tour guide, called Duke, appeared.

I would love to show you a picture of Duke, but he is a registered trademark of Sun Microsystems, and the company doesn't let third parties use him. You can see him by going to one of Sun's sites, for example, **http://java.sun.com/Series/Tutorial/ui/drawing/imageSequence.html**.

Duke looks like an old Star Trek insignia, with a big red W.C. Fields nose—hard to imagine, but really cute. The user could move him through the Green Team's house just by touching the screen. Programming the device and the related consumer electronics was easy. For example, to program the VCR, all the user had to do was move to the virtual living room, touch the virtual *TV guide* on the coffee table, flip through the magazine, select a movie, drag the movie to the virtual VCR, and the VCR was programmed to record the movie selected.

In September 1992 a new company, FirstPerson Inc., was formed to build and market the new technology. But things didn't go as planned. The chip for the device was too expensive to manufacture, and there were other problems at Sun. Ultimately, the Green Team effort was a failure, and the company dissolved it in 1994. However, that is obviously not the end of the story.

Back in 1992, Bill Joy, one of the co-founders of Sun, opened a small Sun research site in Aspen, Colorado. Joy saw Oak as an opportunity for Sun to move into the exploding market of the World Wide Web. He put Gosling and Naughton back to work on the Oak project, convincing Sun management that the project was worth saving. It was Joy's plan to release Java for free on the net, much like Netscape is marketed. Since Oak was very close to the name of another product, in January 1995 Oak officially became Java.

In December 1995 Microsoft signed a letter of intent with Sun to support Java and implement it in their Internet Explorer. This provided exactly the push Java needed. With support from Microsoft, Java became the standard language for applets across the World Wide Web. It served as a common, powerful, uniform language that was truly platform independent and would run in anybody's browser. This was "pure" Java—a critical idea.

Since then, though, Microsoft has moved away from this position, trying to create its own version of Java that includes some Microsoft-specific code and is no longer platform independent. Their new action could defeat one of the most useful and powerful aspects of Java, the fact that it will run anywhere there is a Java Virtual Machine—in its pure form.

Java has become one of the most interesting tools on the Net—and a very powerful addition to the HTML you have already learned.

The Three (Two) Flavors of Java

In most bistros Java-named things come in three flavors, regular, decaffeinated, and extra-crispy. Okay, sorry! Somebody had to say it, right? Really, the two flavors of true Java are:

1. **Java**, a complete and powerful programming language.
2. **Java applets**, a subset of Java used to create miniature programs that are called from an HTML program and run on the browser, or client side.

Then there is **JavaScript,** a specialized language used to build programs that are embedded in an HTML document and perform simple tasks. This language is not one of the Java family. It is not Java. It was simply named JavaScript. We will look at this language briefly later on, but we are not going to discuss Java or Java script in detail. Rather, we will focus our attention on Java applets, the part of Java that is of greatest importance to Web weavers.

Java—The Complete Language

Java is a programming language that is moving quickly into the world of professional programming. It is an object-oriented language in the flavor of C++, but it has more platform independence than other high-level languages. It is very sophisticated and much more tightly controlled than most other programming languages. For example, C++ uses **pointers**, variables that contain the address of other data, to access much of memory. In C++, tables of these pointers, rather than arrays are used to store subscripted data. Java doesn't have pointers; it calls everything, including subroutines, by name. Calling by name makes verification much easier and the application much more secure. Java is also much more **robust** than most other programming languages, that is, more strongly constructed.

Java Applets—The Subset of Java

An applet is a small Java program that is designed to run within the environment of a browser (or an applet viewer). Because the applet is designed to run within a browser, it can rely on the browser to take care of the **graphical user interface (GUI)** and screen handling. Applets also run in what is called a **secure environment,** meaning they are prevented from writing to the disk drives or causing overflow errors. Since they cannot write to the drives, they cannot act like a virus.

It is important to remember that applets are designed to run from within an HTML program as it is displayed in a browser. An applet is called from your HTML code just like the images you use. The Java-compatible browser downloads the applet from the server just as it downloads any other element of the page. Then the Java Virtual Machine begins executing the Java bytecode to perform whatever task it was designed to do.

Because of the way Java was designed, it is a very secure way to perform application-type operations within the HTML environment. A Java applet must pass through four different layers of security before it is allowed to run on a user's system. First the code must be compiled by the **Java compiler,** which changes it from Java source code into bytecode. The bytecode file is called a **class file.** If the programmer tries to take any nefarious actions, like addressing an array out of bounds or making system calls, the compiler will prevent that code from compiling.

The bytecode is kept at the server, and this is what is transferred across the Net to the browser. Once the bytecode is downloaded to the browser, and Java is started at the browser, the downloaded class file is passed through the **bytecode verifier**. In a very complex process, the verifier checks to make sure that the bytecode is in fact a valid Java class. Then it passes the bytecode through several checks to ensure that the code follows all the rules of correctly formed Java. After passing the bytecode verifier, the code is considered relatively safe.

Next, the **class loader** moves the class into a specialized name space controlling where the code is placed and what it can do. Finally, the **security manager** runs at all times, enforcing the rules of applet behavior. For example, if the applet tried to access the hard disk, the security manager would prevent that access. Obviously, then, Java is a fairly secure environment. Theoretically it is not impossible to damage a computer using a Java applet, but it is extremely difficult to do so and a rare event.

In the next chapter we will look at some nifty applets that we can harvest from the Net. Then, in the last chapter of the book, we will build a very simple applet so you can see the actual construction.

JavaScript

First and foremost, JavaScript is *not* Java. It is a completely different language, designed by Netscape Communications Corporation to extend the capabilities of HTML in the Netscape browser. It was originally called LiveScript, but when the folks at Netscape saw the popularity of the Java programming language, they changed the name to JavaScript.

JavaScript is designed to allow the HTML programmer some real programming tools like looping and conditional statements. It is popular, but it does have some serious limitations. For example, JavaScript does not support graphics, parse user input, or read from text files. Currently, the programmer who cannot access the cgi-bin is the one most likely to use JavaScript to perform some of the same actions that could be done with a CGI script.

Object-Orientation Concepts

Some specialized concepts are involved in an **object-oriented programming (OOP)** language like Java. Let's explore some of these OOP subjects.

Class

In OOP, a class is not what you are in at school, nor is it a prestigious quality. Rather, a **class** is the template, or model, for specifying the state and behavior of an object at run time. Everything about a particular program is defined by the class that contains that program. A class can pass on public data and methods to its subclasses.

All Java variables must be members of a class, and a class can encapsulate (a term we will explain in a moment) variables to provide a method of inheritance (another term we will define). We will see how this actually works in a later chapter when we build an applet. Just to make life easier, the Java compiler also creates a file that has the extension of **.class** when it builds the bytecode during compilation of the Java source.

Thus, a class is, in essence, the description of a general form of program. You can build programs using existing classes, or you can "extend" a class by using parts of an existing class and adding new features to it. We will do this when we create an applet. Extending an existing class provides the opportunity for inheritance that is one critical feature of an object-oriented language.

Object Instance

An **object instance** is a particular occurrence or use of a class. Whereas, the class defines a set of variables and procedures that can be used in creating a program, the instance of that class is the actual program. An instance also has instance variables, which define the exact state of the program or routine during the running of the program. An instance of a class is called an **object!** Now we know the basic unit of *object*-oriented programming!

Abstraction

An **abstraction** results from taking the essential characteristics out of an object and creating data to represent those characteristics. Refining the general features of some collection of data to capture just those features that are essential allows the object-oriented programmer to create a set of procedures that perform data manipulation cleanly and easily.

Encapsulation

The data that must be processed are critical, but the procedures that process those data are also important. One central idea, or tenet, of object-oriented programming is that of **encapsulation,** in which the data and the operations necessary to manipulate those data are collected together into a usable module, or unit. In the case of Java, we can call one of these encapsulated data/procedures modules a *class.* In addition to having the data and code, an encapsulated object enforces some access restrictions in most object-oriented languages, including Java.

Inheritance

This term **inheritance** is used the same way when talking of the different species in the animal kingdom or Java routines. We can trace the inheritance of a timber wolf, for example, from *Chordata,* the phylum of all animals with a backbone, through the intermediate steps to the actual genus and species of *Canis lupus.* Here is the pathway of inheritance:

> **Phylum *Chordata* => Class *Mammalia* => Order *Carnivora* => Family *Canidae* => Genus and Species *Canis lupus.***

A wolf inherits characteristics from all the steps in the list above, starting with a spinal column in the *Chordata,* then fur from the mammals, pointy teeth from the *Carnivora,* a bushy tail from the *Canidae,* and a long muzzle and a penchant to howl from the *Canis.* These characteristics are inherited. In the parlance of OOP, a wolf is an instance of the class *Canidae.*

In the same fashion, inheritance in Java means that one class can receive data structures and methods or procedures from a previous class. Usually the key word **extends** indicates this inheritance. Unlike some other, more confusing object-oriented languages, Java allows a single level of inheritance. A new class can extend only one previous class, which makes Java much easier to use and debug than other object-oriented languages.

Here is an example of a new class, **HelloWorldApplet,** created using the data structures and methods already in place in the class **Applet**:

```
public class HelloWorldApplet extends Applet {
```

This line defines the new class called **HelloWorld** and describes its relationship to an existing class called **Applet**. Through this statement, HelloWorld inherits all the data and methods that Applet has, and it can add new features as well.

Inheritance is a very important property for Web professionals, because it means that Web weavers need not reinvent the wheel each time they want to build a new program. They can take an existing class that has most of what they want and extend that class. The functions are already defined, so they need to invent only the new things that the class doesn't already do. Inheritance is a very useful property indeed!

Polymorphism

Polymorphism is a Greek term that means "multiple shapes." It is a long name for a rather simple concept. All it means is using the same name for more than one, usually related, methods. There are two types of polymorphism. The simpler type is called **overloading**. Here several methods within the same class have exactly the same name but each has a different number, or type of parameter, so that the compiler can tell them apart. At compile time the Java compiler can look at the parameter list and decide which of the different methods to use.

A very helpful place to use this type of polymorphism is in input and output (I/O) routines. It would be clumsy to have to code a different output routine to print a **floating-point number** (a number with a decimal point, like 4.5) than to print an **integer** (a whole number, without a decimal point, like 5). Because Java supports overloading, there can be more than one print (number) method. Depending on the type of number you are trying to print (either a floating-point number or an integer), the compiler selects the correct print method. This is a handy, often transparent, and not very interesting type of polymorphism.

The other type of polymorphism is called **overriding,** and it is much more interesting. We can define a method in both a **parent class,** also called a **superclass,** and in an **extended class,** also called a **child class** or **subclass.** If we invoke the subclass, the definition in that subclass will be used. On the other hand, if the subclass does not define the method, then the method invoked will be that of the superclass, or parent. When a choice is possible, the lowest or most recent, method will be used. This decision is made at run time and so is very dynamic. There is a technical term, **late, or delayed, binding,** that means "choosing the correct method to handle the object at run time."

A Java Applet Example

Here is one version of the famous "HelloWorld" applet: Long, long ago, in a galaxy far, far away, some programming professor required his students to write a simple first program that printed the magical words "Hello World" on the screen. For some unknown reason, the practice suddenly became *"The Thing To Do,"* and ever since, programming professors seem to have a need to present the "Hello World" program as the first program their students write. In keeping with this honorable and totally silly practice, Figure 12.1 presents a simple applet that prints the words "Hello World" on the screen.

```
import java.awt.Graphics;
import java.applet.Applet;
public class HelloWorldApplet extends Applet {
     public void paint(Graphics g)  {
          g.drawString("Hellooo  World !", 20, 30);

                                       }
               }
```

Figure 12.1 Java code for the HelloWorldApplet.

The code for this applet is all that is necessary to perform the fantastically complex operation you see in the browser example in Figure 12.2. The first two lines bring sophisticated collections of code into the build of the applet. The third line, which starts with **public class,** creates a new class that extends the applet class. The next line defines a function that uses the graphics from the Abstract Windowing Toolkit (**awt**). The last line of actual code draws a string on the screen that contains the words **"Hellooo World !"**. The two numbers that follow those words are the X and Y coordinates at which to start drawing the text. The **drawString** is a method.

This applet, then, invokes some graphical tools to draw a string of characters on the screen, starting at a point 20 pixels in and 30 pixels down from the top left corner of the area defined. Figure 12.3 presents the convoluted HTML necessary to invoke an applet. The only new container in this complex example is the <APPLET> container. We will examine this container in detail shortly. Notice that <APPLET> defines the space in which the applet works. As we will see, there are many more attributes that can be coded within the <APPLET> container. Look again at Figure 12.2 to see how Netscape Communicator presents this applet. Remember, it is necessary to have a browser like Netscape Communicator that runs under a platform that can run Java. Usually, only UNIX machines, Macintosh computers, and boxes running Microsoft Windows NT or Windows 95 will provide Java capabilities.

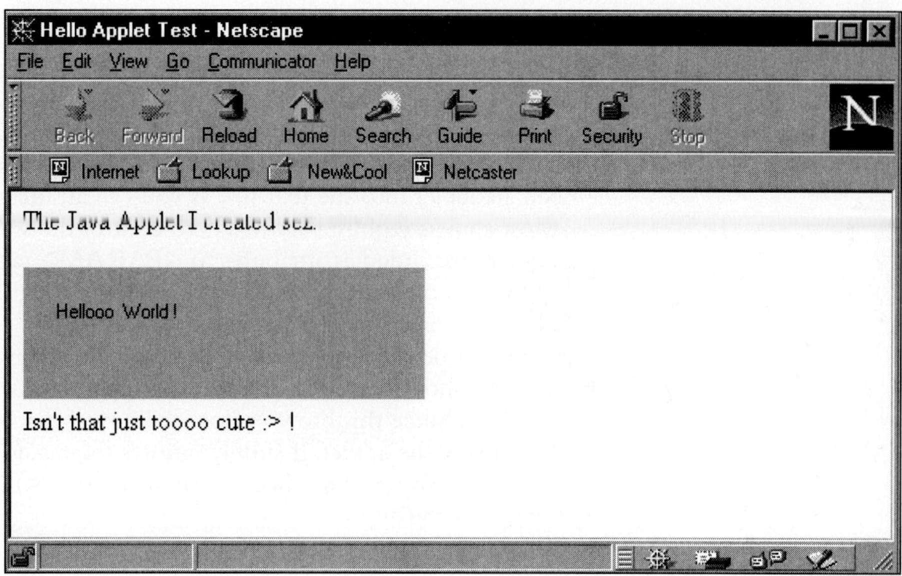

Figure 12.2 Netscape's presentation of the HelloWorld applet.

```
<HTML>
<HEAD>
<Title> Hello Applet Test </TITLE>
</HEAD>
<BODY>
<P>The Java Applet I created sez: <BR>
<BR>
<APPLET CODE="HelloWorldApplet.class" WIDTH=250 HEIGHT=80>
</APPLET>
<BR>
Isn't that just toooo cute :> !
</BODY>
</HTML>
```

Figure 12.3 HTML code necessary to invoke the HelloWorldApplet.

<APPLET>

The <APPLET> container is used to invoke a Java applet. This container is very similar to the <IMG> tag, and it has many of the same attributes. When the browser encounters the <APPLET> tag, it downloads the class code and inserts it into the document without breaking the text flow. Therefore, you can embed an applet into the text just as you can an image.

Most applets require parameters to control the way they work. These parameters are coded as attributes to **<PARAM>** tags, contained within the <APPLET> container. In addition, you can put regular HTML code inside the <APPLET> container. Browsers that don't support applets will ignore the tags they don't understand and dutifully display the output of the code instead. Figure 12.4 shows how the HelloWorld applet looks in a browser that doesn't support Java. Since this browser doesn't know what an <APPLET> tag is for, it cannot display the applet. It simply ignores the tag. (There are three blank lines between the two text lines because there are two
s, one coded before and one after the applet.)

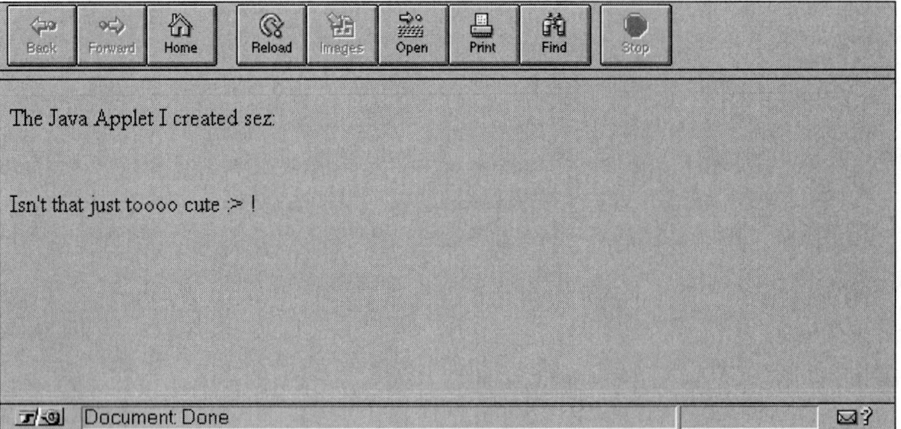

Figure 12.4 The HelloWorld applet as seen by a browser that does not support Java.

If we changed the code in the HTML document to include some text telling the users what they are missing, the browser would display that text, as shown in Figure 12.5. This may not be the most politic way to inform your users that they need to upgrade their operating system, but it illustrates the use of a few lines of text within the <APPLET> container.

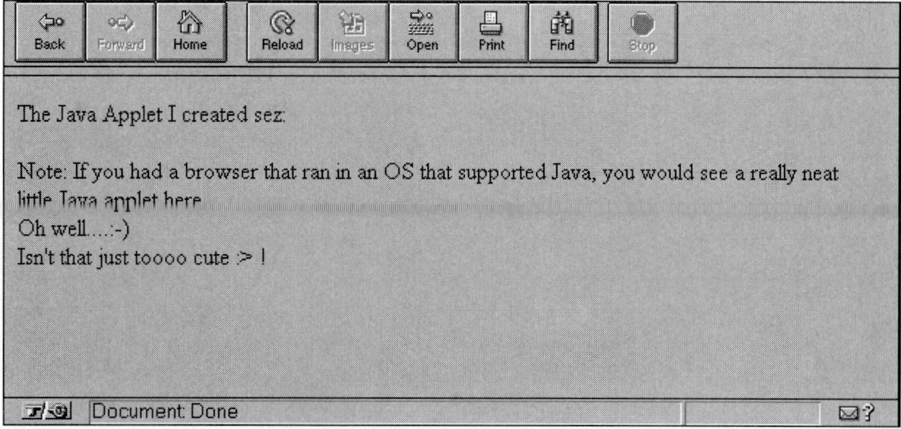

Figure 12.5 HelloWorld HTML that informs users of what they are missing since their browser does not support Java.

Figure 12.6 presents the modified code that produces the screen in Figure 12.5 for browsers that don't support Java. Look at the "Note: . . ." coded within the <APPLET> container. Browsers that support Java will ignore the HTML code embedded within the <APPLET> . . . </APPLET> container.

```
<HTML>
<HEAD>
<Title> Hello Applet Test </TITLE>
</HEAD>
<BODY>
<P>The Java Applet I created sez: <BR>
<BR>
<APPLET CODE="HelloWorldApplet.class" WIDTH=250 HEIGHT=80>
Note:  If you had a browser that ran in an OS that supported
Java, you would see a really neat little Java applet here..<BR>
Oh well....:-)
</APPLET>
<BR>
Isn't that just toooo cute :> !
</BODY>
</HTML>
```

Figure 12.6 HelloWorld HTML code that informs users of what they are missing since their browser does not support Java.

Now let's look at the attributes for the <APPLET> container.

ALIGN

The **ALIGN** attribute for <APPLET>, like the same attribute for <IMG>, has the following values to control positioning: TOP, TEXTTOP, MIDDLE, ABSMIDDLE, BOTTOM, BASELINE, ABSBOTTOM. Like an image, the applet is aligned with the text by means of these values. Also like an image, the applet is placed so that text flows around it on one side or the other by means of the LEFT or RIGHT attribute.

ALT

The value for the **ALT** attribute should be a quoted string that tells the user that something went wrong with the applet. As with the ALT attribute for the <IMG> tag, a value is displayed when the applet is broken for some reason. It is important to note that this attribute will be used only by browsers running on an operating system that supports Java. For other operating systems, this attribute will be ignored, because it is part of a tag that is ignored.

CODE

CODE is the only required attribute for the <APPLET> container. The browser needs to know the URL of the applet it is supposed to run. If the applet is located at the same place as the HTML page, then all that needs to be coded is the name of the applet. The browser infers the **.class** extension. Let's look at a simple case. If the HTML document is located at

http://www.fred.org/index.html

the applet **ticker.class** would be specified as

```
<APPLET CODE="Ticker">
```

and the browser would create the complete path of

http://www.fred.org/Ticker.class

to retrieve the applet.

If, however, the applet is located in a different directory than the HTML code, you will need to specify a **package** to point to the applet class file. A package is a set of directory names, starting from the URL, with each element of the package separated from the others by a dot. The browser would then take the base URL of the page and add directories as specified by the package in order to form the complete path name.

For example, suppose the applet is located in the following directory structure:

/etc/applets/stocks/Ticker.class

The <APPLET> container, with the fully qualified package, would be

```
<APPLET CODE="etc.applets.stocks.Ticker">
```

and the browser would add the base URL and create the following URL to retrieve the applet:

http://www.fred.org/etc/applets/stocks/Ticker.class

The **base URL** is the URL of the page that invokes the applet, unless the CODEBASE attribute is coded.

CODEBASE

The **CODEBASE** attribute allows the application to use an applet that is stored on another machine (at a different URL than that of the HTML document) or in a different directory from the HTML document. It provides a base URL for the browser to use to go find the applet using the techniques discussed in the preceding section. Generally speaking, as with images, it is best to have the applet at the same site as the page that invokes it. However, there are exceptions to this rule, and the CODEBASE attribute allows for those special cases. The attribute overrides the document's base URL but does not replace or reset it. CODEBASE is used only to retrieve the applet for which it is coded.

If the applet is simply in a different directory, you can code the CODEBASE attribute to point to that directory rather than using the fully qualified package. If you use the CODEBASE to specify another directory, you can code either the absolute URL, like

```
<APPLET CODE="Ticker"
```

CODEBASE="http://www.fred.org/etc/applets/stocks/">

or, usually better, you could use a relative URL, like

```
<APPLET CODE="Ticker"
```

CODEBASE>"/etc/applets/stocks/">

In the latter case, the browser fills in everything necessary (the name of the machine and so forth).

HEIGHT

The **HEIGHT** attribute for <APPLET> is coded just like the HEIGHT attribute for <IMG>. Specified in pixels, it determines the height of the applet's display region or applet window on the screen. Some applets adjust their display to the size of the applet window; others require a specified window size. Carefully read the documentation on the applets you choose to use, in determining the applet window size.

In the HelloWorld applet, the size of the applet window is critical. Because the applet starts its display 20 pixels in and 30 pixels down from the top of the applet window, a window that is too small will not allow space for the applet's text to show. One applet-debugging technique is to remove any HEIGHT or WIDTH attributes and see what the applet does.

WIDTH

As with HEIGHT, coding the correct **WIDTH** is sometimes important. The WIDTH attribute is coded in pixels, as it was for the <IMG>. Check the documentation for the applets you choose to use to ensure that you are giving them sufficient space when you define the applet window.

NAME

The **NAME** attribute is not often used. It allows the Web weaver to give a unique name to a specific instance of an applet. This allows each instance of the applet to be referenced somewhere else in the document. Suppose you had two different instances of an applet that displayed a message in a ticker tape box. Based on some information supplied by the user, you want to change the text in one of the applets. Without a way of uniquely identifying them, you would be unable to specify which of the applet instances you wanted to modify. The NAME attribute gives you that ability.

HSPACE

The **HSPACE** attribute, along with the VSPACE attribute, are counterparts to the attributes of the same name for the <IMG> tag. Normally the browser tucks the text close to the applet window, because <APPLET> does not cause a line break. The HSPACE attribute, coded in pixels, provides space to the right and left of the applet window, giving the applet some breathing room and setting it off from the surrounding text.

VSPACE

Like the HSPACE attribute, the **VSPACE** attribute sets the applet window off from the text above and below it. It is coded in pixels, as is the attribute of the same name in the <IMG> tag.

<PARAM>

Many applets need some information from the user to function correctly. A clock applet may need to know the time zone. A ticker tape applet may need to be given the text to display. Some sophisticated applets may need to know what language to use to display prompts or comments. Any of these different data can be supplied using the **<PARAM>** tag. It is an empty tag that has two required attributes that form a NAME = VALUE pair. The browser will pass the name and value of each parameter to the applet. However, the browser does no error checking. It is the responsibility of the Web weaver to ensure that (1) the name is one that the applet uses and (2) the value is of the correct type (text, integer, floating-point) and within the correct range for the applet.

Figure 12.7 presents the code that invokes an applet to provide scrolling text in a marquee. The text will move in different directions within the applet window defined. This applet has eight parameters. They include the different text lines, the different directions they move, the type and size of the font, the colors of the background and text, and the delay length between displays. If the Web weaver using this applet miscoded one or more of these parameters, the result could be disappointing at best. Good documentation and/or a good working relationship with the author of the applet is essential to writing good code for applets.

```
<applet  code="Marquee" width=400 height=30>
  <PARAM NAME="leftText" VALUE="Unix, the only true operating
system!!! ;-)">
  <PARAM NAME="upText"  VALUE="Linux is COOL!!!">
  <PARAM NAME="downText" VALUE="Powered by Linux 5.0">
  <PARAM NAME="font" VALUE="Helvetica">
  <PARAM NAME="fontsize" VALUE="24">
  <PARAM NAME="FGColor VALUE="cyan">
  <PARAM NAME="BGColor" VALUE="black">
  <PARAM NAME="pause" VALUE="25">
</applet>
```

Figure 12.7 HTML code showing the use of the <PARAM> tag within an applet.

NAME

The required attribute of **NAME** is the name of a variable the applet expects to be given. It is specific to a particular applet. It is the first half of a NAME=VALUE pair. The name should exactly correspond to the variable name inside the applet, in both case (upper and lower) and spelling. Misspelling or changing the case of a variable is the most frequent reason for applet failure.

VALUE

VALUE is, of course, the other half of the NAME=VALUE pair. The name is separated from the value by an equal sign. If the value contains embedded spaces or punctuation, it should be enclosed in quotation marks to preserve its integrity. (It is usually a good idea to put values for attributes in quotes—this is not a rule, just a good idea.)

Platform Independence

One of the very best features of "pure" Java is that it is a write-once, run-anywhere language. Pure Java can be run on a variety of machines. It has **platform independence.** That means that a Java program written on a Sun workstation can run on an Intel computer, a Macintosh machine, a UNIX mini or personal machine, all without changing the coding at all. Along with all the other wonderful features of this language, platform independence makes it remarkable.

Unfortunately, some people would corrupt this pure Java for commercial ends. It has been the bane of many of the "standardized" programming languages of the past that one company, seeking to increase its market share, will add "features" to the language to make it a more attractive tool. Programmers who then use these enhancements lose the portability of the standardized language to gain a few advantages. The process continues over and over with every new release of the language until it is no longer standardized and will compile only with the selected vendor's compiler. Portability is lost.

It is important that we keep Java pure. Resist the appeal of the "variant" flavors of Java, and write *pure* Java code that will maintain platform independence.

We are not speaking here of JavaScript, which you will recall, is not a variant of Java, but rather a separate programming language created to enhance HTML. Using JavaScript is fine, as it was designed by one company and as yet is a standardized language, quite apart from Java.

The Future of Java

Will Java be the next great programming language, or will it follow the path of other "greats" like APL (A Programming Language, written by Dr. Iverson)? Okay, you can admit it: you never even *heard* of APL. Yet in the late 1970s it was touted as the next great language after FORTRAN and COBOL.

The pundits do not all agree, but Java applets are an important part of the Web, and they will most likely be a part of a Web weaver's job for sometime to come. **DHTML (Dynamic HTML)** may provide the capacity to perform some of the animation features currently available only through Java, but that standard is not yet finalized. Many applications are being written in Java, and the language is gaining popularity among business programmers. It looks as if Java is here to stay, because, at least in its pure form, it is relatively platform independent, as well as being a very powerful and flexible programming language that is popular with programmers of varying levels of skill. Java applets, our focus in this text, will continue to be a powerful addition to HTML for the foreseeable future.

Exercises

12.1. Cruise the Net and find four or five small, interesting Java applets. Check with the Web weaver at that site, or with the copyright holder if it is different from the Web weaver, and ask permission to download and use the applets on your Web page. (If you don't have Web access, you can examine the applets on the CD that accompanies this textbook.)

12.2. Carefully examine the code that invokes the applet to see if it uses parameters and to see what those parameters do. Write a brief description of the parameters used by the applet.

12.3. Find and download the JDK (Java Development Kit). Many sites have it. One is **http://java.sun.com**. There are usually several different versions of the JDK available, and it is best to find the most recent version. Familiarize yourself with the JDK by reading the documentation files that are packaged with it.

CHAPTER thirteen

Looking at Java

Now that you know what Java looks like, let's look at how you can use Java to accent and add interest and programming power to your Web page. As with CGI scripts, there are three ways to obtain a Java applet: you can write your own, pay someone to write one for you, or get a complete applet from somewhere else. We will assume for this chapter that you have already obtained an applet. In the next chapter we will look at places to find fun applets, see how to modify them once you get them and even how to write a very simple applet.

What Applets Can Do for You

Applets provide a way to add features and capabilities to your page that never existed before. You can offer your users opportunities to play games or to interact with software in other ways—for example, to see what different colors of background and foreground look like together. You can present your users with a nice clock showing the time. And not only can applets provide a visually exciting medium, they can also bring sound to your pages. We discussed the problem of pushing sound over the Net in the Chapter on multimedia. We concluded that sound is an expensive addition and should be avoided unless it is really necessary. Well, the rules are more relaxed when it comes to applets, because the sounds are delivered by the applet. The user need not have specialized plug-ins; the applet takes care of it. And usually the applet needs only a handful of small sounds. You will see an excellent example of this in the UFO game we will discuss later.

In other words, because applets are executable programs, they can do much more than HTML is currently capable of in terms of dynamic content, including interactivity, sound, animation, and, in general, providing programmed capacity to your Web page. What do each of these qualities mean to your user? Let's see.

Dynamic Content

The term **dynamic content** covers the spectrum of what Java is all about. Before Java, users could click on a link and display a picture, hear a sound, or go to a new page. The most active feature was an animated GIF. With Java, all that has changed. Java applets are actually small programs that begin executing when they are downloaded to the browser. Exactly what is done with them is limited only by the imagination of the Java programmer. Applets can perform nearly every function that any other program on a computer can perform, from displaying three-dimensional graphics to providing the user with a spreadsheet application or a game to play. All this is done live. The user need not be involved, although it is generally considered better to let the user play with the game than have the game play itself! Games that just play themselves are usually considered selfish and will not be given high marks in the "plays well with others" category.

Java allows the Web weaver to add a vast array of software tools to her Web pages. We will look at some of them that were in existence when this book was being written. Understand that with the dynamic growth of the Net, new applets are being added every day. This is another place programmers can "make their mark on the world." Designing, developing, and then giving a "way cool" applet to the Net community is a way to become known across the world.

Real Interactivity

As we mentioned before, pre-Java **interactivity** was limited to the user clicking on a button to go somewhere, see a picture, hear a sound, or, at best, to fill out a form that generated a new but also static page. This was fine as long as there was nothing better. Then came Java. Now the user can actually play a game, live, on the Net. Unlike a CGI script, the applet runs locally, so it can provide much more consistent and rapid response to the user. Generally speaking, applets work at the speed of the browser, whereas CGI scripts work at the speed of the connection(s) and the server.

As an example of what Java can do, let's look at a simple tic-tac-toe (or Naughts and Crosses) game the user can play. The static nature of a book won't allow you to see the dynamic nature of this game, so you will need to either take the application from the CD that accompanies this book or go to the Web site created for this book.

What's important about this example is that the game is played in the browser window on the user's computer (see Figure 13.1). All that is required of the server is that it download the Java applet code once! Rather than using something like CGI, where the user is essentially interacting with the server, Java applets provide interactivity at the local level. This is a very important difference.

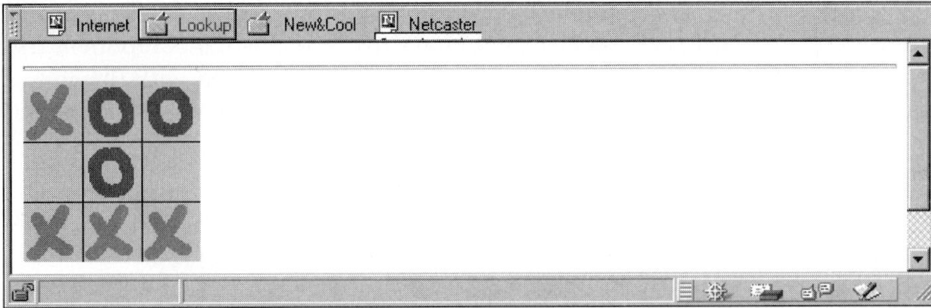

Figure 13.1 Netscape's presentation of the tic-tac-toe applet.

In this applet, the computer takes turns starting, and it always plays Os. It is possible to beat the computer in the version that comes with Sun Microsystem's **Java development kit (JDK)**. But there is another version of this applet on the Net that is unbeatable.

Universal Consistency

As you cruise the Web, it becomes obvious that HTML is a constantly evolving, changing tool. Although it provides Web weavers with an opportunity to do more and more on their pages, it also has the disadvantage of being, in a sense, a moving target. Your great page, written to the new HTML-proposed standard, may work in only the most recent version of one of the browsers. If your Aunt Annie wants to see what you are doing with your time, she must go to the trouble of downloading that particular browser and installing it on her machine before she can view your page.

The changing nature of HTML is less of a problem with Java. While it is true that Aunt Annie must have a machine that runs Java (she is a pretty cool lady, so she is most likely running Linux anyway), the Java Virtual Machine she has will run your applets just fine. This is why it is so important to keep Java pure and not get caught in the "special version of Java for one browser" trend. Not only will your applet run on Aunt Annie's machine, but it will work on her friend's machine, too, and it will look just the same. Using pure Java allows consistent delivery of content over the Net, across multiple browsers. As the Java Virtual Machines are created for other platforms, the power of Java will spread, and more and more people will be able to use this tool.

Adding Sound

Web pages with sound can be more exciting than those that don't have this new dimension. However, downloading large sound files does take some time. You will notice, if you download one of the applets on the Web site for this book, that when the applet tries to play a sound the first time, it takes a few seconds to download the sound. After that, the sound is kept locally and so is fast to play. Downloading large sound files is not normally practical, nor is it good practice from a "netcology" point of view. **Netcology** is the conservation of net resources (like ecology is the conservation of natural resources). However, smaller sound bites that add an aural component to an applet cause little impact. Some smaller sounds, when coupled with the animation of an applet, allow good play with little expense across the Net. Some of the applets discussed in this section have sound capability, yet adhere to the principles of good netcology.

Animation and Graphics

Animated GIFs add movement to a Web page, making it more interesting—for a while. After watching an animated GIF for 45 minutes, nonstop, the user may decide that watching clothes go round and round in one of those big, glass-fronted dryers is infinitely more exciting. The problem with animated GIFs is that although they are cute, they just keep doing the same thing, over and over and over and over and . . . umm, well, you get the idea. What is needed is something that changes a little, something that is somewhat different each time it occurs. That is what an applet can provide. Applet animations are driven by a program and can therefore react to the input of the user. For example, applet animations can react when the user's mouse passes over some area of the screen.

You may have noticed that you can watch waves at the beach, or the flames of a fire, or the water in a waterfall for a long time without finding the sight tiring. That is because the sight is changing, though ever so slightly, all the time. All flames are not the same, and the patterns of the waves and falling water are subtly different from second to second. Some applets, like the frog applet discussed in this chapter, can provide almost the same kind of limitless viewing experience. At least they don't repeat themselves exactly, over and over. Other applets, like the ticker tape animation, do repeat, but the effect is better than with an animated GIF, and they don't repeat as often.

Animation applets provide a nice addition to your Web page, but they, too, can be overdone. It is a good design idea to use no more then two or three on a page, lest your page look crowded and busy. Too many animations can distract from the important content of your page. Again, as with images, not everyone can appreciate your applets. Users who aren't running from platforms that support Java can't see your applets, and people who have visual problems can't see your animations. The same rule applies to applets as to images: don't put important content only in an applet, or you may deny access to some of your users.

From the Simple to the Complex

Applets can provide an almost limitless number of applications. The examples we will examine here are simple ones, but there are applets out there that perform complex database searches, do sophisticated calculations of interest payments, and provide full-blown spreadsheet applications. Applets are beginning to perform some very substantial tasks, and it seems that the evolution of powerful applets is just beginning. This is a place where a Java programmer can still make a very significant contribution to the world of the Web, especially in regard to the user interface. The examples shown here have some degree of sophistication themselves, but there are many, far more powerful user-driven applets as well.

Education

Some of the most significant combinations of the three Java features of sound, animation, and interactivity are those that provide educational opportunities across the Net. One of these applets allows users to rotate a model of a molecule. Another allows users to build a circuit and then test the results of the circuit. One applet of interest allows users to control a nuclear power plant during a crisis. If you successfully manage the problem, the reactor simply shuts down; but if you make a mistake, the reactor core melts. Another interesting applet allows users to dissect a frog—without getting their hands messy. And, speaking of dissection, there is also an applet that allows you to see inside a human body, as if the body had been sliced into very thin slices.

Applets are an elegant and powerful educational tool. Not surprisingly, applets that teach are a fast-growing segment of the Java universe. It would be well worth your time to cruise the Web and find some of these applets. Besides learning something, you will find they are fun to use.

Commercial Applications

Java applets can really make a difference in business. The most obvious place they are used is in advertising. Animated GIFs quickly became the de facto standard in advertising banners on the Net, but as more and more of the online population begins using platforms that support Java, the percentage of Java-based advertisements is increasing. However, the business uses of Java go far beyond advertising. Java stock-market applications can display a stock's history, act like a stock ticker tape, or even graph the market performance of a company. Some companies build online games or interactive environments to promote their products. Others have put applets on the Web as a commercial service to new and existing clients. For example, some mortgage and loan calculators can tell potential home buyers whether they can afford to purchase a particular house or a car and give them the monthly payment amounts.

Commercial applications of Java will likely be the fastest-growing ones for two reasons. First, there is a strong financial incentive to create them; they can bring in business to a company. Second, there is strong support growing for their use as the user base moves toward Java-enabled platforms.

Restrictions

Although applets are powerful tools, they are restricted in some ways. They must work inside a browser window, so they don't have any direct input or output coded. They can't access the user's disk drives, so they can't read from or write to permanent storage. Each execution starts afresh. "But," you say, "the applet seems to be locally stored on my hard drive once it has run!" True, even though the applet cannot read from or write to the disk, the browser will store the parts of the applet in the cache space set up for the browser. This is why the first time you run an applet it is slow, while the parts are loaded, but after that first run, it is much quicker to execute. It runs faster because the parts it needs—the source code, images, and sound files—are already stored locally in cache and are quickly accessible. If you bear in mind that you are dealing with code that can run only within the window of a browser and cannot modify the environment on the client machine, you will understand the environment of the applet.

Sample Applets

The applets that will be described here represent just a small smattering of the types available on the Net. These were chosen because they illustrate some of the different ways applets can add interest or content to a Web page or, in some cases, just because the author of this textbook happens to like them.

Clocks

Some of the earliest applets were clocks. People seem to have a fascination with time and a liking for computer-screen clocks that look like real clocks. Let's look at two different clock applets. The one in Figure 13.2 looks like a traditional analog clock, and the one in Figure 13.3 looks like a digital clock. The analog clock, Bill's Clock, even has a moving second hand.

A static picture in a book cannot do justice to these applets, so use your imagination, or go to the Web page for this book. Or you can load these applets from the CD that accompanies this textbook to see how they really work. Figures 13.2 and 13.3 show you what a snapshot of the applets would look like. They don't pretend to represent the full functionality of the applets. You will need to actually use them to see how they work. Go play!

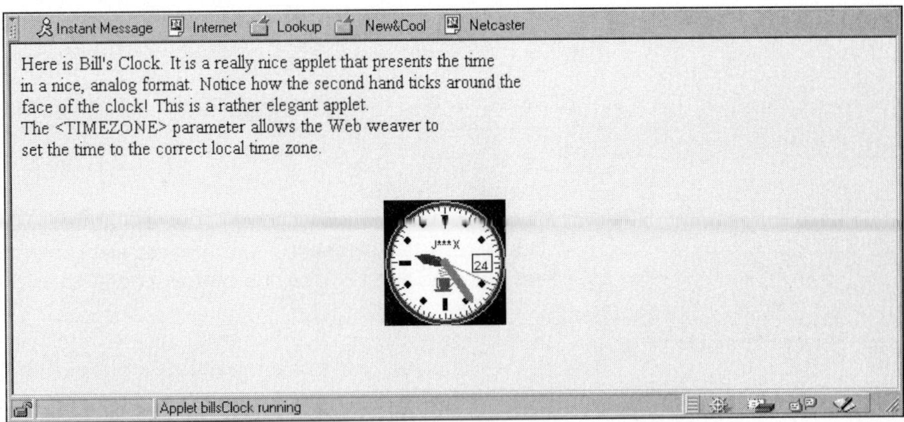

Figure 13.2 Netscape's presentation of an analog clock, Bill's Clock.

Figure 13.3 Internet Explorer's presentation of a digital clock: Digital Java Clock.

Bill's Clock is somewhat sophisticated. It has several different parameters that can control the look of the clock. As you remember from our discussion of the <APPLET> container, **parameters** are tags that give the Web weaver some control over how the applet works. In the case of Bill's Clock, there are several. Different parameters control the colors of the background and face of the clock; the colors of the hour, minute, and second hands; the text color; and the image that appears as a picture on the face of the clock. There is even a parameter to set the time zone. All this parameter control allows the Web weaver to customize the way the clock looks on his site without having to code any Java at all. Figure 13.4 presents the HTML code that invokes Bill's Clock.

```
<HTML>
<TITLE> Bill's Clock Demo </TITLE>
<BODY BGCOLOR="#DDEEFF">
Here is Bill's Clock.  It is a really nice applet that
presents the time<BR>
in a nice, analog format.  Notice how the second hand ticks
around the<BR>
face of the clock!  This is a rather elegant applet.  <BR>
The &lt;TIMEZONE&gt; parameter allows the Web weaver to <BR>
set the time to the correct local time zone.<BR> <BR> <BR>
<CENTER>

        <applet code="billsClock.class" width=100 height=100
ALIGN=MIDDLE>
        <param name=BGCOLOR value="000000">
        <param name=FACECOLOR value="FFFFFF">
        <param name=SWEEPCOLOR value="FF0000">
        <param name=MINUTECOLOR value="008080">
        <param name=HOURCOLOR value="000080">
        <param name=TEXTCOLOR value="000000">
        <param name=CASECOLOR value="000080">
        <param name=TRIMCOLOR value="C0C0C0">
        <param name=LOGOIMAGEURL value="java.gif">
        <param name=TIMEZONE value=5>
        </applet>
</CENTER>
</BODY>
</HTML>
```

Figure 13.4 HTML code that invokes an analog clock. Notice the parameters.

Figure 13.3 shows the digital clock applet, not quite so fancy as the analog clock. This one, too, has some parameters. They control the background color, whether the clock shows seconds, whether the clock works in 12-hour or 24-hour format, what time zone the clock displays, the background GIF the clock applet uses, and what the digits actually look like. Figure 13.5 presents the code for this Digital Java Clock.

```
<HTML>
<HEAD>
<TITLE> Digital Clock </TITLE>
</HEAD>
<BODY BGCOLOR="#DDEEFF">
<CENTER>
<H1>Digital Clock demo</H1>
This is a Digital Java Clock that allows you to choose what
kind of digits you want to display.  You can change the
appearance of the clock by designing your own set of digits
and background.  <BR><BR>
<applet code="dclock.class" Width=224 Height=100>
<param name=bgcolor value="0000FF">
<param name=seconds value="yes">
<param name=24hour value="yes">
<param name=background value="panel4.gif">
<param name=digits value="bit2.gif">
<param name=timezone value="+0600">
</applet>

</CENTER>
</BODY>
</HTML>
```

Figure 13.5 HTML code that invokes a digital clock.

A clock is a nice feature, and using an applet that creates a clock is sometimes useful for your user. Let's look at another general category of applets now, those that provide animation to create exciting, or at least interesting, additions to a Web page.

Animation

As mentioned earlier, animation is a good way to catch the user's eye and create interest on your page. However, animated GIFs don't always have the desired effect, because they are often very repetitive, and that can become boring. Following are three different applets: one that is designed to be watched, one that is actually a rather neat game, and one that—well, the third is just for fun. All of them fall into the category of animations because they display activity. Be careful with the second animation, the UFO game. Once you download it, it can become quite addictive!

The first animation, shown in Figure 13.6, is a rendition of a frog catching flies. What makes this applet interesting is that the flies seem to move at random, and the frog will catch one only if it comes close and if it hasn't just caught another fly. Again, the static nature of a book cannot do justice to this applet. Look at it on the Web page, download it, or take it from the CD that accompanies this text and watch it. It may not be the great American animation applet, but it does have an element of randomness that makes it very "watchable"—much more so than an animated GIF. There are no parameters to set with this applet; it just runs as an entertainment item. All the Web weaver needs to do is set the size of the applet window. Figure 13.7 presents the code. Notice that the animation is provided by only one line. All the Web weaver needs to specify is the size of the applet window.

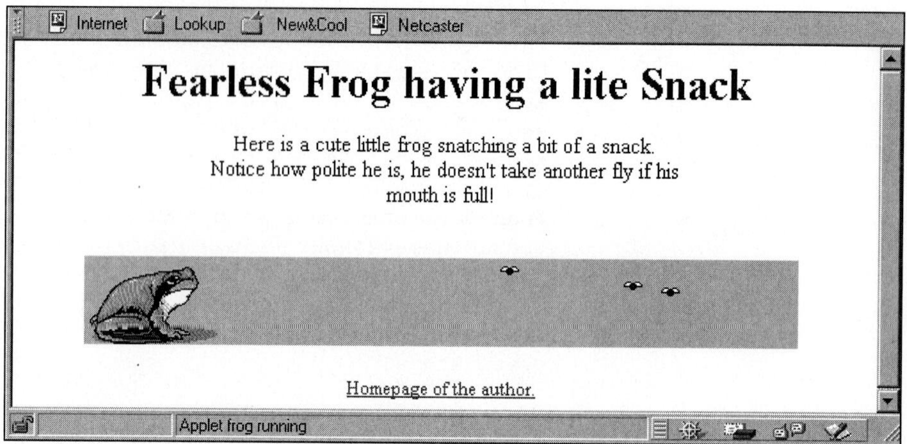

Figure 13.6 Netscape's presentation of an applet showing a frog enjoying a snack.

```
<HTML>
<HEAD>
<TITLE>Feeding the Frog</TITLE>
</HEAD>
<BODY>
<CENTER>
<H1>Fearless Frog having a lite Snack</H1>
Here is a cute little frog snatching a bit of a snack.<BR>
Notice how polite he is, he doesn't take another fly if
his<BR>
mouth is full! <BR><BR><BR>
<APPLET CODE="frog.class" width=500 height=60>
There are no parameters.
</APPLET>
<BR><BR>
<FONT SIZE=-1>
<A HREF="http://www.tdb.uu.se/~karl">Homepage of the
author.</A>
</FONT>
</CENTER>
</BODY>
</HTML>
```

Figure 13.7 HTML code to include the Frog applet on a page.

Some applets allow the user to interact with them, like the tic-tac-toe game we saw earlier. Such games can be far more sophisticated than our tic-tac-toe example. The applet shown in Figure 13.8 is moderately sophisticated. It allows the user to manipulate rockets to intercept and blow up descending UFOs. If a

UFO lands, the game is over. It also keeps track of the number of UFOs the player has destroyed.

One of the powerful features of this applet is that it allows the player to control the path of the rocket in flight. This feature would not be possible if the applet were running on the server. With server-based code, the time delay between the user moving her mouse, the browser sending the mouse movements over the Net to the server, and the server updating the screen image would make the game unplayable. The scientists at NASA faced this same problem when trying to "drive" the Mars Pathfinder. It was impossible for the scientists to drive the Mars pathfinder live, because of the transmission delay. Java applets have allowed this type of interactivity for the first time.

In addition to having some great graphics, the applet in Figure 13.8 incorporates sound. If you play across the Net, you will notice that the applet pauses a couple of times during the first minutes of play. The first time it pauses is to download the "rocket launch" sound. Then, when you blow up your first saucer, it pauses again to download the "blowing up" sound. Once the sounds have been downloaded, the browser has them available to use over and over. As was mentioned before, the static nature of a book does not allow you to experience the fun of this applet. To see the animation and hear the sounds, you need to go "interact" with it yourself. See if you can beat your humble author's score of 22! (Well, okay—that won't be too tough to do; his son can beat him regularly!)

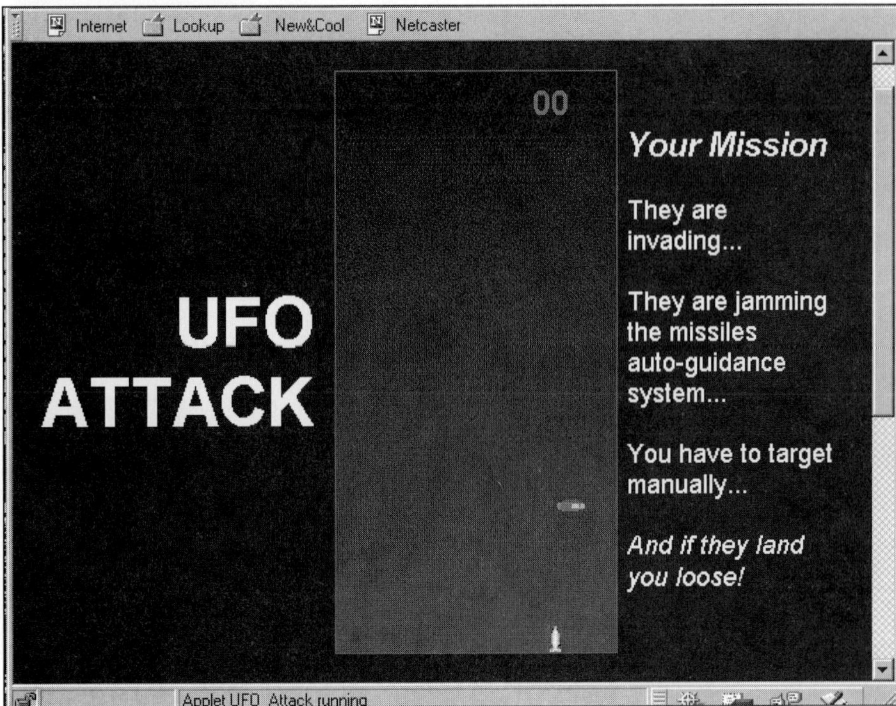

Figure 13.8 Netscape's presentation of the UFO game applet.

Our third example of an animation applet is the Dumb Ball in Figures 13.9 and 13.10. This is a take-off on the old "magic eight ball" that has been a popular toy for some time. This applet has the user interacting on two different levels. On one level the user simply clicks on the Dumb Ball and asks it a question. On the other level, the user is supposed to become "psychically linked" to her computer so that the Dumb Ball applet will know what question she is thinking of. Well, um, err, it could happen! This applet has no parameters. It simply sits there, waiting for the user to ask for a prediction. Figure 13.9 is a screen capture of the Dumb Ball before it is asked a question, and Figure 13.10 shows it after the question has been submitted.

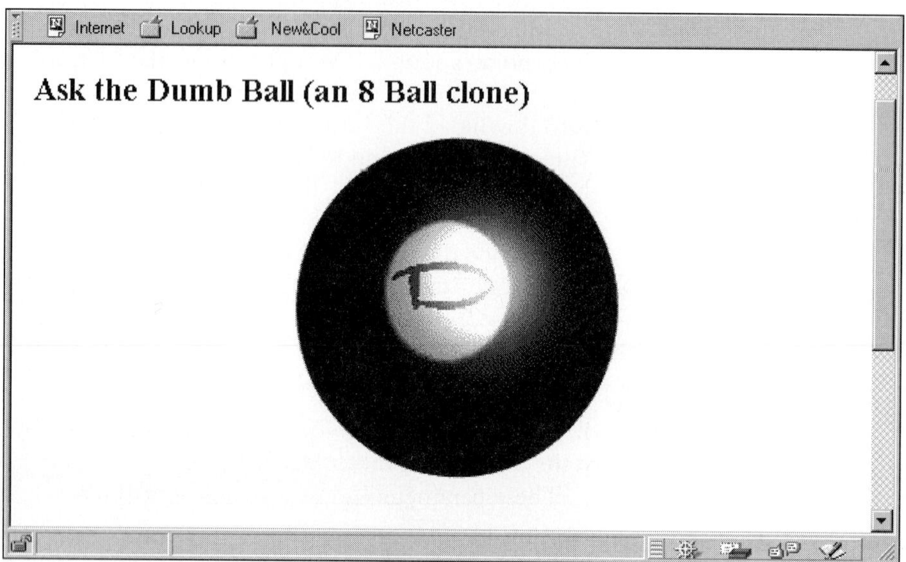

Figure 13.9 Netscape's presentation of the Dumb Ball applet before it is asked a question.

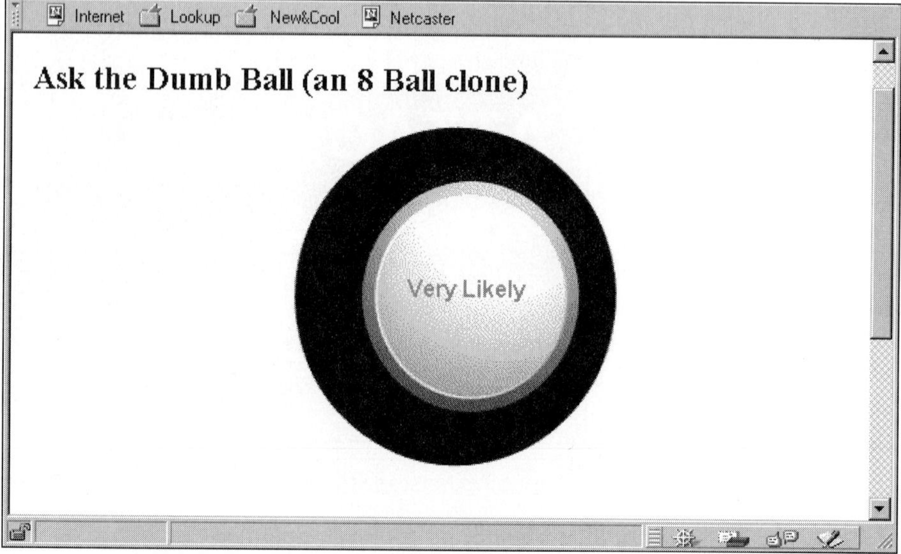

Figure 13.10 Netscape's presentation of the Dumb Ball applet replying to a question.

Animations like those shown here are fun. They add interest and excitement, and even arcade-style interactivity, to a Web page. The next category of applets are among the most common and represent probably the most frequent type of advertising applets on the Net.

Text Applets

Making text do fun or funny things by means of animation is a very common use for Java applets—it is a sure way to catch the user's eye. But the problem with many text animations is that they often repeat to the point of becoming tedious. Be careful with this type of applet. It is best to choose one that will allow different messages to be displayed, perhaps even in different ways, than to have the same effect presented over and over.

The applet represented in Figures 13.11 and 13.12 causes the text to move in an interesting pattern, somewhat varied to keep it interesting. The parameters on this applet give the Web weaver an opportunity to customize it to some extent. Obviously, the actual text to be displayed must be specified. But, in addition to that, the Web weaver can specify several other features. For example, two different types of animation are available: the text can blink, or it can appear to wave. Blinking text seems to shrink and grow at the same rate. With waving text, the letters shrink and grow in a wave across the text field. It is also possible to change the color of the background and the text, plus the text font, the style of the text (plain, bold, or italic), the size of the steps as the text size changes, the delay between updates, the largest and smallest font sizes, and the alignment of the text within the applet window.

These parameters allow a significant degree of customization of the applet. Avoid using too large a text string in this type of applet, however, because a large text line that is animated can quickly become overpowering in some browser windows. The two screen captures in Figures 13.11 and 13.12 show how the applet changes the size of the text in a wave that moves across the text line. It is an effective attention getter.

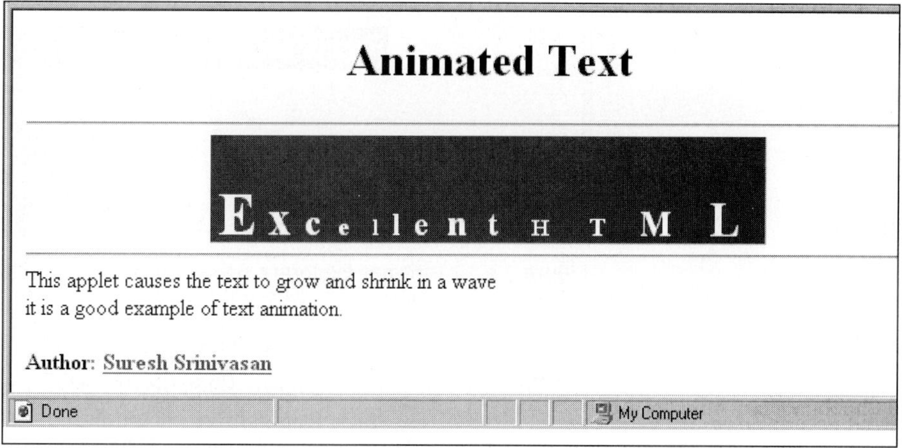

Figure 13.11 Internet Explorer's presentation of a text-animator applet in one of two screen captures.

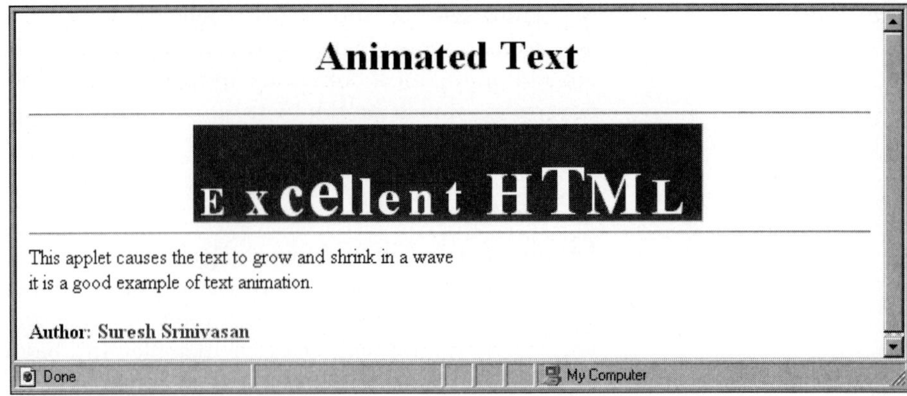

Figure 13.12 Internet Explorer's presentation of a text-animator applet in the second of two screen captures.

Our next example of a text-animation applet, shown in Figures 13.13 and 13.14, is more flexible than the first, because it can display text moving in different directions. This is one of the many text-animation applets that fall into the scrolling **marquee** category. This applet also has several different parameters. Parameters control the color of the background, the color of the text, and the different text strings that move in the different styles and directions.

The screen captures in Figures 13.13 and 13.14 show two of the three different messages presented by the applet.

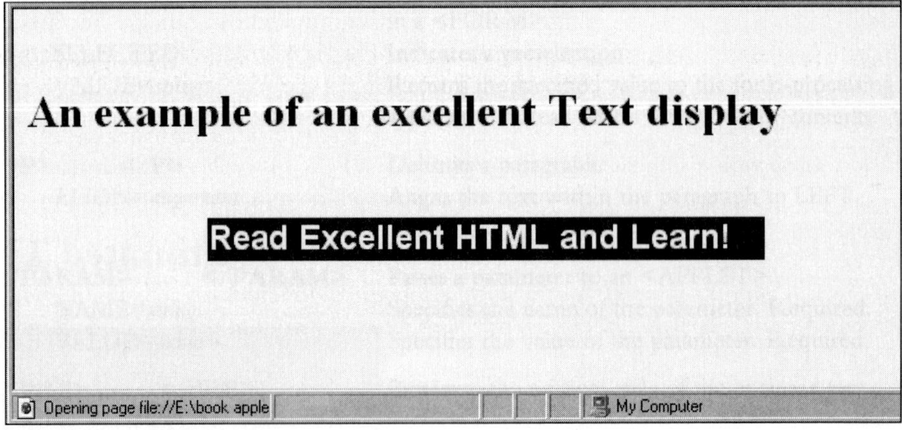

Figure 13.13 Internet Explorer's presentation of a scrolling-text applet in one of two screen captures.

The text message in Figure 13.13 scrolls from the right to the left side of the browser window. The text message in Figure 13.14 scrolls from the top to the bottom. The Web weaver could have made the window the same color as the background so the text would have appeared to just scroll across the screen. A third type of text animation moves text like a TelePrompTer or a Teletype. These applets are also very good attention-getters, provided that the message is not too long. You don't want your user to have to sit there for extended periods of time, waiting as line after line after line of text data are displayed. This type of applet can be a useful way to present important information to your users in a small footprint on a Web page. Figure 13.15 shows a Teletype applet. As you can see, it allows a lot of text to be put in a small area.

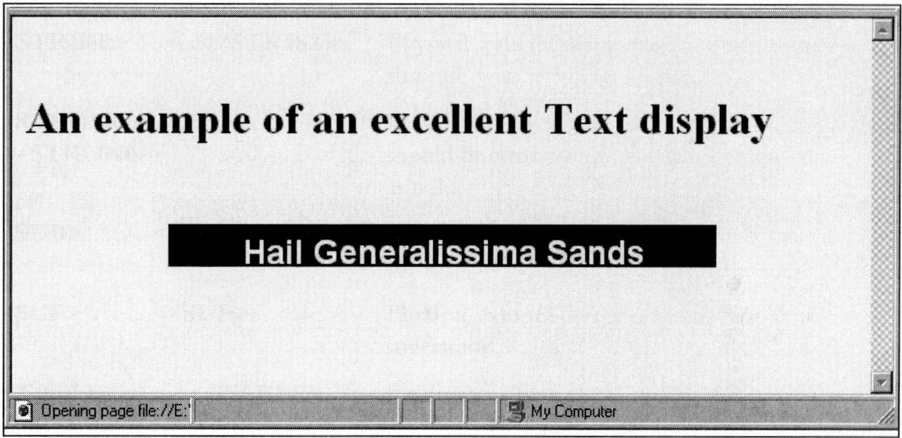

Figure 13.14 Internet Explorer's presentation of a scrolling-text applet in the second of two screen captures.

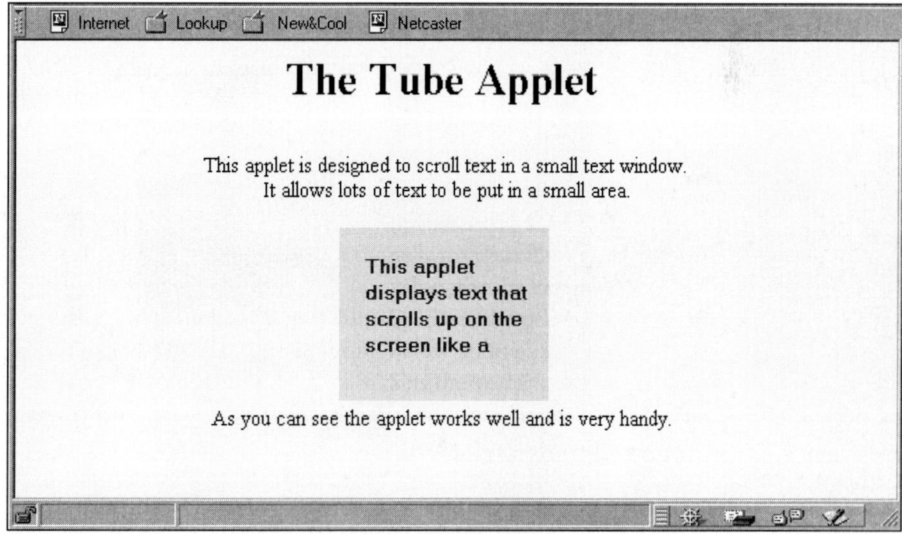

Figure 13.15 Netscape's presentation of a Teletype applet displaying part of a message.

Text display applets are very helpful to provide information in an interesting way to your users. Remember, though, like all the other graphic tools we have discussed, text applets are not accessible to users with nongraphical browsers. Nor are they accessible to users whose browsers do not support Java. Therefore, a conscientious Web weaver will always ensure that the information available in a text applet is also made available in some other way.

Utility Applets

One of the fastest growing categories of applet development are the **utility applets**. These can range from simple calculators to sophisticated and powerful spreadsheets and database search engines. Even at this early date in the development of Java on the Net, books could be written about utility applets. The vast majority of these tools are available only as commercial packages. Just a small number are available as free downloads for private (not business) use. Utility applets are an important segment of the growing market for good Java applets. If you write a marketable utility applet, you could make a tidy sum selling it.

One of the few utility applets not designed for commercial sale is presented in Figure 13.16. This applet allows the user to test different color backgrounds and text colors. It provides both the RGB (Red, Green, Blue) values and the hexadecimal codes for the colors. This sophisticated applet allows the user to either use the slider bar or to click on a color. The user can control the intensity of the color as well. The screen capture in Figure 13.16 doesn't show the range of colors available in this applet, but it does give an idea of the layout.

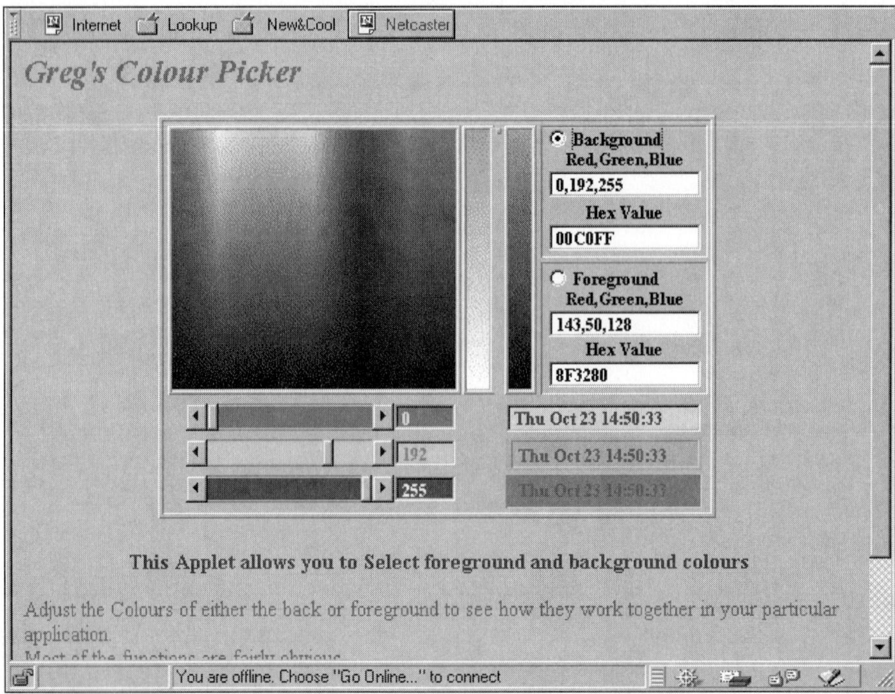

Figure 13.16 Netscape's presentation of a utility applet.

Viewing Applets

An applet can be viewed with a browser or an applet viewer. Many of the specialized Java development environments, like Symantic's Java Cafe, contain applet viewers. These are the environments where Java programmers play, and they will be addressed further in the next chapter.

Netscape

Netscape is one of the most common Internet browsers on the market. Since way back in version 2.0, it has supported the display of Java applets on platforms that can support a Java Virtual Machine. Netscape was the first commercially successful major browser to make the commitment to support Java. Currently those platforms include UNIX, Windows 95, Windows NT, and Macintosh. Figure 13.17 presents the frog applet as viewed in Netscape.

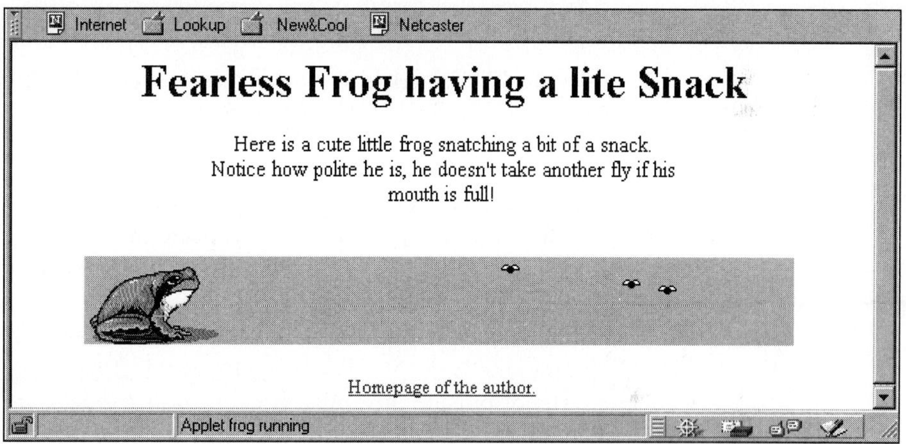

Figure 13.17 Netscape's presentation of the frog applet.

Internet Explorer

Microsoft's Internet Explorer is another popular browser that supports Java applets. Some specialized additions written for Internet Explorer make Java less compatible across the Net. Figure 13.18 shows the froggie applet as viewed with Internet Explorer. One interesting note: in this version of Internet Explorer, on some machines, the frog is blue and pink. In all the other browsers it is gray.

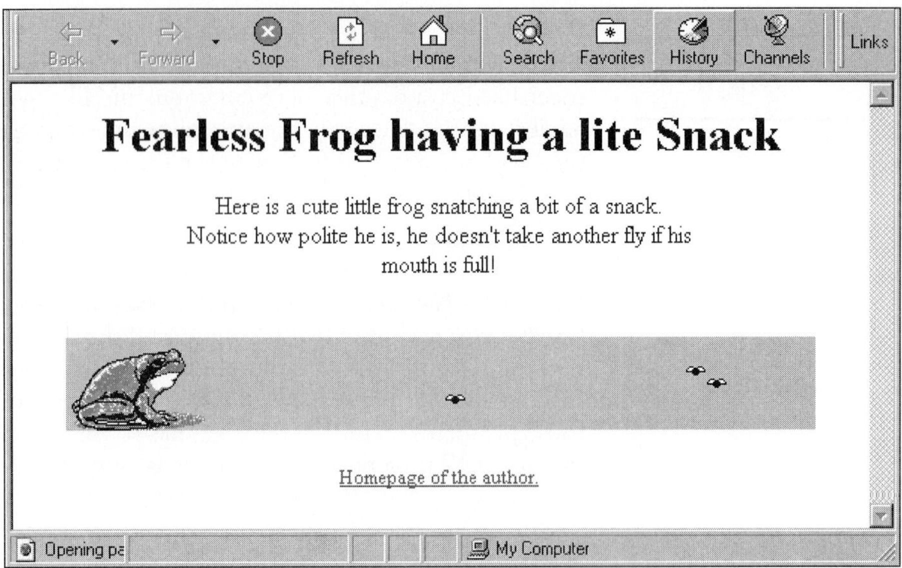

Figure 13.18 Internet Explorer's presentation of the frog applet.

HotJava

Sun Microsystems wrote a browser that breaks the mold of browser design. Unlike the standard browsers (Lynx, Mosaic, Netscape, Internet Explorer), **HotJava** can learn new rules and protocols. That makes it a new type of browser. Browsers of this new generation give a new meaning to the idea of flexibility of design. Oh, yes, HotJava is written in Java, of course! Figure 13.19 shows the frog applet as viewed with HotJava. Notice that in HotJava, our frog extends outside the applet box on the left side. Each browser displays the applet in a slightly different way.

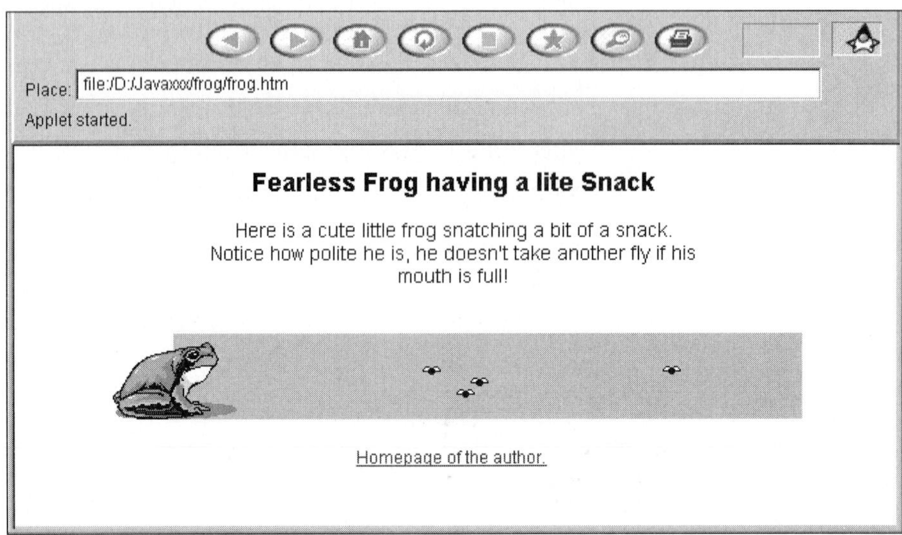

Figure 13.19 HotJava's presentation of the frog applet.

Applet Viewers

Many of the Java development kits (JDKs) provide an **applet viewer** so that you can view applets without a browser. With a multitasking operating system like UNIX, it is less onerous to have multiple windows open, one of which can be a browser. However, for the purist, applet viewers are a little easier to use. Some applet viewers, if they have a built-in windowing system, show only applet code. Others need to use the display tools built into HTML, so they take an HTML document as input. If you have an applet viewer, you will not need to use a browser to see your applet in action. Nevertheless, it is best to use a browser so you can see how your applet looks in the context of the page it will be presented on. It is also a good idea, as you know by now, to view your applet-enhanced pages with several types of browsers to ensure that the majority of your users will find the page useful.

Copyright Issues

As with any other resource on the Net, applets have been designed, developed, and refined by someone. That someone has the right to decide how the applet is distributed. Some applet developers look at the Net as a shared resource. They view their work as a contribution to the general good, giving back to the Net community as they have taken from it. Others view their work as a commercial venture. These folks want to try to make some money from all their hard work. And building an applet can be very hard work. They reason that if they can be compensated financially, they can afford to continue to develop applets. Both of these views should be respected. Applets are intellectual property and should be treated as such.

Many applet authors will allow you to use their applets in a noncommercial setting for little or no fee. And many are very liberal about sharing their work. For example, all the applet authors contacted for this textbook project were happy to have their applets included in the book, on the Web page for the book, and on the CD that comes with the book.

Do be aware, however, that many pages on the Net display applets unethically harvested. If a person who stole an applet gives you permission to use it, that permission is not valid. Look at the code for the applet. Usually the applet author will put his or her name and usually an e-mail address as comments inside the applet code. If that name is different than the name of the owner of the page where you found the applet, you need to ask permission from the owner of the applet. By the same token, if you develop applets, it would be a good idea to put your name and e-mail address inside them.

The bottom line is that applet authors deserve the same respect as other developers of intellectual property. Although most applet authors will not track you down and confront you for using their work, you should refrain from taking advantage of them. Be nice.

Exercises

Note: These exercises assume you have a browser that will display Java. If not, see your instructor for applicable exercises.

13.1. Cruise the Web and find at least two applets from each of the categories described in this chapter. Make a list of the URLs and the name of the applets.

13.2. Create a page, linked from your home page, that contains one or two applets that you have harvested from the Net. Make sure you have permission to use the applets you have found.

13.3. Modify the page you created in Exercise 13.2 to serve as example, or demonstration page. Show how different values for some parameters will change the way the applet works. Also demonstrate that several occurrences of an applet on a page can slow the download of that page.

13.4. Run your applet page, created in Exercise 13.3, in Netscape, Internet Explorer, and HotJava browsers to observe the differences in presentation.

13.5. Using each of the different browsers, go back and view the pages you found in Exercise 13.1. Make notes on how different browsers present the page and applets differently. If you have not done so recently, also review your own Web site and check how your pages look in the different browsers. Correct as necessary.

CHAPTER fourteen

ADDING APPLETS TO YOUR PAGE

14

As discussed in the last chapter, there are three ways to obtain applets to put on your pages: write them, have someone write them for you, or get them from the Net. It is fairly easy to find applets to add to your pages if you know where to look. Until you have spent the time necessary to learn Java and thus are able to write your own applets, you will most likely harvest applets from the Net to include in your pages. Let's look at some places to find applets.

Where to Find Applets

Every day, it seems, there are new places to find applets on the Net. More and more people are writing and collecting applets to display on their pages. In your cruising of the Net you have undoubtedly found sites that have many applets. Following are some of the classic sites that provide collections of applets. You should be able to find more as you continue to cruise the Net. Remember, these sites were correct when the book was written, but they may have changed, moved, or gone out of business by the time you get to them. As always with the Net, YMMV (Your Mileage May Vary).

Sun Microsystems

Sun Microsystems wrote Java, so it stands to reason that the Sun site boasts a wealth of good applets. Point your browser at **http://java.sun.com/applets/js-applets.html** to see the latest and greatest of the Sun applets. Some of these applets are available for free download; others are commercial products. Read the descriptions to determine which is which.

Sun has made a commitment to keep Java pure. Besides providing great applets, **java.sun.com** is a good place to visit on a regular basis to get the most current information on the dynamic language of Java.

Gamelan

Gamelan has a good collection of applets and many other tools available as well. Gamelan is a good resource for serious Web weavers. Its URL is **http://www.gamelan.com.** Gamelan has an interesting approach to ownership of the applets. It provides a showcase for applet authors to present their code. Most of the applets have the author's name and a link to the author's home page or e-mail address.

Java Boutique

Java Boutique is another site like Gamelan. It has a large collection of applets, some written by the owners of the page, and many that have been collected from across the Net. Like most of the applet-collection sites, Java Boutique has grouped the applets into categories to speed your search. The URL for Java Boutique is **http://www.javaboutique.internet.com/appindbut.html.** This is a good site to find applets, for new ones appear fairly frequently.

Applet Orchard

The California-based site of Applet Orchard seems to be trying hard to become one of "the" applet-collection sites on the Net. Many applets are available here that are not found elsewhere. The URL for the Applet Orchard (cute name!) is **http://amadeus.ccs.queensu.ca/orchard.** One of the aims of this site is to list only freeware applets. Check out this site for some interesting applets.

JARS

The **Java Applet Review Service** (**JARS**) attempts to put a measure of worth on new applets. Applets that are rated highly by JARS are usually well written and useful. The JARS page has grouped its applets by their ratings, top 5 percent or top 10 percent, and so on. Within that rating, the applets are grouped by function. You can submit an applet that you write for them to rate, and if it is "good enough," you too will have a JARS-rated applet. JARS URL is **http://www.jars.com.**

In addition to applets, the JARS site has JavaBeans resources, JavaScript resources, ActiveX resources, VRML resources, and even Perl scripts. JARS is well worth your time to research. At last count, it had over 2000 applets, grouped into nine major categories.

Search Engines

Search engines are the best way to find the newest applets on the Net. Any of the search engines are fine for this purpose. Depending on your particular wants, you will need to specify different parameters, but with a little patience (okay, sometimes it takes a lot of patience), you can find new and exciting applets from across the world.

When you harvest an applet, try to also obtain the documentation for that applet. If you have both the applet and the documentation on the way to use it, you will save a great deal of time in experimentation. Also, you may need the documentation to enable you to use features that are not obvious.

Source versus Executable Code for Applets

When you harvest an applet, you sometimes have two choices as to what you actually collect. You can download the Java source code or the executable program, the **.class file**, also referred to as **bytecode.** Some applet authors make only the .class file available because that protects their work from being copied and modified. However, many authors make the Java source code available as well.

If you choose to download the Java source code file, you will need to use the Java compiler (Javac) to create the .class file that the Java Virtual Machine uses. If you download the .class file, you save the compilation step. You don't need to have a Java compiler if you always harvest .class files. Indeed, most Web weavers simply download the bytecode (.class) files and store them on their server.

Just as linking to images across the Net is a very bad idea, so too is linking to someone else's applets on another server. This practice increases Net traffic and slows applet loading. Web weavers new to Java usually choose to use "ready-made" applets and download the executable .class files. There are already many applets that have been built to perform a wide variety of tasks and will do an excellent job just as they are. For example, the froggie applet in Chapter 13 is a complete package that needs nothing done to it. The same is true of the TelePrompTer applet. These applets give the Web weaver great flexibility in determining how they look and act. They have many parameters that control different aspects of applet behavior. When you begin to build applets to use on the Net, keep this adaptability in mind, and design yours with many such parameters to control their function. We will look at applet parameters next.

<PARAMETERS>

There are two ways to change what an applet does, or how it looks. You can change the actual Java source code and recompile the applet. Or, if the applet was designed to be changed, you can simply code different parameters into the <APPLET> container. To do this, you need to know the names of the parameters, so you can code the correct **<PARAMETER>** tags. Also, you need to know the acceptable values for each parameter.

Usually an applet will simply ignore a parameter it doesn't recognize and will use a default value for a parameter that has an incorrect value coded. The default values are set by the author to be used when the user doesn't specify a value. Sometimes, however, an applet is designed in such a way that coding an incorrect value for a parameter causes the applet to fail or to behave in a strange manner. Thus, correctly coding the parameters is essential.

For example, consider an applet that displays text in one color on a background of another color. Suppose the Web weaver codes the text color as "black" and the background color as "whiet." Obviously the background color is misspelled. If the applet has a default background color of black, and uses that, then the black text will be displayed on a black background. That might be just a little difficult to read.

It is important to learn the available parameters for any given applet, plus the allowed values for those parameters. Those data are usually available from one of four sources as follows. First, the most straightforward place to find such information is in the documentation included with the applet, usually in the form of a README file or in comments in the HTML code that invokes the applet. When you download applets from well-designed pages or collections, you will often find the applet and its associated files packaged together in a **zipped**, or compressed, file. The README file is usually part of that package.

Figure 14.1 presents part of the documentation from the Java Digital Clock applet in Chapter 13. It happens to appear in a sample Web page that displays the clock. Notice that the author has told us the names of the parameters, the possible values for the parameters, and the default values as well. This is an example of good documentation. And that brings us to another point to remember when designing you own applets: you should always create documentation that explains what the applet does and how to use it.

```
Parameters:
bgcolor: Background color (in standard RGB Hex) of your
applet.(default: 000000)
digits: Filename of your custom digits. (default: bit1.gif)
background: Filename of your custom background.
seconds: "yes" if you want to show seconds, or "no"
otherwise. In the case of "no", the seperator will flash.
(default: yes)
24hour: "no" if you want the clock to show am/pm. (default: no)
timezone: Use standard GMT offset, i.e. -0800, +0530, etc.
Ignore this field if you want to show the local time.
Note: You can simply ignore all parameters to use the default
value.
```

Figure 14.1 Sample applet documentation.

The second source of data on parameters is the Java source code itself. You can tease this code apart to see what the parameters are and what different values are used. The process is a little tedious and takes longer than just reading the documentation, but it does work. Figure 14.2 presents a snippet of the source code from the text-animator applet in Chapter 13. It includes two different parameters: the font for the text and the style to be displayed. Looking at this code, you can see these two parameters shown as "font" and "style". If there is no value for them, (s == null), or if the Web weaver uses a value not recognized, (the final ELSE function), the applet supplies the default value. "TimesRoman" is the default font, and "PLAIN" is the default style. Further examination of the code shows that there are four recognized fonts: TimesRoman, Courier, Helvetica, and Dialog. The next section of code mentions three possible styles: PLAIN, BOLD, and ITALIC.

```
s = getParameter("font");
if (s == null)        fontString = "TimesRoman";
else if (s.equalsIgnoreCase("TimesRoman")) fontString =
"TimesRoman";
else if (s.equalsIgnoreCase("Courier")) fontString =
"Courier";
else if (s.equalsIgnoreCase("Helvetica")) fontString =
"Helvetica";
else if (s.equalsIgnoreCase("Dialog")) fontString = "Dialog";
else fontString = "TimesRoman";
s = getParameter("style");
if (s == null) style = Font.PLAIN;
else if (s.equalsIgnoreCase("PLAIN")) style = Font.PLAIN;
else if (s.equalsIgnoreCase("BOLD")) style = Font.BOLD;
else if (s.equalsIgnoreCase("ITALIC")) style = Font.ITALIC;
else style = Font.PLAIN;
```

Figure 14.2 Sample applet code showing parameter values.

Dissecting the applet code is more time-consuming than reading documentation, but it does not take as long as the third option, experimentation. If you don't have anything but the bytecode, the .class file, and one example of the use of the applet where you found it, you can either use it as is or experiment with different values for the parameters that were used in the initial invocation. Such experimentation is not only time-consuming but can be frustrating. Yet, it may be the only choice you have if you want to modify the way the applet works.

A final option is to try to find the e-mail address of the applet author. (You might already have that address because you may have used it to get permission to use the applet on your page.) Authors are usually happy to provide information you want. They may even offer to make slight modifications to the applet if you need some special feature. The only problem with this method is that the e-mail address might not be right or might not be available. Always try to find the documentation before you bother any authors, unless you are contacting them to use their applets or to tell them how wonderful their applets are.

Changing an Applet

If an applet doesn't work the way you want it to, and if the change is outside the realm of the parameters, you may need to go into the Java source code and modify it. This book is not intended to give you the knowledge you need to create Java programs from scratch. However, even to make simple changes to an existing program, you need to be able to read the Java source code enough to identify what needs to be changed. There are several different packages available to help you write Java applets, but for our purposes here, we will simply use a text editor, like Notepad in the DOS environment, or vi in the UNIX environment, to make small changes to the applet we are modifying. It is important that you use a text editor to modify the code, not a word processor, because a word processor will add additional codes that the Java compiler cannot understand.

Modifying the Source Code

Figure 14.3 presents the code for the HelloWorld applet that we first saw in Chapter 12. We will modify this applet to give it a bit of a Southwestern flavor. First, let's look at the applet a line or two at a time to figure out what is going on here. The beginning two lines,

```
import java.awt.Graphics;
import java.applet.Applet;
```

bring in two important collections of code to our applet. The first adds all the features of the **AWT** (**Abstract Window Toolkit**), which includes user interface features like windows, dialog boxes, buttons, checkboxes, menus, scroll bars, lists, and text fields. We need to use the last tool, text fields, in our current applet. The second import line brings in the Applet package. This allows for construction of the applet as well as information about the lineage of the applet and sound and motion tools as well. Both these collections are important to our applet.

```
import java.awt.Graphics;
import java.applet.Applet;
public class HelloWorldApplet extends Applet
{
      public void paint(Graphics g)  {
            g.drawString("Hellooo  World !", 20, 30);
                                              }
}
```

Figure 14.3 Java code for the HelloWorld applet before modification.

Now comes a very complex line:

```
public class HelloWorldApplet extends Applet
{
```

The keyword of **public** means that the code being generated is available to other applications either as a **direct call** (using the name) or through the import statement. That means that another applet could extend this one.

The keyword of **extends** means that our applet will inherit all of the features of the existing class, **Applet**. Everything in the Applet class is available to our new class, called **HelloWorldApplet**. This inheritance feature of object-oriented programming facilitates the building of applets.

The opening curly brace (or French brace, if you want to be formal) shows where the actual applet starts:

```
public void paint(Graphics g) {
```

This line invokes the **Graphics** portion of the AWT, and calls the created object **g.** This object is used in the next line to access the **drawString** method:

```
g.drawString("Hellooo  World !", 20, 30);
```

The keyword of **void** indicates that this routine will not be returning a value.

Now we invoke the drawString method that is part of the Graphics object passed from the Graphics tool from the AWT. The drawString tool takes three parameters: the text it is to draw and the X and Y coordinates of the starting point. The numbers that make up the X or Y coordinates give the starting point for the baseline of the text string that will be painted. The top left corner of the applet window has an address of 0, 0:

```
                                }
      }
```

These two closing curly braces—okay, French braces—mark the end of the paint method and the applet itself, in that order. Now let's look at the applet as it appears when invoked from an HTML page and seen in a browser. Figure 14.4 shows the applet as it appears in HotJava.

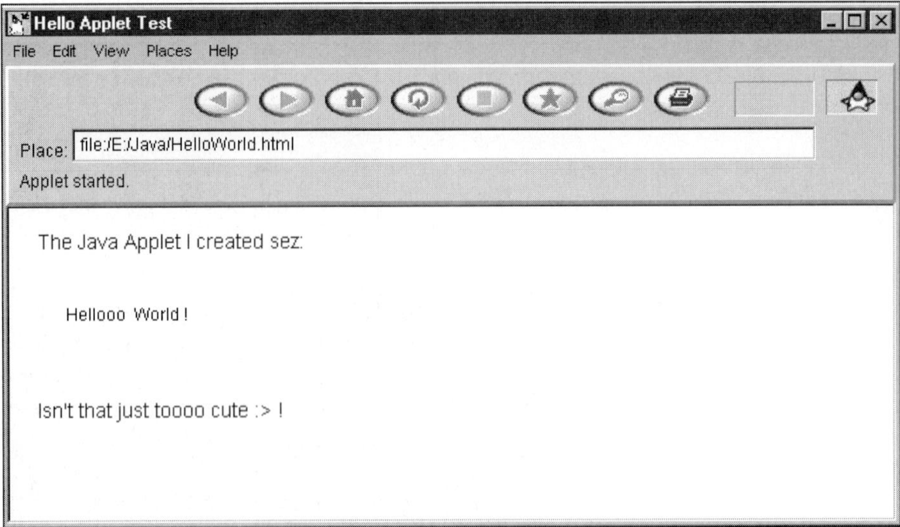

Figure 14.4 The original HelloWorld applet shown in a HotJava browser.

This is a fine applet, but it doesn't reflect the speech patterns of your humble author. Being created in the great state of Texas, the applet should reflect that state's dialect. The first step in changing the applet is to bring up the source, **HelloWorldApplet.java,** in an editor. We will use the vi editor as it has been ported to Windows NT. Notice, in Figure 14.5, that we have changed the text line, as well as the starting point of the applet within the applet window. After making the changes to the text, we save the file, changing the name to **HowdyWorldApplet.java**.

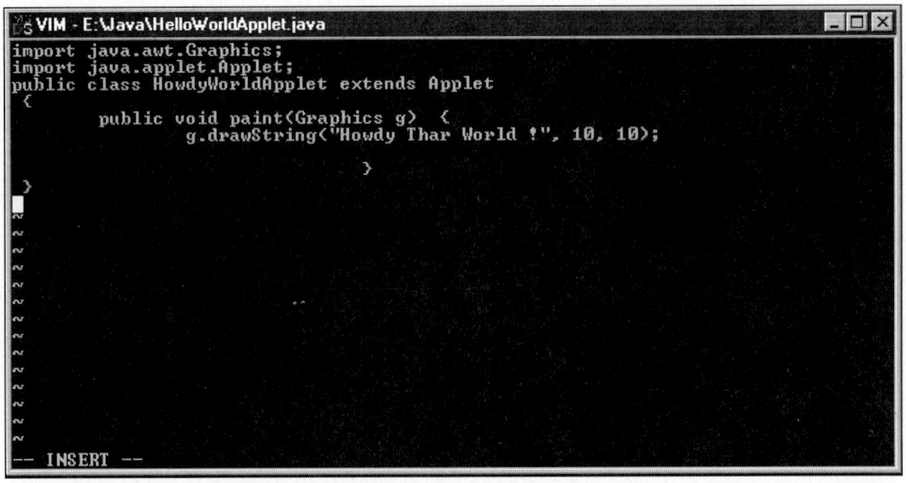

```
VIM - E:\Java\HelloWorldApplet.java
import java.awt.Graphics;
import java.applet.Applet;
public class HowdyWorldApplet extends Applet
 {
        public void paint(Graphics g)  {
                g.drawString("Howdy Thar World !", 10, 10);
                                }
 }
-- INSERT --
```

Figure 14.5 Using the vi editor to change the applet.

Compiling the Source Code

The next step is to compile the Java file to create the bytecode, or .class file. Let's see the result in Figure 14.6. Oops! It seems we made a small error. The Java compiler didn't understand the code we had written. We need to fix the problem and then recompile the source. Perhaps the Java compiler is case-sensitive. Notice that we spelled the applet name HowdyWorldA*P*plet, not HowdyWorldA*p*plet. That uppercase *P* could have caused the problem.

```
Command Prompt

E:\Java>javac HowdyWorldAPplet.java
HowdyWorldAPplet.java:3: Warning: Public class HowdyWorldApplet must be define
in a file called "HowdyWorldApplet.java".
public class HowdyWorldApplet extends Applet
             ^
1 error

E:\Java>_
```

Figure 14.6 Results of compiling the modified applet, HowdyWorld.

After changing the *P* to *p* and compiling again, we see the results in Figure 14.7. Notice the copious and verbose amount of information the Java compiler shows when the file compiles correctly (joke!). This is very UNIX-like. When it works, there is no need to tell the user that it worked; the user can see that it worked.

Figure 14.7 Results of compiling the modified applet, HowdyWorld, after correcting mistake.

Testing the Applet

Now that we know that the applet compiles correctly, let's see how it looks. Figure 14.8 shows the new applet running in a HotJava browser. Obviously, the code was changed to reflect this new, Southwestern flavor.

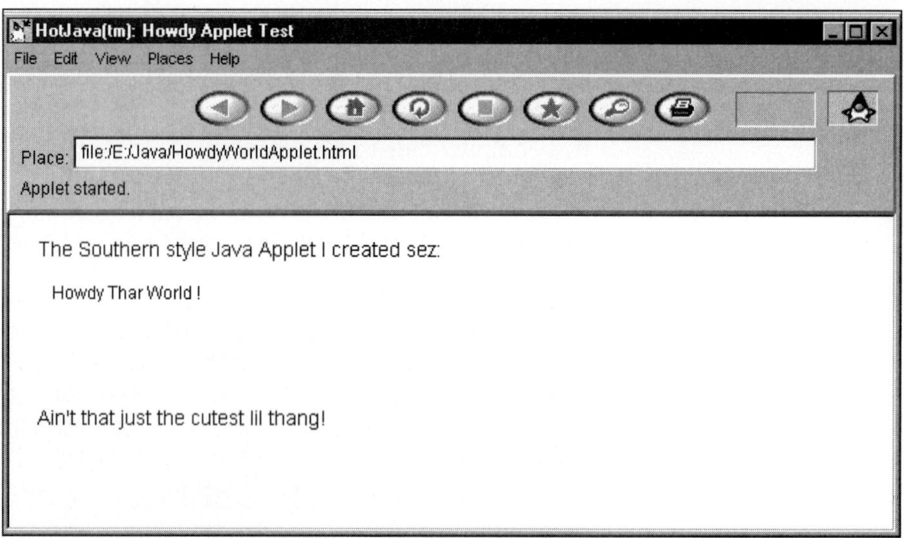

Figure 14.8 The modified applet, HowdyWorld, running in a HotJava browser.

Debugging the Applet

There isn't much that can be "buggy" in a small applet like this, but just as you found with your HTML pages, once something seems to work, then the "fixin" starts. Applets have more power and flexibility than HTML, so there are more things you can do with them—more "bells and whistles." Consequently, the debugging/fixing-up/making-neater phase is longer for applets than for HTML pages. If you thought you could spend a whole bunch of time getting the background color of your HTML page exactly right, just wait until you start playing with writing applets. Each time you get a new feature to work, it seems that the process just demands you create another enhancement. The project can be endless. This book will spare you that fate—we won't get any deeper into applet development than to mention some of the interesting tools that you can use to create, modify, and test your applets.

Applet Development Tools

When Java took off like a rocket, several companies quickly developed tools, or suites of tools, that made writing, testing, and debugging Java code easier. Three of the more popular development environments are discussed here. You don't need a fancy development environment to write Java programs or applets. All you need is a text editor and a Java compiler. Actually, you don't even need the compiler, since there are sites on the Web that will compile your Java code for you. However, having a Java development environment can make your task easier and your efforts much more efficient.

The JDK (Java Development Kit)

Since Sun Microsystems invented Java, it stands to reason that it has a premier Java development environment. The **Java development kit** (JDK to its friends) is a complete Java tool kit. It has a Java compiler (**Javac**), a Java bytecode interpreter to run stand-alone programs (**Java**), a Java debugging tool that helps find errors in Java code (**jdb**), and a tool that allows you to see how your applets are working without having to invoke a Web browser (**applet viewer**). For many people this provides the complete environment they need to produce outstanding code. True to its commitment to Java, Sun makes the JDK available by download to private developers for free.

In addition to the JDK, you will need some sort of text editor. It can be as simple as Notepad for the Microsoft platform or vi for the UNIX world. Actually, there are faux UNIX tools that run in other operating system environments, such as Microsoft Windows NT. With a little judicious looking, you can find tools like that on the Net.

Symantec's Java Cafe

The folks at Symantec look at developing Java programs from a different point of view. They have created an integrated environment designed to build whole Java projects, that is, a related set of applets. This is a windowing environment that uses the JDK as the primary engine but puts a nice windowing front end on the process. There are windows for editing code, browsing the code, and debugging. There is also a file management system to keep track of the files you are working with.

The Java Cafe uses the applet viewer to display the running applet. It even provides a **wizard** to help you design and build Java code. The wizard identifies errors in your code, going so far as to highlight the line of code that contains a specific compiler error. The Java Cafe is a nice package, that, at the time of this writing, retails for under a hundred dollars. Some new users may find it a little overwhelming, but with practice it becomes a useful tool.

Microsoft's J++

Microsoft also has an entry in the Java development tool market. Its J++ development environment looks very much like its Visual C++ development tool. This series of tabbed screens allows the user to build, test, and debug Java applications. A wizard is included to help with development. Rather than using the JDK's applet viewer, the J++ package uses Microsoft's Internet Explorer to run applets. That means you need to have this browser available, and you have to load it each time you want to view an applet. Loading the browser makes this tool somewhat slow to use. However, users who have taken the time to become comfortable with Microsoft's Visual C++ development package will be immediately at home with this tool as well. At the time of this writing, Microsoft's J++ sells for just under a hundred dollars.

Other Applet Environments

There are other, smaller, development environments available to the applet builder all across the Internet. Some are free, and some are commercial products.

Designing with Applets

The strongest caution about using applets on your page is to make sure you need them. Like images and other inclusions into your HTML code, applets should be included because they are necessary, not just because they are there. Don't fall into the trap of loading up your page with applets just because you visited the JARS site and found 20 really cool ones. That is folly. Use applets to bring needed interaction to your pages and to perform tasks you cannot perform without them. In addition, consider placing the applets on pages other than your home page. You need to keep your home page small and fast to load; applets can make it load more slowly. If you use applets on your home page, use small ones that don't require large downloads to work.

For example, the UFO applet in Chapter 13 would not be good on your home page. It would be fine on another page at your site, linked from your home page, but not on your home page itself. Applets that can work well on your home page include things like a clock, a counter that keeps track of hits to your page, one small animation applet that pertains to the theme of your page, and maybe one of the new news ticker-tape applets.

Your home page should not be loaded up with lots of anything—images, links, applets—that cause it to look busy or cluttered. Your home page should gently bring users into your site, giving them an overview of what is there and some nice, clear navigation instructions. It should not overwhelm users with lots and lots of busy applets, all competing for their attention.

Exercises

14.1. Check with your instructor or system administrator to see if a JDK is available on your system or perhaps one of the integrated environments, like Java Cafe or J++. If you don't have a suitable Java development environment, you may be allowed to download the latest JDK from Sun Microsystems. In any event, the object of this first exercise is to identify or create a Java development environment consisting of an editor, a Java compiler, and a way to view applets, either an applet viewer or a browser that is Java-enabled.

14.2. Use your editor to create the **HelloWorldApplet.java** Java file. Check your work, Java is case-sensitive, so everything must be spelled and capitalized exactly as it is in the example. Compile the applet to create a **.class** file.

14.3. Build a small Web page to display your applet. Just put a line or two of text in front of the <APPLET> tag and a line after. Horizontal rules are fine if you don't want to write text lines. Test the applet.

14.4. After you make sure the HelloWorld applet works, modify it. Change the text that is displayed, change the position that the text starts, add another line of text. Experiment! After each change, recompile the applet and display it to see your changes.

14.5. Look across the Net and find another simple applet. With permission, copy the source code to your computer. Compile it into bytecode to ensure that it works with your version of the Javac compiler. Then look at it and make some changes to it. Recompile and test it again.

appendix A

html color names chart

Both Netscape Navigator and the Internet Explorer allow you to change the colors of various elements in the documents you produce. Some of the elements you can change are shown in Table A.1.

ELEMENT	TAG AND ASSOCIATED ATTRIBUTE
Document background color	<BODY BGCOLOR=COLOR VALUE>
Normal text in the document	<BODY TEXT=COLOR VALUE>
Active hyperlinks (Netscape only)	<BODY ALINK=COLOR VALUE>
Visited hyperlinks	<BODY VLINK=COLOR VALUE>
Regular hyperlinks	<BODY LINK=COLOR VALUE>
Block of text (not whole document)	<FONT COLOR=COLOR VALUE>
Table contents (Internet Explorer only)	<TABLE BGCOLOR=COLOR VALUE>
Table rows	<TR BGCOLOR=COLOR VALUE>
Table data	<TD BGCOLOR=COLOR VALUE>
Table headers	<TH BGCOLOR=COLOR VALUE>

Table A.1 Some HTML tags used to change colors.

You can always specify a color as a mixture of Red, Green, and Blue. The color must be specified as a hexadecimal number (six digits). The first (leftmost) two digits are the Red intensity, the second two digits are the Green intensity, and the last two (rightmost) digits are the Blue intensity.

A value of 00 means that the color specified by that position is turned off (intensity of zero). A value of FF hexadecimal, which corresponds to 255 in decimal form, indicates maximum intensity. That means that a color value of "#FF0000" is bright red, "#00FF00" is bright green, and "#0000FF" is bright blue. White is "#FFFFFF", and black is "#000000". When you specify color values in hexadecimal form, you should always precede the number with the octothorp, or number sign (#), and enclose the value in quotation marks.

You can create over 16 million colors by specifying slightly different values for these three main colors. (255 × 255 × 255). Thus, you can spend a great deal of time getting the colors on your page "just right." Finding just the right hexadecimal code for a specific color, like "#41A4D1", which is a rather nice bluish gray, can be difficult and time-consuming. It is also hard to communicate and remember a string of hexadecimal numbers. Fortunately, the folks at Netscape and at Microsoft also thought there should be an easier way. Accordingly, both Netscape Navigator and Internet Express support the use of color names.

Color names can be used in place of the hexadecimal numbers to specify color values. However, you should be aware that some of these colors may look a little different—and sometimes a lot different—on different screens. For example, with one browser on one machine, "red4" looks very much like a yellow green!

Some of the color names are actually a series of different color variants. For example, there are four azures: azure1 through azure4. Azure1 is the lightest, and azure4 is the darkest. The gray series is the largest series, running from gray1, the darkest gray, to gray100, the lightest. Usually if you use the color name from a series without any number, it will be the same as the first level of that range. For instance, "gold" looks just like gold1. Again, gray is the exception. "Gray" is closest to gray75.

The color names in Table A.2 are supported by Internet Explorer and seem to work with Netscape as well. The color names in Table A.3 are supported by Netscape.

As with most other things on the Internet, YMMV (Your Mileage May Vary) when using these color names. Different versions of the browsers will most likely support different name sets, or the same name set will give you different colors on different browsers. Moreover, different hardware will allow different expression of the colors for any given name. If you want to play it safe and just use hexadecimal codes for your colors, see Table A.4 for some standard Windows palette colors with their approximate hexadecimal values.

aqua	navy
black	olive
blue	purple
fuchsia	red
gray	silver
green	teal
lime	yellow
maroon	white

Table A.2 Internet Explorer color names.

aliceblue	darkturquoise	lightseagreen	palevioletred♣
antiquewhite♣	darkviolet	lightskyblue♣	papayawhip
aquamarine♣	deeppink	lightslateblue	peachpuff♣
azure♣	deepskyblue♣	lightslategray	peru
beige	dimgray	lightsteelblue♣	pink♣
bisque♣	dodgerblue♣	lightyellow♣	plum♣
black	firebrick♣	limegreen	powderblue
blanchedalmond	floralwhite	linen	purple♣
blue♣	forestgreen	magenta♣	red♣
blueviolet	gainsboro	maroon♣	rosybrown♣
brown♣	ghostwhite	mediumaquamarine	royalblue♣
burleywood♣	gold♣	mediumblue	saddlebrown
cadetblue♣	goldenrod♣	mediumorchid♣	salmon♣
chartreuse♣	gray	mediumpurple♣	sandybrown
chocolate♣	green♣	mediumseagreen	seagreen♣
coral♣	greenyellow	mediumslateblue	seashell♣
cornflowerblue	honeydew♣	mediumspringgreen	sienna♣
cornsilk♣	hotpink♣	mediumturquoise	skyblue♣
cyan♣	indianred♣	mediumvioletred	slateblue♣
darkblue	ivory♣	midnightblue	slategray♣
darkcyan	khaki♣	mintcream	snow♣
darkgoldenrod	lavender	mistyrose♣	springgreen♣
darkgray	lavenderblush♣	moccasin	steelblue♣
darkgreen	lawngreen	navajowhite♣	tan♣
darkkhaki	lemonchiffon♣	navy	thistle♣
darkmagenta	lightblue♣	navyblue	tomato♣
darkolivegreen	lightcoral	oldlace	turquoise♣
darkorange♣	lightcyan♣	olivedrab♣	violet
darkorchid♣	lightgoldenrod♣	orange♣	violetred♣
darkred	lightgoldenrodyellow	orangered♣	wheat♣
darksalmon	lightgray	orchid♣	white
darkseagreen♣	lightgreen	palegoldenrod	whitesmoke
darkslateblue	lightpink♣	palegreen♣	yellow♣
darkslategray♣	lightsalmon♣	paleturquoise♣	yellowgreen
♣ = color series (i.e. blue1-blue4)			

Table A.3 Netscape color names.

Color Description	Hexadecimal Value
black	"#000000"
blue	"#0000FF"
cream	"#FFFBF0"
cyan	"#00FFFF"
dark blue	"#000080"
dark cyan	"#008080"
dark gray	"#808080"
dark green	"#008000"
dark magenta	"#800080"
dark red	"#800000"
dark yellow	"#808000"
grass green	"#C0DCC0"
green	"#00FF00"
light blue	"#A6CAF0"
light gray	"#C0C0C0"
magenta	"#FF00FF"
medium gray	"#A0A0A4"
red	"#FF0000"
white	"#FFFFFF"
yellow	"#FFFF00"

Table A.4 Windows palette hexadecimal color codes.

All in all, it is fun to play with colors, and they can introduce some real variety into your pages. But remember the cautions we discussed in Chapter 2. Your user can override your color choices with some browsers. Also, you may be asking a browser to display a color that is not available on the machine in use. In either case, you could create problems for your user.

appendix B

html tag list

Here is a quick reference list of the HTML tags covered in this textbook. The list provides only a brief description of each tag, not a complete one. If you have any question as to how to use the tag, please refer to the text itself. The information in this list is only the actual tag (on the left margin and in bold) and the list of associated attributes, indented, following the tag. Deprecated tags are not listed.

<A> . . . </A>	Anchor; creates a hyperlink (HREF is attribute) or fragment identifier (name anchor).
HREF=*URL*	Hypertext reference specifying the URL of a hyperlink target. Required if not a name anchor.
METHODS=*list*	Specifies a comma-separated list of browser-dependent presentation methods.
NAME=*string*	Specifies the name of a fragment identifier. Required if not an HREF.
REL=*relationship*	Indicates the relationship going from a document to the target.
REV=*relationship*	Indicates the reverse relationship going from the target to a document.
TARGET=*name*	Defines the name of the frame or window to receive the referenced document.
TITLE=*string*	Provides a title for the target document.
URN=*URN*	Specifies the location-independent URN (Universal Resource Name) for this hyperlink.
<ADDRESS> . . . </ADDRESS>	Enclosed text appears as an address.

Tag / Attribute	Description
<APPLET> . . . </APPLET>	Defines and invokes an applet at this point in the document.
ALIGN=*position*	Aligns the applet, like an image, to TOP, MIDDLE, BOTTOM, LEFT, RIGHT, ABSMIDDLE, BASELINE, or ABSBOTTOM of current text line.
ALT=*string*	Specifies alternative text to be displayed if the applet doesn't work for browsers that support applets. Should always be used.
CODE=*class*	Specifies the class name (applet name) to be executed, required.
CODEBASE=*URL*	Defines the URL from which to retrieve the code used if code is not on the local machine.
HEIGHT=*pixels*	Specifies the height of the applet space.
HSPACE=*pixels*	Specifies the horizontal space around the applet space.
NAME=*string*	Defines a specific instance of this applet.
VSPACE=*pixels*	Specifies the vertical space around the applet space.
WIDTH=*pixels*	Specifies the width of the applet space.
<AREA> . . . </AREA>	Creates a mouse-sensitive area on a client-side image map.
COORDS=*list*	Defines a comma-separated list of the coordinates of the edges of the area.
HREF=*URL*	Identifies the URL of the hyperlink target that is associated with the defined area.
NOHREF	Indicates that no link is associated with this area. Clicking has no effect. *Very* confusing to users.
SHAPE=*shape*	Defines the shape of the area as CIRC, CIRCLE, POLY, POLYGON, RECT, or RECTANGLE.
<B> . . . </B>	Physical style causing the enclosed text to appear **bold.**
<BASE>	Defines the base URL for all relative URLs in the current document.
<BASEFONT>	Specifies the font size for all text following.
SIZE=*value*	Sets basefont size as 1–7. Default is 3. Can also be set relatively (i.e., +2).
<BIG> . . . </BIG>	Physical style changing the size of enclosed text to a bigger type size.
<BLINK> . . . </BLINK>	Physical style causing enclosed text to blink. Very annoying tag. Use only when absolutely necessary.
<BLOCKQUOTE> . . . </BLOCKQUOTE>	Logical style causing enclosed text to appear as a quotation, right/left indented. May be in italics.
<BODY> . . . </BODY>	Defines the start/end of the body of an HTML document.
ALINK=*color*	Changes the color of the active link. Use hexadecimal "#AABBCC" or color name.

BACKGROUND=*URL*	Points to the image to be used as a background for the document.
BGCOLOR=*color*	Sets the background color for the document. Use hexadecimal "#AABBCC" or color name.
BGPROPERTIES=*value*	If value is set to FIXED, will prevent scrolling of background image.
LEFTMARGIN=*pixels*	Sets the width of the left margin of the document.
LINK=*color*	Changes the color of links not taken. Use hexadecimal "#AABBCC" or color name.
TEXT=*color*	Changes the color of the actual text. Use hexadecimal "#AABBCC" or color name.
TOPMARGIN=*pixels*	Sets the size of the document's top margin.
VLINK=*color*	Changes the color of links that have been visited. Use hexadecimal "#AABBCC" or color name.
** **	Adds a line break. Text flow continues on the next line.
CLEAR=*margin*	Breaks the line and moves down until the requested margin—LEFT, RIGHT, or ALL, is clear.
<CAPTION> . . . </CAPTION>	Creates a caption for a table.
ALIGN=*position*	Netscape sets the vertical position of the caption to TOP or BOTTOM. Internet Explorer sets the horizontal alignment of the caption to either LEFT, CENTER, or RIGHT.
VALIGN=*position*	Internet Explorer sets the vertical position of the caption to either TOP or BOTTOM.
<CENTER> . . . </CENTER>	Centers the text within the container.
<CITE> . . . <CITE>	Logical tag indicating that enclosed text is a citation.
<CODE> . . . </CODE>	Logical tag indicating that enclosed text is a code sample.
<DD> . . . </DD>	Logical tag indicating that enclosed text is the definition part of a definition-list element.
<DFN> . . . </DFN>	Logical tag indicating that enclosed text is a definition.
<DIR> . . . </DIR>	Creates a directory-style list using <LI> tags.
COMPACT	Makes a list more compact if possible. Usually ignored.
<DT> . . . </DT>	Logical tag indicating that enclosed text is the term part of a definition-list element.
<EM> . . . </EM>	Logical tag indicating that enclosed text should have additional emphasis. Usually rendered as bold.

<FONT> . . . </FONT>	Sets the characteristics of the enclosed text.
COLOR=*color*	Sets the color of the enclosed text. Use color hexadecimal values or names.
FACE=*list*	Sets the typeface to the first available font in the comma-separated list of font names.
SIZE=*value*	Sets the size to an absolute size of 1 to 7 or a size relative to the <BASEFONT> size using +*n* or −*n*.
<FORM> . . . </FORM>	Delimits a form.
ACTION=*URL*	Specifies the URL of the application to process the form. Required.
ENCTYPE=*encoding*	Specifies how the form element values will be encoded.
METHOD=*style*	Specifies the parameter-passing style as either GET or POST (required).
<FRAME> . . . </FRAME>	Delimits a frame within a frameset.
MARGINHEIGHT=*n*	Adds *n* pixels of space above and below the frame contents.
MARGINWIDTH=*n*	Adds *n* pixels of space to the left and right of the frame contents.
NAME=*string*	Names the frame.
NORESIZE	Disables user resizing of the frame.
SCROLLING=*type*	Adds scroll bars or not, as follows: always (YES), never (NO), or add when needed (AUTO).
SRC=*URL*	Defines the URL of the source document for this frame.
<FRAMESET> . . . </FRAMESET>	Defines a collection of frames or other framesets.
COLS=*list*	Specifies the number/width of frames within a frameset.
ROWS=*list*	Specifies the number/height of frames within a frameset.
<H*n*> . . . </H*n*>	Defines a level *n* heading: for level *n* from 1 to 6.
ALIGN=*type*	Specifies the heading alignment as either LEFT (default), CENTER, or RIGHT.
<HEAD> . . . </HEAD>	Delimits the beginning and ending of the document's head.
<HR>	Inserts a horizontal rule, breaking the text flow.
ALIGN=*type*	Specifies the alignment of the rule as either LEFT, CENTER (default), or RIGHT.
NOSHADE	Specifies to not use 3D shading and to round the ends of the rule.
SIZE=*pixels*	Sets the thickness of the rule in pixels.
WIDTH=*value* or %	Sets the width of the rule to either an integer number of pixels or a percentage of the page width. Percentage is preferred.

<HTML> . . . </HTML>	Contains the whole of the HTML document (usually first and last tags).
VERSION=*string*	Indicates the HTML version used to create this document. Not usually used.
<I> . . . </I>	Physical style changing enclosed text to an *italic* typeface.
<IMG>	Inserts an image into the current text flow.
ALIGN=*type*	Aligns an image to the TOP, MIDDLE, BOTTOM (default), LEFT, RIGHT, ABSMIDDLE, BASELINE, or ABSBOTTOM of the text.
ALT=*text*	Provides a text description of the image for non-image-enabled browsers. Should always be used.
BORDER=*pixels*	Sets the thickness of the border around images contained within hyperlinks. Default size is 3.
CONTROLS	For Internet Explorer only. Adds playback controls for embedded video clips.
DYNSRC=*URL*	Specifies the URL of a video clip to be displayed.
HEIGHT=*pixels*	Specifies the height of the image. Forces image height.
HSPACE=*pixels*	Specifies the horizontal space to be added to the left and right of the image.
ISMAP	Indicates that the image is mouse-selectable when used within an <A> tag (server side).
LOOP=*value*	Sets the number of times to play the video; the value may be an integer, or it may be INFINITE.
LOWSRC=*URL*	Specifies a low-resolution image to be loaded by the browser first, followed by the image specified by the SRC attribute.
SRC=*URL*	Specifies the source URL of the image to be displayed. Required.
START=*start*	Specifies when to play the video clip, either FILEOPEN or MOUSEOVER.
USEMAP=*URL*	Specifies the map of coordinates and links that defines the hypertext links within this image (client side).
VSPACE=*pixels*	Specifies the vertical space added above and below the image.
WIDTH=*pixels*	Specifies the width of the image.
<INPUT TYPE=CHECKBOX>	Creates a checkbox-input element within a <FORM>.
CHECKED	Indicates a preselection.
NAME=*string*	Specifies the name of the parameter to be passed to the form-processing application if this element is selected. Required.
VALUE=*string*	Specifies the value of the parameter sent to the form-processing application if this element is selected. Required.

<INPUT TYPE=FILE>	Creates a file-selection element within a <FORM>.
MAXLENGTH=*chars*	Specifies the maximum number of characters to accept for this element.
NAME=*string*	Specifies the name of the parameter that is passed to the form-processing application for this input element. Required.
SIZE=*chars*	Specifies the number of characters to display for this element.
<INPUT TYPE=HIDDEN>	Creates a hidden element within a <FORM>.
MAXLENGTH=*chars*	Specifies the maximum number of characters to accept for this element.
NAME=*string*	Specifies the name of the parameter that is passed to the form-processing application for this input element. Required.
SIZE=*chars*	Specifies the number of characters to display for this element.
VALUE=*string*	Specifies the value of the element that is passed to the form-processing application. Required.
<INPUT TYPE=IMAGE>	Creates an image input element within a <FORM>.
ALIGN=*type*	Aligns the image to either the TOP, MIDDLE, or BOTTOM of the form's text.
NAME=*string*	Specifies the name of the parameter to be passed to the form-processing application for this input element. Required.
SRC=*URL*	Specifies the source URL of the image. Required.
<INPUT TYPE=PASSWORD>	Creates a content-protected, but not secure, text-input element within a <FORM>.
MAXLENGTH=*chars*	Specifies the maximum number of characters to accept for this element.
NAME=*string*	Specifies the name of the parameter to be passed to the form-processing application for this input element. Required.
SIZE=*chars*	Specifies the number of characters to display for this element.
VALUE=*string*	Specifies the initial value for this element.
<INPUT TYPE=RADIO>	Creates a radio button within a <FORM>.
CHECKED	Indicates a preselection.
NAME=*string*	Specifies the name of the parameter that is passed to the form-processing application if this input element is selected. Required.
VALUE=*string*	Specifies the value of the parameter that is passed to the form-processing application if this element is selected. Required.
<INPUT TYPE=RESET>	Creates a reset button within a <FORM>.
VALUE=*string*	Specifies an alternate label for the reset button. Default is RESET.

<INPUT TYPE=SUBMIT>	Creates a submit button within a <FORM>.
NAME=*string*	Specifies the name of the parameter that is passed to the form-processing application for this input element.
VALUE=*string*	Specifies an alternate label for the submit button. Also modifies the value passed to the form-processing application for this parameter if this button is clicked.
<INPUT TYPE=TEXT>	Creates a text-input element within a <FORM>.
MAXLENGTH=*chars*	Specifies the maximum number of characters to accept for this element.
NAME=*string*	Specifies the name of the parameter that is passed to the form-processing application for this input element. Required.
SIZE=*chars*	Specifies the number of characters to display for this element.
VALUE=*string*	Specifies the initial value for this element.
<ISINDEX>	Creates a "searchable" HTML document.
ACTION=*URL*	For Internet Explorer only. Provides the URL of the program that will perform the searching action.
PROMPT=*string*	Provides an alternate prompt for the input field.
<KBD> . . . </KBD>	Logical tag causing enclosed text to appear as keyboard-like (usually monospaced) input.
<LI> . . . </LI>	Container for a list item in list containers, <OL>, <UL>, <DEF>, and <MENU> lists.
TYPE=*format*	Sets the type of this list element to the desired format. For <LI> within <OL>:A (capital letters), a (lowercase letters), I (capital Roman numerals), i (lowercase Roman numerals) or 1 (Arabic numerals, the default). For <LI> within <UL>:CIRCLE, DISC (default) or SQUARE.
VALUE=*num*	Changes the number for this list item to *num* (starts or restarts counting with *num*).
<LINK>	Establishes a link between this document and another coded in the document <HEAD>.
HREF=*URL*	Identifies the URL of the target document.
METHODS=*list*	Defines a list of browser-dependent display methods for this link (comma delimited).
REV=*relation*	Indicates the relationship from this document to the target.
TITLE=*string*	Provides a title for the target document.
URN=*URN*	Specifies the Universal Resource Name (URN) for the target document, location-independent.
<MENU> . . . </MENU>	Defines a menu list containing <LI> tags.
COMPACT	Makes the list more compact. Usually ignored.

<META>	Provides meta (additional) information about a document.
CONTENT=*string*	Specifies the value for the <META> information. Required.
HTTP-EQUIV=*string*	Specifies the http-equivalent name for the <META> information and causes the server to include the name and content in the http header for this document when it is transmitted to the client.
NAME=*string*	Specifies the name of the <META> information.
<NOBR> . . . </NOBR>	Turns off automatic line breaks at the browser window boundary for the enclosed text.
<NOFRAMES> . . . </NOFRAMES>	Defines content to be presented by browsers that do not support frames. Should be used in all framed documents.
<OL> . . . </OL>	Defines an ordered list containing numbered (ascending) <LI> elements.
COMPACT	Presents the list in a more compact manner. Usually ignored.
START=*num*	Starts or restarts numbering the list at *num* instead of 1.
TYPE=*format*	Sets or resets the numbering format for the list to either 1 (Arabic numerals, default), A (capital letters), a (lowercase letters), I (capital Roman numerals), or i (lowercase Roman numerals).
<OPTION> . . . </OPTION>	Defines an option within a <SELECT> item in a <FORM>.
SELECTED	Indicates a preselection.
VALUE=*string*	Returns the specified value to the form-processing application instead of the <OPTION> contents.
<P> . . . </P>	Delimits a paragraph.
ALIGN=*alignment*	Aligns the text within the paragraph to LEFT, CENTER, or RIGHT.
<PARAM> . . . </PARAM>	Passes a parameter to an <APPLET>.
NAME=*string*	Specifies the name of the parameter. Required.
VALUE=*value*	Specifies the value of the parameter. Required.
<PRE> . . . </PRE>	Preserves the original style of the enclosed text, keeping line breaks and spacing more or less like the original.
WIDTH=*chars*	Sizes the text so that *n* characters fit across the display window if possible.
<S> . . . </S>	Physical style causing enclosed text to be struck through with a horizontal line.
<SELECT> . . . </SELECT>	Creates a multiple-choice menu or scrolling list within a <FORM>, containing one or more <OPTION> tags.

MULTIPLE	Enables the user to select more than one <OPTION>.
NAME=*string*	Specifies the name for the <OPTION> values that, if selected, are passed to the form-processing application. Required.
SIZE=*num*	Displays *num* items using a pull-down menu for SIZE=1 (without MULTIPLE specified) and a scrolling list of *num* items otherwise.
<SMALL> . . . </SMALL>	Physical style rendering enclosed text in a smaller typeface.
<STRIKE> . . . </STRIKE>	Physical style rendering enclosed text as struck through with a horizontal line.
<STRONG> . . . </STRONG>	Logical style indicating that enclosed text should be strongly emphasized. Usually renderd as bold.
_{. . .}	Physical style rendering enclosed text as a subscript.
^{. . .}	Physical style rendering enclosed text as a superscript.
<TABLE> . . . </TABLE>	Delimits the bounds of a table. Will not work if closing tag is left off.
ALIGN=*position*	Aligns the table either LEFT or RIGHT and flows text around the table.
BGCOLOR=*color*	Sets the background color for the entire table. Use either hexadecimal "#AABBCC" or color name.
BORDER=*pixels*	Creates a border so many pixels wide around the table.
CELLPADDING=*pixels*	Sets pixels of padding around each cell's contents.
CELLSPACING=*pixels*	Sets spacing of pixels between cells.
HSPACE=*pixels*	Specifies the horizontal space to be added to the left and right of the image.
VALIGN=*location*	Specifies the vertical location of the text in the cells to either the TOP or BOTTOM. Sets these values for the entire table.
VSPACE=*pixels*	Specifies the vertical space to be added above and below an image.
WIDTH=*size*	Sets the width of the table in either pixels or a percentage of the window width. Percentage is preferred.
<TD> . . . </TD>	Describes a table data cell.
ALIGN=*type*	Aligns the cell contents to the LEFT, CENTER, or RIGHT.
BGCOLOR=*color*	Defines the background color for the cell. Use either hexadecimal "#AABBCC" or color name.

Tag / Attribute	Description
COLSPAN=*cols*	Sets the cell span at a certain number of adjacent columns.
NOWRAP	Turns off automatic wrapping of text in this cell.
ROWSPAN=*rows*	Sets the cell span at a certain number of adjacent rows.
VALIGN=*type*	Vertically aligns this cell's contents to the TOP, CENTER, BOTTOM, or BASELINE of the cell.
WIDTH=*size*	Sets the width of the table in either pixels or a percentage of the whole table width. Percentage is preferred.
<TEXTAREA> . . . </TEXTAREA>	Creates a multiline text-input area within a <FORM>. Content initially coded in the <TEXTAREA> tag is the default value.
COLS=*bytes*	Defines the text-input area to be so many bytes wide. Should always be coded.
NAME=*string*	Defines the name for the text-area value that is passed to the form-processing application. Required.
ROWS=*lines*	Defines the text-input area to be so many lines tall. Should always be coded.
WRAP=*style*	Sets word wrapping within the text area to OFF, VIRTUAL (display wrap but do not transmit to server), or PHYSICAL (display and transmit new lines to server).
<TH> . . . </TH>	Describes a table header cell. Contents are usually bold and centered.
ALIGN=*type*	Aligns the cell contents to the LEFT, CENTER, or RIGHT.
BGCOLOR=*color*	Defines the background color for the cell. Use either hexadecimal "#AABBCC" or color name.
COLSPAN=*cols*	Have this cell span *cols* adjacent columns.
NOWRAP	Does not automatically wrap and fill text in this cell.
ROWSPAN=*rows*	Have this cell span *rows* adjacent rows.
VALIGN=*type*	Aligns this cell's contents vertically to the TOP, CENTER, BOTTOM, or BASELINE of the cell.
WIDTH=*size*	Sets the width of the table in either pixels or a percentage of the whole table width. Percentage is preferred.
<TITLE> . . . </TITLE>	Creates the HTML document's title. This tag is very important and should always be used (unless the document is part of a frameset).
<TR> . . . </TR>	Describes a row of cells within a table.
ALIGN=*type*	Aligns the cell contents in this row LEFT, CENTER, or RIGHT.

BGCOLOR=*color*	Defines the background color for the cell. Use either hexadecimal "#AABBCC" or color name.
BORDER=*pixels*	Creates a border so many pixels wide.
VALIGN=*type*	Aligns this cell's contents vertically to the TOP, CENTER, BOTTOM, or BASELINE of the cell.
<TT> . . . </TT>	Physical style that formats enclosed text in Teletype-style, monospaced font.
<U> . . . </U>	Physical style that underlines enclosed text. This is very simple underlining of text, spaces, and tabs.
<UL> . . . </UL>	Creates an unordered list of bulleted <LI> elements.
COMPACT	Presents the list in a more compact manner. Usually ignored.
TYPE=*bullet*	Sets the bullet style for this list to either CIRCLE, DISC, or SQUARE.
<VAR> . . . </VAR>	Logical style indicating enclosed text is a variable's name.
<WBR>	Defines a possible word break point within a <NOBR> section.

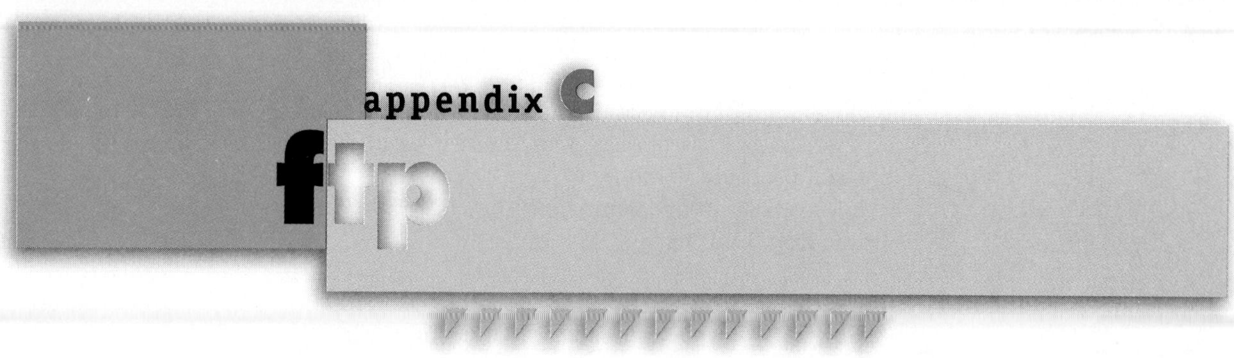

File **T**ransfer **P**rotocol (ftp) is both a tool and a protocol. One of the browser protocols supports ftp as a way to move files from a remote site to your computer (this is how you are able to download files using a browser like Netscape or Internet Explorer). Ftp is the tool most often used to send files between computers, across the Internet. You can use ftp to move interesting files from other places on the Net to your account on the local machine. Or you can use ftp to copy files on your local machine to other computers on the Internet. You can retrieve or send text files, images, icons, and other information with ftp.

There are ftp clients for most operating systems, but it was originally a UNIX tool, so the commands for standard ftp look very UNIX-like. Many enhanced ftp tools are available to make it very simple to transfer files. In the first part of this discussion we will look at the UNIX ftp command that is available if you are lucky enough to be working on a UNIX machine. Many other operating systems also support this command line version of ftp.

Following are some of the features of the standard ftp client and some of the standard ftp commands. You may choose to use a more graphical ftp client, which will do more of the work for you, but even then, the steps described here must be accomplished for ftp to work.

Remember, ftp is a specialized file transport tool. Starting an ftp session establishes a link between your computer and a remote computer, but only ftp commands will work during that session. If you want to be able to use all the features of a remote computer, you must use the **telnet** command to start a remote login session on that computer.

Ftp can operate in one of two transfer modes, either moving **ASCII** or **binary** files. If you are moving images, sounds, or programs, you need to move them as binary files. Binary moves take a little longer, but they are usually safer. Use ASCII only for moving text files. If you try to move a binary file in ASCII mode, ftp will try to convert the binary to an ASCII representation. This often involves padding with extra zero bits, which will corrupt a binary file. If you download a program and it doesn't seem to work, chances are you downloaded it in ASCII rather than binary. Download it again, using binary transfer mode, and it will probably work.

Here are a set of ftp commands (they look a lot like Unix because, of course, ftp came from Unix).

Connection commands

open	Open a specific connection using ftp.
close	Close the current connection (ftp continues to run).
bye	Close the current connection and quit ftp.
?	Show a list of all the commands.
help	Give a one-line explanation of the command that follows help.

Switches (like a light switch, if you type the name and if it is on, it turns off; if it is off, it turns it on.)

prompt	A switch that turns on or off confirmation of each file move.
verbose	A switch that gives you statistics on the transfer.
hash	Presents a set of #'s to indicate movement progress. (This is really nice if you are transferring a large file; it lets you know that ftp is really working. It does slow down the transfer slightly. But hey, what price is your sanity!)

Transfer modes

ASCII	Turns on ASCII file transfer mode (use only for text).
bin(ary)	Turns on binary file transfer mode (safe but a little slower).

Navigation commands

cd	Changes the remote directory (just like Unix—surprise surprise!).
pwd	Shows the directory on the remote computer.
lcd	Shows or changes the *local* directory (the one on your box).
ls	Lists the files in the current directory on the remote computer.
dir	Produces a different (longer) version of **ls.**

File transfer commands

put	Sends a file to the remote machine.
get	Retrieves a file from the remote machine.
mput	Sends a series of files to a remote machine (multiple put).
mget	Retrieves a series of files from a remote machine (multiple get).
delete	Removes a file from the remote machine (dangerous!). This command is not usually enabled but you should *never* take chances.

A normal ftp session is shown in Figure C.1. It starts with the ftp command to initiate a connection between the local computer (the one you are sitting at) and a remote computer (the one that either has the files you want or is where you want to send files). In this screen, the user, **ttg,** has connected to **phred,** a UNIX machine that has an ftp server set up for registered users only. Many ftp sites are set up to allow **anonymous ftp** connections in which the user can use the name "anonymous" and thus need no password. In the case of Figure C.1, the user was required to enter his name and then a password. This is the way it will most likely be when you move pages up to your Web server.

```
File  Edit  Setup  Control  Help
clyde% ftp phred
Connected to phred.dcccd.edu.
220 phred.dcccd.edu FTP server (Version wu-2.4.2-academ[BETA-12](1) Wed Mar 5 12
:37:21 EST 1997) ready.
Name (phred:ttg): ttg
331 Password required for ttg.
Password:
230 User ttg logged in.
ftp> cd web-pages
250 CWD command successful.
ftp>
```

Figure C.1 Starting an ftp session.

Ttg types his user ID, then his password, and the ftp server on phred responds with the "logged in" message. Notice that the prompt changes to **ftp>,** indicating that the ftp program is now active. Next, the user changes directories with the **cd web-pages** command, moving to a directory called **web-pages.** This is where the Web pages for that user are stored. Each time the user enters a command, ftp tells him whether the command worked or not. This is an important feature of ftp.

Now that ttg is in the correct directory, he can begin to work. He knows that he wants to download a file that starts with an "h," so he asks the computer to list the files in the current directory that begin with "h," using the command **ls h*,** as shown in Figure C.2. After looking over the list of files, ttg decides that the file he really wants is the **htmllab4.html** file—a file containing the exercises for the fourth lab in an HTML class at his school. Now he wants to download that file to his local PC. Figure C.3 shows the screen capture, which

```
ftp> ls h*
200 PORT command successful.
150 Opening ASCII mode data connection for file list.
htmlextra1.html
htmllab1.html
htmllab2.html
htmllab3.html
htmllab3.old
htmllab4.html
htmllab4.old
htmllab5.html
htmllab5.old
htmllab6.html
htmllab7.html
226 Transfer complete.
remote: h*
164 bytes received in 0.027 seconds (5.9 Kbytes/s)
ftp>
```

Figure C.2 Listing files on the remote computer.

```
ftp> get htmllab4.html
200 PORT command successful.
150 Opening ASCII mode data connection for htmllab4.html (2325 bytes).
226 Transfer complete.
local: htmllab4.html remote: htmllab4.html
2362 bytes received in 0.0097 seconds (2.4e+02 Kbytes/s)
ftp> bin
200 Type set to I.
ftp> put htmllab4.html
200 PORT command successful.
150 Opening BINARY mode data connection for htmllab4.html.
226 Transfer complete.
local: htmllab4.html remote: htmllab4.html
2325 bytes sent in 0.0028 seconds (8.1e+02 Kbytes/s)
ftp>
```

Figure C.3 Downloading a file from a remote server.

is a bit more complex than the one in Figure C.2. First, the user issues a **get htmllab4.html.** The ftp program informs him that the file is 2325 bytes long. Then ftp begins to download the file. Since it is a rather small file, there was no need to turn on the hash function. Notice that the ftp program tells the user the name of the file on both the local and remote computers. Finally, all of 0.0097 seconds later, ftp reports that 2363 bytes have been downloaded. Hmmm, the file seems to have grown by 38 bytes in the download! Why? Ah, ha! Ttg forgot to set the transfer mode to *binary*! Even though the file is actually an ASCII file, as are all HTML files, the ftp program pads the file with some bytes of binary zeros to round things out. This won't make any difference in this case, as we will see in a moment.

This scenario serves only as an example of how to retrieve a file with ftp. Usually the user would do something to the file before putting it back. In this case nothing was done to the file, but ttg finally figured out that he should set the transfer mode to binary. That is the next line in the code. Then he sent the file back to the server with the **put** command. Notice that ftp moves exactly the right number of bytes this time.

This is the normal sequence of events using ftp. It is not a complex tool to use. The biggest problem most students have with ftp is figuring out where the files should come from or where they went when they were uploaded or downloaded. And that problem disappears with a little practice.

There are tools available that make the ftp process even more intuitive. One is called CuteFTP, a program designed to run under Microsoft Windows that creates a "point and click" ftp environment. CuteFTP is a very powerful program with lots of options. At this time, however, we will look at only the bare bones of this tool. CuteFTP is on the CD that comes with this text. It is also available for download from **www.cuteftp.com** with a 30-day trial. CuteFTP is shareware. If you use the product after the 30 days of free trial, you owe the author, GlobasSCAPE Inc., $34.00 to pay for the time and effort necessary to create this product.

The screen captures in Figures C.4 through C.8 show the steps in setting up and using CuteFTP. The first screen shows how to tell CuteFTP to find a particular computer. Here we set up a "way cool site" at IP address 123.123.123.123. (Note: this may or may not be a valid IP address; it is for demonstration purposes only. Don't try this at home. :-}) Notice that we can set the user ID and the secret password as well, so CuteFTP can go to the site and log in for us. In the box below UserID, we can set the radio button to use anonymous ftp if that is the type of site we intend to access.

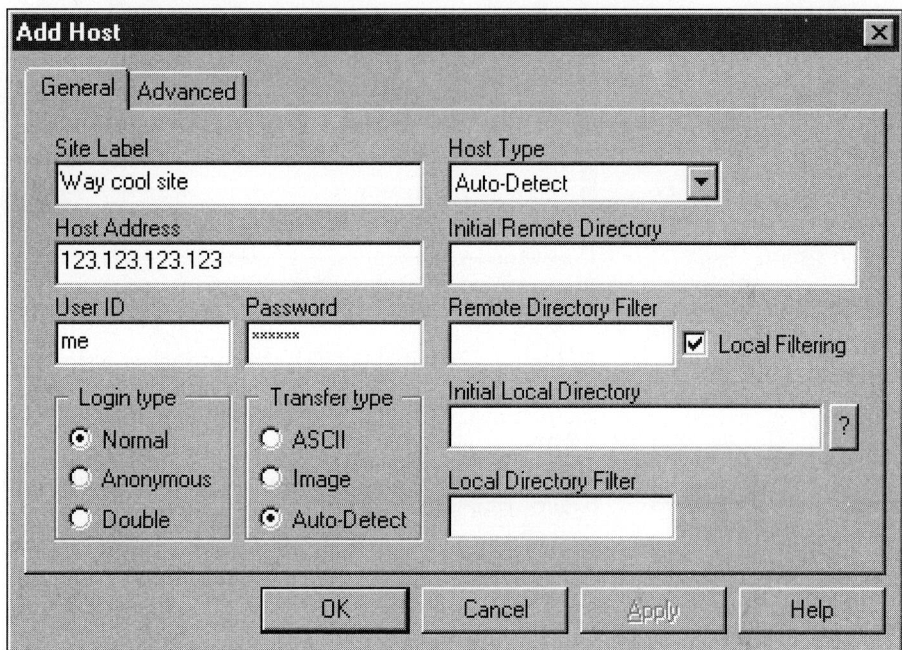

Figure C.4 Setting up an ftp site in CuteFTP.

Figure C.5 shows the first screen we normally see when starting CuteFTP. It allows us to select a site from a series of folders. When we click on that site, CuteFTP will connect us to it. In Figure C.6, CuteFTP has connected to phred, and we have clicked on the **web-pages** subdirectory to open that set of files. Notice that the interface is complete GUI. In this example we want to download a file from phred to our local computer.

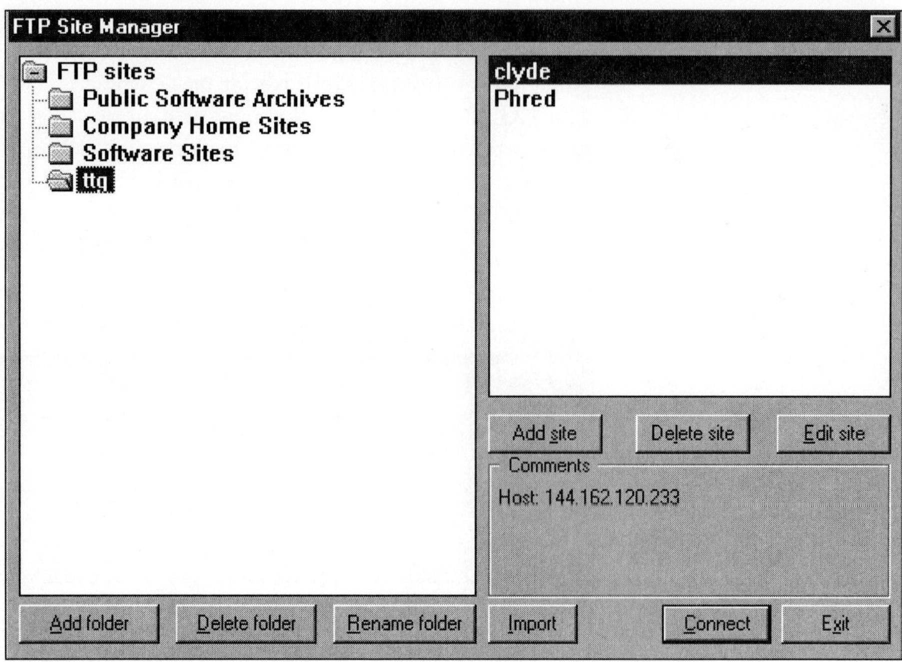

Figure C.5 The initial CuteFTP screen to select a site.

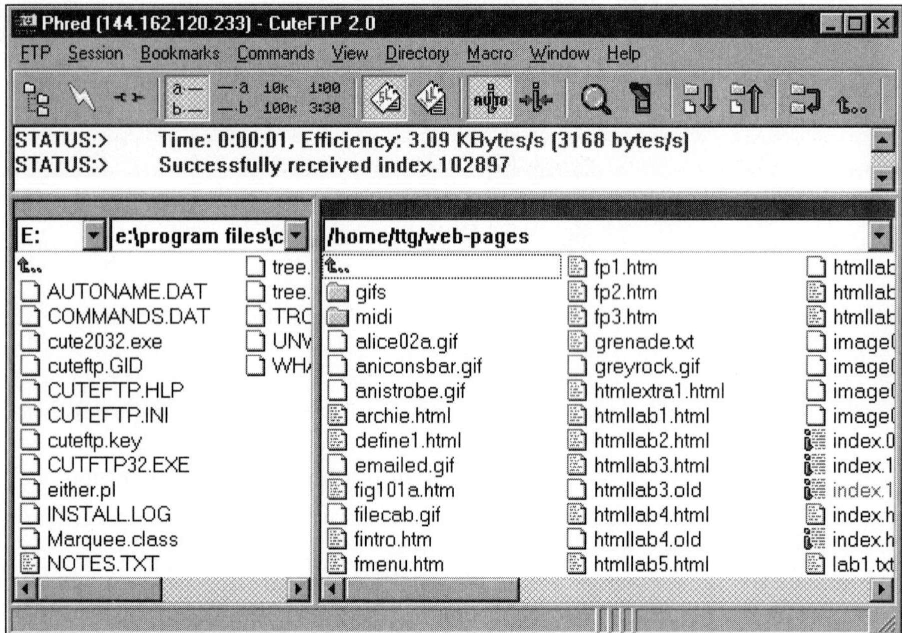

Figure C.6 Starting an ftp session after being connected by CuteFTP.

As Figure C.7 shows, the file we want to download is a syllabus file from the server. To download, we simply double-click on the filename. If we click on the server side, CuteFTP will download the file to our PC. If we click on the local side (left), CuteFTP will upload the file to the server. It really makes the ftp process simple.

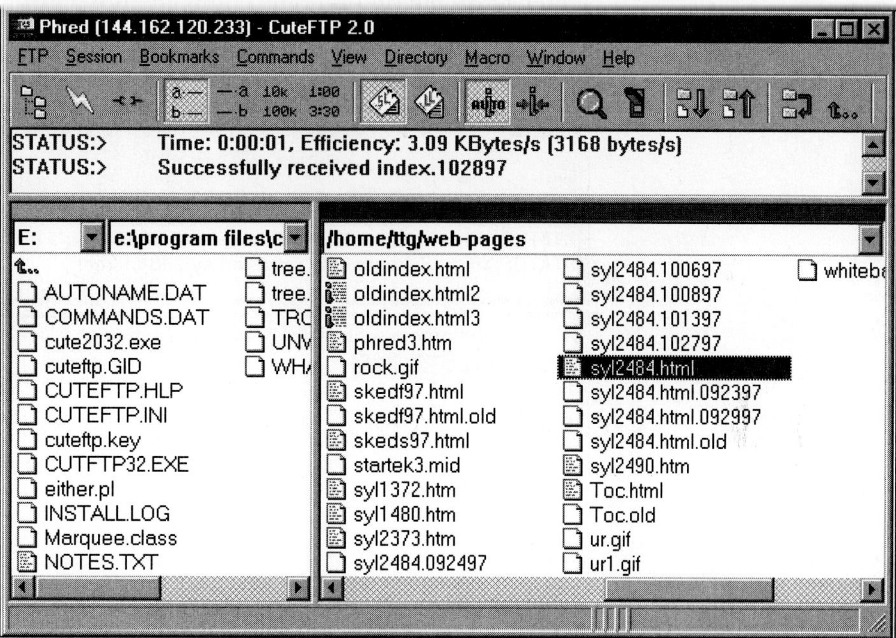

Figure C.7 Selecting a file to download.

In Figure C.8, CuteFtp has successfully downloaded the file from the server to our PC in 5 seconds—not as fast as the ftp example earlier, but in that example the two computers were directly linked to the Internet. Here CuteFTP was working over a dial-up connection.

Programs like CuteFTP make it much easier to move files across the Net. Even a hard-core UNIX bigot like your humble author owns a copy of CuteFTP to use on his home computer. It is a great tool that makes ftping much easier.

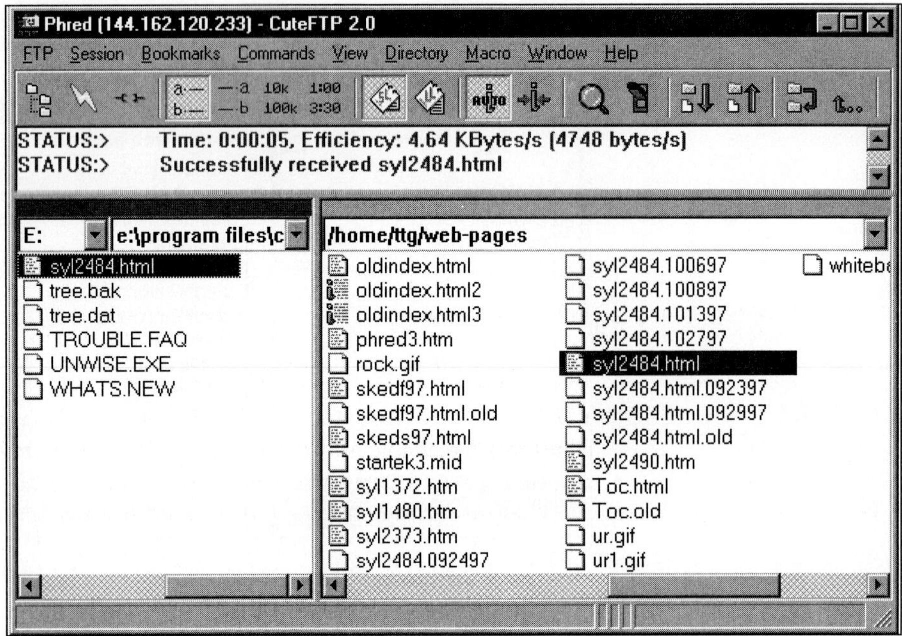

Figure C.8 File successfully downloaded.

appendix D
style guide

Style—we all feel we have it when we are building our pages, and our pages always look good to us. But there are some guidelines that will make your Web pages more readable and more usable. Or, as Robert Burton (1576–1640) said, "It is most true [that] *stylus virum arguit,* our style bewrays us."

These style guidelines—and they are just that, guidelines not rules—come to you from a number of different sources. First, they reflect the page-design experience of the author of this textbook, plus the experiences of his students. Some of these student endeavors worked, and some serve as good examples of what not to do.

Second, these guidelines come from many different style guides found across the Net. They are too numerous to mention, but a collection of some URLs that served as resources appears at the end of this section. Third, these guidelines were derived from rants and raves of many users who have written in mail groups, left messages, and generally made their feelings clear about what they like and don't like about different sites.

General Guidelines

• **Be consistent.** Consistency is critical. Decide on things such as how you are going to use headings, what colors will mean, how site navigation will be accomplished, and then stick with that design across all your pages. In addition, use consistent images when you mean the same thing, and use a consistent background to tie all your pages together (or use a different but consistent background to identify related collections of pages.) Use the same navigational controls on all your pages.

• **Always design for both graphical and nongraphical browsers.** All the world doesn't use a graphical browser, so if you want your information to be accessible to all users, design your pages to be accessible to nongraphical browsers. In fact, in large areas of the world, most folks depend on fast, small, text-only browsers. Always look at your page in Lynx or another text-only browser to see what it looks like. One site recently visited looked like this in Lynx:

[LINK]

[LINK]

[LINK] [LINK] [LINK]

[LINK]

That is not very helpful, now, is it?

- **Don't try to be "slick."** Fancy, powerful, animated images and applets are wonderful toys, but most users don't appreciate a page full of distracting elements that get in the way of finding what they need on your page. Creating pages that use the very latest Web technology will probably be of value only to the minority of users who are on the cutting edge. For the majority of users, your innovations will either be invisible, at best, or render your page useless, at worst. Don't design pages to simply show off how complex you can make a page. Always remember that your primary goal should be to create a page that enables users to efficiently and enjoyably find the information they seek.
- **Use big pages and images only when necessary.** Size *is* important! Big, slow-to-load pages do not reflect good design. If you need to display a large image, put it on a page by itself, and give the user a link to that page. Make sure you tell the user how big the image is and how long it may take to download. Your home page should download very quickly. A good rule of thumb is to keep your home page with all its images smaller than 1 megabyte of disk space. That way it will be relatively quick to download. A good test is to link to your page from a browser connected through a modem, and see if you can hold your breath until your page fully loads. If you can't, consider making the page smaller.
- **Maintain your page!** If you have spent the time to create a page, you need to ensure that all the links on that page work and that the other elements of the page are correct. Plan to spend some time each week checking your page. It is always more fun to create new content for your pages, but your users deserve to find a good, useful, accurate page when they make the effort and take the time to come to your site. Make sure your links work and that the information you put on your page is accurate.
- **Don't change the colors of the linking text unless your design absolutely forces you to.** If that happens, look long and hard at your design before changing these colors. It might be better to change your design. Coding ALINK, LINK, and VLINK attributes for different colors than the defaults can confuse your users. Even though the default colors are not necessarily the very best, and there may be good arguments for changing them, users still expect unvisited links to be blue and visited links to be purple. Stick with that color scheme whenever possible.
- **Use background images with care.** A background image will, without a doubt, interfere to some extent with the readability of your page. Use background images when necessary, but know that you will be reducing, albeit slightly in some cases, the readability of the text on your page.

• **Use light backgrounds with dark text when you can.** They are easier to read than dark backgrounds with light text. If you doubt this, ask yourself if it is easier to drive a car during the day or at night. Dark backgrounds make seeing more difficult. In addition, white text on a dark background will not usually print out if the user tries to print your page. White text doesn't show up well on a white page!

• **Use color sparingly.** Color is a powerful tool, but too much color on a page is worse than no color. Color can focus the attention of your user, or it can distract from the content. One of the glaring mistakes that novice Web weavers make is to create pages that are a veritable riot of colors. Bright colors for text and background, color images, initial caps in a contrasting color to the rest of the text, color, color, color everywhere. Those pages are visually brutal to view and downright difficult to read. Subtle use of color is always better than the assault on the senses employed by some Web weavers.

• **Always provide a way for the user to get in touch with you.** You will want your users to be able to tell you of problems they found or give you kudos for things they liked. Your address should be on your home page or on the main page of a collection. This way, since all the other pages will have navigation links back to the home page or to the central link for a series of pages, the user can always get to the page with your address by means of the **mailto:** link. Make sure that the mailto link is documented as well. A cute, animated GIF is nice, but it is invisible in a text-only browser.

• **Cross-link all the pages in your site.** Avoid dead-end paths that force users to use the "Back" button on their browser. If you have a worthwhile page, someone will bookmark it. When she comes back to your page using a bookmark, she will need to be able to move back to the rest of your site. She must have a set of navigation tools to do that. One of the more useful tools is a small one-row table at the bottom (or top) of each page that contains links around your site.

• **Date your pages.** Always include the date on your pages so your user knows when the site was last updated. For example, it does him no good to have a site that lists all the important astronomical events for 1994. It might be interesting in a historical context, but not of much interest to the user who is trying to find out when to look for the next Perseid meteor shower.

You owe it to your readers to date your page. Besides, it may encourage you to keep your page up to date if the time of your last update is noted there for everyone to see. Along this same line, when you put the date on your page, use the formal style of "Last updated March 4, 1998" rather than "Last updated 03/04/98." Why? Because in Europe that date means April third, not March fourth. (Europeans place the day number first, then the month number.)

• **Don't have several links to the same content on the same page.** It is horribly confusing for your user to see links to *interesting material,* more *interesting material,* even more *interesting material,* all of which point to exactly the same page. In fact, you should beware of using too many links as a general principle. A page that is filled with too many links of any type can be very confusing for the user. Link to important sites, but don't overdo the links—unless you are creating a page of links, that is. A page of links is usually not a good use for a Web page, but in specialized cases it can be useful. If you are going to have a page of links, consider putting them in a table to better arrange them for your user.

• **Make sure your page is unique.** Okay, this sounds like a social issue, not a style issue, but your page should exist only if it supplies some unique content to the Net. It is not sufficient to be a page of links, or a page of quotes from other pages, or a page of images, ahem, "borrowed" from other sites. Your page should provide something unique to the world. If it doesn't, why should it take up space on the Net? Perhaps the only thing unique about your page is your history, your vision, and a collection of your holiday pictures. Well, let's forget that last bit—but the first two items are reason enough to create a Web page. No one else has your exact history and vision.

The point is, your page should provide something new to the Web, something that is available only on your pages. Without that, all the rest of these issues become merely smoke.

Looking at the HEAD

• **Use a title, and make it a meaningful one.** Often the title is all a potential user has to go on to determine if she wants to go to your page. Make your title descriptive and accurate. A good title is usually less than 50 characters long. Remember, if users save your page in a Bookmarks file, your title is the description that will be stored to help them find your page again.

• **Include <META> tags that contain complete and accurate data.** An example of a good <META> tag follows:

<META NAME="KEYWORDS" CONTENT="Keywords like style guide, excellent>

These tags help indexing packages like Alta Vista search your page and create accurate links to it. The list of keywords will often be displayed by the search engine as well.

In the BODY

• **Use headings in level order.** <H1> headings are important, main ideas. <H2> should come next, then <H3>, and so on. Always use headings in order. Don't skip a level unless your design forces you to. And if it does, consider changing your design.

• **Don't pad your page with blank lines.** Use other text-dividing tools. If you need a little more space between lines, use a paragraph container instead of inserting extra
s to create blank lines. Never have more than two
s in a row.

• **Leave your eyepatch and Jolly Roger at home when you cruise the Web and when you design and code Web pages.** There are a plethora of wonderful images and applets and animated GIFs and backgrounds out there that people have spent a great deal of time and effort to create. Don't pirate them for your site. Take only those that are clearly marked as free, and always give credit to the site where you found them.

• **Don't link to images or multimedia across the Net unless the owner of the site requires it.** Linking will slow the loading of your page and create additional congestion on the Net as well. Always harvest the images or other resources you are going to use and host them locally. Of course, you must have permission from the owner of the resource before you harvest it.

- **Be careful about the content of your pages.** In the United States we have the Constitution to protect our right to free speech. This is not a universal right. Some countries restrict the content of any material allowed across their borders. In addition, many organizations and parents are beginning to use blocking software to limit access to sites on the Net. If you have valuable content to share—and why else would you have a Web page—you don't want access to your site blocked because you have used offensive language or graphics. If you are compelled to use language or graphics that a significant portion of your audience may find offensive, put it on a page or pages of its own, and tell your users what they are linking to. Remember, as well, that unless you own your own Internet feed, the computer that is hosting your page, and all of the content on that page, somebody else may feel responsible for what you post.
- **Put equal spacing between elements of equal importance.** Add extra spacing between elements that are of distinct categories.
- **Use horizontal rules to separate different elements on the page.** Horizontal rules, <HR>, provide a good visual break. But don't code them with too large a SIZE attribute. It is also considered bad form to code more than one <HR> in succession.
- **Keep your pages to a reasonable length.** There is great debate on what is a "reasonable" length for a page. It is like when Abraham Lincoln was asked how long should a man's leg be, and he gave the famous reply, "Long enough to reach the ground." Your Web page should be long enough to reach the ground too. Hmmm . . . okay, how long would that be? How about long enough to cover the concept or idea you are presenting? If the page is too short, the user wastes time waiting for it to paint up. (However, sometimes it is an excellent idea to have small pages that serve as footnotes to your larger page.) If the page is too long, users may not want to view all of it. There is some evidence that most users will not scroll down more than one or at the most two screens on a page. That is a good measure for your home page, as well as for index pages or pages at the head of a set. Yet, it makes little sense to break up the posting of a scientific paper that runs to 15 screens just for the sake of brevity. If you are putting a book on the Net, it is usually a good idea to break it down by chapters, or even by large sections, but you shouldn't break it into 20 line chunks and force your reader to flip from page to page to follow your narrative. The proper length, then, is dependent on the use to which the page is put. But it should always be long enough to reach the ground.
- **Always have a table of contents for your site.** If you have a complex site with several different areas of interest, try to have a main table of contents (TOC) that links to the sublevel TOCs. That way your user can navigate about your site more easily. Each page should have a link back to the sublevel TOC at a minimum. It is better to also have a link to the main TOC. A series of pages should have links from each one to the next. It makes little sense to force the user to bounce back to the TOC to see each successive page of a document. The pages should have "next" and "back" links to help the user navigate.

• **Test your page with the Lynx browser.** Lynx is available for download to your server (check with your systems manager) or available to use from several sites. The Web page for this book has a link to Lynx in case you can't find one closer to home.

• **Print your page.** This sounds like a really simple test, but it is sometimes amazing how bad a page can look when printed. A good Web weaver will always consider the printed version of her page even though the Web is designed to save trees.

• **Always indicate the status of your page.** Some pages are created for a specific purpose and require no updating. You should tell your user when the data on your pages are final versions and not subject to revision. On the other hand, most pages are constantly under revision. If that is the case, tell the user so, and give him some idea as to when the next update will happen. However, don't use the cute "under construction" GIFs or, worse, the "under construction" *animated* GIFs. Everybody knows that everyone's pages are almost always "under construction"; you don't need to include those ugly graphics.

• **Always use the shortest URL you can get away with when referencing pages within your site.** Remember that the browser will complete the left portion of the URL if you allow it to. Use relative URLs whenever possible.

• **Don't use <BLINK>!** There really isn't any compelling reason to, now is there?

• **Pay attention to the people who take the time to write to you with complaints about your page.** For every one that writes, there will have been dozens who left your page in frustration.

Language and Writing

• **Write in gender-neutral language whenever possible.** For example, the line

"A wise Web weaver always checks **his/her** links."

is gender-neutral but seems clunky, obvious, and interrupts the text flow. A better choice might be

"Wise Web weavers always check **their** links."

• **Spell-check your pages!**

• **Proofread your pages.** A spell-checker can only check spelling. As you cruise the Web, you will notice sites where the Web weaver did use a spell-checker but probably never reread the page. Eye yam shore ewe no thee kinks of problems eye yam tanking abut! My spell-checker had *no* problem with the preceding line.

• **Make sure the text within an <A> container explains the target of the link.** Remember, some text-only browsers display link text just like any other text, so the explanation is critical.

• **Avoid regional slang.** You are writing for an international audience, and using slang can cause serious problems for non-native speakers of your language. As regional dialects continue to evolve, non-native speakers may include people from the other half of your country as well as folks from outside your national borders.

• **Don't use the phrase "click here."** Not only is the effect obnoxious, but the phrase assumes the user has a mouse. Don't use it.

• **Try to avoid politically inflammatory, racist, or religiously biased language on your page.** If you feel compelled to use any of this kind of language, put it on pages that your users can choose to link to, and be sure to tell users what they are linking to. For example:

> These are my *feelings* about the UNIX operating system. Note: I'm a UNIX bigot!

That line tells users that they will be linking to a page that is probably a pro-UNIX rant. If they don't want to read it, they don't have to. Don't put rants on your home page, forcing users to see them when they first come to your page.

Some Style-Guide URLs

The following sites contained style guides at the time this book was written. With the rate of change on the Net, some of these sites will have disappeared by the time you read this. However, other sites will have come online. Searching with a search engine like Alta Vista or HotBot will allow you to find others.

www.mcs.net/~jorn/html/net/checklist.html
www.useit.com/alertbox/9612.html
www.sun.com/960416/columns/alertbox/index.html
www.tlc-systems.com/webtips.shtml
www.sysmag.com/web/html-style.html
www.w3.org/Provider/Style/All.html

The most important thing you must do as a Web weaver is be considerate of your users, first, last, always, and design your pages for them.

appendix E

cougar, html 4.0 specifications

As Melissa Etheridge says in the song "Change" on her *Your Little Secret* CD, "The only thing that stays the same is change." That seems to be true of HTML. It continues to grow and change and expand. At the time of this writing, the most recent standard is a new specification called **COUGAR.** The copy I am using was released on December 18, 1997 and is 258 pages long. Based on this release of the standard, it looks as if the changes discussed in this appendix were implemented. It is another example of the growth of HTML since it was first created way back in 1989. There may be an update by the time you read this, or there may even be a new standard. Read the actual specifications and see proposals for new changes at **http://www.w3.org.** The W3 Consortium are the folks in charge of standardizing HTML. They are led by researchers at MIT (Massachusetts Institute of Technology), CERN (European Laboratory for Particle Physics), and INRA (French National Institute for Research in Computer Science and Control). It is well worth bookmarking the W3 Consortium page and dropping in once in a while to see what is new in the world of HTML.

Here, then, is an overview of the proposed new standard.

Deprecated Tags

Almost every release of HTML deprecates some tags. COUGAR deprecates those in the following list. While these tags will still work, the new specification recommends that they no longer be used.

<APPLET>	<BASEFONT>
<CENTER>	<DIR>
<FONT>	<ISINDEX>
<MENU>	<STRIKE>
<S>	<U>

The function of several of these tags is being replaced by a new way of handling the layout, text, and colors of pages. In most cases, using the new construct called **style sheets** (discussed later in this appendix) is the recommended way to accomplish the same functions. In the case of the <APPLET> tag, COUGAR identifies the <OBJECT> container as the way to include dynamic code to enable the page to respond to the user. Java applets are still a very useful and powerful part of the Web; there are just different ways to invoke them.

Obsolete Tags

COUGAR suggests that the three tags listed next be considered obsolete—no longer supported by browsers that are in strict compliance with the standard. It is proposed that existing pages with these tags be updated to eliminate them and that no new pages include them.

<LISTING>
<PLAINTEXT>
<XMP>

These tags were deprecated in a previous version of the HTML standards. Now they are to be considered obsolete.

New Tags

There are several new tags in the COUGAR specification. They add new functionality to our pages, and they reflect a change in the direction that HTML is going. To quote section 2.2 of the specifications,

> HTML 4.0 extends HTML with mechanisms for style sheets, scripting, frames, embedding objects, improved support for right to left and mixed direction text, richer tables, and enhancements to forms, offering improved accessibility for people with disabilities.

The most significant change seems to be the inclusion of style sheets. This topic is addressed in the next section. Other than styles, the following are the new tags proposed as additions to the set:

<ACRONYM>—allows authors to specify that a particular group of letters, like WWW, is indeed an acronym. This new tag also provides a place to list the expansion of the acronym. For example:

```
<ACRONYM TITLE="World Wide Web">WWW</ACRONYM>
```

<BUTTON>—allows the creation of a new type of button. If the value is either SUBMIT or RESET, this button behaves like the <INPUT TYPE=SUBMIT> or <INPUT TYPE=RESET> input areas currently available in forms. However, this new tag also can trigger a client-side script if its type is <BUTTON>.

<COLGROUP>—gives the author the ability to set the width of a column and the number of columns that are grouped into this column group. In HTML 3.2, a column in a table was always defined by the widest cell in that column. COLGROUP allows the author to specify the vertical and horizontal alignments of data within the cells of the grouped row(s).

<DEL>—used to mark up text that has been deleted in a different version of a document. This container is the opposite of the <INS> container.

<FIELDSET>—allows the author to group related fields in a form to create a thematically related group of data input elements. The <LEGEND> tag establishes a caption for the <FIELDSET>.

<INS>—used to mark up text that has been inserted in a different version of a document. This container is the opposite of the <DEL> container.

<LEGEND>—used to create a caption on a <FIELDSET>. <LEGEND> can be placed above, below, on the right, or on the left of the <FIELDSET>.

<Q>—provides a new way to indicate short, inline quotations. <BLOCKQUOTE> is still available for longer quotes that should be indented, but the <Q> container is designed for short quotations that don't require a paragraph break.

Table Changes

The new standard proposes many changes to tables, some of which have been eagerly awaited by Web weavers. One proposed change would allow alignment of the cell data on characters like the decimal point and the colon. In another change, the body of long tables, <TBODY>, would be scrollable between a fixed head, <THEAD>, and/or a fixed footer, <TFOOT>. This way the data would always be presented below a descriptive header that would stay in the browser window and/or above a descriptive footer that would also stay in the browser window.

The new standard would give the Web weaver greater control over the frames and rules that divide the cells in the table. Like many other elements in the proposed standard, tables would be defined by a style sheet specifying many layout, alignment, and coloring features. Style sheets are going to be very important in HTML 4.0 and beyond.

Forms Changes

Many changes and enhancements are proposed for forms in the new standard. The specifications speak of the "controls" in a form that respond to and accept user input. The <BUTTON> is an example of a new control. One significant proposed change would deprecate the GET method. The proposal states that this method is being deprecated "for reasons of internationalization" but would still be supported for backward compatibility. The new standard also proposes deprecating the <ISINDEX> element in favor of the <INPUT TYPE="TEXT"> element.

A new attribute proposed to be added to many of the controls is DISABLED, which would turn off the action of the control. This attribute could be useful during development of a form. It could also be used to limit the use of some controls on some versions of an existing form. The <FIELDSET> and <LEGEND> elements described earlier are two other new attributes proposed.

The new specifications propose that forms have direct keyboard access, providing the page with a way to react to control key sequences (like control-C) by moving from field to field. In addition, Web weavers could mark a field as "read-only" and thereby prevent the user from changing its contents.

Style Sheets

One of the most significant changes in the proposed new specifications are style sheets. Style sheets will begin to change the mantra you have heard throughout this book, "The Web weaver controls the content; the BROWSER controls the format." The major reason for style sheets seems to be to give the Web weaver greater control over the placement and appearance of various elements on the page. Style sheets also give the Web weaver the ability to create aural entries on the page.

A significant tenet of the proposed standard is to provide greater accessibility to users who have some sort of sensory limitation. Throughout the proposed specifications Web weavers are cautioned to include descriptions with images, tables, and other visually oriented constructs that are not of value to visually impaired users or users with nongraphical browsers. Style sheets are composed of **rules** that define specific elements of the document. These rules are placed in the head of the document to which the style sheet applies. A rule is composed of two main parts: a selector and a declaration. Each declaration has two parts as well: the property and the value to be assigned to that property. A selector can have one or more declarations. An example of a cascading style of rule with three different declarations is

```
H1 { font-family: Helvetica;
     color: blue;
     font-size 120% }
```

This rule specifies that all <H1> (header level 1) elements be displayed in the Helvetica font, in a blue color, and with a font size 20 percent larger than the font currently in use. In the parlance of the specification, **H1** is the selector; and

font-family, color, and **font-size** are all properties of declarations. **Helvetica, blue,** and **120%** are the corresponding values. With this style in the cascading style sheet for a document, all the headers at level 1 would have the same appearance.

HTML 4.0 will not require the Web weaver to create style sheets, because each browser or user agent will have a default style sheet defined. However, by using style sheets, the wise Web weaver will have control of about 100 properties that can determine the presentation of a document. This new specification, when finally adopted, will provide us with some powerful new tools to better design our pages.

glossary

Absolute path—also called absolute URL, the complete description of the path to a resource.

Absolute width—width measured in pixels. *See also* Relative width.

Abstract Window Toolkit (AWT)—includes user interface features like windows, dialog boxes, buttons, checkboxes, menus, scroll bars, lists, and text fields.

Abstraction—results from taking the essential characteristics out of an object and creating data to represent those characteristics.

AIFC—*See* AIFF Compressed Format (AIFC).

AIFF—*See* Audio Interchange File Format (AIFF).

AIFF Compressed Format (AIFC)—sound format developed by Apple because AIFF required so much storage space. Compression is lossy.

American Standard Code for Information Interchange (ASCII)—standard for representing text in a machine; understood by most machines. *See also* Text file.

Analog sound—sound in which values flow from one to another continuously.

Anonymous ftp—allows use of ftp without entering password; user gives "anonymous" as the login ID.

Applet viewer—allows user to view applets without a browser.

ASCII—*See* American Standard Code for Information Interchange (ASCII).

ASCII editor—produces an ASCII file without the embedded special codes produced by a word processor.

Attributes—HTML elements that modify tags.

Audio Interchange File Format (AIFF)—sound format developed by Apple and used most often by Macintosh and Silicon Graphics to store high-end audio data. It has uncompressed format, and it supports stereo.

Audio/Video Interleave (AVI)—provided by Internet Explorer for inline movies.

AVI—*See* Audio Video Interleave (AVI).

AWT—*See* Abstract Window Toolkit (AWT).

Base URL—the URL of the page that invokes an applet (unless the BASE attribute is coded).

Baseline—imaginary line that runs across the bottom of the text letters, not including descenders.

Binary file—file of machine-readable code.

Bits per pixel (bpp)—determines the number of colors in an image.

Bits per second (bps)—a measure of modem speed.

BMP—standard Microsoft Windows image format usually created by Paintbrush program and used for the wallpaper in Windows. It supports 1, 4, 8, and 24 bits per pixel. It is usually not compressed.

Bpp—*See* Bits per pixel (bpp).

Bps—*See* Bits per second (bps).

Browser—software that translates the HTML codes into a presentation on the screen; used to cruise the World Wide Web.

Browser pane—the part of the screen that is normally visible to the user.

Bulleted list—list with items bulleted instead of numbered or lettered.

Buttons—elements that perform some action when activated.

Bytecode—intermediate code between Java source code and actual executable code that can be run by a specific processor. Bytecode is generated by a Java compiler.

Bytecode verifier—checks to make sure that bytecode is a valid Java class and follows all the rules of correctly formed Java.

Cache—to store in memory.

Call—request for a program.

Calling document—page that contains the link that brings up a search page or other document.

Cards—HyperCard pages.

Carriage-return line feed (CrLf)—starts a new line of text.

Cell—intersection of a row and column in a table.

CGI script—a program written in any one of several popular languages, most often Perl, to process data sent from an HTML form.

Checkboxes—type of input item that allows a user to make more than one selection, usually by clicking on a box.

Child class—a subclass in object-oriented programming; allows inheritance.

Class—template, or model, for specifying the state and behavior of an object at run time (in object-oriented programming).

Class file—bytecode file.

Class loader—moves the class into a specialized name space that controls where the code is placed and what it can do.

Client software—program that is resident on your computer but interacts with other programs or data across the Net.

Client-side map—image map controlled by client rather than server.

Comments—documentation of choices made in a program, with explanations of those choices.

Common Gateway Interface (CGI)—program that passes data sent in on a form to the program written to handle it.

Compiler—program that translates higher-language programs into machine language.

Containers—used to modify the contents placed within them. They consist of a beginning and closing tag that surround the contents.

Content—what a document says versus how a document looks (layout).

Content-based style—*See* Logical style.

CrLf—*See* Carriage-return line feed (CrLf).

Default value—the choice that the program will make for you if you fail to specify a value.

Definition list—list formatted like a dictionary or glossary.

Delayed binding—choosing the correct method to handle an object at run time.

DHTML—*See* Dynamic HTML (DHTML).

Digital sound—sound in which values are represented by numbers rather than by a continuous stream.

Digital video—created by capturing analog video at regular intervals and saving each capture as a distinct image called a *frame*. Frames can then be played back to give the appearance of motion, that is, to create a movie. Digital video files may have audio tracks associated with the frames.

Direct call—retrieving a file by name.

Discrete data—data represented by numbers (digital data).

Distributed program—runs on computers across the Internet—for example, an HTML browser.

Dithering—replacing one uniform color with repeating patterns of other colors that approximate the initial color, or blending two colors to create a third color. Dithering can reduce compressibility.

DNS—*See* Domain Name Server (DNS).

Document—the HTML code for a page.

Domain Name Server (DNS)—program that translates domain names into IP addresses.

Domain name—substitutes for the numeric IP address; an alphabetic name, such as "WWW.McGraw-Hill.com."

Domain—the computer that runs the server software.

Downloading—copying a computer-readable file from another computer to your computer.

Driver—master document that builds the frames of a framed document.

Dublin Metadata Core Element Set (Dublin Core)—one standard for the META tags.

Dynamic content—refers to the spectrum of active features, including images, sound, animation, and interactivity.

Dynamic document—document with active features that could include images, sound, animation, and interactivity.

Dynamic HTML (DHTML)—provides the capacity to perform some of the animation features formerly available only through Java.

Empty tag—a tag that does not have a closing tag associated with it; for example, <BR>.

Encapsulation—feature of object-oriented programming in which data and the operations necessary to manipulate those data are collected together into a usable module.

Executable file—binary file.

Extended class—child class or subclass in object-oriented programming; feature of inheritance.

Extends—inherits all the features of the existing class.

File Transfer Protocol (ftp)—software used to move files across the Net.

Firewall—program that protects security of networked computers.

Floating image—an image that can be placed (in either margin) by the browser.

Floating-point number—a number with a decimal point.

Flood filling—creating a large colored area by using HEIGHT and WIDTH attributes to expand a very small image across the screen.

Form—an HTML document, or part of an HTML document, that allows the user to provide input to a CGI script for processing.

Frame (1)—created by capturing analog video at regular intervals and saving each capture as a distinct image. Frames can be played back to create a movie.

Frame (2)—one section of a framed document, one part of a <FRAMESET>.

Ftp—*See* File Transfer Protocol (ftp).

GIF—*See* Graphic Interchange Format (GIF).

Graphic Interchange Format (GIF)—most common image format on the Web, supporting 8-bit color and having lossless compression. The three types of GIF are plain, transparent, and animated.

Graphical user interface (GUI)—program that uses images to facilitate users' selections of commands.

Grep—(Global Regular Expression Print) a UNIX tool that searches in a file or files for a specified string.

GUI—*See* Graphical user interface (GUI).

Harvest—to collect resources from the Net, most often used to refer to the collection of images, sounds, or applets.

Hierarchical—structure in which larger parts are composed of smaller parts.

Home page—the highest level page on a Web site.

Hot spots—areas in image maps that can be selected to invoke associated HTML documents.

HREF—*See* Hypertext reference (HREF).

HTML—*See* HyperText Markup Language (HTML).

HTML author—the person who creates or weaves a Web page.

HTML editor—produces HTML code.

HTML text-file converter—converts existing ASCII or word-processor files to HTML code.

HTML verifier—software that makes sure your links are valid and your HTML syntax and grammar are correct.

Http—Hyper Text Transport Protocol, the protocol used to send HTML documents across the Net.

Hyper document—document that contains links.

Hypertext document—document that contains links to other resources, usually written in HTML.

HyperText Markup Language (HTML)—the tool used to build Web pages; not a true programming language.

Hypertext reference (HREF)—a required attribute of the LINK tag; it points to some valid http address.

Image map—image that serves as a map in that users can click on various parts (links) of the image to retrieve information. There are two types: server-side maps and client-side maps.

Inheritance—feature of object-oriented programming in which one class can receive data structures and methods or procedures from a previous class.

Integer—a whole number, without a decimal point.

Intellectual property—material resulting from ideas, or mental processes; usually protected by a copyright.

Interactivity—exists when the user can input information to a page and receive a response. Java provides a degree of interactivity that allows users to play games, live, on the Net.

Internet Protocol (IP) address—numeric address assigned to each machine on the Internet. Consists of four sets of one, two, or three digits separated by periods. *See also* Domain name.

Internet Service Provider (ISP)—company that specializes in providing World Wide Web access.

Interpreter—translates source code into binary code, one line at a time.

Intranet—computer network like the Internet except that it contains only the computers of a specific company.

Intrapage link—link within a single document or page.

IP address—*See* Internet Protocol (IP) address.

ISP—*See* Internet Service Provider (ISP).

Java—programming language that uses object-oriented techniques, works across the Internet, is translated line by line, is safe and hard to crash, runs on many different computer platforms, and does powerful things quickly.

Java applet—small program that serves as an extension to an HTML document, providing visual and other effects, including animation. Applets are a subset of Java. They are called from an HTML program and run on a browser.

Java compiler—translates Java source code into bytecode; called Javac.

Java development kit (JDK)—includes a Java compiler (Javac), Java bytecode interpreter to run stand-alone programs, a Java debugging tool, and an applet viewer.

Java script—specialized programming language for building programs that are embedded in an HTML document and perform simple tasks; not related to Java. Java script gives the HTML programmer tools such as looping and conditional statements.

Java Virtual Machine—Java interpreter.

Javac—Java compiler.

JDK—*See* Java development kit (JDK).

Joint Photographic Experts Group (JPEG)—image format on the Web that supports 8-bit and 24-bit color and is available on all browsers. Compression is lossy. "Progressive" JPEGs create an effect similar to an animated GIF.

JPEG—*See* Joint Photographic Experts Group (JPEG).

Just-in-time programming—involves multithreading, in which a program can start running before all of it is downloaded.

kHz—*See* Kilohertz (kHz).

Kilohertz (kHz)—a thousand samples per second.

Late binding—choosing the correct method to handle an object at run time.

Latin-1 character set—list of common letters, numbers, symbols, and punctuation marks used in Western languages, each with a numeric value and some also with names; designed by the International Standards Organization (ISO).

Layout—how a document looks versus what it says (content).

Link—specially marked place on the screen that will cause something to happen when you activate it. Links can open another HTML document, move you to another place in the current document, display a picture, play a sound, or run a video clip.

Links—elements that perform some action when clicked with mouse button or activated by some other means.

Local action buttons—buttons that cause the browser to perform specific actions on the client computer instead of involving the CGI script on the server.

Logical style—describes the way the text within a container is used.

Lossless compression—compression that keeps all the data bits in the image so that image or sound quality does not degrade.

Lossy compression—compression in which some pixels are discarded, causing image or sound quality to degrade.

Lynx—the most common text-only browser.

Mailto—the electronic mail (e-mail) address used as a link in HTML documents.

Marquee—display of animated (moving) text.

MIME—*See* Multipurpose Internet Mail Extensions (MIME).

Modular—self-contained.

Monaural sound—single-channel sound as opposed to multiple-channel (stereo).

Monospaced font—font in which each letter takes up the same amount of space. *See also* Proportionally spaced font.

Movie—digital video file, sometimes accompanied by audio file. *See also* Audio/Video Interleave (AVI).

Moving Picture Experts Group (MPEG)—video or audio format with the best compression algorithms, providing high-quality online files.

MPEG—*See* Moving Picture Experts Group (MPEG).

Mu-law (μ-law)—sound file originally developed for UNIX, now an international standard for compression of voice-quality audio, supported by almost all operating systems. Does not support stereo. Extension is "au."

Multimedia—includes sound, pictures, and animation.

Multipurpose Internet Mail Extensions (MIME)—tells the browser what kind of file is being sent across the Net.

Multithreading—allows a program to start running before all of it is downloaded or to perform several actions at the same time.

Nesting lists—lists within lists; lists with sublists.

Netcology—conservation of Net resources; coined from the term *ecology*.

Newline—term used in UNIX to describe a carriage-return line feed.

Object—basic unit of object-oriented programming. Each object is an instance of a class; it has a state and a behavior.

Object instance—a particular occurrence or use of a class (in object-oriented programming).

Object-oriented programming (OOP)—building programs using object-oriented constructs and design.

OOP—*See* Object-oriented programming (OOP).

Open standard—a standard that is still developing; anyone is free to use it.

Ordered list—list with items numbered or lettered.

Overloading polymorphism—where several methods within the same class have exactly the same name but each has a different number, or type of parameter, so that the compiler can tell them apart.

Overriding polymorphism—where a method is defined in a parent class (superclass) and a child class (or subclass).

Package—set of directory names, starting from the URL, with each element of the package separated from the others by a dot.

Page—what you see when a document is displayed on your screen by a browser.

Parameters—attributes that give the Web weaver some control over applets.

Parent class—a superclass in object-oriented programming; feature of inheritance.

Parent window—the window containing the hypertext reference.

Parse—to divide into component parts.

Path—set of directory names that lead to a specific document.

PCX—image format on the Web that was developed by Zsoft for the PC Paintbrush program. Supports 1, 4, 8, and 24 bits per pixel but does not seem to support compression.

PDF—(Portable Data Format) image format on the Web that is created with a special software package called Acrobat from Adobe. PDF documents look like a magazine page, with multiple columns. PDF documents support "on page" searching.

Perl—highlevel programming language often used to write CGI scripts.

Physical style—describes the way the text within a container looks in a browser.

Pixel—stands for "picture element"; one of the many tiny dots that make up the display on your screen.

Platform—describes the specific type of computer and its operating system, browser, and so forth.

Platform independence—can be run on a variety of machines.

Plug-in—additional software program that works with a browser and is required to display multimedia.

PNG—*See* Portable Network Graphics (PNG).

Pointers—variables that contain the address of other data.

Polymorphism—having the same name for more than one, usually related, method. The two types are overloading and overriding.

Port number—specified only when the server is set up to receive http traffic on a network port other than the default port.

Portability—characteristic of being able to run on many different computer platforms.

Portable Network Graphics (PNG)—image format on the Web that supports 8-bit and 24-bit color but is an open standard and is not supported by all browsers. Compression is lossless.

Procedural approach—traditional approach to program design in which data are separate from instructions and the programmer lists the steps needed to solve a problem.

Proportionally spaced font—font in which some letters take up more space than others. *See also* Monospaced font.

Protocol—tells the browser what kind of resource it is accessing; allows different machines or programs to communicate.

Public—available to other applications either as a direct call or through the import statement.

Public domain—not copyrighted; can be used for free, without obtaining permission.

Pull technology—describes a situation where the Web page requests new or updated information from the server; the data are pulled to the browser.

Push technology—describes a situation where the server sends data to the browser without a request for update from the browser; the data are pushed to the broswer.

Radio button—type of input item that ensures that only one of a series of choices can be selected by the user.

Relative width—width measured as percentage of the screen. Relative width is the preferred way to specify sizes or widths. *See also* Absolute width.

Resource Interchange file format Waveform Audio Format (RIFF WAVE)—proprietary sound file format sponsored jointly by Microsoft and IBM and most commonly used on Microsoft Windows products. It is supported by most operating systems, has uncompressed format, and supports stereo. File extension is "wav."

RIFF WAVE—*See* Resource Interchange file format Waveform Audio Format (RIFF WAVE).

Robust—strongly constructed or a reliable environment.

Rules—part of a style sheet.

Script—program.

Searchable document—document containing ISINDEX tag; it allows the user to search one or more files on the server.

Secure environment—created by a programming language that does not write to disk drives or cause overflow errors; an environment safe from viruses.

Security manager—runs at all times in Java to enforce the rules of applet behavior.

Server redirection—technique for returning a CGI script in which a "Location:" header is coded instead of a "Content-type:" header.

Server-side map—image map data are processed by server; that is, the server decides what client should do.

SGML—*See* Standard Generalized Markup Language (SGML).

Snail mail—regular postal service.

Source—origin of a link.

Stacks—HyperCard documents.

Stand-alone program—runs on a single, local machine and is complete on that machine.

Standard Generalized Markup Language (SGML)—language for coding Web pages that can be viewed by all types of computers, all across the world.

Static Web page—page containing no links.

Stereo sound—multiple-channel sound as opposed to single-channel (monaural).

Style—describes a way to set off a group of characters from the surrounding text block.

Style sheets—part of the new HTML 4.0 standard giving the Web weaver more control over the placement and appearance of various elements on the page and the ability to create aural entries.

Tagged Image File Format (TIFF)—image format used to exchange documents between different computer platforms. Supports 1, 4, 8, and 24 bits per pixel.

Tags—HTML codes that are enclosed in angle brackets and are used to format the text. *See also* Containers.

Target—end of a link.

Telnet—allows you to work remotely on computers across the Net.

Text file—file consisting of just text, with no embedded word-processing codes; consists of ASCII characters.

Thumbnail image—very small version of the actual image.

TIFF—*See* Tagged Image File Format (TIFF).

Tiled—repeated image.

Uniform Resource Locator (URL)—the Internet address, or location, of a resource, whether it is a Web page or a specific part of a Web page.
Universal Resource Name (URN)—a more general identifier for Web resources not yet completely defined.
Unordered list—*See* Bulleted list.
URL—*See* Uniform Resource Locator (URL).
URN—*See* Universal Resource Name (URN).
Utility applets—useful, practical applets usually designed for commercial sale.

Virus—self replicating software that destroys other software or damages the computer.
Void—will not return a value.

Web weaver—the person who creates a Web page.
What You See Is What You Get (WYSIWYG)—term for word processing and desktop publishing that shows what the end result will look like.
White space—extra spaces, tabs, and blank lines.
Wizard—program that helps you code and may identify errors in your code.
WYSIWYG—*See* What You See Is What You Get (WYSIWYG).

Zipped file—compressed file.

index